The Thousand-Mile War

The Thousand-Mile War

World War II in Alaska and the Aleutians

Brian Garfield

Foreword by Terrence Cole

Aurum

First published in Great Britain
2004 by Aurum Press Ltd
25 Bedford Avenue, London WC1B 3AT

Published by arrangement with University of Alaska Press

First published in the US by Doubleday 1969

This revised edition published in the US
by University of Alaska Press 1995

A catalogue record for this book is available from the British Library.

ISBN 1 84513 019 7

1 3 5 7 9 10 8 6 4 2
2004 2006 2008 2007 2005

Designed and typeset in New Caledonia by
David Fletcher Welch at SS Graphics Limited
Printed by MPG Books, Bodmin, Cornwall

Contents

Acknowledgments

MARSHALL FREERKS WARNED ME at the outset, "With the whole campaign under a fog figuratively and literally, it is not surprising the records are a little clouded." Freerks was right; there was not enough material in available documentary sources to make it possible to complete this book. Therefore I reinforced the available records with tape-recorded interviews and lengthy correspondence with scores of veterans of the Aleutian Campaign.

Hundreds of people provided sine qua non help in the research and preparation of this book. My most sincere thanks to each correspondent and interviewed veteran, a partial list of whom appears in the bibliography.

I owe deep and very special thanks to Admiral James S. Russell, the gentle wise mentor without whose immense contributions this book would have been far less complete. Admiral and Mrs. Russell took me in as their house guest in Tacoma with warm hospitality. The admiral opened to me his basement full of transcribed Japanese and American records; submitted to a fusillade of questions; helped obtain information from his high-ranking Japanese friends; prepared the way for my eye-opening trip to Alaska and the Aleutians (where I was welcomed as the first voluntary civilian tourist in years); and spent long hours meticulously correcting errors in the final manuscript with generous good-natured patience.

Particular thanks, as well, to:

Senator Ernest Gruening and Admiral Thomas C. Kinkaid, USN Retired, who granted far longer interviews than their busy schedules might have permitted;

Major General Albert E. Brown, USA Retired, who not only contributed personal recollections of the Battle of Attu but also induced the Defense Department to open wide the records of his relief from command and the events surrounding it;

Vice Admiral Robert M. Griffin, USN Retired, who engaged with me in a long good-natured argument about the causes of the Battle of the Pips, in which he commanded a U.S. Navy task group;

Major Generals Archibald V. Arnold, Wayne C. Zimmerman, Frank L. Culin, and Albert V. Hartl, USA Retired, who provided detailed recollections, files, and records of the Battle of Attu;

Brigadier General Benjamin B. Talley, USA Retired, whose only fault has been in insisting that credit for the remarkable engineering achievements in the Aleutians belongs to everyone but himself;

Brigadier General Earl H. DeFord, USAF Retired, who filled important gaps in the nebulous record of Bomber Command operations;

Colonel William Alexander, USA Retired, who has sent me an enormous avalanche of recollection and detail in scores of long letters;

Colonel William H. Willoughby, USA Retired, whose recollections of Scout Battalion operations at Attu were amiably provided along with the hospitality of the Willoughby home;

Lieutenant Colonel Lawrence Reineke, USAFR, whose gift of cartons of yellowing files is exceeded only by the overflowing hospitality of himself and his family;

Lucian K. Wernick, former Air Force major, whose skill in our card games has been no less than his former skill at the controls of a four-engine bomber, and whose recollections, corrections, and photos have been of great value;

Marshall C. Freerks, former Navy lieutenant commander and PBY squadron leader, who provided both insight and hospitality at his home in St. Louis;

Robert C. Reeve, long-time (since 1932) Alaskan bush pilot and owner-operator of Reeve Aleutian Airways, who granted several interviews and gave me VIP treatment on the long journey from Anchorage to Attu and back;

Robert Atwood, editor-publisher of the Anchorage Times and a close friend of Simon Buckner, who handed me the key to Alaska and indispensable reminiscences;

Captain Hank Orth, the Reeve pilot whose phenomenal aerial skill made the Aleutian journey fascinating and safe (Orth is possibly the only man alive who has flown a DC-3 backward—he once took off into a 110-knot Aleutian headwind);

And the late Captain Billy J. Wheeler, USAAF, whose vibrant diary of the 36th Bombardment Squadron was the cornerstone on which this book was designed.

DOCUMENTARY RESEARCH MATERIAL FOR THIS book came from many private and governmental archives. They include:

The Japan Defense Agency in Tokyo.

Shemya Air Force Base, Shemya Islands, Aleutians.

Alaskan Command (Elmendorf Air Force Base, Anchorage).

Office of the Chief of Military History (Fort Lesley J. McNair, Washington, D.C.).

Navy Office of Information (Pentagon Bldg., Arlington, Virginia).

Office of the Chief of Naval Operations, Classified Operational Archives (Navy Yard Annex, Washington, D.C.).

Air Force Archives and Air University Library, Maxwell Air Force Base, Alabama.

World War II Records Division (primarily Air Force), National Archives Collections, Alexandria, Virginia.

National Archives, Washington, D.C.

National Personnel Records Center (Military Personnel Records), St. Louis, Missouri.

Aerospace Audio-Visual Service (MAC), Washington, D.C.

Navy, Army Signal Corps, and Air Force photo libraries (in Washington, Arlington, and the Pentagon).

The U.S. Superintendent of Documents (Washington, D.C.).

The Air Force Museum (Wright-Patterson AFB, Ohio).

The National Air and Space Museum of the Smithsonian Institution (Washington, D.C.).

Historical Department, the Boeing Company (Seattle, Washington).

Files of Wide World Photos, Inc., *The New York Times, Time, Life,* other newspapers and magazines.

Private files of Admiral Russell, General Hartl, Colonel Reineke, and many other veterans.

FOR GUIDANCE AND ACCESS TO files in the archives of the U.S. Defense Department and other agencies, I am above all indebted to Lieutenant Colonel Robert A. Webb, USAF, Chief of the Book Branch, Magazine and Book Division of the Office of the Assistant Secretary of Defense, in the Pentagon.

Colonel Webb guided me through the maze of official records without once losing temper or patience, and I cannot overstate my gratitude for his help and forbearance. He not only located many records, but had them declassified for my use.

The following individuals also provided great assistance:

At the World War II Records Division of the National Archives, Alexandria: Herman G. Goldbeck; Thomas E. Hohmann; Caroline Moore; Mr. Andrews; Mrs. Livingston.

At the Office of the Chief of Military History: Colonel H. A. Schmidt; D. H. Finke; Hannah M. Zeidlik.

At the Classified Naval Operational Archives: Dean C. Allard

At the Air Force Museum: Royal D. Frey.

At the Boeing Company: Harl V. Brackin, Jr.

At Elmendorf AFB: Colonel Carroll V. Glines (himself an oft-published historian); and Dr. John M. Weidman, official historian of the Alaskan Air Command.

At Shemya Air Force Base: Colonel George V. Kreamer; Major Donald L. Sigl; Staff Sergeant David L. Youngman.

At Seattle Naval District Headquarters: Lieutenant Commander Haig O. Cartozian.

At Sitka, Alaska: Charles Q. Conway.

At U.S. Naval Station, Adak Island: Lieutenant Ralph H. France II, USNR.

At Anchorage: Lieutenant Colonel Marvin R. "Muktuk" Marston, AUS Retired.

At San Bruno, California: Jack O. Haugen.

My debt is also great to my good friend Rear Admiral Robert Granville Burke, USNR, who obtained introductions and quarters for me at various stops on the long trek toward the completion of this two-year project; to Priscilla Shames, who enthusiastically ripped into the rough drafts so that the final draft would be better; to my friend Harold Kuebler, senior editor of Doubleday & Co., who has nursed the project with patience and enthusiasm; and to Shan Botley, who has suffered through the slow painful construction of research, organization, rough drafts, and final manuscript.

Foreword

A B-24 BOMBER PILOT WHO flew raids over Kiska in 1942 called the little known Aleutian campaign of World War II "the weirdest war ever waged," a three-sided battle among the United States, the Japanese empire, and a force that proved to be more powerful than either Washington or Tokyo: the weather.1 A giant low pressure system hovers over the Aleutian Chain in the North Pacific like a permanent hurricane, earth's version of Jupiter's giant red spot, often blanketing the entire region with rain and fog or winds of up to 100 miles an hour or even greater. "Despite all human courage and mechanical genius, the forces of nature in the Aleutians could always call the turns," Brian Garfield wrote. "No general or admiral was as powerful as the weather."[2] In the thousand-mile-long battleground between Dutch Harbor and Attu, the weather dictated that both sides would spend most of the war searching for each other, usually without success.

The Thousand-Mile War is Brian Garfield's masterful narrative history of the blind war fought in the wind and the fog of the Aleutians in 1942–1943. Published in late 1969—and nominated for the Pulitzer Prize in history in 1970—Garfield's book was the first independent study ever written about the only campaign of World War II fought on North American soil and is still the finest one-volume history of World War II in Alaska. The University of Alaska Press Classic Reprint Series is pleased to issue this newly revised and expanded edition of Garfield's gripping narrative on the 50th anniversary of the end of World War II.

1. Ira F. Wintermute, "War in the Fog," *American Magazine*, August 1943, p. 9.
2. Brian Garfield, *The Thousand-Mile War*. (See page 35.) Dr. Glenn Shaw of the University of Alaska Fairbanks Geophysical Institute noted the comparison between the Aleutian Low and Jupiter's red spot.

Brian Garfield is best known as a popular western and suspense novelist and screenwriter for television and Hollywood. He has written more than seventy novels, which have sold on the order of twenty million copies and have been translated into seventeen different languages. His most famous work is probably *Death Wish* (1972) which inspired a series of five bloody feature films starring Charles Bronson. Like many viewers, Garfield said he "reacted with revulsion" to the glorification of violence in the big-screen treatment of his original novel. A more light-hearted mystery called Hopscotch won the 1976 Edgar Award from the Mystery Writers of America—the acclaimed film version starred Walter Matthau and Glenda Jackson.

Born in New York in 1939—his maternal grandmother was a relative of Mark Twain—Garfield's writing career began after he graduated from the University of Arizona in 1959. He published his first novel, *Range Justice,* in 1960. In the years that followed he learned his craft writing dozens of westerns and mysteries under both his own name and an army of pen-names including Bennett Garland, Alex Hawk, Jonas Ward, Brian Wynne, and Frank Wynne. A handful of his titles include: *The Rimfire Murders, Massacre Basin, Letter to a Gunfighter, Savage Guns, Seven Brave Men, Call Me Hazard, The Last Outlaw,* and many others. Often he published two or three books in a single year.[3]

Garfield came to write *The Thousand-Mile War*—his first work of nonfiction—while searching for a topic for a new novel about World War II. "It all started," he explained, "simply because a publisher had suggested I write a World War II novel and I said I was sick of reading about 8th Air Force bomber pilots or naval battles in the Coral Sea, and he said, 'Why don't you find yourself a battle that hasn't been written up?' So I did."[4]

The battle for the Aleutians and Alaska was then one of the least known episodes in the history of the war. Though fragments had been published over the years, no one had ever put the whole story of the battle for Alaska together in a comprehensible fashion. In the 1940s government censorship had stifled news of the war in Alaska, and as a result many Americans had never heard of Dutch Harbor, Adak, or Attu. Several embarrassing military blunders, including the tragic invasion of Kiska, made some of the top brass of the U.S. armed forces less than eager to publicize their exploits in the North Pacific. Those who knew about the Aleutian campaign tended to downplay its significance. In his

3. For a listing of Garfield's books and a brief biography see his entry in *Contemporary Authors* (New Revision Series), Vol. 6. pp. 182-183.

4. Brian Garfield to Terrence Cole, April 22, 1980.

fifteen-volume history of the U.S. Navy in World War II, historian Samuel Eliot Morison had called the Aleutians the "Theater of Military Frustration" and claimed that nothing that went on there "accomplished anything of great importance or had any appreciable effect on the outcome of the war." According to Morison, servicemen sent to the Aleutians "regarded an assignment to this region of almost perpetual mist and snow as little better than penal servitude. Both sides would have done well to have left the Aleutians to the Aleuts for the course of the war."[5]

The inclement weather which cloaked the region also made it difficult to decipher what had actually happened in the Aleutians. Reconstructing the story of a battle is difficult enough even with recognizable landmarks, let alone when both sides are utterly lost, blindly groping for each other in the fog. Furthermore, many of the official government documents from the war remained classified until Garfield requested they be released in the 1960s. As one former PBY pilot warned him at the beginning: "With the whole campaign under a fog figuratively and literally, it is not surprising the records are a little clouded."[6]

The more Garfield learned about the brave men who had served in the Aleutian theater, the more compelling the story became, so he abandoned his idea for a novel and decided to tackle instead the job of researching and writing the first in-depth history of the Aleutian campaign. As he wrote the brother of one veteran after publication of *The Thousand-Mile War*, "the subject-matter grabbed me in a grip an ape couldn't have pried loose. Compulsions like that don't come along every day."[7]

Brian Garfield spent two years—longer than the actual battle itself—refighting the Aleutian campaign. He tirelessly searched libraries, museums, and government archives for every scrap of relevant information. He advertised in the *New York Times* and tracked down dozens of surviving veterans who had served in the Aleutian theater and were eager to share their stories. His extensive interviews and correspondence—he lists forty-three primary interviews in his bibliography—provided Garfield with a wealth of detail that only eyewitnesses could have recalled. Garfield visited Attu in 1967, where he was the first "voluntary

5. Samuel Eliot Morison, *Aleutians, Gilberts and Marshalls June 1942–April 1944,* in *History of United States Naval Operations in World War II* (Vol. 7), (Boston: Little, Brown, 1951), pp. 3-4.

6. See Acknowledgments, page v.

7. Brian Garfield to Reverend Laidlaw, May 17, 1970. Garfield's old correspondence and manuscript files are located in the Garfield Collection in the archives of the University of Oregon at Eugene.

civilian tourist in years," and tramped in the mud where the thousand-mile war was fought a quarter-century earlier.

Upon its publication in 1969, readers and reviewers found *The Thousand-Mile War* to be thoroughly researched but written with the drama and suspense of a high-tension thriller. Garfield's expertise in crafting historical fiction gave him the ability to make the characters in his history come alive. "I never studied history in the formal sense," he wrote in 1972 to one reader who had served in the Aleutians. "I guess the last history course I took was in high school. But when you write enough novels and movies... at least you learn how to tell a yarn."[8] Another Aleutian vet commented that the "poor bastard author" would probably not make enough money in royalties "to pay his researchers, assistants, aids, even postage." Garfield's response was: "Would that I'd had researchers, assistants, and aids. But if I had, they'd probably have missed good stuff; it's always better to do it yourself. Anyhow, I had nobody to pay except the airlines and the post office and the suppliers of recording-tape and typewriter ribbon, and the lady who typed the damn thing when I finished it."[9]

In a review in the *New York Times,* noted World War II historian John Toland praised Garfield's book "for its fresh scenes, its original ingredients." Garfield had removed the "veil of anonymity" which had for so long hidden what took place in the Aleutians and uncovered the dramatic story of "one of the most difficult operations in American military history."[10] Even a skeptical reviewer, who dismissed the Aleutian campaign as "usually boring, occasionally ridiculous, and essentially one of the least significant of the war," praised Garfield's dramatic depiction of the "demoniac weather" as the unseen enemy.[11] But the most gratifying response came from veterans who had served in the Aleutians. Many wrote and offered him their stories of the war for future editions (Garfield confessed that if he had used all of the anecdotes he had received even before publication his book would have been six volumes long). Others wrote and thanked Garfield for finally letting them see the big picture of the war in Alaska for the first time. Some readers impressed by the realistic details of Garfield's history believed that the author must have served in the Aleutians and wondered to which outfit he had belonged.

8. Brian Garfield to Bill Robinson, April 26, 1972, Garfield Collection, University of Oregon Library.
9. Ibid.
10. *New York Times Book Review*, February 8, 1970, p. 16.
11. *Library Journal*, Feb. 15, 1970, p. 663.

"I'm most flattered the book gave you the feeling I must have been there," Garfield wrote one veteran. "I was there, of course, but in 1967, not 1941–1945…."[12]

In the quarter-century since the first publication of Brian Garfield's book, dozens of scholars have followed in his footsteps and published many excellent studies of various aspects of World War II in the north (see the bibliography). This flood of historical research has done nothing to diminish the achievement of *The Thousand-Mile War,* the book that first brought to life the modern memory of the so-called "Forgotten War" in Alaska.

—*Terrence Cole*
History Department
University of Alaska Fairbanks

12. Brian Garfield to Col. Samuel R. Dows, April 14, 1971, Garfield Collection, University of Oregon Library.

Preface to the 1995 Edition

THE FIRST PRINTING OF *The Thousand-Mile War* was published in 1969 by Doubleday, in a hardcover edition that included eighty-two photographs and several maps. A less expensive edition (same printing, cheaper boards) was published by the History Book Club.

Unfortunately those editions went out of print before long.

During the past twenty-five years several companies have published mass-market reprint editions. Most of these paperbacks contained no photographs, although one edition sported a front cover picture of a tank leading an infantry charge across a snowscape. I felt obliged to point out to the publishers that no tanks had been used in combat in the Aleutians.

The experience suggested we still have a good deal to learn about that war.

Subsequent jacket illustrations were more credible, but by the early 1990s even the latest of the many Bantam paperback editions was no longer in print.

Meanwhile various smart-mouthed friends were asking, "When are you bringing out the sequel?"

I hope they're not too disappointed to see that this present book is not the sequel; it's not even the remake. It's still the original vessel, with a few leaks plugged and a few refinements added fore and aft. I am deeply grateful to the University of Alaska Press for providing this opportunity to restore old illustrations and add new ones, to update readers about some relevant events that have occurred during the past twenty-five years, and of course to correct some of the original book's mistakes.

In that regard I'm embarrassed to admit that my errors began in paragraph one of chapter one—where I said one of the carriers that attacked Dutch Harbor was avenging damage inflicted on it by the 1942 Doolittle bomber raid on Tokyo. Several sharp-eyed correspondents on both sides of the Pacific were quick to correct this gaffe. The carrier that attacked Dutch Harbor in June 1942—the *Ryujo*—was not the same ship as the carrier that was hit by Doolittle's bombs in Tokyo Bay—the *Ryuho*. (I come from Arizona, where Spanish is the second language, and if the letters "J" and "H" are interchangeable in Spanglish, well then, why not in translations from the Japanese?)

The *Ryujo-Ryuho* confusion and several other errors have been pointed out by astute readers. I am grateful for their help; I also am pleased, conceitedly, because most of the book's mistakes seem to be more trivial than that one.

Veterans and historians have sent not only corrections but reminiscences and additions. Much of their material could be added appropriately to the contents of *The Thousand-Mile War* and without doubt would make the book more comprehensive but it also would require that we make a multi-volume work out of it. *The Thousand-Mile War* was always intended as a narrative overview rather than a day-by-day record and several of its gaps have been filled by the many books and articles that have been published since this book appeared in its original version. Those new publications—as many as I've been able to track down—are listed in an expanded bibliography at the back of this edition.

A good amount of unpublished Aleutians-related material has come along. As I did with the sources I collected while writing the first edition, I am depositing all these documents and tapes with the archivists of the University of Oregon Library at Eugene, so that veterans and interested researchers may have access to them.

The Oregon archives also include formidable gifts from dedicated and generous benefactors whose contributions include unit histories, records, wartime letters home, reminiscences written and taped, photos, drawings, paintings and other artifacts.

One hard-working team of veterans congregated in 1988 to compile a detailed summary of the activities of their 406th Bombardment Squadron, an outfit which (regrettably) is hardly mentioned in this book. The 406th was one of the first to reach Alaska after commencement of hostilities; it served "for the duration" and only returned to the Lower 48 a year and a half later after the end of combat in the Aleutians. The courageous warriors of the 406th Squadron flew Hudson A-29s and Mitchell B-25 medium bombers on perilous deck-level submarine-chasing missions and on long-range bombing sorties over the Japanese bases on the Aleutian islands of Kiska and Attu. Despite an excellent record and plenty of heroic action, and the loss of numerous airplanes,

Squadron 406 experienced no combat fatalities. If for that reason alone, it ought to deserve a spotlight in any illumination of the Aleutians campaign.

Colonel Harold D. "Doug" Courtney, president of the 406th Bombardment Squadron Association, sent me a complete print-out of the veterans' reconstructed 406th war diary and it provides an invaluable complement to the stories that are sampled in *The Thousand-Mile War.*

The record of the 406th is striking to say the least; but it does not seem to change the structure or emphasis of the book. So, with regret, I have sent it and other materials on to the University of Oregon without replicating them in this book. They are left out not because of neglect or ignorance but because of limited space. Fortunately, a growing number of these materials has been showcased in excellent recent publications from such dedicated writers (and esteemed colleagues) as John Cloe and Stan Cohen.

With regard to those and other such additional materials, I hope the extended bibliography and the updated afterword at the back of this edition will help readers find sources that may satisfy their interests.

—Brian Garfield

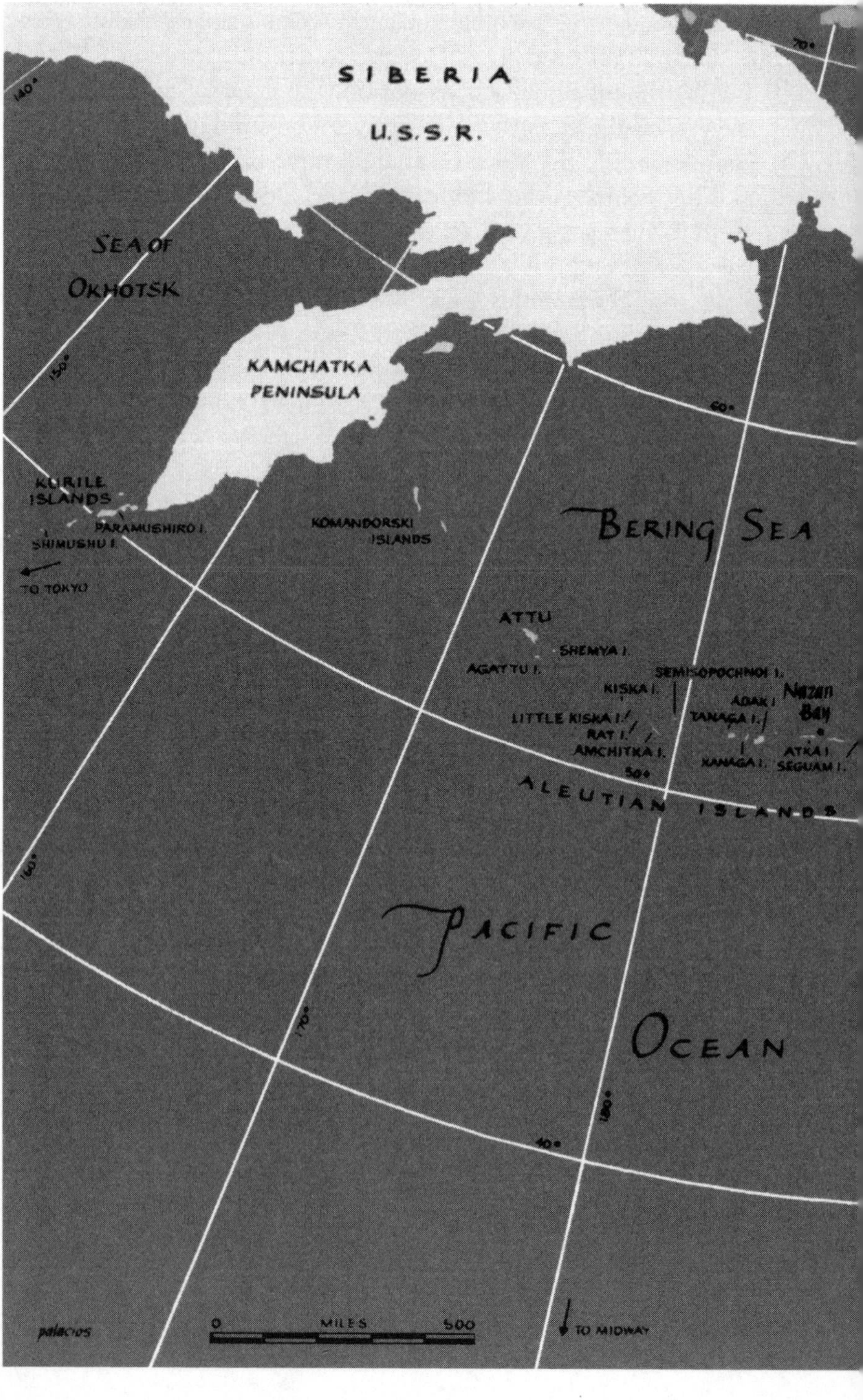

SIBERIA
U.S.S.R.
70°
140°
SEA OF OKHOTSK
150°
KAMCHATKA PENINSULA
60°
KURILE ISLANDS
PARAMUSHIRO I.
SHIMUSHU I.
TO TOKYO
KOMANDORSKI ISLANDS
BERING SEA
ATTU
SHEMYA I.
AGATTU I.
SEMISOPOCHNOI I.
KISKA I.
ADAK I.
Nazan Bay
LITTLE KISKA I.
TANAGA I.
RAT I.
AMCHITKA I.
KANAGA I.
ATKA I.
SEGUAM I.
50°
ALEUTIAN ISLANDS
160°
PACIFIC
170°
OCEAN
180°
40°
palacios
0 MILES 500
TO MIDWAY

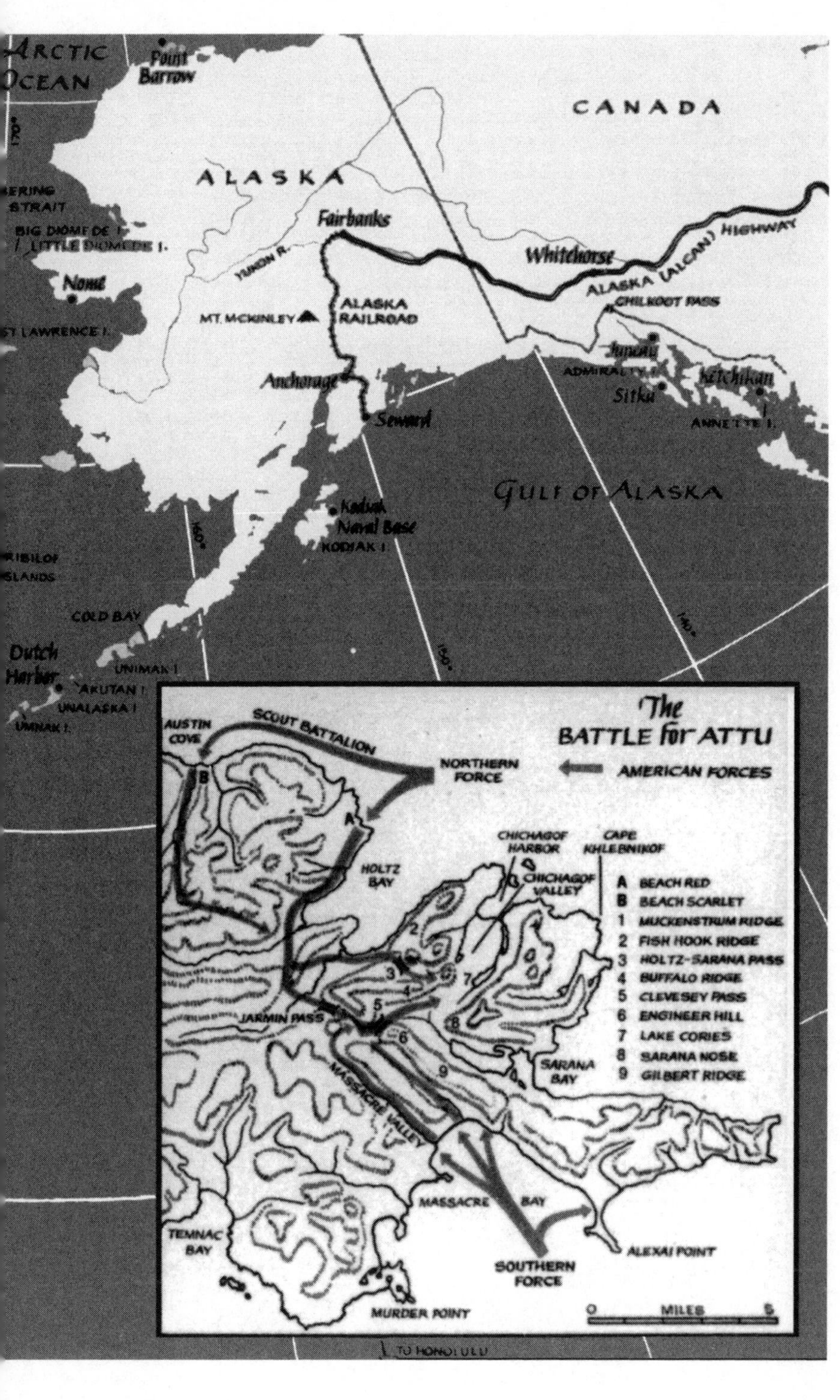

ARCTIC OCEAN
Point Barrow
CANADA
ALASKA
BERING STRAIT
BIG DIOMEDE I.
LITTLE DIOMEDE I.
Nome
YUKON R.
Fairbanks
Whitehorse
ALASKA (ALCAN) HIGHWAY
MT. MCKINLEY
ALASKA RAILROAD
CHILKOOT PASS
ST LAWRENCE I.
Juneau
ADMIRALTY I.
Ketchikan
Anchorage
Sitka
Seward
ANNETTE I.
GULF OF ALASKA
Kodiak Naval Base
KODIAK I.
COLD BAY
Dutch Harbor
UNIMAK I.
AKUTAN I.
UNALASKA I.
UMNAK I.
The BATTLE for ATTU
AMERICAN FORCES
AUSTIN COVE
SCOUT BATTALION
NORTHERN FORCE
HOLTZ BAY
CHICHAGOF HARBOR
CAPE KHLEBNIKOF
CHICHAGOF VALLEY
A BEACH RED
B BEACH SCARLET
1 MUCKENSTRUM RIDGE
2 FISH HOOK RIDGE
3 HOLTZ-SARANA PASS
4 BUFFALO RIDGE
5 CLEVESEY PASS
6 ENGINEER HILL
7 LAKE CORIES
8 SARANA NOSE
9 GILBERT RIDGE
JARMIN PASS
SARANA BAY
MASSACRE VALLEY
MASSACRE BAY
TEMNAC BAY
ALEXAI POINT
SOUTHERN FORCE
MURDER POINT
0 MILES 5
TO HONOLULU

Author's Note

It is about a thousand miles from Dutch Harbor, near the Alaska Peninsula, to Attu at the far western tip of the Aleutian Island Chain. They are the most brutal thousand miles in the Pacific Ocean. Here, for fifteen months in 1942–1943, was fought one of the toughest campaigns of World War II.

In the context of global war it was relatively small. About 500,000 men took part—Americans, Canadians, Russians, Japanese. Its battles were fought on land, at sea, and in the air. It cost scores of ships, hundreds of airplanes, and perhaps ten thousand lives. It was the only campaign of World War II fought on the United States' own North American soil. And it gave the United States her first theaterwide victory over Japan.

Few Americans recall even its highlights. This is the first history of the Aleutian campaign to be published.

This is not an authorized history. That is, it has not been directed, commissioned, subsidized, or in any way controlled by any agency, government or private. But I must add that I have received great assistance from many individuals and agencies without whose help I could not have written this book. I owe each of them a great debt of gratitude.

At the same time, I take full responsibility for any errors of fact or interpretation.

PART ONE

Buckner's War

CHAPTER
ONE

Japan Steams North

COLD FOG SWEPT ACROSS THE pitching flight deck of the Japanese aircraft carrier *Ryujo*; it stung men's exposed faces with brittle needles of wind-driven spray. The Aleutian fog brought midnight close against the ship—and with it, the grave risk of collision with the seven other Japanese ships nearby.

On the bridge of the flagship stood her skipper, Captain Tadao Kato, bundled in a heavy fur coat. Kato scanned the low black sky intently, keyed-up and grim: on the deck of the fifteen-year-old warship a gathering of bombers were warming up, and soon Captain Kato would have the honor of launching a bomb attack on the U.S. Army and Navy bases at Dutch Harbor, Alaska.

It was the night of June 2, 1942.[1] *Ryujo's* bomber strike would set in motion a full-scale, fifteen-month war for the Aleutian Islands—the only military campaign of World War II fought on North American soil.

SAILING OFF *RYUJO'S* QUARTER WAS the brand-new carrier *Junyo*. Together the two flattops carried an armada of eighty-two attack planes. Close by in the swirling North Pacific fog were the escorts—heavy cruisers *Takao* and *Maya*, three destroyers and an oiler. And supporting the task group not far to the west were the ships of Vice Admiral Boshiro Hosogaya's Northern Force: cruisers *Nachi, Abukuma, Kiso,* and *Tama,* nine destroyers, three transports carrying 2,500 Japanese Army invasion troops, and a screen of submarines.

1. The Japanese record the date as June 3, 1942. Since Japan lies west of the International Date Line, all dates of events in Japanese records are one day later than those in American records. For simplicity, all dates used in this book are American dates.

A foggy cold-weather front was tracking eastward across the North Pacific at about 20 knots, and the Japanese carrier force stayed just within it, to avoid detection by American patrol planes. On flagship *Ryujo,* Captain Kato and Rear Admiral Kakuji Kakuta, the task force commander, had been alerted earlier in the day by sight of a patrol plane in the soup overhead. It could have been an American PBY Catalina flying boat; then again it might have been a Russian plane—the Soviets, who had pirated the PBY design from the Americans, patrolled regularly off the Siberian coast. There was no way to be certain; but to avoid discovery, Admiral Kakuta had turned his carriers and escorts into the leading edge of the storm, and had stayed with the front all afternoon and evening. Now, just before midnight, Kakuta stepped onto the open bridge, a thick bodied man with batwing ears and a small mustache. Captain Kato noticed him look at his watch: the success of the admiral's impending operation depended on its timing, for the assault on Dutch Harbor—scheduled to take place in a few hours, in the early morning of June 3—was meant to divert massive American naval forces north toward Alaska. On the following day, June 4, the main body of Admiral Isoroku Yamamoto's Combined Imperial Fleet would make its massed attack in the vicinity of Midway Island, 2,000 miles to the south of Kakuta.

Kakuta's tough *Ryujo* force was not as large as the fleet that had attacked Pearl Harbor six months before, but all signs pointed toward an equally devasting success. The only possible trouble was the afternoon's reconnaissance by the nebulous patrol plane, if in fact it had really been an American plane, and if it had detected the fleet sliding through the fog below. Captain Kato mentioned the plane once again, and the admiral gave him a reassuring smile; in any event there was nothing they could do about it now. All they could do was keep close track of the time. Kakuta looked at his watch again.

The *Ryujo* fleet was now on the last leg of a fast four-day dash from Ominato in North Honshu, where it had waited a week before outfitting at Hashira anchorage near Hiroshima. There, in mid-May, the Northern Force had loaded heavy Arctic gear in the midst of a harbor filled with virtually the entire Imperial Navy: sixty-eight capital warships and almost uncounted escort vessels and transports, massed for the largest naval operation in Japanese history. Admiral Yamamoto was deploying more than 190 warships and 700 airplanes against the United States Pacific Fleet.

For Japan, which had not lost a naval battle in more than a century, the operation would prove to be one of history's most disastrous strategic mistakes.

JAPAN'S PREMIER, THE STOLID AND determined General Hideki Tojo, had come to office on a path paved with assassinations, terror politics, and the back-room power of the tough Army establishment. His military shogunate had led the nation into a world war, much against the practical misgivings of officers like Admiral Yamamoto; now Tojo aimed his biggest guns toward Midway—and toward the Aleutian Islands. In so doing, Japan embarked on a new program of expansion and conquest while she had not yet secured her immense victories of the first six months of the war.

The record of conquest was phenomenal. Within days after the attack on Pearl Harbor on December 7, 1941, Japan had swallowed up Guam, Indochina, Thailand; she had sunk the only major Allied warships west of Midway—the British leviathans *Prince of Wales* and *Repulse*. By Christmas she had taken Wake and Hong Kong. Within two months she had occupied Manila, Singapore, Malaya; in February at Java Sea she sank ten Allied ships; in March the Allies lost Java and Burma, and Japanese armies were in the Owen Stanley Mountains of New Guinea with the coast of Australia almost within sight. Japan had driven the British fleet from the Indian Ocean and the Pacific; she had sunk nearly every American battleship in the Pacific Fleet; and at the end of April Japan still had lost nothing bigger than a destroyer.

In May 1942, Corregidor surrendered and the Philippines fell; Japan invaded the Solomons. She had swallowed Southeast Asia and the islands of the South Pacific; she had crushed all Allied strength in the western ocean.

By the end of May, the Allies were at the low point of the global war. In Africa, Rommel had retaken Benghazi; in the Atlantic, German U-boats had sunk almost five hundred ships off the North American coast, many of them within sight of the U.S. shore. Japanese submarines and planes had bombed and shelled forests, refineries and installations on the U.S. Pacific Coast. American sea power, what was left of it, had been driven back to Hawaii and the West Coast, and the Japanese knew that U.S. strategy had to be restricted to a policy of holding fast on a fragile line of defense that began in New Guinea, extended through Samoa and Midway, and was anchored at its northern end at Dutch Harbor in the Aleutians.

There had not been a single setback to muffle Japanese enthusiasm. Heady with conquest, the Imperial General Staff brushed off warnings from junior officers just home from the field, who felt that the newly acquired territories must be secured, even at the expense of further expansion. Even the forceful Yamamoto, Japan's star naval strategist who had masterminded the attack on Pearl Harbor, was convinced that Japan could not hope to win a long war. Yamamoto had spent too much time in the United States to underestimate the massive industrial strength of America. He saw clearly that there was only one hope for Japanese victory, and that was to draw out and destroy the remnants of the U.S. fleet at a time when the Japanese fleet was far superior to it in total strength. The American Navy could be reinforced quickly by new construction; it had to be smashed irrevocably in 1942—or not at all. If Yamamoto could destroy American naval power, and particularly the four American carriers then in the Pacific, he felt Japan could persuade the United States to sign a peace that would insure the security of the expanded Japanese Empire.

By April 1942, Yamamoto's naval strategy had crystallized into an obsession to scuttle the U.S. Navy in one massive stroke. Army commanders disagreed with him; they wanted to press forward in the South Pacific and invade Australia. The staff was at loggerheads, until April 18—the day of the Doolittle raid. That day bombs fell on Tokyo, and the Imperial Staff forgot its infighting in a rush to the wall charts. Officers crowded around the maps, trying to guess where the Doolittle bombers had come from.

Some officers argued that Doolittle's twin-engine Army bombers might have been launched from aircraft carriers. Others pointed to the north: Alaska was the only area from which American land-based planes could reach Japan. The Aleutian Islands, off Alaska, lay only 650 miles from Paramushiro in the Japanese Kuriles. The Doolittle raiders could have taken off from the western Aleutians. One staff colonel recalled that Doolittle himself, identified by intelligence, had grown up in Nome, the son of an Alaskan gold rush miner.

The mystery was never solved; it was not until after the war that the Japanese learned that Doolittle's raid had been launched from "Bull" Halsey's carriers in the Central Pacific. Meanwhile, during the closing days of April, the Imperial Staff agreed with Yamamoto that American sea power must be destroyed. But, they added, it was also necessary to protect their Aleutian flank against further raids like Doolittle's.

Yamamoto moved fast. His first attempt to ambush the U.S. fleet took place in early May with the Battle of the Coral Sea, where he sank the carrier *Lexington* and inflicted crippling damage on the carrier *Yorktown*. Yamamoto was elated; of the four American carriers in the ocean, he had put two out of the war. Two more, and the job would be done. (It was not until later, after Midway, that the Naval Staff stopped to reconsider Coral Sea, and realized that the battle had been a standoff. Despite the victory, Japan had been checked at Coral Sea; the battle had halted her naval expansion so that Japanese troops could never reach Australia.)

Meanwhile Yamamoto's brilliant Senior Operations Officer, Captain Kameto Kuroshima, drew up a far-reaching plan for the "M I Operation"—Midway and the Aleutians. It called for a deployment of the entire Combined Fleet in a wide sweep of the Central and North Pacific, to capture the Aleutians and trap the rest of the U.S. fleet. Twenty admirals and more than 100,000 men would take part. Flagship would be the awesome super-battleship *Yamato*, 64,000 tons of big guns and armor plate.

In the Aleutians, multiple task forces under stolid Vice Admiral Boshiro Hosogaya would strike a paralyzing blow at Dutch Harbor while an occupation group landed troops on the islands of Adak, Kiska, and Attu. The operation would draw the American fleet out of hiding from Pearl Harbor; it would steam north toward Alaska, and Yamamoto would wait for it at Midway. Hosogaya's attack on the Aleutians would give Yamamoto time to conquer Midway, so that when the American fleet arrived he would have the island base secured for use by his own attack planes. Meanwhile the Northern Second Mobile Force—Admiral Kakuta with his carriers—would complete its diversion at Dutch Harbor and swing west to support the occupation of the western Aleutians. Thus Japan would gain both the protection of her northern flank and the eagerly desired annihilation of the U.S. Pacific Fleet.

On May 5, Imperial General Headquarters issued Navy Order Eighteen, formally authorizing the operation by calling in part for "the invasion and occupation of the western Aleutians...in order to prevent enemy forces from attacking the homeland."

Less than a month later, the intricate plan went into operation.

ON THE NIGHT OF JUNE 2, as his carrier force made its final highspeed dash toward Dutch Harbor under cover of the eastward-tracking storm, Admiral Kakuta studied his latest intelligence about the island he was about to attack.

Japanese Intelligence was not so good as it might have been, because no Japanese spies in Alaska had communicated with Tokyo for months. The eight or ten spies had been interned in the States, along with hundreds of innocent Nisei. But Kakuta still had several sources of information. He had himself launched eight planes during the day, to scout ahead 250 miles; but they had stayed away from Dutch Harbor to avoid alerting the Americans.

Kakuta's principal reconnaissance eyes belonged to a handful of Japan's I-class submarines. Bigger than their counterpart American fleet boats, these super-submarines were designed to make the round trip from Tokyo to Los Angeles without refueling—and several of them had already done so. Although their living conditions were cramped and demoralizing, they displaced about 5,000 tons and their deck hangar space was big enough to carry as many as three folding-wing seaplane bombers. The unique I-boats were effective weapons of war. Their usefulness was limited only by the nature of the missions assigned to them; for the most part Japan never used her I-boat fleet to best advantage. But the big undersea craft had recorded a few encouraging successes. In early January one of them had torpedoed the American freighter *Absaroka* just outside the harbor of Los Angeles. On February 23 an I-boat fired twenty-five high-explosive shells into a refinery near Santa Barbara, California, destroying an oil well and pump. Planes launched from I-boats periodically reconnoitered Seattle and Canadian West Coast ports; and once an I-boat's plane bombed a National Forest in Oregon, on orders from Admiral Yamamoto, who had been talked into the notion that a few incendiary bombs set off in the great forests would cause a holocaust of flame and destruction that would sweep down the Pacific Coast and wipe out the major cities.

Admiral Kakuta had three I-boats scouting for him, as well as several smaller RO-class submarines. One of the I-boats had launched its scout plane over Dutch Harbor on May 29; the seas were so rough that the plane had cracked up when it tried to land by the I-boat. Now on June 2, the submarine itself ran silently past Dutch Harbor at periscope depth, and that night Kakuta had its radio code report in front of him. Meanwhile two other submarines were patrolling to the east, near Cold Bay, after reconnoitering Kodiak (by periscope) and Kiska (by plane).

Kakuta now learned that some of the intelligence estimates he had been given in Japan were incorrect. He had believed an entire combat division of American troops was stationed at Dutch Harbor; now he learned there were no more than 5,000 troops, most of them service and support personnel. He sent a last-minute signal to Admiral Yamamoto, requesting permission to divert the invasion force from the western Aleutians and instead invade and capture Dutch Harbor, which was the principal American military base in the Aleutians—indeed, as far as he knew, it was the only one. But Yamamoto vetoed the suggestion; Dutch Harbor was too far from Japan, too difficult to supply.

And with the vast commitment at Midway and to the south, there weren't enough ships available to guarantee the security of Dutch Harbor once it had been taken. No; the plan would proceed as originally ordered.

Kakuta put the radiograms away and sent for the captain, Tadao Kato.

The two men met on *Ryujo's* bridge; and Kakuta gave Kato the order to proceed with the execution of Plan A O.

LESS THAN 170 MILES FROM Dutch Harbor, *Ryujo* and *Junyo* increased speed to 25 knots to break through the forward edge of the storm into the clear, where they could launch their planes. Shortly after 2:00 a.m. the warmed-up engines of the torpedo-bombers were switched off so that the gas tanks could be topped up with fuel. On *Ryujo's* flight deck, Lieutenant Masayuki Yamaguchi, the flight leader, climbed into his cockpit, and flight crews stood by to spin propellers on the contact signal to start engines. Pilots checked their gauges and their radios; there was no banter. Behind them had been cold nights with nothing to do but play cards and sip tea. Ahead was action—what they had come for. Deck crews stood about, envious because they must stay behind.

Ryujo's deck was silent except for the rush of wind. Lieutenant Commander Masatake Okumiya paused at the ship's shrine, then went on up to the bridge. Admiral Kakuta glanced at him and muttered something about the weather. Okumiya looked out at the fog; it seemed as impenetrable as ever. The admiral turned to him and said he was worried about the lack of daylight. In these northern latitudes the sun ought to be up. The admiral asked Okumiya's opinion; Okumiya, the staff Aviation Officer, was one of the most highly regarded pilots in the Japanese Navy—it was he who had bombed the American gunboat *Panay* and three Standard Oil tankers in the Yangtze River in China in 1937, providing one of the international incidents that led to unavoidable war.

Okumiya suggested they wait a few minutes longer for the fog to lift; that was what delayed the daylight. It was 2:28 a.m.; Kakuta was already an hour behind schedule. He began to pace the bridge.

On the flight deck, the bombers held 1,000-pound bombs, the fighters 250-pounders.* Pilots laced into their life jackets: life expectancy in these frigid waters was measured in minutes, but a submarine north of Dutch Harbor had orders to pick up downed Japanese pilots.

Watching the flight-deck activity, Kakuta displayed his nervousness; his pacing quickened. His hands were rammed in his pockets against the cold. The loudspeaker ordered all hands to launching stations; then the

---

*1995 ADDENDUM: In the 1960s, my information about these armaments came from American sources. The reported sizes of the bombs are wrong, partly because English-speaking military historians had a tendency to miscalculate the ratio of pounds to kilos. In the 1990s, as 11th Air Force historian John Cloe points out, we know that "The Japanese horizontal bombers were armed with one 550-lb and four 150-lb bombs. There were no 1,000-lb bombs."

bullhorn roared again: "Start engines."

From the bridge, the admiral watched the black fog coil around the ship. The bow was barely visible, lighted momentarily by the reflected glow of engine exhaust flames. The deck floodlights came on, bright yellow, punctuated by the flickering red and green wing lights of the motionless planes. Fog blanketed the deck.

At 2:43 in the morning, light carrier *Junyo*, a thousand yards distant, steamed out of the fog into plain sight. Blinker signals flashed from the flagship, and Okumiya swung his green launching lamp overhead in a wide semicircle. *Ryujo* plunged straight ahead into the wind; aircraft engines wound up to full power. Lieutenant Yamaguchi rumbled down the deck and roared off the square bow, banked upward into a spiral and orbited while his flight formed up behind him. Off *Junyo*, Lieutenant Yoshio Shiga completed the same maneuver.

One bomber from *Ryujo* stalled during the moment of take-off and crashed into the sea directly in front of the slicing bow of the flagship. The lives of the three-man crew were saved when a destroyer nudged the wrecked plane out of the carrier's path and dropped scaling nets to the fliers.

Kakuta watched from the bridge while the first wave of thirty-five airplanes formed overhead. The low cloud ceiling, jammed down at 400 feet, prohibited long formation flight. As they flew out of sight of the fleet, the planes separated to fly independently to Dutch Harbor.

Kakuta turned his ships back into the protective curtain of the storm. Now he had to wait. *Ryujo* moved slowly with the storm front, lashed by heavy rain and chilling wind. Captain Kato and Commander Okumiya told the admiral several times that they had nothing to worry about; Japanese Intelligence was convinced the nearest landbased American planes were at Kodiak, hundreds of miles from Dutch Harbor.

Within a few hours Kakuta's pilots would suffer badly from this mistake in intelligence.

CHAPTER
TWO

"You Will Be Governed by the Principle of Calculated Risk"

AS EASTERN AND WESTERN POWER converged toward Dutch Harbor, Yamamoto expected to achieve the complete surprise of a second Pearl Harbor. He was wrong.

The flying boat Admiral Kakuta had seen at noon June 2 had indeed been an American patrol plane. It had been dead reckoning for hours through heavy storms; its pilot could not give an exact fix, but he did radio a coded contact report to the Naval Air substation at Dutch Harbor. There the latest intelligence bulletin from Seattle—WAR DEPARTMENT REPORTS INDICATIONS OF ENEMY CARRIERS LESS THAN 400 MILES SOUTH OF KISKA—had just been logged, though it was already twenty-four hours out of date. American radio teams had been monitoring heavy enemy wireless traffic all day; by nightfall, Intelligence placed the Japanese task force somewhere in the waters about 250 miles southeast of Dutch Harbor.

The atmosphere at Dutch Harbor was one of tension, but not surprise. The United States had been tracking Admiral Kakuta ever since Tokyo had issued his initial orders.

ON MAY 15, JUST THREE WEEKS before Kakuta launched his planes toward Dutch Harbor, a team of U.S. Navy cryptanalysts in a Honolulu basement had broken the top-secret Japanese naval code.

From fragmentary interceptions, Lieutenant Commander Joseph J. Rochefort Jr. pieced together the information that Yamamoto intended to occupy Midway and the Aleutian Islands. Armed with this information, Rochefort went directly to the gentle, accessible Commander in Chief of the Pacific Fleet (CINCPAC): Admiral Chester W. Nimitz, the scholarly fifty-five-year-old Texan who was to oversee, from afar, all Allied operations in the Aleutian theater.

To Nimitz, the news came at a bad time. The enemy was pounding the Allies on every front. In the Pacific the ultimate outcome of the war appeared alarmingly doubtful. Europe and North Africa had first call on manpower and equipment; on Nimitz's Japanese front, Allied forces were depleted and weak, spread thin across the entire Pacific.

Even in that context, the defenses of Midway and the Aleutians were inadequate. Midway, a tiny pair of flat atolls, was a nightmare to defend; as for the northern outposts, the War Department had assigned defense priorities to Hawaii, the Panama Canal, and Alaska—in that order.

The Alaska Defense Commander, Major General Simon B. Buckner Jr., had pointed out with no exaggeration: "We're not even the second team up here—we're a sandlot club." Alaska[1] was hopelessly unready for war, in spite of Buckner's strenuous efforts to beef it up with all he could get—tiny Army garrisons, a scatter of air fields guarded by a few bombers and fighters, and a Navy fleet of ancient World War I destroyers and wooden "Yippee" boats which, in the words of their commander, the colorful Squeaky Anderson, "would sink if they got rammed by a barnacle."

According to Nimitz's codebreakers, the Imperial Combined Fleet would sortie from Japan around May 20; the attack on Midway and the Aleutians could come at any time after May 24. Nimitz had to decide whether to concentrate his outnumbered fleet at Midway, or divide it to meet both threats. He was down to two carriers—*Enterprise* and *Hornet*. (*Yorktown*, crippled at Coral Sea, was not expected to be repaired before August.) Against these carriers and a handful of cruisers and destroyers, the Japanese arrayed an enormous fleet spearheaded by six aircraft carriers and eleven battleships.

To concentrate the U.S. Fleet at Midway would mean a surrender of the Aleutians, and perhaps all Alaska, by default; yet to split the force offered little chance to halt the enemy either at Midway or Alaska.

High-speed signals flashed from Nimitz's Hawaiian headquarters to Washington, where the Joint Chiefs of Staff met in emergency session to examine Commander Rochefort's *Fleet Intelligence Bulletin 4–42*, the deciphered evidence of enemy plans. In hot arguments, officers who knew Alaska insisted that it would do little harm to let the Japanese have the Aleutians. The climate there was unlivable. To defend them, Japan would need to invest enormous manpower and equipment, and her

1. The Aleutian Islands had always been an integral part of the political and geographic entity of Alaska. Strategically, no distinctions were made between the archipelago and the mainland, any more than a distinction would have been made between Long Island and the mainland part of New York State.

troops would suffer torture trying to live there. Surely Midway, with its strategic location, was far more important to the Allies than a string of barren volcanoes in the Bering Sea?

But global strategists argued that the best U.S. shipping route to Siberia lay across the narrow strait of Unimak Pass, a tidal slot commanded by the guns of Dutch Harbor. If the Japanese captured Dutch Harbor, they would isolate most of Alaska and leave it open for occupation, and they would cut off the United States' best sea lanes to Siberia when Lend-Lease shipments by that route had just begun.

The Soviet Union might go to war against Japan at any time; the United States was trying (unsuccessfully) to persuade Stalin to join in the Pacific war, to take some of the pressure off China and the Western Allies.[2] It would be folly to abandon the Lend-Lease route to Russia just when it was becoming vital. America had to do everything possible, the Joint Chiefs concluded, to keep Japan from driving a wedge between Alaska and Siberia. Dutch Harbor, the key to the Bering Sea, had to be kept out of Japanese hands.

The decision flashed from Washington to Hawaii. But by then Nimitz had held his own staff consultations and had decided independently to go ahead and defend Alaska with a small force. He felt he could spare five cruisers and four destroyers; the action at Midway, he was sure, would be like the recent Battle of the Coral Sea—a duel between aircraft carriers, out of sight of each other and far beyond gunnery range. His judgment would soon prove correct.

On May 21, 1942, the nine-ship North Pacific Force[3] steamed out of Pearl Harbor at 22 knots and headed for Kodiak Island, headquarters of the Alaska Naval Sector. In command was the crusty former Commander of Destroyers, Pacific Fleet: Rear Admiral Robert A. Theobald.

The portly Theobald ran up his flag on cruiser *Nashville* and made the run to Kodiak in five and a half days. En route he received from Nimitz a peppering of dispatches which did nothing to improve his acidulous

2. In 1939, Japan had lost 18,000 men in a short war against Russia. It had ended with the Hitler-Stalin non-aggression pact, but Hitler had broken the pact since then, and his Japanese ally was expected to attack Russia at any time.

3. In one form or another, this North Pacific Force was to exist for more than four years, under a bewildering variety of names. To avoid confusion this book assigns one consistent designation to each organization. Air Service, Air Corps, Army Air Forces, all were names given to the service this book calls the Air Force. As another example, the Eleventh Air Force mentioned throughout the book was at various times called the Alaskan Air Force, the Eleventh Army Air Force, Task Group 16.1, the Alaskan Air Command, and the Alaskan Command...For similar reasons, the ranks and ratings of personnel are those contemporaneous with the events described.

disposition—they told him that he was to "oppose the advance of the enemy in the Aleutian-Alaskan area, taking advantage of every favorable opportunity to inflict strong attrition," and "be governed by the principle of calculated risk"—which meant to some of Theobald's staffers that their force was to sacrifice itself if that would stop the Japanese.

> 25 MAY 1942
> FROM: CINCPAC
> TO: COMNORPACFOR
>
> THE JAPANESE HAVE COMPLETED PLANS FOR AN AMPHIBIOUS OPERATION TO SECURE AN ADVANCED BASE IN THE ALEUTIAN ISLANDS...FOLLOWING ESTIMATED JAPANESE TASK FORCE HAS LEFT JAPAN WITH PROBABLE OBJECTIVE ALEUTIAN ISLANDS AND/OR ALASKA: 2 AIRCRAFT CARRIERS, 2–3 SEAPLANE TENDERS, 3 HEAVY CRUISERS, 2 LIGHT CRUISERS, 12 DESTROYERS, 8 SUBMARINES, HEAVY BOMBERS (PROBABLY FLYING BOAT TYPE) AND TRANSPORTS AND CARGO VESSELS...ON 25 MAY THE ABOVE FORCES WILL ARRIVE IN NORTHERN JAPAN, FUEL, AND PROCEED TO THE ALEUTIANS.

"Two aircraft carriers" was what caught Theobald's attention. He insisted that to fight the enemy without carriers or strong land-based air forces of his own would be suicide. PLANES ALONE CAN ASSURE DECISIVE TACTICAL RESULTS, he pointed out in a terse dispatch to CINCPAC. But Nimitz had no carriers to spare, and there was no time left to send additional air reinforcements into the Aleutians. Theobald would have to make do.

At sea on the way to Kodiak, Theobald made plans for the defense of Alaska. Despite his nickname, Fuzzy Theobald had a quick mind which caused him at times to be caustic and insulting with lesser wits. He had ranked near the top of the Naval Academy class of 1907; he had a wide, square face, and at fifty-four had put on so much weight that his trousers looked baggy, though he wore neatly pressed uniforms—a habit that would set him apart from most officers in the Aleutians, who wore whatever was warm enough for comfort.

His new command included the nine ships with which he steamed north, as well as all Navy, Canadian, and U.S. Air Forces already stationed in Alaska. But his jurisdiction stopped short of the Army—the Alaska Defense Command and its muscular, ebullient Major General Buckner.

Hard, strict, and brilliant, Simon Buckner had spent two years building Alaska's defenses from scratch. In his opinion, CINCPAC had made a mistake by taking the Alaskan Air Force away from him and assigning it to a new admiral who was bound to make the costly mistakes of a stranger to the area's unique character.

Buckner and Theobald first met—and clashed—when Theobald arrived at Kodiak on May 27. At the first meeting, papers kept spilling off the crowded desk until Buckner asked Theobald to "nail those damned maps up on the wall." Theobald ordered a yeoman to "batten the charts to the bulkhead," thus emphasizing that it was a Navy base, and in Theobald's view a Navy war.

Buckner refused to back down. Theobald quickly sent a request to Nimitz for clarification of the command roles. He received a distinctly unhelpful reply:

> THE COMMAND RELATIONSHIP BETWEEN...ALASKA DEFENSE COMMAND UNDER GENERAL BUCKNER AND THE NORTH PACIFIC FORCE IS TO BE BY MUTUAL COOPERATION.

Judged by its results, that decision was one of Admiral Nimitz's few important mistakes. Buckner and Theobald would never achieve anything like mutual cooperation. In the months ahead, their bristling rivalry became such a vital issue that it all but superseded the conflict between American and Japanese forces in the Aleutians. The clash of powerful personalities reinforced the natural intramural jealousy between Army and Navy; officers immediately chose sides, so that there was a quick shutdown of the usual informal channels of interservice communication. It all added a great deal, in time and effort and even lives, to the cost of the campaign.

While the Japanese attack fleet made its final battle preparations at Ominato in northern Japan, Theobald and Buckner sat down at Kodiak and tried to agree on plans to meet the enemy threat. Theobald's first task was to picture the battleground where he would have to fight. This was not easy; most of darkest Africa had been charted more accurately. Much of Alaska, and all the Aleutian Islands, had never been mapped in any detail.

Air Force pilots still used Rand McNally road maps. Naval charts of Aleutian waters, "based on the Russian survey of 1864," were so inaccurate that a sailor passing over the charted location of mountainous Bogoslof Island could see no island within the visible horizons, not even on a clear day (if one could be found). Alaska's 34,000-mile coastline, longer than the combined coasts of the entire continental United States, was largely unexplored, and vulnerable to attack almost anywhere.

Theobald did not share Buckner's faith in the accuracy of CINCPAC's Intelligence predictions that the enemy's most likely target for attack would be Dutch Harbor on Unalaska Island, not far from the Alaska mainland. Buckner proposed that they concentrate all their defenses around Dutch Harbor and wait for the Japanese to come. Theobald disagreed. He found it unthinkable to base his entire plan on unconfirmed guesswork; all he really knew was that the Japanese planned to attack, as CINCPAC had advised, with "probable objective Aleutian Islands and/or Alaska." If Theobald committed everything to the defense of Dutch Harbor, what would happen if the enemy bypassed it and struck elsewhere?

If the Japanese took Hawaii, they would still be 2,400 miles from the nearest targets on the U.S. mainland. But if they took Alaska, they would be within three hours' bombing distance of the great Boeing bomber plant and Bremerton Navy Yard at Seattle. In the other direction, they would be within point-blank striking distance of the Soviet Union: at the Bering Strait, Alaska and Siberia were separated by a scant 57 miles of ocean.

The geography of it was alarming. Japan could take Alaska without straining her supply lines; indeed, Alaska was closer to Tokyo than to New York; yet a Japanese beachhead on the Alaskan mainland would threaten the entire United States and Canada.

With all that at stake, Theobald could not risk all his defenses at Dutch Harbor. He proposed, instead, that the Alaskan Navy station a picket line of patrol boats and submarines in a wide arc across the Aleutian chain, where it could provide advance warning of enemy movements. The pickets, and sector-patrolling Catalina flying boats, would alert headquarters when the enemy fleet approached, and U.S. bombers could then engage the Japanese carriers before they came within striking distance of the Alaskan mainland.

It was a logical plan; but in voicing it, Theobald fell into an armchair strategist's trap, as General Buckner pointed out bluntly.

Buckner had traveled most of the length of the Aleutian chain several times. On a map it looked like the Florida Keys, but there was an important difference. Arching along the 55th Parallel, the Aleutians made a 1,200-mile line from the tip of the unsettled Alaska Peninsula. From Anchorage to the far end of the chain was almost 2,000 miles. There were more than a hundred islands; even the fifteen islands of strategically important size, where the enemy might seek a toehold, were scattered along the length of the chain. Theobald's plan, Buckner observed, did not take into account the sheer vastness of the area he would have to patrol.

Besides, Theobald's submarines and picket boats had no radar, nor did many of his planes. He would have to rely on visual contact to find the enemy carriers in a huge ocean where even in clear weather his tiny group of ships and planes would need luck. But the weather would not be clear. On May 29, while the Japanese fleet sortied out of Ominato and the American commanders continued their meeting at Kodiak, a series of fast-moving fog fronts and rainstorms moved in from the west. They socked in the entire chain and would continue to do so for two weeks without a break. Weather reports from Siberia and the western Aleutians confirmed Buckner's moist-finger estimate that Theobald's sailors would be lucky to see as far as the bows of their own ships. The picket-line operation, Buckner said, had no chance at all.

Theobald replied flatly that he had no choice. The picket line would be thrown up.

The forces deployed fast. First to move out, Captain Oswald Colclough's squadron of six antique S-boat submarines fanned out on patrols so grueling that officers and men on surface watch had to be lashed to the bridge to keep from being swept off the conning tower by icy high seas. Inside, condensation dripped from the cold hulls and drenched the crewmen.

Following the submarines, a litter of commercial fishing boats put their prows into the heavy westward seas. They had been painted Navy gray and designated "patrol craft," but there was little military character to the Yippee boats. Their crews had been trained by Dutch Harbor's captain-of-the-port, Commander Carl "Squeaky" Anderson, a Swede whose nickname described his loud, piercing voice. Squeaky was said to be the only sailor alive who really knew Aleutian waters.

The Alaskan Navy, in the person of Captain Ralph C. Parker, had a squadron of eight destroyers—tin cans of the First World War four-stack type. The biggest weapons they had were torpedoes and old three-inch guns. These tin ships, commanded by Commander Wyatt Craig, accompanied the Yippee boats out from Kodiak, but they went only as far as Dutch Harbor. Here they turned into nearby Makushin Bay and dropped anchor; Admiral Theobald wanted them to stand by, to defend Dutch Harbor against any enemy landing attempts.

The rest of Theobald's Navy—the five cruisers and four destroyers he had brought from Pearl Harbor—would deploy in the gulf south of Kodiak Island. When Theobald announced this, General Buckner observed loudly that the waters where Theobald planned to cruise were a full 500 miles east of Dutch Harbor. Theobald retorted that he had no intention of taking his cruisers near the enemy's carriers. The Japanese force was bigger, stronger and more concentrated than any task group Theobald could possibly put together—the enemy, now fast approaching from Honshu, had twelve destroyers, six cruisers, and a variety of other vessels in addition to the two deadly aircraft carriers. Theobald's only chance, he felt, was to wait until his landbased bombers could take those carriers out of the fight; only then would he commit his surface ships. In the meantime, he would keep his cruisers within range of Kodiak's land-based air support, where they would have some defense against the Japanese carriers.

Everything narrowed down to those enemy carriers. It was the carriers that gave the overwhelming advantage to the Japanese; it was the carriers Theobald would have to stop. For that job, he called on Alaska's Eleventh Air Force.

The fledgling Eleventh, America's smallest and youngest overseas Air Force, had only four heavy four-engine bombers with enough range and payload to hit the enemy at any real distance from base. It also had thirty-one medium-range twin-engine bombers (B-26 Marauders, never tried in combat, and obsolete B-18 gooneybirds that had been hastily redesigned from DC-3 cargo planes), and several squadrons of short-range P-40 Warhawk fighters. None of Brigadier General William O. Butler's pilots had ever flown in combat; virtually none of his planes were equipped to fight an enemy task force bristling with antiaircraft guns, screening vessels and deadly Zero fighters; but it was the only Air Force Theobald had, and he proposed to use it.

Theobald wanted to move the Eleventh Air Force's fighters and bombers to forward bases in the Aleutians. From there, they could attack the carriers far out at sea, as soon as the picket boats or patrolling PBY flying boats located the enemy. But Theobald met immediate resistance from General Butler of the Air Force. Butler, an earnest slow-moving walrus of a man, told Theobald that the two forward bases where Theobald wanted to post the planes were "in an unfinished condition," not ready for combat use.

The air fields in question were at Cold Bay, on the peninsula 180 miles east of Dutch Harbor, and at Umnak Island, 40 miles west of Dutch (there was no runway at Dutch Harbor itself; the rugged terrain would have made it too expensive, the War Department had ruled). The new air fields had been built in secret, and were still secret—to the enemy, and to most of Butler's pilots as well.[4]

Butler had kept most of his planes off the new fields for a sensible reason. The runways at Umnak, made of perforated steel matting and not yet paved, were so unstable that fighter planes bounced thirty feet in the air on impact when they landed. When heavy bombers landed, the flexible steel mats rippled up ahead of them in waves. The same thing happened on take-off, making the operation hazardous if not deadly. Captain Russell Cone, commander of the 36th Bombardment Squadron, had been flying his B-17 Flying Fortress in and out of the Umnak base for a week, and gave graphic testimony to the trampolinelike springing and buckling of the mats. "It felt like landing on an innerspring mattress."

General Butler told Theobald flatly that he would not order his combat squadrons forward until the Army Engineers laid concrete pavement over the steel mats. But there was no time, and no concrete, to do that overnight. The Air Force could not do Admiral Theobald much good if it had to base at its present headquarters, Elmendorf Field at Anchorage—that was nearly 800 miles from Dutch Harbor. Therefore, Theobald ruled, the pilots would just have to take their chances. He overruled Butler and ordered the planes forward to Cold Bay and Umnak.[5]

The Air Force began to move its squadrons on May 28—at the expense of rear-guard air bases. Thinking of such vulnerable targets as the forty-three 50,000-gallon steel gasoline storage tanks at Anchorage, Generals Butler and Buckner pressed for immediate reinforcements to defend the mainland. They were assured by the Western Defense Command in California that planes were on the way—an assurance of doubtful value, based on past experience—and the Royal Canadian Air Force responded by placing several combat squadrons at Theobald's

---

4. See Chapter Five. Umnak had no harbor; Dutch Harbor, on the adjoining island, had no air field. As Senator Ernest Gruening observes, the situation was "something like what happens when a blind man carries a lame man on his back. It worked, but not very well."

5. The curious command relationship established in Alaska was such that Buckner's Alaska Defense Command was separate from Theobald's North Pacific Force, while the Eleventh Air Force—a subsidiary of Buckner's command, created by Buckner—was assigned to both commands, for them to use as needed. In a state of "fleet-opposed invasion" the Air Force was Theobald's to rule; if Japan secured a beachhead on the mainland, a state of "ground-opposed invasion" would then exist, and control of the Air Force would pass to Buckner.

disposal. The RCAF 115th Fighter Squadron was already stationed at Alaska's Annette Island[6]: now the 8th Bomber Recon Squadron (Bolingbrokes) and Canada's 111th Fighter Squadron (P-40 Warhawks) roared in from the Yukon, a few of them flown by war-hardened veterans of the Battle of Britain.

The Canadians deployed along a string of mainland bases to replace the rapidly disappearing American planes; by June 2, the eve of the Battle of Dutch Harbor, more than half of Alaska's combat air force had roared into the Aleutians—much against General Butler's misgivings: planes had to make their way into Umnak through steel-colored fog and icy rain that fell sideways and sometimes upside-down, driven by freak gale-force air currents called "williwaws" that swept through and around the volcanic gorges of the Aleutian Islands. Thick damp air plugged up carburetors; ice coated wings; engines became so sluggish that pilots complained about "airplanes that can do everything but fly."[7]

At Dutch Harbor, Cold Bay, and Umnak, williwaws sucked planes out of their revetments and blew them away or flipped them over. One bomber pilot, Frederick R. Ramputi, recalls, "The initial moves to Cold Bay and Umnak found us sleeping in or under the aircraft.... It got real sporting when aircraft taxied by."

For most of the pilots it was their first glimpse of the Aleutians, described as such "a desolate spot that even Mrs. Roosevelt has not visited." Lieutenant William S. M. Johnson, keeper of the unit log of the (U.S.) 11th Fighter Squadron, wrote:

> We lived in tents which were always blowing down. The kitchen was housed in a wall tent which always blew over at mealtime; the food was mostly chili or corned beef or powdered eggs. A plane chose our flour supply as a landing spot, and there was no bread for days; the cooks could be seen running out and begging for help,

6. An American customs official at Annette had amazed the Canadian pilots when they arrived in early May. Mentally paralyzed by bureaucratic regulations, he had refused to allow them out of their planes unless they paid duty on their arms and equipment. A frenzy of communications erupted from this idiocy. It was abated only when U.S. Secretary of State Cordell Hull signaled from Washington that the Canadian fliers were to be exempted from customs duties as Distinguished Foreign Visitors.

7. All this rapid repositioning of air units, from May 28 to June 2, 1942, was accompanied by a great increase in radio code traffic, which led some intelligence officers in Japan to suspect that the United States knew Admiral Yamamoto's plans. Yamamoto, a habitual poker player who tended to run thin bluffs and overplay his hand, studied the information, expressed regret that his staffers hadn't learned the dispositions of Allied forces in Alaska and the Aleutians, but ordered the operation to proceed as scheduled.

> shouting that the kitchen was blowing away... The only transportation in the entire squadron was one jeep, which we had acquired illegally, so that the usual way of going places was by foot... There was a small tent-exchange store, but it had little or nothing to sell. It seemed to deal mostly in shoestrings. One day, however, the store got in a large supply of white civilian shirts, which were as useful as tits on a boar hog... The Navy men who flew over to Dutch Harbor tried to bring back cigarettes, but the little they brought could not reach around... The hospital was in tents, and every time aircraft took off or landed, the hospital blew down. Patients used gas masks to survive the fumes of the coal stoves. Only the periodic collapse of the tents relieved the monotony.

Major Jack Chennault, son of China Flying Tigers General Claire L. Chennault, commanded the 11th Fighter Squadron (and he also painted snarling tiger jaws on the snouts of his Warhawks); he noted that "We fueled our own planes from drums, slept in rude huts and bedrolls, and froze all the time." Temperatures were in the thirties, but dampness and wind chill drove them down another twenty degrees or more. Visibility in the Aleutians was measured not in miles but in feet. The ceiling varied, at five-minute intervals, from 500 feet to zero.

The primitive airplane revetments had not yet been floored; hardstands belied their name, for the heavier planes mired in whenever the ground was wet, which was all the time. Captain Russell Cone, commanding the 36th Bombardment Squadron, had his Flying Fortress parked on the only paved space; the other planes were scattered along the mud shoulders of the mile-long runway at Umnak. Every day from May 28 on, Cone flew the well-worn B-17E ("Old Seventy") the length of the chain, and saw nothing but endless miasmic mists, with an occasional 6,000-foot volcano poking up through the clouds. The picket search patrols were flown every day, ordered by Bomber Command's Colonel William O. Eareckson, who did not want to be "caught with my planes down."

Eareckson's bomber patrols augmented the sector sweeps of big Captain Leslie E. Gehres' patrol wing of twenty-three PBY flying boats. The huge twin-engine Catalinas operated from four seaplane tenders anchored at Dutch Harbor and nearby bays. The PBYs flew search patterns through howling storms in which even seagulls were grounded; williwaws smashed one of them to fragments at Dutch Harbor (and scattered the lashed-down lumber yard across three islands). Some of the

PBYs, and two of the Army bombers, were equipped with British-type radar, primitive and unreliable but vital in the constant fog of the Aleutians. To Admiral Theobald, airborne radar seemed to offer the only real hope of finding the Japanese fleet in time; he ordered the radar planes in the air virtually twenty-four hours a day.

The PBYs were big and capacious; they could stay aloft around the clock and carry heavy bomb loads. But their cruising speed of 95 knots did not encourage their use in combat; they were primarily search craft. Theobald's only real battle strength lay in his thirty-one medium bombers and four heavies—two of them obsolete prototype B-17 models, the other two LB-30s (B-24 Liberators converted for export to the English R.A.F.). It made for something less than an armada, so that an eager enthusiasm swept the Kodiak command when word came down that seven brand-new B-17E bombers had reached Fairbanks from the States and were on their way to Kodiak. But the frenzy of keen hope died quickly: fog grounded five of them at Anchorage on June 2, a sixth was held at Fairbanks for a compulsory 100-hour inspection, and only one plane reached Kodiak.

The delay of the new bombers by a vital twenty-four hours crushed the Allies' last hope of reinforcement before the Japanese attack. But Theobald himself was not aware that the promised Fortresses had not reached the front, and that he would have to fight with no more than what he had on hand. On June 1 he had departed in cruiser *Nashville* for a rendezvous with his cruisers and destroyers about 400 miles south of Kodiak. The rendezvous would take place on the morning of June 3, at just about the moment when Dutch Harbor opened fire on the first wave of Japanese bombers from *Ryujo*. From here on, Theobald was isolated completely by the rule of radio silence.

He was not the only incommunicado commander. Generals Buckner and Butler had gone back to Anchorage headquarters, almost 800 miles from Dutch Harbor. Navy Air commander Gehres, and Air Force tactical commander Colonel Everett S. Davis, were at Kodiak, still hundreds of miles from the impending battle. And their communications with the front were anything but dependable. The various services used different radio frequencies and codes; the equipment itself was primitive, more so as it approached the front. At Dutch Harbor the Army had a portable radiotelephone set in a deserted Aleut Indian shack. This weak short-range transmitter was beamed toward another set on top of Mount Ballyhoo (fancifully named by Jack London during a stay at Dutch Harbor, locale of *The Sea Wolf*). This set was supposed to relay transmissions through a Rube Goldberg system to a battery radio at the air base 40 miles away at Umnak. The battery set, liberated from a gunboat, weighed 100 pounds but put out such a weak signal that Ballyhoo could only receive it when conditions were ideal. Dutch Harbor could not pick it up at all.

To operate this strange thread between imperiled Dutch Harbor and its only hope of quick defense at Umnak, the Army had no personnel trained in code; all messages had to be broadcast vocally, using the phonetic alphabet instead of a cipher.

The reason communications were so ludicrous was the same reason behind the trouble the American forces had getting aviation fuel and other necessities to the new forward bases. It was, simply, the newness of war for Americans in 1942. They were inexperienced; they were excited; most of the junior officers responsible for details were recent arrivals from civilian life. And their problems were compounded by oversight, top-level interservice rivalries, and the pressures of time. They made mistakes more often than they made excuses; but one of their mistakes left the three forward Aleutian bases—Dutch Harbor, Umnak, and Cold Bay—without reliable radio communications.

Under the circumstances, the weight of combat command fell on small-unit commanders, forced to act independently in a situation that demanded nothing so much as coordination and cooperation. Not surprisingly, a number of them spent the night of June 2 making out their wills.[8]

AT COLD BAY, THE FORWARD tactical air commanders prepared for the fight: Colonel Norman D. Sillin of Fighter Command; Colonel William O. Eareckson of Bomber Command; Lieutenant Commander James S. Russell of PBY Squadron 42. Eareckson and Russell had their bunks in the radio tent. If an urgent signal came in, the radioman could poke the officers' feet without moving from his headset.

---

8. Soon after the Battle of Dutch Harbor, Theobald's headquarters assigned Bomber Command chief Eareckson to compose a report on the lack of Army-Navy cooperation during the battle. Admiral James S. Russell recalls being at Cold Bay at the time: "On my way from my squadron command tent to the six-holer latrine, I passed Bill's (Eareckson's) tent and heard the clacking of his portable typewriter. I stuck my head through the tent fly and asked if he'd given up flying for a stenog's job; he replied that he was writing a report on non-cooperation between Army and Navy at the direction of higher command. That should be interesting, said I. Yes, said he, I'll give you a copy of it. It will be on flimsy paper and—noting that I was en route to the latrine—you can do what you like with it." Unquestionably there was great wasteful interservice rivalry at the flag level, but at tactical unit level, cooperation was good. Eareckson's report didn't prove what Theobald wanted; it was shelved, never sent forward.

Russell's PBYs were fueled and armed at all times, with crews alerted for immediate take-off from their anchorages in the Aleutians (at and near Dutch Harbor). They flew regular search sweeps on June 1 and 2, in spite of blasting storms; it was one of the Navy's pilots who turned in the first contact report on the enemy fleet at noon June 2. But by evening the weather was so furious that even williwaw-toughened veterans stayed aground. The roaring winds drove stinging rain across the ugly barren flatlands of Cold Bay and the volcanic canyons of Umnak and Dutch Harbor.

Gale warnings were posted—but at Dutch, Ensign Marshall C. Freerks took off anyway, and at Cold Bay, Lieutenant Jack Bingham got airborne just after dark. These two were almost the only American planes to get off the ground on the evening of June 2, while Admiral Kakuta's carriers were lining up to launch their planes against Dutch Harbor. The two PBYs patrolled all night. "We may not have been very far from the Japs," Freerks recalls, "but we never got clear of the storm."

At sea, Admiral Theobald was trying to sleep in *Nashville's* pitching flag-country while the cruiser plowed south toward an impotent rendezvous with the task group. Submarines and picket boats tumbled helplessly on frothy seas, manning a useless picket line—Kakuta, unseen, had already passed through it. Far to the west, on Kiska Island, Navy Aerographer's Mate William C. House and his nine-man crew of weather observers huddled within a flimsy storm-lashed shack; for them it would be a short and bitter war.

Just before dawn, tall, cheerful Ensign Freerks racked his PBY back into Dutch Harbor, tied it down with cables, and rolled up exhausted in a bedroll. The storm began to die down; sunrise filtered weakly through heavy cloud cover, and Dutch Harbor awakened for an air-raid drill.

"After the drill," Freerks recalls, "everybody went back to bed and then the Japs bombed us."

CHAPTER
THREE

The Battle of Dutch Harbor: The First Day

MOORED AT DUTCH HARBOR AT 0540 hours on June 3, 1942, the U.S. seaplane tender *Gillis* picked up more than a dozen fast-moving pips on its radar screen. Coming up from the south above the clouds, they looked like airplanes—range about 10 miles; altitude 10,000 feet. *Gillis* flashed a signal to base, and sounded general quarters.

The captain of the Naval Station, Commander William N. Updegraff, heard the signal come in and spoke tersely to the signalman: "This looks like it." He ordered an air-raid red alert and commanded the six ships in the harbor to get steam up in their boilers.

Air-raid sirens wailed across Unalaska Island from Dutch Harbor to Fort Mears. In the mountain-ringed port six ships—*Gillis*, two Army transports, a Coast Guard cutter, a submarine and an old 1917 four-stack destroyer—went to battle stations and started engines; but none was to clear the harbor in time to escape the first attack. The biggest guns they had were the destroyer's old three-inchers; gun crews ripped the tarpaulins off these and every other weapon on the decks.

In the five minutes that followed *Gillis'* first contact report, the Americans moved fast. Around Dutch Harbor, antiaircraft muzzles cranked skyward and machine-gunners manned the roofs of Fort Mears. Soldiers swarmed pell-mell into prepared defensive positions. Aircraft spotters in flat tin-hat helmets of First World War vintage trained their binoculars on the southern sky. In the harbor, Lieutenant Jack Litsey was already warming up his Catalina mail plane with two passengers aboard; Litsey gunned his engines to take-off power and began to pick up speed across the bay. Nearby in a cove, Ensign Hildebrand started his PBY moving before the last of his crew had even scrambled aboard.

In the Dutch Harbor radio shack a yeoman tapped a hurried message—ABOUT TO BE BOMBED BY ENEMY PLANES. The plain-English message reached out to wireless sets at Cold Bay, Kodiak, Anchorage, and Admiral Theobald's *Nashville.* At Cold Bay, P-40 fighters were airborne within four minutes of the radio flash, heading out across the 180 miles of volcanoes and choppy seas that separated them from Dutch Harbor.

At nearby Umnak, the air field was serene and untroubled. The Rube Goldberg communications system had failed. Pilots on alert waited by the radio tent for a message that never came. A poker game in the operations shack proceeded without interruption.

AT 10,000 FEET IT WAS DAMP and icy cold; but by the whim of fate, the eye of the storm was just passing over Dutch Harbor. At 0545 hours fifteen of *Ryujo's* Japanese attack planes broke out of the clouds and found visibility unchecked across a panorama from Mount Ballyhoo to Fort Mears.

Flight leader Lieutenant Masayuki Yamaguchi lowered the flaps of his torpedo bomber and peeled off to attack. His bombs and bullets were the opening rounds of what history would record as an "incident"—yet it was powerful enough to influence the course of the war. Dutch Harbor was only a diversionary attack; but because of it, Japan would lose the balance of power at Midway: she would lose a major battle within forty-eight hours, if not the war, because Yamaguchi and his comrades were at Dutch Harbor instead of Midway.

On the ground at Dutch Harbor, an American chief petty officer recognized the diving planes and bellowed the order to fire. His guns puffed dark chunks of flak into the sky. Battery commanders all over the harbor found his aiming point and started shooting. Flak bursts walked up toward the enemy bombers, seeking the range; machine-gun tracers crisscrossed in arcs of flame as the Japanese planes thundered across the harbor.

Jack Litsey's Catalina was almost airborne at the end of its take-off run when tracers from two Zeroes drummed into the PBY, killed both passengers instantly and set the plane afire. Litsey skidded the burning wreck to a wild crash stop on the beach and scrambled for his life. He reached the rocks and ducked for cover just an instant before the plane blew up.

It was first blood.[1] The Japanese planes slid through heavy flak to beat up several Catalinas moored in the bays, but Ensign Hildebrand was already off the water and climbing when the Zeroes found him. Hildebrand

1. The first actual shot was fired a day earlier. The U.S. Army transport Fillmore had come into Dutch Harbor maintaining radio silence, appearing suddenly from the fog. The

rumbled under a Zero's belly and his waist gunners blazed away murderously. Hit simultaneously by plane and ground fire, the Zero spiraled into the harbor in a spectacular dive. Hildebrand wheeled up a mountain draw where the fast Zeroes could not follow, and climbed for the nearest cloud cover as fast as the waddling PBY could take him.

Japanese bullets ricocheted off the steel plating of the ships in harbor. The diving Zeroes pulled out and zoomed over the Naval Station toward Fort Mears as antiaircraft gun barrels wheeled to follow them. Four of the bombers rumbled steadily through flak at 9,000 feet, took careful aim and released their thousand-pounders with lethal accuracy: they smashed the tank farm and a truck to rubble, and blew up an Army barracks, killing twenty-five men and badly injuring as many more. Choking on smoke, men crawled coughing from the debris.

For twenty minutes the enemy pounded Dutch Harbor, planes slaloming through a fury of antiaircraft bursts to flatten several shore installations and batteries. To the Japanese pilots and observers, Dutch Harbor was a maelstrom of racket and smoke and flying rubble; it looked half-destroyed from the air.

But things on the ground were not so bad as they looked from overhead. Under the rolling smoke, most of the base was untouched. Bombs from the wing racks of Lieutenant Samajima's "Kate" bombers bracketed the radio shack, half-burying it in mud and rocks (the U.S. Navy radio operator signaled, "That one knocked me off my chair") but the shack and its equipment were not damaged. Except for the mangled bodies in the smashed Fort Mears barracks, hardly anyone was hurt.

The American fighters from Cold Bay, halfway to Dutch Harbor with throttles wide open, hoped they would reach the scene before the fighters from Umnak finished the fight. They did not know that Umnak had never been alerted.

The Japanese pilots held the sky uncontested. They returned to the attack until all their bombs dropped; then, with deliberate efficiency, Lieutenant Yamaguchi herded his air group south into a driving rain

---

harbor defense battery fired across her bow to halt the ship pending identification.

To some observers aboard Fillmore, including one who wrote a blistering letter published later in the Chicago Times, it seemed the gunners were rattled. Unsigned, the letter accused the U.S. forces of confusion and cowardice—and prompted commander Paul F. Foster, FDR's observer on the scene, to write to Navy HQ in Washington, "The letter contains misstatements of fact…(which) I consider to be a libel."

Actually the harmless across-the-bows shot had been the prudent step of an alert battery commander, but the press report was never corrected for the record; it added undeserved spice to several popular accounts of the Battle of Dutch Harbor.

squall, dissolving from sight less than ten minutes before the Cold Bay fighters swept over Dutch Harbor. The short-range P-40 Warhawks found nothing to fight but fog, and in angry frustration returned to base without firing a shot.

Smoke settled at Dutch Harbor; damage-control officers came out of their revetments and sent shore parties to inspect the base. In the harbor, ships took stock of their injuries and found they had virtually none. The American base had weathered the opening skirmish of the Aleutian Campaign without much physical damage; Dutch Harbor's defenses had not been impaired. About fifty-two Americans—one percent of the Dutch Harbor force—had been killed or injured. Before the first attack ended, Dutch was ready to take on another; but it would have to wait until the next day for a chance to hit back.

The first attack in the Aleutians had given Japan a minor tactical success but no real victory. Kakuta's pilots had been hampered by their lack of air-recon photos and intelligence; they had known almost nothing about the layout of the American base until the actual bombardment. They had picked targets of opportunity and let fly almost at random. Strategically, in terms of the power contest between East and West, the importance of the attack was that it had taken place at Dutch Harbor and not at Midway, where at this hour—early on the morning of June 3, 1942—a PBY pilot had just sighted part of Admiral Yamamoto's fleet steaming eastward toward the great battle that would soon erupt.

UNPURSUED, THE JAPANESE CARRIER planes droned south from Dutch Harbor. Their course took them into steadily worsening weather until Lieutenant Yamaguchi found it impossible to maintain formation. He broke the flying group into smaller flights and told the pilots to find their way home independently by staying close to the ocean, where they could judge wind-blown drift by the direction of the wave crests.

It was not the first time the weather had turned against them; earlier, the planes launched by carrier *Junyo* had lost their bearings in the fog and turned back. Yamaguchi's *Ryujo* planes had faced Dutch Harbor's guns alone.

Yamaguchi had been surprised by the enemy response; it was as if the Americans had been expecting the attack. He had been amazed by how fast the American antiaircraft had opened up, and by the lethal concentrations of flak. It had been nothing like Pearl Harbor.

Still, he felt pleased. Dutch Harbor, he was sure from the noise and smoke, was a shambles. All it would take to destroy the base would be one more bombing attack. He would advise Admiral Kakuta of that as soon as he got back to *Ryujo*—if he made it. For the storm, as bad as any he had ever flown, kept getting worse.

It was an experience that would be shared by every pilot in the Aleutians, American and Japanese alike, in the years to come. Despite all human courage and mechanical genius, the forces of nature in the Aleutians could always call the turns. No general or admiral was as powerful as the weather. From this point on, men would expend most of their bravery and strength in search, not in battle. Everyone had to look for everyone else, and no one was ever easy to find.

Junyo's pilots had already learned that; they had not been able to find Dutch Harbor. Now Lieutenant Yamaguchi learned it too. Down on the ocean surface, Yamaguchi crawled along with his plane's engine half-choked by cold salt spray; he shivered in the unheated cockpit while he peered through his mist-crusted windshield at the desolate ocean. For a long time he saw nothing but ugly greenish swells, lashed into froth. The thought of crashing down in that white foam, out of fuel, ran through his mind; he knew a man could last only moments in that churned-up sub-freezing water.

He checked navigation again and glanced bleakly at the unwinding fuel gauge. He was only 50 feet off the water—to the eye it seemed much closer—and he had no safety margin of glide if the engine should quit.

Then, abruptly, he sighted a ship slicing through the waves—*Ryujo*, her flight deck into the wind. He was home.

ADMIRAL KAKUTA KEPT COUNT AS HIS planes slammed onto the carrier deck, hooked the arresting cables and caromed to a precipitous halt. He knew of only one plane lost over Dutch Harbor. Now a last Zero bounced to a stop on deck, and he stopped counting. There would be no more arrivals: thanks to good luck and skillful pilots, he had recovered all his planes.

He sat in on the pilots' debriefing, listening with care to their description of the raid. One of the pilots, passing Makushin Bay, had sighted a squadron of four-stack destroyers waiting in obvious ambush; the pilot had counted the ships and radioed ahead to the fleet, and Admiral Kakuta had already launched a second air strike to bomb the discovered American ships. He had used *Junyo's* air group, which had returned one-by-one after getting lost in the fog earlier. Just before 9:00 Kakuta had sent the planes out again, accompanied by four catapult-launch seaplanes from the escort cruisers.

Somewhere in the course of the next twenty minutes the *Junyo* group had crossed paths with *Ryujo's* homeward-bound planes, unseen in the soup. The second group pressed on, but by now the eye of the storm had passed beyond Dutch Harbor. The weather was terrible. In the swirling squall not a single Japanese pilot found the American destroyers in Makushin Bay. They could not even find Dutch Harbor. When they called for help to find their way back to the carrier, a Japanese-speaking American radioman on the ground gave them instructions, and elated Dutch Harbor with the belief that he had sent an entire enemy air group to oblivion, out of fuel over the empty sea; but in fact the American's accent had not fooled the Japanese pilots. They sorted out real signals from false, and headed home.

The four Japanese float planes, catapulted from cruisers *Takao* and *Maya*, had worse luck. They found themselves off course, lost, and in bad trouble: they emerged from the edge of the storm within sight of Umnak Island.

On the secret air strip, Private George Stanley of the 11th Fighter Squadron was washing hospital bed linen outside the hospital tent. The abrasive GI soap stung his eyes, and he paused to throw his head back and clear them. When he looked up, he had a perfect view of four enemy planes turning in a tight circle past the distant clouds.

Private Stanley gave the alarm—and went on washing sheets.

Fighter Command responded to Private Stanley's shout by scrambling its twenty-one P-40s. The Warhawks swarmed up after the intruders. The Japanese, expecting no American planes in these skies, did not see them until it was almost too late. Lieutenants John B. Murphy and Jacob Dixon cut one Japanese plane out of the night and chased it down over Umnak, where they shot it down in flames in full sight of cheering American airmen on the ground. It plummeted vividly into the churning waters of Umnak Pass. The P-40s slashed into the remaining three enemy ships, thoroughly machine-gunned one of them and drove all three into the clouds.

The crippled Japanese plane crashed at sea on its way home; the other two found their cruisers, but neither pilot could suggest where the American fighters could have come from so quickly. For the moment, the location of the American air field remained a secret, but it was clear there was a base somewhere in the vicinity.

Near noon, the last stragglers of *Junyo's* strike group appeared, low over the water and almost out of gas. The admiral recovered his planes and retired southwest into the storm; he refueled his aircraft, studied strike reports and the riddle of the American fighters, and called a staff meeting to decide what to do next.

FROM DUTCH HARBOR, THE EMPHASIS of action now shifted elsewhere. Five hundred miles away, Admiral Theobald was finally linking up with the last of the nine ships in his cruiser-destroyer force in the pea-soup fog. By now Theobald knew that Dutch Harbor had been bombed, but he could do nothing until he could find the Japanese carriers.

To that end, big, blustery Captain Leslie E. Gehres at Kodiak had sent a coded message to his forward operations officer at Dutch Harbor. Misled by fragmentary clues, Gehres believed the enemy carriers were somewhere north, in the Bering Sea; he ordered all available PBYs to concentrate the search in the north.

Only two PBYs went southwest, where the Japanese were. The first of the two, piloted by Lieutenant (jg) Jean Cusick, had been in the air seven hours after leaving Umnak at three in the morning. About 200 miles from Dutch Harbor, Cusick blundered into *Junyo's* combat air patrol.

The Zeroes attacked. Tracers wounded Cusick, knocked out his starboard engine, and set the wing on fire. Cusick fought the burning PBY to a flat landing in the sea. The stricken flying boat quickly filled with water. Three crewmen jumped into an inflated life raft, only to have it sink, full of bullet holes. The icy swell swept all three men under to their deaths. The plane sank with a dismal sucking noise; Cusick and the remaining four crew members crowded into a two-man raft.

Within an hour Cusick and an enlisted man died of exposure and wounds. Drenched and frozen, the co-pilot, Lieutenant (jg) Wylie M. Hunt, drifted in the storm with the two surviving crewmen. There was no radio, no hope of rescue. They waited to die.

At noon the Japanese heavy cruiser *Takao* steamed out of the mist and sighted the three men in the bobbing raft. Soaked and numb, Wylie Hunt and his half-conscious companions were taken aboard the ship and separated in isolation.

Hunt hoped his two fellow crew members had kept silent. He pleaded ignorance to Japanese questions. On the second day, after a second Japanese strike at Dutch Harbor, a pilot slammed into Hunt's cell and cuffed him around. The pilot was enraged: he had been jumped by fighters from the unexpected base at Umnak. He demanded to know where the American planes had come from.

Interrogating officers threatened to kill Hunt if he refused to talk. They blindfolded him and took him up on the weather deck, tied a huge metal weight to his belt and led him out onto an extended platform: walking the plank. The blindfold was whipped off and an officer told Hunt in uncertain English that if he did not answer questions he would be shoved over the side.

Hunt had given himself up for dead twenty-four hours earlier in the plane crash. He refused to answer. He knew all about Umnak—he had come from there—but his act was so consistent that it finally convinced the Japanese. They untied him and took him below.

Hunt remained on the ship three weeks before he was taken to a prisoner of war camp in Japan, where he and his two companions sat out the rest of the war.

WHEN CUSICK AND CO-PILOT Hunt failed to return from their sector, Lieutenant (jg) L. D. Campbell took off from Dutch Harbor to look for them (and the enemy). Campbell reached the limit of his gas supply without finding Cusick's plane, and was turning back when he sighted the Japanese carrier force steaming across the Pacific in full battle order. The radioman's fingers tapped his key with staccato fever while Campbell fed details to him from the cockpit—number of ships and types, dispositions, position, course, speed. Then Campbell wheeled the ponderous Cat toward the protection of the clouds. But Admiral Kakuta's screening Zeroes had closed in.

Kakuta did not know that atmospheric static had garbled Campbell's broadcast; nor did he know that his Zeroes' bullets had wounded Campbell's waist gunner, severed the PBYs rudder wires, and made a sieve of the starboard gas tanks. At 5,000 feet with Zeroes chasing him through the clouds, Campbell rewrote the engineers' text that called the PBY a "directionally unstable aircraft" which would go into an uncontrollable spin without the guidance of its rudder. Campbell kept equilibrium with ailerons and elevators alone. The Zeroes made five passes at him; Campbell shook off all five by magnificent maneuvering at a speed of 120 knots. Finally he lost the fighters in the clouds and set course for Umnak, with gasoline running out of the holed starboard tank. He set his carburetors on their leanest mixtures and told the crew they probably weren't going to make it. Bucking the storm, he climbed in an effort to get above the worst weather and gain altitude so that if fuel ran out short of base, there might be a chance to glide several miles into the nearest sheltered harbor.

He made it halfway home. Then both engines quit, out of gas.

He had only been able to climb to 5,000 feet. From that altitude, dead-stick without power or rudder, Campbell manhandled the PBY down in an instrument glide through gale-force gusts. He came out under the clouds at 300 feet, righted the banking ship, and settled on the choppy sea.

Riddled with bullet holes, the flying boat immediately began to take water. Campbell and the crew stuffed rags and life jackets into the holes and kept the ship afloat by bailing; but the gunner was wounded, there was no heat, and they were adrift in the storm.

Campbell sent out a radio SOS and repeated his earlier contact report on the enemy ships. Nearby, Coast Guard Cutter *Nemaha* picked up Campbell's radio signal and set about to find the downed Catalina. Within twenty minutes the cutter hove into view, picked up Campbell and all his men.

Nemaha's skipper had orders to maintain radio silence and patrol his sector for forty-eight hours more. It was not until three days later that she put into Sand Point in the Shumagin Islands, and Campbell was able to make a personal report. In the meantime he had broadcast two exact contact reports—but static had garbled them both, and Dutch Harbor still knew nothing of the enemy's position. Campbell received the Distinguished Flying Cross; every member of his crew was awarded the Air Medal; but the American commands were no better off than they had been.

ALL DAY LONG, FLIGHTS OF AMERICAN planes sortied from Cold Bay and other bases on unsuccessful search missions. There was a moment of heart-swallowing terror at Umnak when one returning Marauder crashed on collapsing landing gear; its torpedo broke loose and tumbled with a hair-raising clatter, end-over-end down the steel mat runway. The racket sounded like a death rattle for the whole island. But the torpedo did not explode.

The six new B-17 bombers from the States came into Kodiak during the afternoon, but they didn't get off the ground again that day; the weather closed in fast from the west, enough to convince Eleventh Air Force Chief of Staff Colonel Everett S. Davis to ground the valuable Fortresses. By late afternoon the rain and fog were so thick at Umnak that ground crews could not even see landing planes until they had taxied half the length of the runway.

In the cold flapping mess tents, pilots wearing rumpled clothes and five o'clock shadows attacked tin cups of coffee like drug addicts snatching an overdue fix. As soon as their PBYs and Marauders were refueled they dragged themselves back into the cockpits and took off once again into the brawling night.

The first day of battle was ended. The second began just like it, with aerial adversaries groping through the Aleutian weather, blindly trying to find one another.

CHAPTER FOUR

The Battle of Dutch Harbor: The Second Day

JUNE 4, 1942: THE MORNING BROKE rainy, with a low black overcast. At Umnak and Cold Bay, combat crews exhausted by grueling night-search flights had to cook their own breakfasts in bivouac areas swollen with mud and oozing muskeg; even the insides of the tents were six inches deep in the stuff. Pilots and gunners, their ground crews left behind at rear bases, had to fill their own aircraft from heavy 55-gallon gasoline drums, change their own oil and make baling-wire repairs.

One Liberator had spent the night on a fruitless eight and one half hour patrol; Lieutenant Billy Wheeler wrote in the 36th Squadron war diary,

> At approximately 6:30 this morning Lieutenant Andrews landed at Kenai with only a few minutes' fuel. The landing was made on a runway studded with barrels that had been placed there to prevent enemy aircraft from landing. Andrews accomplished an unbelievable feat, since the ship touched nothing in its landing roll.

Andrews was lucky; another night patrol—a PBY flown by young Ensign Hildebrand, who had helped shoot down the only Zero hit at Dutch Harbor the previous day—ended in death. Hildebrand's patrol sector took him into the fiercest storm area of the night; he, his crew and his airplane disappeared and were never heard from again.

Young, green, terrified by the gale-force storm, and frustrated by the enemy's elusiveness, the dogged air crews kept the search going through the day. Air commanders made regular head counts and were amazed that more tragedies hadn't occurred. So far, nobody had cracked up on the unfinished steel-mat runways that had worried General Butler.

One of the few veteran Aleutian fliers in the air on the morning of June 4 was Ensign Marshall C. Freerks, all arms and legs and grin, a PBY magician who volunteered for the toughest missions—and always came back. "I always left something undone," he explains, "so I knew I'd have to come back." This time it was a half-written letter home.

At 9:00 in the morning, eight hours out and about 160 miles southwest of Umnak on the return leg of his patrol, Freerks' radar man reported a contact. The screen's pale green surface showed blips where no islands or ships were supposed to be. Freerks put the Catalina into a gentle dive to go down for a look.

He had found the Japanese carrier force.

FREERKS COUNTED THE SHIPS IN Admiral Kakuta's second Mobile Force, radioed back an exact fix and description, waited until his signal was acknowledged, and then reluctantly broke off the contact after a look at his fuel gauges. He reached Cold Bay in time to see ground antiaircraft batteries filling the sky with flak—they were shooting at the six new B-17s that had emerged from the clouds overhead. The hapless Fortresses took violent evasive action; Freerks gave them a wide berth. With his engines sputtering out, he glided into nearby Cannery Cove and landed on the water. Behind him, ground gunners belatedly recognized the American bombers and stopped shooting. They had not scored any hits.

Delayed by interservice confusion and slow radio relays, Air Force bombers headed into the air from Cold Bay and Umnak to attack the Japanese fleet that Freerks had located. In the meantime, Commander Russell's exec, Lieutenant Charles E. "Cy" Perkins, had flown out of Dutch Harbor to take over Freerks' contact with the enemy carriers and shadow them until a bomber strike could arrive. Perkins, who had a crusading fervor to win the war singlehanded, had his PBY festooned with a torpedo and two 500-pound bombs; he found the enemy carriers by radar an hour before noon.

Perkins sent back a report of position, course and speed; and added a remark that chagrined, but did not surprise, those who knew him:

"Going in to attack."

One slow flying boat against seven men-of-war, Perkins went into a screaming dive, leveled off above the water, and prepared to launch his torpedo against carrier *Junyo*. Japanese antiaircraft orchids blossomed fast; one flak burst blew up Perkins' starboard engine and all but pitched the PBY into the sea. Perkins righted it at deck level, disgustedly jettisoned bombs and torpedo, and ducked into a squall. To lighten the plane more, he dumped half his fuel; he limped home on one engine. Perkins' valiant attempt earned him the Navy Cross, but the Japanese fleet was still untouched. Air Force bombers had reached the area, but without radar their only chance of finding the carrier force in the storm was to be guided in by a radar-equipped pathfinder.

While Captain Owen Meals, with six B-26 Marauders from Umnak, circled blindly in search of the phantom enemy, a third PBY arrived to cover the Japanese force and guide the bombers to target. Lieutenant (jg) Eugene W. Stockstill found the fleet with his radar, but by then *Ryujo* had launched an umbrella of fighters. The moment Stockstill came in sight, Zeroes swarmed across his course and shot Stockstill down in flames with all hands. He had no chance to make radio contact with the Air Force attack planes.

It left the bombers without eyes. The B-26s went down to wave-top level several times, desperately hunting the invisible enemy. The weather was broken—not a continuous storm, but a close-bunched series of violent squalls, separated by patches of fog. Meals did not stay long on the deck; he and his pilots had too much respect for altitude, the only defense against sudden wild downdrafts.[1] The first enemy, as always, was the weather. It was not Japanese cleverness, and not American blundering, that kept the opposing forces from joining in battle; it was the power of Aleutian nature.

At Cold Bay, hot-blooded Colonel Eareckson of Bomber Command had lost patience with the inactivity of the radio shack, where he had spent twenty-four hours trying to coordinate air missions. Eareckson turned the job over to a subordinate, strode down the muddy runway and climbed into the cockpit of a B-26 Marauder. His Air Force crews had taken instruction from Commander Russell's Navy airmen in how to arm their bombers with torpedoes; now, with the belly-hung torpedoes clearing the steel runway by only four inches, Eareckson led a six-plane formation off the ground, out across a drumming southwesterly course aimed at the area where the enemy had been reported by the PBYs.

As Eareckson's flight approached the target area it plowed into a murderous black fog that hung all the way down to the water. There was no choice but to climb over it. In the process, one pilot lost sight of the

---

1. A year earlier, after a practice diving attack, the Eleventh Air Force had recorded its first operational obituary for a victim of Aleutian weather. The official report said, "The formation hit such turbulent air at 4,000 feet that all the planes fell out of control to 1,500 feet. Lieutenant (William A.) Anderson's plane fell into Chatham Bay in three pieces."

formation. Lost, Captain George W. "Wayne" Thornbrough, Operations Officer of the 73rd Bomber Squadron, decided to go ahead independently.

Alone, Thornbrough found the Japanese carrier force. He made two unsuccessful torpedo passes, then put the B-26 into a shrieking, wing-straining dive, hoping his speed would arm the torpedo's water impeller in the air; there was no room to launch a torpedo between the Japanese screening vessels, but if he could arm the torpedo by diving, and use it like a bomb, he might be able to hit a carrier.

The dive whined up speed until the bomber shook violently. Below, the carriers heeled into desperate flank-speed turns, swinging their bows toward him to present the narrowest targets. Deliberately, Thornbrough aborted his approach, pulled out of the diving attack and wheeled around at deck level, waiting for a broadside target. He only had one torpedo; he wanted it to count.

On the bridge of *Ryujo*, Air Officer Masatake Okumiya stood watching with awe while the American bomber leveled off just above the sea and burned in toward him at full combat speed, flying dead level with seeming contempt for the solid wall of antiaircraft flung at him by every ship in the Japanese fleet.

The seas were running heavy, too rough to permit the launching of fighters; *Ryujo's* deck heaved up and down several yards with each wave swell. Unable to do anything but stand and stare, Okumiya watched the thundering B-26 barrel toward the ship in a clean run across *Ryujo's* deck, watched the torpedo—dropped like a bomb—fall free of the plane, and watched the gleaming missile arc toward *Ryujo*, dead amidships.

Ryujo pitched into a wave trough; the deck heaved down—and the sizzling torpedo slipped over the dropping deck and plunged into the sea some 200 yards beyond, throwing up a huge geyser.

Okumiya slumped with relief. In the air, Thornbrough was furious. He cut away through heavy flak bursts and zigzagged into the soup, setting course for the Aleutians with one ambition: to rearm his bomber and come back for the kill.

The uncertainty of navigating through Aleutian fog brought him out of the clouds at Cold Bay, although Umnak was closer to the Japanese fleet—Eareckson and the rest of the flight were landing at Umnak after their fruitless search, but Thornbrough went on into Cold Bay and waited impatiently while excited ground crews loaded his B-26 with 500-pound bombs and gasoline. He wrote out a complete description of the composition, disposition and location of the enemy task force; Commander Russell immediately broadcast it.

Thornbrough climbed back into the bomber, determined to sink at least one Japanese carrier before the day was over.[2] When he disappeared into the foggy gloom, it was the last anyone ever saw him alive. Shortly before midnight Cold Bay picked up his voice radio: *"Over station, nine thousand feet on top, trying to find a hole."*

On the ground, Commander James S. Russell heard the distress call, made contact with seaplane tender *Casco* and talked with the skipper. *Casco* tried to coach the Army pilot down by using the ship's direction finder on Thornbrough's radio. It almost worked: Thornbrough was trying to land on the radio-range signal when he crashed. A month later the wreckage was found on the beach of the peninsula about 40 miles from Cold Bay.

THE SEARCH WENT ON. In the early afternoon two B-17s—"Old Seventy" and an early prototype Fortress on loan from the Cold Weather Lab at Fairbanks—joined the dozens of varied craft searching the region from which Freerks, Perkins, and Thornbrough had radioed. The two four-engine bombers were the next to confront Admiral Kakuta, who by now was amazed by the strange one-at-a-time attack tactics of the Americans.

The two B-17s had radar. Determined, hotshot Captain Jack L. Marks, in "Old Seventy," was leading the two-plane flight; his wingman was Lieutenant Thomas F. Mansfield. The two found Kakuta's carrier fleet by radar. Marks went down to 900 feet and made a bomb run through scattered fog. He dropped his five big bombs from such low altitude that the blasts tossed the old B-17 and shook up the crew; nevertheless the worst damage done was to splash water on the Japanese ships.

Marks climbed out of the barrage of flak and orbited. Mansfield told him by radio that he would attack at closer range. He went down to deck level and headed for cruiser *Takao* (on whose deck Navy Lieutenant Wylie Hunt was being questioned by Japanese interrogators). Mansfield was ready to release his bombs when his plane blew up in a sheet of flame; he had flown right into a flak burst. The old Fortress smashed into

---

2. The official Eleventh Air Force history and other records made rumor into myth when they recorded the story that Thornbrough's first attempt on Ryujo failed because the Navy had not shown him how to use his torpedo (not true), and that Colonel Eareckson "advised" Thornbrough not to take off on his second flight, but that Thornbrough disregarded the advice and went away anyway, to his death. First, Eareckson would have given orders, not advice; second, Eareckson was at Umnak and Thornbrough landed at Cold Bay, and there is no evidence the two officers ever communicated with each other after Thornbrough lost formation during the first sortie.

the water just short of *Takao* and sank so quickly that nobody was able to get out.

Overhead and out of bombs, a stunned Captain Marks radioed back to base, and turned "Old Seventy" home.

On Marks' signal, weary Captain Owen Meals, who had already flown one patrol that day, climbed back into his cockpit and led his six B-26s from Umnak back to the same waters he had searched all morning. This time Meals and two of his wingmen found the carriers.

All three Marauders went in with torpedoes. Two aimed for *Ryujo*, the third for *Junyo*. They bored in from opposite directions and released their fish; the torpedoes plunged into the water and sizzled toward the carriers.

That night the elated unit historian of the 36th logged the claim, "Today a B-26 sank an enemy cruiser with a torpedo." The claim was confirmed officially—but in fact none of the torpedoes scored a hit, let alone a sinking, and at the end of this final attempt to blow him out of the water, Admiral Kakuta was still in possession of a totally unscathed fleet.

IF THE UNCOORDINATED AMERICAN efforts to find and sink the enemy seemed to be a slapstick series of vaudeville frustrations, the Japanese performance was equally confused. Kakuta had made a dizzying number of course changes, some of them meant to evade air attack by keeping to the cover of storms, others made because the Japanese staff had trouble deciding what to do next. In the early morning hours, Kakuta had fueled his destroyers from the accompanying oiler and set out westward to bombard the island of Adak in a pre-invasion softening-up. Those were his orders from Admiral Yamamoto. But the fog had become so heavy that Kakuta had to reduce speed to less than 10 knots, and his weathermen had predicted that it would get worse the farther west he went.

Back at Dutch Harbor the weather was likely to be better. During the morning Kakuta canceled the attack on Adak and reversed course once more to head for Dutch Harbor. The miserable weather hid him from search planes and American picket boats, some of them at times passing within a few thousand yards of him.

Kakuta's maneuverings lost him time and headway; at no time before noon was he close enough to launch a bomber strike against Dutch Harbor. Finally, after shooting down Stockstill's PBY, Kakuta decided he had to make speed. Despite the risk of increasing knots in the fog, the primary mission was still to keep pressure on Dutch Harbor—enough to persuade the U.S. fleet headquarters at Pearl Harbor to send ships north in defense of Alaska. At this point in time, before noon on June 4, neither Kakuta in the North nor Yamamoto in the Central Pacific knew that the U.S. Pacific Fleet had already passed safely through Yamamoto's submarine screen—and that within a very few hours Admiral Raymond Spruance's U.S. carrier planes would close with the Imperial Fleet at Midway.

Kakuta set course on a straight line for the American base, knowingly risking discovery by a large enemy air group. This was when he was attacked by Thornbrough, Marks, Mansfield, and the others who finally found him because he was no longer taking evasive action.

Just before three o'clock Kakuta judged he was close enough to hit Dutch Harbor again; but even now, the weather was so bad that he only allowed his best pilots to take off. He launched a single combined wave, seventeen bombers and fifteen fighters, from both carriers.

When the planes were halfway to target, a terse coded message reached Kakuta. Admiral Yamamoto's signal implied that the battle at Midway was going badly; it ordered Hosogaya and Kakuta to postpone the occupation of the Aleutians, and instead steam south at top speed to join the Japanese reserve force north of Midway.

Puzzled, Kakuta replied that he would comply as soon as possible. He did not understand what Yamamoto meant. What could possibly have gone wrong at Midway? The plan had been foolproof.

Baffled, he looked out past the bridge into the Aleutian haze. At any rate he could not obey the order immediately; his planes were en route to target, and he could not steam away before recovering them. Perhaps by then there would be clarification from Midway.

AT DUTCH HARBOR, BASE DEFENSES had been ready all day. The harbor had been cleared of ships, except for one vessel: the old station ship *Northwestern,* deliberately beached by a civilian contractor for use as a barracks for workers.

At four o'clock the Japanese planes came in from two directions. Fighters strafed the naval station; Kate bombers leveled off at high altitude to drop sticks of high explosives and incendiaries.

Two bombs made direct hits on the decks of the grounded *Northwestern*, throwing sheets of flame through the ship. Waves of Zeroes strafed the fifty-year-old liner until the rolling mass of smoke became so thick they could no longer find the target. Beneath the thick cloud, fire-fighting crews and damage-control parties went grimly to work, with more dedication than might have been expected. She was old and beached, but the veterans loved the ancient troop ship. Since 1909 she had served as an Alaska Steamship Company vessel, and her reputation was phenomenal—she had run aground sixteen times in the Inside Passage, but always survived. She would survive Japanese thousand-pounders as well: fast-working crews flooded the engine room, and ultimately *Northwestern* was saved. For many months thereafter her engines were to supply power, steam and heat to the community.

Flames and black oil smoke from the burning ship half-obscured the village of Unalaska and the Navy base while Japanese planes swept over Dutch Harbor and Fort Mears in steady waves, smashing installations. An oil tank shot spinning into the air. A steel building twisted slowly, sagged, and collapsed under a stick of bombs. HE bombs demolished one wing of the base hospital; incendiaries set fire to a warehouse, gutting it. Four U.S. Navy men were killed instantly when a bomb blew their antiaircraft emplacement to fragments. Then, with an ear-splitting thunder of explosions, four big fuel storage tanks blew up. More than 750,000 gallons of fuel oil went up with a roar loud enough to alert crews at Umnak, 40 miles distant. Searing heat flashed through Dutch Harbor, flinging new eruptions of thick black smoke over the embattled community.

But in the twenty minutes of savage destruction, only eighteen men lost their lives; twenty-five others were injured. Dutch Harbor's defenders were well dug in.

Heavy antiaircraft flak scored no hits on the wheeling enemy aircraft, but the Japanese did not escape untouched. The Rube Goldberg radio had failed to get through, but Umnak had been alerted by noise, and by the Japanese choice of the west end of Unalaska Island as a rendezvous point to rally after each attack. Now eight Japanese planes from Junyo had formed up in plain sight of the Umnak runway—and eight Flying Tiger Warhawks scrambled to meet them.

American fighters corkscrewed through the enemy formations, striated the sky with tracers, and sent one dive bomber into a spin, surrounded by a white vapor that turned black and erupted before the bomber torched into the water.

Lieutenant John J. Cape, a good-natured boyish twenty-three-year-old pilot who loved to drive an old tractor around Umnak, watched a Japanese dive-bomber swell in his gunsight until, at pointblank range, he triggered a burst that hammered the enemy plane into a ball of flame and sent it down in fragments. Then a snapped warning in his radio headset made him look behind: he had a Zero on his tail. He zoomed upward, hung desperately on his propeller, and rolled over on his back in a wild attempt to evade the Zero.

In 1942 the United States had no fighter capable of outmaneuvering the Japanese Zero. When Cape righted his P-40 he found the Zero still with him. The panel instruments blew apart in Cape's face. Ammunition exploded in his gun racks and fumes rolled through the cockpit. Engulfed in flame, Cape fell into Umnak Pass, unable to get out of the spinning airplane.[3]

As Cape went down, Lieutenant Winfield E. McIntyre tried to break away from another pursuing Zero. The Zero's guns knocked out McIntyre's engine and set it afire. McIntyre put the ship into a screaming dive, trying to blow out the fire; he could not get the engine restarted, and almost went into a spin before he glided to a crash-landing on the Umnak beach. He put the burning P-40 down so skillfully that he climbed out of it and walked unaided into camp.

Overhead, the Japanese broke off and fled through the clouds; they had lost two planes in dogfights, and two more were so badly crippled that they crashed at sea before reaching their carriers.

Meanwhile, four of the homeward-bound Zeroes spotted an American PBY flying low on the water. The PBYs waist-blister gunners raked the sky with tracers that seemed to have no effect on the diving fighters. But three of the Zeroes broke off and headed away, too low on fuel to stay for the finish. One stayed behind to finish off the PBY: Flight Petty Officer Tadayoshi Koga, a slim young man with an abiding hatred for Americans. Koga blew the plane apart in the air with his guns. The Catalina splashed into the ocean, but Koga stayed to make sure. Finally one man (Aviation Machinist's Mate W. H. Rawls) crawled out of the burning wreckage and paddled away in a life raft.

Rawls, the blister gunner, had put a machine-gun bullet into Koga's plane, though Koga did not know he had been hit. That one bullet, a third of an inch in diameter, was to bring the Allies a decisive prize of war. Koga circled the bobbing rubber raft and machine-gunned Rawls to death in the water.

Koga climbed into the soup after that, but at that moment the needle of his oil-pressure gauge dropped to zero. Convinced his engine was about to pack up, Koga turned toward the nearest land—Akutan Island.

---

3. Cape was awarded a posthumous Distinguished Flying Cross, and the air field at Umnak was later named Cape Air Force Base in his honor; at the same time the Cold Bay air field was named Thornbrough AFB in memory of the bomber pilot who had been lost the same day after his second attempt to sink *Ryujo*.

He sent out a voice broadcast to the I-boat submarine which he had been told was standing by to pick up downed pilots. Coming in over the island, he prepared to make a forced landing on the flats.

He made the mistake of lowering his landing gear; his wheels caught in the boggy muskeg, snagged and flipped the Zero on its back. The crash broke Koga's neck.

The alerted Japanese submarine searched the coast by periscope, but could not find Koga's plane. (The Zero remained undisturbed on the lonely island until a month later, when a U.S. Navy PBY sighted it. Navy crews were immediately dispatched to collect the prize.)

Aside from a few dents, Koga's Zero was intact. Its only damage was a single bullet hole, from A/M Rawls' gun, severing the oil return line. The pressure gauge showed a loss of oil, but the engine was unharmed. American crews quickly dismantled the Zero and shipped it back to the States.

(Tadayoshi Koga's fighter was the first Zero captured intact by the Allies in World War II. The apparently trivial loss cost Japan dearly. American engineers, with this opportunity to fly and study the war's fastest, deadliest and most secret fighter aircraft, would learn a great deal from its specifications.)*

ADMIRAL YAMAMOTO WAS TAKING a terrible beating at Midway; that much was evident from the dispatches that reached Admiral Kakuta and his immediate superior, Admiral Boshiro Hosogaya of the Imperial Northern Force. Within hours, Yamamoto was to lose all four of the aircraft carriers he had committed at Midway, along with 332 planes and one-third of Japan's combat pilots; all told, Japan would lose more than 3,500 lives at Midway.[4] Midway lay in flames; but Japan had suffered her first major Naval defeat in more than a century.

It appeared to Yamamoto that without success at Midway, the Aleutian operation lost its meaning. So thinking, he had ordered Kakuta to bring his carriers south, to cover the withdrawal from Midway. But

*1995 ADDENDUM: The first edition erroneously stated that the captured Aleutian Zero provided the model for the design of the Navy's F6F Hellcat fighter. Allan M. Lazarus effectively exploded "The Hellcat-Zero Myth" in his summer 1989 Naval History magazine article of the same title. The Hellcat was built and ready to be test-flown by the time the Aleutian Zero was delivered to the lower forty-eight. Nevertheless it remains true that the AGFM-2 "Zeke" model was the first flyable Zero captured during the War, and that aeronautical engineers learned a great deal from it.

4. By comparison, U.S. losses amounted to 307 lives, 150 planes, and the carrier Yorktown which had already been crippled a month earlier at Coral Sea.

while Kakuta's planes were beating up Dutch Harbor, Admiral Hosogaya and Yamamoto's staff officers argued that any victory—even one so small as the capture of the western Aleutians—would be of great value to home-front morale; it would help offset the grievous loss at Midway. Besides, the strategic objective of guaranteeing Japan's northern defenses had not changed.

Yamamoto yielded to Hosogaya and his staff. At 1930 hours Admiral Kakuta received a new set of orders: the Aleutian operation must go on.

The Second Mobile Force reversed course again. Almost immediately there was yet another change in plan. Admiral Hosogaya, who commanded the occupation fleet forces, had orders to occupy Adak Island, less than 350 miles west of Umnak, as well as Kiska and Attu farther west. Now, feeling that he lacked sufficient forces to land on Adak within range of American planes from the unexpected base at Umnak, Hosogaya canceled the Adak occupation. The fleet changed course once more, heading farther west toward Kiska and Attu. Kakuta's carriers steamed along behind the occupation ships, providing air cover. By early morning on June 5, the Japanese task groups had threaded Theobald's picket lines without incident and were well beyond the limits of American air patrols. The fleet crossed into the Eastern Hemisphere before morning. Admiral Kakuta was depressed by the news from Midway, but that could not dampen his pride in the performance of his own officers and men; at a cost of only about fifteen lives and less than a dozen airplanes, he had fulfilled his mission—the harassment and partial destruction of Dutch Harbor and, soon, the occupation of the western Aleutians.*

LOCALLY, KAKUTA HAD DONE WELL. But strategically the Japanese operation in the Aleutians had been a blunder. Steaming away from the disaster at Midway, Admiral Yamamoto may have realized that if he had combined his forces, adding *Junyo* and *Ryujo* to the four carriers at Midway, the outcome would have been far different. The Dutch Harbor diversion had cost Japan the major battle of 1942—perhaps the war.

On the American side, the local cost in the Aleutians had been seventy-eight lives and fourteen airplanes, but Dutch Harbor was still intact, even if it was destined for a shaking-up in reorganizations and new training procedures—shore batteries had fired some 12,000 rounds of antiaircraft, and ships in the harbor had fired several thousand more on June 3, and all they had to show for it was a shared claim (with a PBY

*1995 ADDENDUM: The five Japanese prisoners taken at and after the Battle of Dutch Harbor were the first enemy POWs to arrive in the continental United States.

gunner) of one enemy plane shot down. The Signal Corps was rushed into the Aleutians in strength, to correct the dangerous faults in radio communications

As the fourth of June drew to a close, no one knew the United States was about to lose the western Aleutians; at the moment the result at Dutch Harbor looked like a local stand-off, satisfactory in the face of the great strategic victory at Midway. Still, no one was sure where the Japanese carrier raiders might strike next. Admiral Theobald had listened to radio reports all day; by evening he was erupting with exasperation. Radio silence prevented him from giving any orders beyond line-of-sight blinker signals; when he heard of the second attack on Dutch Harbor, it was too much for him. He cut loose from his cruiser force and made a high-speed run to Kodiak in the *Nashville*. It was early morning (June 5) when he reached base—just in time to receive a PBY's report of two enemy carriers with five escorts steaming toward Dutch Harbor from the Bering Sea.

Theobald scrambled every available plane to scour the Bering, and set out aboard *Nashville* to join in the search. There ensued the "Battle of the Pribilofs," in which the six new B-17 Flying Fortresses saw their first action: with the aid of their new radar, they dropped several tons of bombs on radar targets that looked like a task force on the green screens. When they went down afterwards to find out if they had scored any hits, they discovered they had all but sunk the Pribilof Islands.

There was no Japanese fleet in the Bering Sea, but the game of hide-and-seek would last five days, with Theobald racing in and out of Kodiak to issue bursts of orders before continuing the chase, until finally it became obvious that the patrol plane report had been an error. At the end of the fog-shrouded fifth day, Theobald carried his flag onto the beach at Kodiak and planted it there for good—whereupon he learned that the enemy, undetected and unopposed, had occupied the western Aleutians—an event to which the admiral would react with apoplectic expletives.

"BUT FOR THE FOG," said General Simon Bolivar Buckner Jr. of the Alaska Defense Command, "there go I." He referred to the military commanders at Pearl Harbor who had been scuttled after the December 7 disaster; only the miserable Aleutian weather, he knew, had prevented both sides from suffering great damage.

It was tempting to use the weather as a scapegoat. It nicely masked the fact that conflicting orders, fouled communications, an absentee admiral, and confusion in the untried joint commands had half-paralyzed American reaction to the enemy attack.

Nevertheless, if only because Nimitz's codebreakers had given them warning, the Americans had done far better at Dutch than they had at Pearl Harbor. Alaska had not been touched—although local newspaper reports that a handful of desperate heroes had saved the Territory and kept war from the West Coast seemed more enthusiastic than the facts warranted. In a series of barking dispatches to Stateside commands, General Buckner warned that the only reason the Japanese had not taken Alaska was that they didn't seem to want it at the moment. Next time, he said in a request for reinforcements, the enemy might not be as lenient.

Dutch Harbor had been saved; Midway had been saved, and with it, American naval power in the Pacific. The western Aleutians had been lost, but it would take time to assess the significance of that loss. In the meantime, at the Air Force base at Umnak, the fourth of June ended as it had begun. Wheeler's 36th Squadron war diary concluded,

> Andrews, returning from Kenai in the LB-30, topped off an exhilarating trip when his right landing gear gave way during the landing and this ship joined others in the permanent repair department. No one was injured, but Dick Leow found his tin hat crumpled.

The Battle of Dutch Harbor was over.

CHAPTER
FIVE

Buckner's Beehive

GENERAL BUCKNER HAD REMAINED behind the scenes during the battle. But the defense of Dutch Harbor had required men, planes, equipment, and bases. Without Buckner, none of these would have been there. Dutch Harbor, and Alaska, owed whatever defenses they had to Simon Buckner.

Until mid-1940, Alaska had never had a defense commander. When Anthony J. Dimond, Alaska's voteless delegate to the U.S. Congress, had pleaded for funds to defend the Territory, he had been shouted down with catcalls of "pork barrel" and one Congressman had asked seriously, "Why should anybody want Alaska?"

With the outbreak of World War II in Europe on September 1, 1939, America's twenty peacetime years of isolationism and unpreparedness gave way reluctantly to considerations of self-defense. Unrest in the Pacific, and open war in China, persuaded the Joint Chiefs of Staff to strengthen America's western outposts, and Plan Orange, one of the Rainbow plans for hemisphere defense, established a strategic triangle—Panama, Hawaii, and Alaska. Lieutenant General John L. DeWitt, thin-lipped Commanding General of the Fourth Army and the Western Defense Command at San Francisco, was ordered to prepare the West Coast and Alaska for the possibility of war against the ambitious military regime of Japan.

To provide Alaska with a military commander, DeWitt tapped the Chief of Staff of the 6th Infantry Division, Colonel Simon Bolivar Buckner Jr.[1] Buckner reached Anchorage on July 22, 1940, preceded by some eight hundred troops of the 4th Infantry Regiment, and saw immediately that he had been handed a herculean task.

1. Buckner's father, Simon B. Buckner Sr., had been one of the Confederacy's first generals. Forced to surrender Fort Donelson to Grant after a bitter siege, Buckner Sr. had made a daring storybook escape from Union prison and made his way back to the South, where

Alaskans had been alarmed ever since Japan rolled her divisions into Manchuria in 1931. There was a war on—and Alaska was defenseless. To remedy that, Buckner needed to build everything from scratch: garrisons, air fields, communications, supply lines. At the outset, he had to face all the staggering handicaps of any expeditionary force sent to occupy a vast foreign wilderness—even though this was American soil on the American continent.

Buckner had to contend with the military nightmare of a terrain that ranged from sea level to the 20,320-foot peak of Mount McKinley: glaciers, forests, craggy mountain ranges, tundra, permafrost, muskeg, shifting ice, even jungle-size mosquitoes. There were no good roads or transportation (other than one short railroad). There was almost no electric power. There were no military quarters or defenses, and no communications.

To complete the dismal picture, Alaska's agriculture could not feed a tenth of the resident population, much less an immigrant army. There was one tiny useless infantry post; the Navy had only the most perfunctory of emergency stations; and Buckner did not have a single Air Force plane, let alone air field, in 1940.

IN THE DECADE THAT LED up to Buckner's arrival, Alaska had struggled heroically but unsuccessfully to obtain military defenses against the

---

he was promoted to Lieutenant General, a rank his son would achieve exactly 80 years later.

Buckner Sr. became Governor of Kentucky despite Reconstruction policies. At sixty-two he took a twenty-eight-year-old bride. Buckner Jr. was born near Munfordville on July 18, 1886. At ten, the boy watched his father accept the National Democratic Party's nomination for Vice-President, but the McKinley Republicans won the election and Buckner at seventy-two retired from politics.

Buckner Jr. attended the Virginia Military Institute; in 1903 Theodore Roosevelt obtained his appointment to the U.S. Military Academy at West Point, where Buckner Jr., "Buck" to his classmates, graduated 57th in the class of 1907. During World War I he earned his wings and trained the nation's first combat pilots for the fledgling U.S. Air Service, but did not see action and was later criticized for having risen to high rank without test in battle.

A singularly air-minded infantryman, Buckner Jr. commanded an aviation brigade and served on the Air Staff in Washington between wars. He served twice at West Point, as tactics professor and commandant of cadets. In a letter, the mother of one cadet accused him of "forgetting that cadets are born, not quarried"—he was known as the Army's hardest bargain; he led his cadets on grueling 35-mile marches with full packs and once tossed the two West Point wrestling champs on the mat.

Yet, despite his accent on athletics and his splendid 200-pound physique, Buckner was one of the Army's leading scholars. In a primarily inarticulate profession, he possessed a first-rate vocabulary and an outstanding conceptual talent. His barbed aphorisms were legion; his witty letters were often devastating.

growing threat from the Orient. Warning voices, largely unheeded, cried out in the nearly 600,000-square-mile Alaskan wilderness—voices like that of Air Force prophet Brigadier General William "Billy" Mitchell, who had served in Alaska in his youth. On February 11, 1935, Mitchell had singled out Alaska as "the key point of the whole Pacific," and told the House Military Affairs Committee, "He who holds Alaska holds the world...Alaska is the most strategic place in the world. It is the jumping-off place to smash Japan. If we wait to fight her in the Philippines, it will take us five years to defeat Japan."

Fairbanks, center of Alaska, was within 4,000 miles of London, Berlin, Moscow, and almost every other strategic northern capital. The shortest line between Tokyo and the United States—the Great Circle Route—crossed the Aleutians and Alaska. In the bombers of 1940, Fairbanks was fifteen hours' flying time from New York—or from Tokyo.

Nine hundred miles long, eight hundred wide, Alaska bridged the Pacific across the top of the globe, where the waters of the Bering Strait were only 57 miles wide; trading Eskimos crossed the shifting winter ice on foot, and the American and Russian Diomede Islands faced each other across 2,600 yards of sea. Past that lay the Soviet Union; and from the western Aleutians it was only 650 miles to the northern Japanese military bases at Paramushiro in the Kurile Islands.

Respectable prophets like Vilhjalmur Stefansson, Homer Lea, and Bernt Balchen echoed Billy Mitchell's warnings; in 1937, Anthony Dimond had told Congress,

> Alaska today could be taken almost overnight by a hostile force. It is today without any form of defense. At least $450 million have been spent in the defensive installations [at Pearl Harbor and Hickam Field in Hawaii], and yet the inescapable conclusion to be drawn from the most casual inspection of a globe...is that, so far as the main body of the United States is concerned, the defense of Alaska is of much greater consequence than those all but impregnable defensive works [in Hawaii]...What's the use of locking one door and leaving another wide open?

But three years later the new Territorial Governor, Ernest Gruening, could still state flatly, "A handful of enemy parachutists could capture Alaska overnight."

Gruening had seen for himself: he had visited the sole Army base in pre-Buckner Alaska. As Gruening recalled the trip,

> Chilkoot Barracks had about as much relevance to modern warfare as one of those frontier Indian-fighting posts from the days of Custer and Sitting Bull. It had no road or air connection with the outside world. Its only transportation was provided by a 51-year-old harbor tug. When we went up the Lynn Canal, the terminal fjord of the Inside Passage, we encountered a 30-knot headwind that stopped us cold and stranded us for three days. We had to be rescued by the Coast Guard. If war had come, we'd have had to sue for peace and ask for a wind-check.

Chilkoot Barracks had not changed much in the forty years since it had been built to guard the gold trail to the Klondike. Charmingly situated on the Canadian border, it housed four hundred soldiers who kept leisurely garrison routine, armed with World War I rifles. One old Russian cannon, the only artillery piece in Alaska, served as a flower pot.

BUCKNER FOUND BITTER IRONY in the fact that Alaskans, the most air-conscious people on earth, had no Air Force when war was not only possible but probable. The airplane was Alaska's only alternative to the dogsled as a means of crossing the wilderness from town to isolated town, yet air fields were almost nonexistent—bush pilots landed on frozen lakes, glaciers and mud flats. (During the 1930s a third of Alaska's planes were destroyed in crashes, but pilots learned how to "crack up easy" and only sixty-three people died in the decade. Pioneer glacier pilot Bob Reeve alone survived seventeen air crashes in eight years.)

Though the Territory's history was studded with the names of great aviation pioneers who had flown there—Lindbergh, Balchen, Amundsen, Billy Mitchell, Ben Eielson, Howard Hughes, Wiley Post—few Washington officials had taken note of Alaska's need for air facilities. One of the few officers who recognized it had been Brigadier General Henry H. "Hap" Arnold, chief of the young Army Air Corps; in 1939, Arnold had appeared before a congressional committee to beg funds for a cold-weather aviation laboratory in Alaska:

> Our people have got to be trained how to fly up there. How to start an engine when it's 40 degrees below zero. How to keep the oil from congealing before you get it into the engine. What happens to a metal airplane when you bring it from minus-40 degrees and suddenly put it in a warm hangar. We have every reason to believe the rivets will just fall out.

Congress had voted $4,000,000 for the test lab—the nearest thing Alaska would see to an air-defense appropriation in 1939—but political bickering stalled funds, and when Buckner arrived in mid-1940 construction had barely begun.

Only two weeks before Buckner's arrival, Hap Arnold and Lieutenant Colonel Ira C. Eaker had toured Alaska to spot air field sites and lay out runway patterns four miles from downtown Anchorage, where Buckner hoped to build Elmendorf Air Base. But Arnold had to get the money for it from Congress, and Congress was not yet prepared to oblige.

For Simon Buckner, outspoken, uninhibited and still a colonel at fifty-four partly because he had argued too often with generals, the Alaskan job was his first major command in thirty-three years as an Army officer, and no matter how much the situation infuriated him, he was determined to master it. But it was not easy. From the moment of his appointment, he was faced with a system that gave him a huge job and then prevented him from doing it. Without funds, equipment, or men, he could do nothing but travel around and learn his territory.

He could not sit still. He worked out frustration by hunting duck and bear with his Kentucky setters, by flying a borrowed plane into the Kenai and Bristol Bay wilderness to fish the famous trout streams. At forty-seven he had learned to ice skate; he had been a mountain climber all his life; now, inexhaustible in his mid-fifties, he took up skiing.

When not traveling, Buckner spent his first Alaskan winter in a tent. His orderly used a blowtorch to thaw the ice rime on Buckner's outdoor bathtub each morning. When he finally moved into sturdier quarters he hung a huge Kodiak bearskin on the wall—scuttlebutt said he had yelled at the bear and "it just up and died of fright." No soldier ever complained that he did not hear an order Buckner gave—his normal voice level was one most men would have used only during an artillery barrage. Upright, downright, and loudspoken, Buckner was not known for tact; but there were times when he displayed unexpected subtlety—as when his shrewd silence helped bring Alaska its first real defense funds:

For two years the House Committee on Un-American Activities had been busily "exposing Communists," spurred by the Hitler-Stalin alliance and the fear of war in the Pacific. On April 22, 1940, the American press broke the story that Nazi-Soviet forces (reportedly witnessed by the USCG cutter *Perseus*) were building air and submarine bases on Big Diomede, a few miles from Alaska. Alarmists cried, accurately enough, that the Russians had bases all over the Siberian coast and that the Soviet air base at East Cape was only 150 miles from Nome.

The Hitler-Stalin pact produced a full-scale Red scare. By June it was seriously reported that Russo-German forces were ready to attack Alaska from Big Diomede and elsewhere. Just before Buckner came to Alaska, a suspicious Governor Gruening flew over the Russian "base" in a borrowed plane. He took photos from the window to confirm what he saw: the Soviets were actually building nothing more threatening than a scientific station to study Arctic phenomena. Big Diomede had no harbor that submarines could use, and despite its name the island was too small for a bomber field.

Buckner met the governor at Anchorage, heard Gruening's report, and suggested drily that the Red alarm was "a very useful rumor, don't you think?"

For once, Buckner's voice was conspicuous by its silence: this time he shot down his bear, a Russian bear, with an absence of noise. In a very short time the Red scare induced Congress to vote a record defense budget for Alaska, and within eighteen months Buckner and Gruening had more than $350,000,000 for Alaskan military construction.

THE FIRST CONCRETE RESULT OF Buckner's shouting was an obsolete B-10 bomber which made its screeching landing on the grass runway of Merrill Field, the civilian airport of Anchorage, on August 12, 1940.

It was feeble, but it was a beginning for the war Buckner expected to fight. His entire new Eleventh Air Force stepped out of the plane—Major Everett Sanford Davis, Sergeant Grady, and Corporal Smith. But if Buckner was dismayed he gave no sign of it. Davis hardly had a chance to get his land legs before Buckner was telling him that he wanted air fields set up on a dozen proposed sites throughout Alaska in time for the arrival of combat squadrons—an arrival for which Buckner fixed the tentative date of May 1, 1941, just eight months hence.

Buckner's staff (most of them recruited from the Alaska veterans at Chilkoot Barracks) had misgivings: in ordering the construction of so many fields he was exceeding his authority. But Buckner was in a table-thumping mood; he told them that like the turtle, a man could only advance when he stuck his neck out. As far as he was concerned, war was just around the corner. He did not confuse movement with action, but he knew he would have to do ten years' work in a space of months; and the problems could not be solved with the Maginot Line mentality of many Stateside commanders. To do the job, he would bend a few rules if he had to.

Davis set up his Eleventh Air Force headquarters in a portable one-room wanigan, a cabin on sled runners. He "reformed" a number of infantrymen, commandeered four cargo planes, and within weeks had six air fields surveyed and the Cold Weather Aviation Laboratory activated. To learn Alaska's aerial bag of tricks, Davis put himself on a backbreaking schedule of testing; he often pushed his luck as well as his energy—he wrote: "Three times in six weeks I have been caught between mountains with no radio or emergency fields available, and had to pull up into the soup (never can get up through it), deadreckon to the flattest area available and go down through."

Mechanics and engineers arrived from the States to help—there was a kind of high adventure in the air, in an era when great mechanical challenges could be met by one man, working with his hands, his imagination and a pair of pliers; when blueprints were sketched in hangar-floor dust and their designs manufactured on the spot with sheet metal and acetylene torches; when five gloveless minutes fiddling with a fuel line could cost a man several fingers in subzero cold.

The Eleventh Air Force historian wrote in exasperation: "Oil becomes like jelly, hydraulic systems freeze, and rubber becomes brittle and fractures...." Yet Davis learned so much about Arctic aviation in the following months that he was able to put together a unique and invaluable text which saved hundreds of airmen's lives in the next few years.

RESULTS WERE TOO SLOW—for Buckner, and for the war that was imminent.

During the fall of 1940, hordes of construction men began to ship into Alaskan ports. They were hardly off their boats when Buckner had them at work. At Anchorage, he was building Elmendorf Air Base and Fort Richardson, which was to be his headquarters. At Fairbanks, he built Ladd Field so quickly that by September its new runway was complete; to remain smooth and flat at –60° it had to contain more concrete than there was in every paved street and sidewalk in all Alaska. At Dutch Harbor and elsewhere he constructed antiaircraft sites and ground-troop garrisons; at sites throughout the wilderness he assigned workers to Everett Davis' air field construction projects, where they drilled with jackhammers and broke the permafrost with highpressure steam jets.

Buckner ("The Silver Stallion of Alaska," as he loved being dubbed) never seemed to be more than ten paces from anything. His trousers pressed to a razor edge, he was everywhere, bellowing in his parade-ground voice, badgering civilian contractors to work their crews three shifts a day, seven days a week. When cement shipments sank en route, he told the contractors to use native stone. When shiploads of milled lumber did not arrive on time, he used his Army troops to cut down trees and handsaw them into planks. When rain ruined newly mixed concrete before it could set, he used the soldiers again, putting them to work shoulder-to-shoulder with civilian workers to make up the lost time. With Japan on the march, there was no time to be lost. Buckner, the battling great swaggerer, the performing extrovert, pushed his men harder every day. Ebullient, crusty, bellicose, he had a resonating impact.

With miraculous speed, a massive discordant complex was orchestrated into phenomenal harmony under Buckner's direction. Miles of runway were hewn out of the muskeg, scores of barracks raised and roofed, hundreds of gun emplacements scooped out and revetted. In spite of supply problems, weather, mosquitoes[2] and myriad other handicaps, Simon Buckner changed the face of Alaska virtually overnight.

EVEN A YEAR BEFORE PEARL HARBOR, Alaska was like a country at war. Every ounce of cement, steel, gasoline and Coca-Cola came by sea, through the dangerous channels of the Inside Passage, on battered crowded boats Buckner stole or begged from other commands, and on the creaky old steamers of the Alaska Steamship Company—and even these merchant tramps, loaded to the gunwales with men and equipment, sailed under Navy orders.

The ships had to navigate the foggy fjords by the echoes of their horns; to supply Anchorage, they had to fight the 30-foot tides of Cook Inlet. Within a year at least a dozen sank or ran aground on the treacherous Alaska run. But the convoys kept coming; to Buckner, it was build fast or forfeit Alaska in the war that was sure to come. Civilian Alaskans accused him of warmongering and rabble-rousing; even the War Department regarded him as a pest, although his performance quickly earned him a promotion to brigadier general. But Buckner had no doubts that war would come, or that Alaska would be one of its battlegrounds.

Backed by the new defense budget and the prestige of his new rank, General Buckner received a steadily increasing tonnage of equipment—but this posed a new problem. He could not get the equipment out of his ports.

There were hardly any roads; even Fairbanks and Anchorage had no

---

2. In 1943, an Eleventh Air Force pilot wrote of the infamous Alaskan mosquito, "The flight characteristics of Alaskan mosquitoes have been greatly exaggerated. It is not true that they are as large as vultures. It is not true that antiaircraft outfits fresh from the States have opened fire on them, thinking they were Japanese Zeroes. Their tail assemblage is entirely different."

connecting highway until Buckner had one built.[3] The railroad belt to Fairbanks was almost the only reliable corridor of movement—and the thought of a bomb attack on that slim thread gave Buckner ample cause to thunder and roar.

Shiploads of heavy equipment piled up on the docks. The principal method of getting it to the new inland bases took months: shipped inland by river barge during the fall, machinery then had to wait for winter when tractor-pulled cat trains hauled it on sleds across the freeze-hardened muskeg. To avoid some of these delays, Buckner hired Robert C. Reeve and other bush pilots to haul deliveries into the new air fields. The amiable Reeve often carried five and a half tons of cargo in his trimotor biplane designed to haul two tons. He was often in the air fourteen hours a day, maintaining and repairing the battered Boeing 80-A during brief loading-unloading halts. In five months Reeve alone flew more than 1,100 tons of equipment and three hundred men into the new Air Force field at Northway.

By these means, Buckner laid out his air fields. By the spring of 1941 some were finished, others crude and unpaved, but all of them were ready to operate. On the last day of March he brought to Alaska the combat planes that would use them.

Fifteen B-18 bombers of the 36th and 73rd Bombardment Squadrons flew into Elmendorf Air Base that day. They were quickly joined by twenty P-36 fighters of the 18th Pursuit Squadron, which arrived by sea in crates and had to be assembled by Lieutenant Colonel Norman Sillin's pilots and crews.*

Buckner did not approve of the War Department's investment in antiquity—the B-18s and P-36s were old, slow, and obsolete—but it was a start. Now he had his air fields and he had his airplanes. He needed

---

3. Anchorage was linked to Fairbanks and Valdez (both on the Richardson Highway) by way of the Glenn Highway which runs from near Palmer to Glennallen. A fervent booster of this road link was *Anchorage Times* publisher Robert Atwood.

Simon and Adele Buckner were frequent guests at the Atwoods' in 1941. Buckner's aide, Colonel Edwin Post, would adroitly steer the cocktail conversation to lead smoothly up to some remark that would "remind" Buckner of a story. He had a rich lode of anecdotes but always wanted Post to run conversational interference for him by paving the way for his "ad libs." One of Buckner's favorite legpullers was a fanciful, elaborate recipe for mint juleps that began, "First you go out to a clear mountain creek when the moon is full..." He delighted Anchorage society with his southern charm and gallantry; when offered Scotch whisky he would always bow courteously and shake his white-maned head. "Not," he would roar, "in the presence of bourbon!"

*1995 ADDENDUM: John Cloe's precise research indicates that the first aircraft actually arrived in February 1941, but that the full 36th and 73rd Squadrons did not assemble at Elmendorf until May 1941.

more of both; but more important, he needed leaders to help him prepare Alaska's armed forces for war.

He obtained one such leader in the person of the slim aviator who led the 36th Bombardment Squadron into Elmendorf: Major William O. Eareckson, forty-one, a raffish aviation pioneer who had been piloting fabric-and-wood biplanes when some of his squadron's young officers had been in safety pins. A crack pilot who flew with his fingertips, Eareckson was headstrong and sometimes arrogant; he had a contagious drive and a romantic recklessness that infected his young pilots with the notion that pilots were a breed apart, a race of giants.

Eareckson and his followers had recently shown their contempt for groundlings in typical fashion. Eareckson had invited the entire squadron—planes and all—to come from March Field, California, to his wedding in Reno, Nevada. Frederick R. Ramputi recalls: "Part of the celebration was our fly-over by the squadron. I flew with Major [William M.] Prince down the main street. There was plenty of room for the airplanes, even though I was looking up to second-story windows." Not for some time did Reno forget its sidewalk-level buzzing by a thundering squadron of Air Force bombers.

Thus Buckner had on his hands a group of green young pilots, arrogant with ignorance. Few of them were old enough to have known the days when nomadic barnstormers had slept on the prairie beneath the wings of Jennys, but they were all under the spell of the legends. They had joined the Air Corps, as one of them, Lucian Wernick, puts it, "as insurance against having to slog through the dust with packs on our backs," after the enactment of the 1940 draft law. Few of them had more than a few hours' solo flying experience.

Buckner and Everett Davis picked Eareckson as the man most likely to bring the new pilots through Alaskan training alive. Davis organized the three squadrons into a Composite Air Group, and Eareckson took command of it, with a promotion to lieutenant colonel. His pilots expected a loose and happy ship, but Eareckson soon showed them an altogether new face. He did not propose to lose a single airman for lack of training; the penalty for ignorance or carelessness in the Alaskan sky was unchangeable. The "cheechako" (Alaska greenhorn) pilots trained from reveille to taps on a migraine schedule. They flew endless practice missions; they learned instrument flying, dead-reckon navigation, and a hundred other techniques and abilities.

Davis and Eareckson pressed a number of veteran bush pilots into service to help train their pilots; no one could learn high-country flying by piloting a Link Trainer or reading manuals. Strange air pockets claimed several victims, quickly demolishing five of the B-18s, and subzero flying called for the utmost in skill and special knowledge; a cold carburetor or ice on the wings could cut power or destroy the delicate buoyant airfoil and make an aircraft into a few tons of metal no more capable of flying than an iron safe. Alaska had massive underground mineral deposits that deflected magnetic compasses, fooling even expert pilots and leaving them lost, hundreds of miles from an air field and out of fuel.[4]

An acute problem was the lack of radio-beam navigational facilities by which pilots could "fly the beams"—navigate by tuning radios to directional beams from air fields of known location. Worldwide shortages, and Alaska's low priority, kept Buckner from obtaining transmitters, and the Eleventh Air Force had to settle for seat-of-the-pants navigation, aggravated by the fact that only two of Alaska's civilian airports (Juneau and Anchorage) had night beacons.

Alaska was short of all kinds of electronic equipment. Buckner impressed on General DeWitt the need to demonstrate how feeble Alaskan communications were, and when Japan called up 1,000,000 conscripts on July 2, 1941, DeWitt used it as an excuse for a vivid demonstration of unpreparedness: he called a July Fourth alert from Point Barrow to Panama. Within minutes, Panama and California stood to arms—and in Alaska it took four days for the alert to reach all stations.

---

4. Colonel Harold H. Carr, executive officer of Fort Richardson, got lost in the Yukon while flying a Norseman through a storm from Fairbanks to Whitehorse. Air-search teams scoured the area without success, because Carr had been blown so far off course by compass deflection and high-altitude winds that he had actually come down farther from his destination than he had started. The 36th Squadron history notes, "During the search we flew over terrain that was either completely uncharted or very inaccurately charted at best." When Carr finally turned up safe, General Buckner let out his great ringing laugh and promptly wired, WRONG WAY CARR AGAIN.

Eareckson had a similar experience on an air field inspection flight along the southern panhandle coast. Trapped by snowstorms, he ran low on fuel and had to execute a daring, skillful stall-landing on a thin strip of curving beach. Three days later a Coast Guard cutter found him; the skipper observed, "He must have landed the plane with a shoe horn." But Eareckson persuaded the sailors to bring ashore a few cans of fuel, which he poured into his tanks. The Coast Guardsmen watched amazed when the plane lifted free, cleared the whitecaps by inches and spiraled into the sky.

With only enough fuel to make nearby Yakutat, Eareckson was advised by the radio tower that a wicked crosswind was blowing flakes across the narrow runway strip that had been hurriedly cleared for him; and the tower warned him to please avoid hitting a B-10 bomber parked on the field. In a sarcastic rage, Eareckson shouted, "Why don't you take all the pregnant women in town and put them on the runway too?" The radio operator at Yakutat did not log his own reply. Eareckson somehow landed safely.

Radios were so thinly scattered and so undermanned that airplanes, runners and dogsled teams had to deliver the word to frontier stations.

Buckner and DeWitt made their point. The War Department allocated an emergency fund for the immediate expansion of communications in Alaska.

It didn't mollify Buckner very much. He complained, in a voice like a bassoon, that he was "playing without any cards." Having seen that he could draw attention to Alaska's plight by making enough noise, he fired a fusillade of letters:

To DeWitt, July 13, 1941:

> About twenty years ago, I could have knocked out Joe Louis easily, when he was young and weak. Since he has grown up I would hesitate to meet him in the ring. The same principle applies to hostile expeditions against Alaska. If we hit them while they are at sea and weak, we can destroy them, but if we wait until they are on shore and strong, our chances for the heavyweight championship are not particularly good.... There are two ways of dealing with a rattlesnake. One is to sit still and wait for it to strike. The other is to bash in its head and put it out of business. That is what I favor.

To DeWitt, July 17:

> Only two fields exist in Alaska from which bombers can take off with full loads.

To Chief of Staff, Gen. George C. Marshall, July 24:

> In view of our present available strength, or perhaps I should say weakness, I would rather have one squadron of heavy bombers than a whole division of infantry.

To DeWitt, September 4:

> We must have an air striking force now.

To Marshall, November 28:

> Quick-drying cement does us very little good in speeding up construction unless some quick-drying ink is used on the approval of our plans.

DeWitt said he would support Buckner, "right up to the lynching," and by December the Army promised aircraft, new construction equipment, and warning installations, including radar. The trouble was, no such equipment was actually available for use. As if it would be an adequate sop, the Army promoted Buckner to major general on August 4, but that didn't abate Buckner's disgust with a new Air Force policy—to hold outpost forces to a minimum and concentrate air strength within the States. The announcement came just when two of Buckner's B-18s and half his P-36s were grounded for lack of spark plugs and other small parts; by August 1941, the Eleventh Air Force was down to five obsolete bombers and nine obsolete fighters; by December Alaska was the only theater which still did not have a single up-to-date combat plane. The day before Pearl Harbor, Everett Davis wrote: "By no stretch of the imagination can we be [expected]… to defend the Territory against any attack in force."

In Washington, Buckner's chief ally was General George C. Marshall, but Marshall felt hamstrung by President Franklin D. Roosevelt's attitude toward the Navy ("us") and the Army and Air Force ("them"). The Navy had the Administration's ear—and the Navy, in Washington and in Seattle (headquarters of the Naval District that included Alaska), did not believe Buckner's constant demands for planes and bases were justified.

The Navy, which had opposed Buckner's ambitions from the beginning, had shown no interest in Alaska until 1940. Its Fleet Problem XVI in 1935 had been conducted in the Aleutians (watchfully shadowed by the *Hakuyo Maru*, a Japanese "fishing" vessel), but in 1940 the only armed vessels in Alaskan waters had been a few Coast Guard cutters. At about the time of Buckner's arrival, funds had come through for a general beefing-up of Navy facilities at Sitka, Kodiak, and Dutch Harbor.

Though the Japanese had made a point of exploring the seas around Alaska and the Aleutians,[5] the U.S. Navy had made few efforts to chart the waters or defend the North Pacific frontier. Instead, it had devoted its efforts to fighting Buckner, who insisted that the most serious threat

---

5. Anthony Dimond wrote in January 1941, "Alaska's strategic value was early recognized by the Japanese, who secured from us an agreement, in the Treaty of Naval Limitations of February 6, 1922, not to fortify the Aleutian Islands." The Treaty expired in 1934 but no U.S. naval bases were built west of Dutch Harbor until after the Aleutian Campaign began. Meanwhile the Japanese (whose large angling fleet caught one-fourth of the world's fish) were busy "fishing" Aleutian waters with lines calibrated in fathoms. They took soundings throughout the 1930s, explored many inlets in Alaska, and landed on virtually every island in the chain; they even placed markers on some of the coastlines. By 1939 Japanese

to Alaska came from the air, and that Alaska needed antiaircraft defenses and air bases more than anything else. The Navy had argued from the beginning that the impossible terrain would tie down ground forces, that the defense of Alaska should be essentially a Navy function, and that Buckner's responsibility should be limited to the protection of the three Navy bases then being built.

For several months, the tough Navy stand had kept Buckner from getting authority to build his air bases. He had built them anyway; authorization came after the fact. In the end, the Navy had relented to the extent of letting Buckner build a chain of landing fields on the Alaskan mainland, but it continued to block Army ambitions in the Aleutians (one reason why, a year later, Buckner would defy regulations by building his secret Cold Bay and Umnak air fields with funds diverted from other projects).

In his public pronouncements, Buckner insisted that "Army" and "Navy" were indistinguishable terms in Alaska—that the two comprised a single welded force. He was being less than candid; what truth there was in the statement came from his rapport with Navy Captain Ralph C. Parker, whom the Navy had placed in charge of its newly subdivided Alaskan Sector in October 1940.

Parker, literate and forthright, was Buckner's kind of man. He had come north in his "flagship," the gunboat *Charleston*; it was the only vessel in his Alaskan Navy until Parker purchased three small fishing boats, painted them Navy gray and "converted" them into Yippee-boat patrol craft.

No sooner had the paint dried than Simon Buckner had marched on board *Charleston* and told the startled captain that the matter of first priority was to reconnoiter the Aleutian Islands and see whether air fields could be built there against the possibility of Japanese invasion.

If only to humor the lunatic general, Parker had assigned him a destroyer, and Buckner had set out into the foggy Aleutians. He had ordered the ship into perilous coves and crannies, acted impervious to the howling weather, and terrified the Navy crew; later he himself wrote to General DeWitt:

> The Naval officers had an instinctive dread of Aleutian waters, feeling that they were inhabited by a ferocious monster that was

---

submarines and patrol boats were openly reconnoitering Annette, Nunivak, Unalaska (Dutch Harbor), and no doubt other islands where they were not spotted. The wonder was, with all this busy espionage, that the Japanese did not make better use of their superior knowledge of North Pacific waters in the campaign to come.

> always breathing fogs and coughing up williwaws that would blow the unfortunate mariner onto uncharted rocks and forever destroy his chances of becoming an admiral.

The Aleutians[6] which Buckner blithely set out to explore were the world's longest archipelago of small islands. The westernmost island, Attu, though part of the North American continental shelf, was the only inhabited American island in the Eastern Hemisphere. From here it was five time zones back to the Alaskan capital, Juneau (about the same distance as that between Atlanta and San Diego).

Like war clouds, the tropical Japan Current came up from the south, and met the cold dry Siberian air mass over the Aleutian Chain. Although the warm current kept the ocean ice-free the year round, the clash of forces created the world's worst weather: it was perhaps the only place on earth where high winds and thick fog attacked simultaneously—round-the-clock Aleutian gales sometimes reached 140 miles an hour; yet most of the islands had no more than eight or ten clear days in a year. There was no calm or dry season.

It was not a place Buckner would choose for a battleground. But then, war seldom offered a choice. The climate would be hell on ships, on planes and on men; fliers would have to fight not only the weather, but

---

6. The Aleutian Islands were fixed on Pacific charts in 1741 by Vitus Bering, a Danish explorer in the service of the Russian Czar. The chain was soon crowded with Russian fur traders and murdering looters who systematically slaughtered the Aleuts; the tribes were near extinction when the U.S. purchased Alaska in 1867. (Congress caustically deliberated "Seward's Folly" and finally approved the $7,200,000 Alaska purchase by the slimmest possible margin—one vote. Since the Juneau Discovery of 1879, Alaska has returned in gold alone more than $900,000,000.)

Americans stocked the islands with blue foxes to give the struggling Aleuts a means of livelihood, and established the Coast Guard's Bering Sea Patrol as the symbol of U.S. sovereignty; it brought law, protection, and medical aid to the scattered Native villages. Still, the Aleut condition was poor. There came to each village three whites: missionary, schoolteacher, and white trader. All three were usually at each other's throats and it cannot be said that the Aleuts' best interests were invariably served.

In the 1890s, Japanese pelagic sealing had reduced the North Pacific seal herd—source of "genuine Alaska seal" fur coats—close to extinction; in 1910 an international treaty banned all sealing near the Pribilofs, where the seals had their annual breeding ground. But in 1940 Japan denounced the treaty, and thus began a dead-serious naval tradition that was maintained through the darkest days of World War II and was still in practice in the 1960s: the armed escort by the U.S. Coast Guard of 2,500,000 seals through their migratory waters to the rocky Pribilof Islands in the Bering Sea.

...A note on pronunciations: Although Aleutian is pronounced "*al-ooshin*" or "*al-yooshin*," the tribal designation Aleut is pronounced "*Alley-oot.*" Aleuts were the first North American natives encountered by the Russian explorers, and the word "Alaska" is a Russian approximation of the Aleut word for the Alaskan mainland.

nightmare air pockets created by rough terrain and the steamy craters of hundreds of volcanoes that sent up poisonous hot gases.

It would be a primeval field of battle. There were no trees—wind kept them from taking root. Here and there crouched a wind-stunted shrub. The inland valleys grew thick with rank weeds, coarse wild rye grass, ferns, parsnip, monkshood, fireweed and other wildflowers that blazed forth brilliantly in summer. Beneath all this lay the muskeg—a thin elastic crust of matted dead grasses something like celery, overlying a topsoil of dark volcanic ash which became quicksand whenever it was wet, which was to say all the time. The muskeg's spongy animus would prohibit the movement of men, jeeps, tanks, or airplanes; the mud would suck the boots off an infantryman.

Buckner studied the jagged mountains and sunken bogs of the Aleutians with close care. He did not want to fight here; but if the fight came, he wanted to be prepared. As he traveled through the Chain he made a list of islands on which he felt runways might be built—Umnak, Adak, Amchitka, Kiska, Shemya, Attu. Before the end of the war, American warplanes would be operating from them all.

IN APPRECIATION OF BUCKNER'S fearless leadership of the joint prewar Aleutian survey, the Navy's Captain Parker formally presented him with a commission as "Brevet Brigadier Admiral." For a time, the two commanders' friendship made for easy interservice relations in the Alaska theater. But Parker did not make policy; he only carried it out. In Seattle and Washington, higher Navy officers watched with growing restlessness while Buckner built Alaska into what looked like one big Army and Air base. In the months before the United States went to war, military officials had no one to snipe at but one another. They bickered over Alaska with the same sort of buck-passing, charging and countercharging, and Army-Navy corruption that would soon lead to disaster at Pearl Harbor.

Simon Buckner was not without prejudice, but his was limited to Academy football-team loyalty (and contempt for all indecisive bureaucratic officialdom regardless of service). He never tried to blame the Navy for Alaska's unpreparedness; in fact he supported most Navy efforts to increase sea power in the North Pacific. Advocates of more and bigger naval bases in Alaska had no stauncher supporter than Buckner.

Nevertheless, Alaska's Army-Navy fight came to a boil, and it was a trivial dispute that brought it to a head.

In the fall of 1941, Buckner had committed his few bombers to a vigorous coastal patrol instructed to warn all Japanese craft to stay out of

American waters. The warnings were in keeping with national policy, but the use of Army planes to fly offshore patrols incensed the Navy. Jealous of their prerogatives, Navy officials in Washington demanded sole control over air patrols at sea—and added the punitive demand that since Buckner was not supposed to run the patrols, he therefore should be denied long-range aircraft.

The Navy's arguments seemed overly bold, since the Navy had no planes in Alaska to take over the job. Discreetly, General George C. Marshall mediated the controversy by proposing that Buckner's offshore patrols be phased out as soon as the need was past. The Navy agreed. A few of its PBYs had been stationed intermittently at Sitka, home-based out of Seattle; now patrols were extended as far north as Kodiak,[7] but Buckner steadfastly kept his own patrols flying, and when the Navy objected, he pointed out some figures that indicated the Navy's actual ability to take over coastal reconnaissance and defense: On December 7, 1941, Army forces in Alaska had increased to 22,000, of whom 2,200 were Air Force personnel. On the same day, the Navy had 67 men at Dutch Harbor, 300 at Kodiak, and about 180 at Sitka. The Kodiak Naval Base had only seventeen minutes' ammunition. The Navy had no capital ships in Alaskan waters—and only six PBYs.

IT WAS NAVY OPPOSITION, AND the foot-dragging of the War Department in the face of imminent combat (or so Buckner was convinced), that gave Buckner his excuse to rip the red tape to shreds and issue *sotto voce* orders to bypass the uncooperative twitches of government digits.

In August 1941, a group of hard-bitten civilians landed from ships in Cold Bay, at the southwestern tip of the Alaska Peninsula where the Aleutian Chain began. From here west, the Navy had done everything short of putting up NO ARMY TRESPASSING signs.

Hauling ashore several shiploads of crated construction machinery addressed to *Saxton & Co.*, the tough civilian engineers picked out a site for a "fish cannery" and began leveling and surveying. They ruffled the feathers of an old hermit pensioner who had lived undisturbed on the barren flats with such eccentric comforts as a fur-lined outhouse seat.

7. It was fortunate that the Navy extended its air patrols to the north. On August 25, 1941, fifty miles south of Montague Island, the U.S. Army Transport *Clevedon* was wallowing through a heavy sea when a soldier on board came down with acute appendicitis. Lieutenant Commander James S. Russell, skipper of Patrol Squadron 42, was then at Kodiak with his PBY flying boat; Russell flew out through the storm with an Army doctor, made a daring landing on rough seas, picked up the stricken soldier, and flew into Seward, where the soldier underwent a successful emergency operation.

The construction workers quickly ruined the sourdough's peace, shot a number of pesky brown bears whom he had regarded as friends, and made an incredible amount of noise, building what looked like a road. The sourdough gave up in disgust and moved away.

Saxton & Co.'s crates carried the return-address labels of one *Consolidated Packing Company* in Anchorage. It was well that no Navy officers looked up the two corporations, for neither existed.

In crates marked *Cannery Equipment*, bulldozers and graders came to Cold Bay and were put to work by laconic engineers who gave no answers to questions put to them by the idle curious who watched them drift mysteriously in and out of Seward and Anchorage.

The workers were civilians, all right, but their supervisors were officers of the Civil Aeronautics Authority, their boss was Army Engineer Colonel Benjamin B. Talley, and what they were building was not a cannery but an air field. To pay for it, Buckner had quietly diverted funds and equipment meant for inland base construction at McGrath.

With the work well under way, Buckner formed a new subsidiary, the *Blair Fish Packing Company*, and prepared to move it out to Umnak while he started clever proceedings to embezzle funds from yet another inland project to pay for building the Umnak base. It proved unnecessary; in the States, General DeWitt was in Buckner's confidence, and had sold the Navy and the War Department's Joint Board on the Cold Bay-Umnak plans at last; on November 26 Buckner got official authorization for the two fields. But he went ahead with the clandestine "fish cannery" schemes, using them as cover operations to fool the enemy.

Legitimate funds were held up for a while, but on March 5, 1942, dressed in civilian clothes, the 807th Army Engineers went into the Aleutians, under Buckner's hand-picked engineering officer, Colonel Talley.

Umnak was the third-largest of the Aleutian Islands—675 square miles, about half the size of New York's Long Island. It supported about fifty residents, most of them Aleuts, 15,000 imported Australian sheep, and a herd of reindeer introduced from the mainland. Ruggedly mountainous, it had no trees, and according to early reports its muskeg was "incapable of supporting an aircraft runway." To compound the handicaps, the Otter Point area—the flat area closest to Dutch Harbor—had nothing remotely resembling a natural harbor. It was just a flat spit, poking out into the rolling tides of Umnak Strait and exposed to the full fury of Aleutian gales.

Under any other circumstances it would have been unthinkable to propose an airplane base be built at Otter Point. But Dutch Harbor—

with its excellent port, its command of Unimak Strait, and its existing Army, Navy, and Coast Guard bases—was vital to the defense of the whole vast area: it controlled access to Siberia, Nome, the upper Alaska Peninsula, and the eastern half of the Aleutian Chain. If Japan should attack Alaska (and Buckner never doubted she would), then Dutch Harbor would be a key target. There was no choice but to build an air-defense base as near Dutch Harbor as possible. Otter Point, on Umnak, was the only answer.

To master the impossible muskeg, "incapable of supporting an aircraft runway," Buckner applied his usual ingenuity: he imported 3,000,000 square feet of pierced steel-plank matting, designed to be laid down in an interlocking weave of 80,000 individual 65-pound mat segments. The Marsden matting was still experimental; nobody knew if it would work; but Buckner told his Engineers to try.

Umnak's second handicap, its lack of harbor, was far more difficult to master. The only sheltered landing spot for ships was in Chernofsky Harbor on Unalaska, eleven miles across Umnak Strait from Otter Point. Fierce storms were almost continual. Every man and piece of equipment had to be barged in lighters from freighters in Chernofsky Harbor, across the churning waters of the Pass to the wide open beach. Equipment had to be carried by hand through the pounding surf, and dragged by cat-trains to the runway site. The 807th Engineers fought through several inches of snow and 80-knot winds, working around the clock; on some days they laid as much as 500 feet of runway in twenty-four hours; and by March 31, after just twenty days' work, they had completed a 3,000-by-100 foot strip, and the first plane landed—a C-53 transport, with a passenger on board: the new Commanding General of the Eleventh Air Force, William O. Butler. From that moment forward, Simon Buckner had his hands full trying to persuade Butler to make use of the new runways which the Engineers had done such a magnificent job of building.

"Build us the nests," Buckner had told the Engineers, "and I'll bring the birds." But the birds did not come until after war began, and in the meantime, late in November 1941, warnings from State Department Japanalysts convinced Buckner that the fragile trans-Pacific peace was close to breaking. As of December 1, 1941, the Alaska Defense Command went on a War Alert status.

Buckner fired a shotgun-blast of dispatches at DeWitt, Hap Arnold, and Marshall, urging the delivery of the promised warplanes, requesting authority to move farther west along the Chain and build more bases, and insisting that the Alaska Defense Command "could easily become the

Alaska Offense Command," and that the Aleutian Chain formed a "spear pointing straight at the heart of Japan."

The replies were a long time coming. Meanwhile, early in December, twenty Japanese warships slipped out of Etorfu in the Kurile Islands, and sailed east on a track south of the Aleutians. Buckner's air patrols did not reach out that far, and the Navy had no patrols in those waters. The twenty Japanese ships proceeded without detection along the Aleutian boundary until they turned to starboard somewhere south of Amchitka and set a new course that would bring them, on that Sunday morning of December 7, to Pearl Harbor.

CHAPTER SIX

"The Airfield is for Use Either by Ourselves or by the Enemy, Whichever Gets There First"

THE DAY THAT WOULD LIVE in infamy began peacefully in Alaska. Churchgoers bundled up and trudged to nine o'clock Sunday services, even though the sun would not be up for two hours.

It was 9:30 a.m., December 7, 1941, when radio station KFAR at Fairbanks, with the most powerful equipment in Alaska, picked up a faint signal. Announcer Augie Hiebert pressed the headphones to his ears and listened with disbelief, then wrenched off the headset and put in an emergency trunk call to General Buckner.

At Fort Richardson, in Anchorage, Buckner listened coldly to the news. Japanese carrier planes were attacking Pearl Harbor. Early reports indicated that more than a dozen U.S. Navy ships, including eight battleships, were in flames and sinking.[1] Pearl Harbor was afire; casualties were monstrous.

War had come. At one stroke, discounting only the three American carriers then at sea, Japan had broken the back of the U.S. Pacific Fleet.

And Alaska might well be Japan's next target.

Buckner ordered the guns of Fort Richardson to fire, to summon the men to arms. Radio stations KFAR and KFQD broadcast the news throughout the Territory; to the south, in Juneau, Governor Ernest Gruening answered his phone gruffly—his bags were packed and he was waiting to hear whether the ship on which he planned to leave for Seattle (on a trip to Washington) would leave today in the raging snowstorm.

---

1. At Pearl Harbor, the Japanese attack sank or crippled eight U.S. battleships and nine other warships. It destroyed 230 airplanes, killed more than 3,600 people and wounded 1,500 more. In the harsh, cold terms of military scorekeeping, it was a brilliant and astounding success for its mastermind, Admiral Isoroku Yamamoto. Japan's only—and persistent—strategic mistake was to underestimate the force and will of the American reaction. It was hardly a unique mistake.

The news shook Gruening badly. He was a feisty political antagonist and had fought to implement Alaskan defenses, but the energetic leprechaun-faced governor was above all devoted to peace.

Shortly before ten o'clock he canceled his Washington trip and called Buckner. The two men outlined emergency measures without wasting words; Buckner had already drawn up contingency plans for just such an event.

Trucks with shrieking sirens raced through Anchorage to collect troops from town. All civilian traffic was cleared off the streets, which roared with the rush of armed vehicles and military trucks. Buckner grounded all private airplanes except those on Army-approved emergency flights. The Air Warning Service went into full alert, spurred by rumors of imminent attack. Colonel Eareckson's handful of B-18 bombers struggled into the air with full bomb loads to fly offshore patrols to their maximum range; Colonel Sillin's P-36 fighters flew inshore sectors with armed machine guns.

When Buckner ordered civilian radio stations off the air to expedite military communications, many neighboring Canadians immediately feared that the Japanese had taken Alaska. Canadian broadcasts to that effect reached isolated Alaskan settlements, and the alarm was compounded when Radio Tokyo (audible on short-wave receivers) boasted that Kodiak and Dutch Harbor had been bombed to rubble, that 3,000 people had been killed in air attacks on Fairbanks, and that Anchorage and Sitka were in Japanese hands.

Stores boarded and taped their windows. As the brief subarctic daylight gave way to dusk, Buckner decreed a strict blackout. Civilian workers at Umnak and Cold Bay dug trench shelters. Alaskans gathered two-week food supplies in rucksacks and stood ready to bolt for the hills on a moment's notice; with visions of fighting a civilian resistance campaign from the wilderness, they crowded around shortwave radios to hear the latest reports of the war.

As far south as Puget Sound, farmers armed with shotguns patrolled the beaches. General DeWitt's San Francisco command, acting as if the war were already on its doorstep, enforced full blackouts while searchlights probed the night sky—and Brigadier General William O. Ryan, Interceptor Commander, claimed his fighters had turned back thirty Japanese planes at the Golden Gate. A Seattle street was looted by a mob in panic.

MONDAY MORNING BROKE COLD AND cloudy at Anchorage. Buckner sent a coded dispatch to Hap Arnold in Washington:

> AT DAWN THIS MORNING I WATCHED OUR ENTIRE ALASKAN AIR FORCE TAKE TO THE AIR SO AS NOT TO BE CAUGHT ON THE FIELD. THIS AIR FORCE CONSISTS OF 6 OBSOLESCENT MEDIUM BOMBERS AND 12 OBSOLETE PURSUIT PLANES...SO FAR OUR REQUEST FOR AVIATION GASOLINE HAS ACCUMULATED TWENTY ENDORSEMENTS BUT NO GASOLINE.... OUR CONSTRUCTION HAS BEEN CONCENTRATED IN THE INTEREST OF ECONOMY IN SEWER PIPE RATHER THAN A DIVERSION AGAINST BOMBING.

The President called an emergency meeting of Congress to declare war on Japan; Alaskan Delegate Anthony Dimond told the House, "My people feel that they are occupying a battlefield"; and overnight, Washington seemed to realize how vulnerable Alaska really was. Belated orders were cut to send Buckner emergency aid.

Forty-eight hours after Pearl Harbor, the Eleventh Air Force responded to an air-raid alarm blurted by the jittery Air Warning Service. Two B-18s almost collided at take-off in the thick fog; three fighters shot down a U.S. weather balloon, and then had to go down to treetop level and follow the railroad tracks into Anchorage to find their way home through the soup. The Los Angeles *Times* headlined JAPANESE AIR STRIKES ON ALASKA.

But by midweek, after Navy planes at Sitka had bombed a whale after reporting a "submarine sighting," Alaskans were rediscovering their balance and humor. When Buckner commandeered the swank Mount McKinley Park Hotel as a rest haven for his off-duty men, Robert Atwood reported sarcastically in his Anchorage *Times* that the Army intended to camouflage Mount McKinley, the tallest peak in North America. Finally the Commandant of Fort Richardson, Brigadier General Jesse A. Ladd, threatened criminal prosecution of rumormongers.

Draft Board officials parachuted into remote Eskimo villages, where enterprising missionaries had already signed up confused Natives as conscientious objectors. Sourdoughs in the back country organized vigilante squads armed with hunting rifles, but most Alaskans settled back to their normal routines, even when General Buckner ordered the evacuation of all military dependents from the Territory. The evacuation began in December and did not exclude Buckner's own family; his wife Adele and the two sons he adored went to San Francisco. "If we get hit," Buckner growled, "I want my men thinking about their posts, not their families." The rapid disappearance of the distaff population was nothing new to Alaska, where there had always been a disproportionate ratio of men to women.[2]

What caused greater controversy was the evacuation of Japanese-American residents. Hardly had the smoke dissipated over Pearl Harbor when the West Coast's Hearst press started a banner campaign against the "yellow peril"; it was not long before a full-blown witch hunt was under way. Under pressure from a vast Western public whipped up to the verge of panic, the President authorized the Secretary of War to "exclude" Japanese from military areas. By order of the Secretary of War, Alaska and the Pacific Coast states were designated "military areas."

Men of good sense fought the tide. General DeWitt, not always the most reasonable of men, pleaded for reason and calm: "An American citizen, after all, is an American citizen…I don't think it's a sensible thing to do." Governor Gruening called the proposal "a shocking miscarriage of justice."

But because hysteria compelled it, evacuation began—hurried along by rabble-rousing cries like A. E. Johann's in *Alaska Life*: "Alaska is one of the great reserve territories of the Nordic race." Of the 230 Japanese residents interned in Alaska, more than half were native-born citizens; throughout the West, more than 100,000 people of Japanese ancestry were rounded up and herded into "relocation centers," many of them no better than prison camps hastily thrown together in brutal, inhospitable deserts.

Most of these victims of blind mob fear were born in America, schooled in America, and unquestionably loyal to America. It was not their loyalty that was suspect; it was their race. Only a handful of the Japanese residents of Alaska were found to have suspicious articles in their possession (like detailed topographic maps and charts of Aleutian waters).

General Buckner obeyed his orders without expressing any public opinion[3]; he seemed more concerned by items like Johann's "Nordic race" article, which soon led Buckner's intelligence staff under fast-moving,

---

2. "The lines outside the whorehouses were like chow lines," recalls one veteran. Another adds, "You never talked about prostitutes in the presence of wealthy Alaskans, because their wives were likely to be former ladies of the profession." In Fairbanks the red-light district was a row of log cabins on 4th Avenue, hardly changed from the Gold Rush days; Alaska was still frontier country, realistic and raw.

3. Buckner was a Kentuckian and the son of a Confederate general. He was inescapably conditioned in racial attitudes, although he expressed respect for Japanese military men and never made the mistake of underestimating them; there is little evidence he ever accused the Japanese (at home or abroad) of inferiority. But his racism sometimes stood out sharply. The Army was segregated; a number of Negro construction battalions served in Alaska, and

boyish Colonel Lawrence V. Castner to uncover several Bundist groups, the members of which were arrested along with some White Russian exiles suspected of being Nazi collaborators. Interrogations soon brought to light a small spy organization that took its orders from Hauptmann Fritz Wiedemann, Hitler's one-time adjutant who was then on loan to the Japanese Intelligence command in Tokyo, and who had once served as German consul-general in San Francisco. Once Castner had smashed Wiedemann's embryo spy-saboteur ring, virtually no further intelligence of Alaskan defenses reached Japan. But in the meantime more than two hundred Alaskans who happened to have Japanese blood were subjected to humiliation, injustice, and often inhuman treatment that mocked the principles for which America was supposed to be fighting.

Later in the Aleutian Campaign, several Japanese-speaking Nisei returned to Alaska to fight the enemy; but almost all the Alaskan Japanese spent the rest of the war in internment camps in the Southwest.

THE DAY AFTER PEARL HARBOR, Buckner wrote wearily to General DeWitt at Western Defense Command:

> We were fortunate not to have been included in the official calls paid by the Japanese yesterday.... As usual, I follow my customary practice of sending a radio requesting increased air strength and I have no doubt that you have, as usual, seconded it very heartily. I hope, however, that the unusual may happen in this case and we will get something.

Hap Arnold promised Buckner twenty combat air squadrons, but the Army ordered an "indefinite delay" in delivery, caused by "pressing needs elsewhere"; and only two squadrons were actually assigned. The orders were cut December 10, three days after Pearl Harbor; but the squadrons had to come in from Mississippi and Idaho. It took them two weeks to reach Sacramento, where they were supposed to be winterized. The Army Air Depot was overcrowded with emergency priority work, cold-weather gear proved impossible to obtain, and airplanes on test

---

Buckner segregated the service clubs to keep out Aleut and Eskimo girls. "For the protection of their own virtue," Buckner said; but many disagreed. It was partly over this that Governor Gruening finally cooled toward Buckner and almost broke with him. Gruening went to FDR with the problem, and by mid-1943 Alaska's service and USO clubs were opened to all. By war's end, Gruening had passed through the legislature a series of anti-discrimination laws which (long before their Stateside counterparts) forced establishments to abandon their house-rules of "No Natives allowed" and "No coloreds need apply."

flights cracked up in bad weather. At the end of the year both squadrons were still in Sacramento, although some personnel of their ground echelons sailed into Anchorage December 29 and were greeted by General Buckner: "I know that you and your garrison have the guts to take it, the punch to hand it out and the stuff to carry the war into the enemy's country before 1942 is over."

It was a stirring, saber-rattling speech but the fact remained that Buckner had no aerial sabers to rattle. Since Pearl Harbor he had pushed airmen and airplanes hard. All but one of the P-36 fighters had crashed while patrolling. The 36th Bombardment Squadron had no remaining aircraft of its own; its crews alternated half-day shifts in another squadron's planes, and clearly the few remaining B-18s would not last long if they had to stay in the air eighteen hours a day. Billy Wheeler wrote in the Squadron's unit diary:

> All patrols are flown to the maximum range of the B-18s. The weather is very bad, even for Alaska.... Icing conditions are always present and both men and ships suffer. The P-36 flying air-alert over Turnigan Arm iced up suddenly and spun out of control. The pilot escaped by bailing out....

But enemy submarines were putting in frequent appearances off the Canadian and Alaskan coasts; there was no reason to doubt they were scouting potential landing beaches for an invasion. Buckner had to keep his patrols in the air, no matter how few airplanes he had left.[4]

He wasn't heartened by growing rumors that the War Department had decided to abandon Alaska and leave it to fight with what it had on hand; this was already happening in the Philippines, where a Japanese expeditionary army had landed immediately after Pearl Harbor and was rapidly pushing MacArthur and Wainwright out to sea. Afraid the high command might have the same sacrificial fate in mind for him, Buckner wrote to DeWitt on February 4:

4. Buckner expected the same toughness of his men that he expected of himself. Sometimes he took an almost childish pride in his harshness, as when he trained himself to squint his eyes into narrow pinholes so he could read without glasses. Major General Archibald V. Arnold, second-in-command at the 1943 Battle of Attu, recalls, "General Buckner enjoyed being tough. He...slept on a cot with a very thin mattress with only a sheet for cover." But if Buckner drove men hard, it was not for lack of sympathy. He personally tested varieties of Arctic boot and sleeping bags under the most brutish midwinter conditions before he allowed them to be issued to his troops. He consistently saw as best he could to the feeding, housing, and recreation of his men. Nobody accused him of indifference; he showed an abiding concern for the soldier's welfare, if not comfort.

> I fear the War Department is obsessed with an unfortunate degree of optimism and dismisses Alaska with the thought that "if anything happens, we'll rush a lot of planes up there and take care of the situation." The point which is not taken into consideration is that planes cannot be rushed to Alaska....

In Washington, General Marshall advised the President that the Japanese might well attack Alaska "at any moment" and launch a full-scale occupation.

The battle of channels produced results, but the first of them was absurd: the War Department sent Buckner a new Table of Organization for his Air Force, providing for a huge increase in headquarters personnel, with a lieutenant general in command and a major general as chief of staff.

Buckner, himself a major general, snorted at the memorandum and returned it to Washington with a curt, scrawled note: *When we get enough planes for such a headquarters, we can ask for it.*

Taking up Buckner's battle cry, Alaskan civilians started to buy Defense Bonds for a new B-17 bomber to be called *The Spirit of Alaska.* Within four months they had surpassed every state in the Union by oversubscribing their War Bond quota by 300 percent. But it took a long time to build a Flying Fortress.

EARLY IN JANUARY THE 11TH Pursuit Squadron's twenty-five P-40s, and the 77th Bombardment Squadron's thirteen B-26s left Sacramento for Spokane, on the first leg of an incredible voyage to Alaska.

Commanding the fighters was Lieutenant John S. Chennault, son of a famous father, a big friendly twenty-eight-year-old Louisianan with a white scar on the right side of his face. Jack Chennault was a good pilot and a good leader, but when General DeWitt told him to fly the 11th Squadron to Alaska he was asking for a miracle. Chennault wrote:

> My three flight commanders had less than eight months' experience; eighteen of my pilots averaged less than eight hours apiece. It is obvious that we were poorly trained for a trip of such magnitude. We lost three planes before we even left the United States....

The short-range Warhawks followed a new patched-together Northwest Staging Route—up the eastern slope of the Canadian Rockies and across through Whitehorse into Alaska along the Yukon. Only five primitive staging bases had been leveled along the Canadian route, none of them complete. On some legs the P-40s had to fly to the limits of their fuel to reach the next air field, and some of the fields did not even have radio transmitters.

January—and it was one of the severest winters on record. Chennault's shivering fighter pilots plunged north out of Spokane into a melee of snowstorms and icy fog, and before they finished the journey they gave emphatic proof to Simon Buckner's statement that "Planes cannot be rushed to Alaska." Plowing blindly through subzero storms, the Warhawks lost one another, lost radio contact with the ground, lost their bearings, and a week later were scattered all over western Canada, out of gas on frozen lakes and farm fields.

It was six weeks before all the surviving Warhawks gathered at Fairbanks. Eight of them did not make it at all, though all the pilots eventually reached Alaska unhurt.

Meanwhile the thirteen Marauders of the 77th Bombardment Squadron had left Sacramento on New Year's Day under command of Major Robert O. Cork. It took four weeks for the first of Cork's Martin bombers to limp into Fairbanks; en route, one plane crashed in Canada, and four others cracked up between Edmonton and Fairbanks in a mountain bowl that soon came to be known, accurately, as Million Dollar Valley.[5]

It was mid-February before all the surviving new planes had regrouped at Fairbanks, and even then they had to be overhauled and rewinterized. Mechanics at Ladd Field worked at full speed to make use of the four winter hours of daylight, and then worked at night under floodlights in temperatures that went down to 40° below zero. Every piece of equipment, even coal to fuel the stoves, had to be thawed before use.

When the two new squadrons—twenty-five planes out of the thirty-eight that had started out for Alaska—finally went into patrol operation in March, Buckner did not fail to point out that it had taken four months to get them there. And he objected bitterly to the Air Force's choice of bombers: the B-26 Marauder was a new and untried design with such a

---

5. The 77th Squadron was plagued thenceforth by crackups. Within the next year it would lose twenty-seven officers and men in noncombat crashes, not to mention the total loss of thirteen airplanes in addition to the five demolished on the way to Alaska. The principal cause of these disasters was that many bugs had not yet been worked out of the new B-26 design. When Colonel Eareckson's Marauders went into battle at Dutch Harbor in June, it was the first combat anywhere for B-26s.

high wing-loading that it needed extra-long runways to take off and land. Long runways were precisely what Buckner's budget-dwarfed air fields did not have.

The B-26s had an effective round-trip range of less than a thousand miles—hardly adequate for long-range patrols over the vast North Pacific and Bering Sea. Buckner demanded heavy bombers with greater range; and by unorthodox *sub-rosa* tactics, General DeWitt provided them: he diverted from a British Lend-Lease shipment four LB-30 Liberators capable of flying 2,200 miles from runways of normal length.

This time Buckner refused to take chances with green pilots. He sent Colonel "Eric" Eareckson, with four Alaskan air crews, to California to pick up the new planes. Eareckson and his Alaska veterans flew the four heavy bombers from McChord Field, Washington, to Anchorage in one nonstop eight-hour flight.

It proved the value of using experienced Alaska pilots on ferrying flights; the method immediately put a stop to the horrible attrition of airplanes in transit.

Delivery of the first squadrons had been delayed by the need for winterization at the crowded Sacramento Depot. By spring, Buckner was certain the Japanese would attack before another winter set in. He prevailed on the Air Force to disregard regulations and send him planes whether or not they were modified for cold-weather flying. His demands had an urgent tone, for patrol accidents were frequent and unavoidable. Two of the four Liberators cracked up within weeks (the parts were used to keep the other two fyling), and planes piled up on the junk heaps faster than replacements could be ferried in.

DeWitt and Arnold sent a bit more help. By May 1942, two of Buckner's squadrons were equipped with new Marauders, leaving only the 36th with its tired old B-18s. Buckner persuaded the Cold Weather Laboratory to give up its one experimental B-17 Flying Fortress, and shuffled it quickly into the pack.

It still wasn't enough. When the secret Umnak runway went into operation in March, Buckner wrote to DeWitt:

> My greatest concern now is to get a squadron of P-40's on the field at Umnak. The field there is for use either by ourselves or by the enemy, whichever gets there first.... It is a splendid place from which to defend Dutch Harbor, but it is an equally good place from which to attack it.

BUCKNER HAD BEEN CRYING FOR airplanes; now, incredibly, he found that he would have to ground some of the airplanes he had if he could not get more pilots.

His airmen were sharp, well-trained; Jack Chennault's fighter crews regularly had six P-40s in the air within four minutes after a practice alert sounded. But daily combat patrols exhausted even the hardiest pilots; as Billy Wheeler noted in the 36th's diary, "The majority of our members have spent almost a year flying under adverse weather conditions, lacking accurate charts, in constant icing conditions...." Some of them began to crack under the pressure. One fighter pilot was sent back to the States with a deliberate self-inflicted wound, and morale ebbed steadily. On April 1, Buckner notified Washington that his Air Force needed at least 135 more pilots and three hundred more crew members. He was granted sixty pilots; but by the time they arrived, Buckner was at war.

In place of the badly needed pilots, the Air Force sent Buckner one forty-seven-year-old brigadier general whose qualification was that he was a rated balloon pilot: William O. Butler, former Chief of Staff of the Fourth Air Force.

The bureaucrats in their flyspecked wallboard offices in Washington were still obsessed by the Table of Organization which Buckner had already rejected. They seemed incapable of regarding his Air Force seriously unless it could be commanded by a general, no matter how dubious his qualifications for Alaskan combat air command. The two experienced Alaskan officers who might have taken over—Everett Davis and "Eric" Eareckson—had only recently reached full colonelcy; by the book, they did not have enough time-in-grade to warrant further promotion to brigadier general. And so in March the Air Force sent in "Bruce" Butler, methodical and placid, to assume command of the Eleventh Air Force.[6]

The new air chief toured the forward bases at Umnak and Cold Bay and turned in a cautious report that was hardly calculated to win Buckner's approval:

---

6. William Ormon Butler, born in Virginia on September 23, 1895, suffered constant confusion with William Olmstead Eareckson and Simon Buckner because of the similarities in their names. The coincidence did not stop there. Simon Buckner's father had been a nominee for Vice-President. General William O. Butler, also of Kentucky, had been the Democratic nominee for Vice-President in 1848.

Butler, a 1917 West Point graduate, had earned the Croix de Guerre as an Infantry officer in France in World War I. He had spent the next twenty years in the Air Service as a balloonist and staff officer. Late in 1941 he had planned and carried out the first mass flight of land-based airplanes from California to Hawaii; it was just Butler's bad luck that many of the planes were bombed to junk at Hickham Field when the Japanese hit Pearl Harbor.

> Tactical units should not move into and operate from a base which is not fully prepared to service them. Full station complement with complete equipment including transportation, signal communication and station equipment must be on the field and operating before the tactical units move in.

The report came just when Buckner had overruled time-consuming plans to pave the runways at Umnak and Cold Bay (in favor of using steel matting alone); it showed Buckner immediately that he would have a hard time reaching a meeting of the minds with the new Air Force general. His answer was to shunt Butler subtly onto the sidelines. By diplomacy and shrewd rhetoric, Buckner persuaded Butler to put Colonel Everett Davis in charge of the field headquarters at Kodiak. As a result, Davis kept tactical control of operations, with Eareckson working closely under him.

The maneuver worked well enough for a time, mainly because Butler realized he needed time to get used to his new command. But by late May he had developed confidence enough to move ponderously back into the center of activity, whence for more than a year Simon Buckner would attempt unsuccessfully to dislodge him.

BY THE SPRING OF 1942, Allied interest in the Aleutians had quickened. British Prime Minister Winston Churchill wrote to President Roosevelt on March 5: "Particularly I shall be glad to know to what point your plans for operating from China or the Aleutian Islands have advanced."

The answer was that War Department planners were designing a strategy to attack Japan by way of Nome, Siberia, and Kamchatka. The plans depended on Russian cooperation; Roosevelt was doing all he could to obtain it. The planning board ordered the Army to map a railroad route from Prince George, British Columbia, to Nome. Bush pilot Bob Reeve surveyed the route, but by then it was clear the Soviets were not happy with the idea, and planners switched their attention to the Aleutian Islands.

The Allies were not even holding their own in the Pacific; as Buckner was constantly being told, there were not enough men and planes available to give him an adequate defense force, let alone launch a quick invasion of Japan. Still, it was long-range planning that decided wars. If the United States could someday invade Japan, it would need to move its troops and equipment to bases within striking distance of the enemy. The Aleutians were close enough to Japan, but a quick solution had to be found to one great obstacle: there was no land route—no railroad, no highway—between the United States and Alaska.

As early as 1928 an Alaskan engineer, Donald MacDonald, had mapped out a practical Alaska-Canada Highway route; President Herbert Hoover had ordered a study; but on Pearl Harbor Day the road had not yet been surveyed, much less built. In 1940–1941, joint American-Canadian staffs had debated various routes, but the Canadians pointed out that once the Alaska Highway was built it would lead in two directions. Unless the United States could supply enough troops to defend it against use by the enemy as a ready-made invasion route, the highway would be more peril than asset. Lack of money, machinery, and manpower forced the two nations to shelve the plan; but when Pearl Harbor brought America into the war, officials like Buckner and Governor Gruening felt the time had come to build the road.

On Monday, February 2, Brigadier General Clarence L. Sturdevant, Assistant to the Chief of the U.S. Army Engineers, reported to the War Department in Washington and was told that the decision to build a military highway to Alaska had finally been made.[7] The job was his.

On Wednesday, after forty-eight hours in shirtsleeves with a coffee logged team, Sturdevant produced a complete, detailed program for surveys and construction. Men and equipment were mobilized with high-priority speed. On March 9, Engineers began to flow into the Dawson Creek end of the Canada railroad system. From here they deployed with paratroop precision along the 1,645 miles of mountains and forests through which the road had to be cut. After years of controversy over the choice of routes, the Alaska-Canada (Alcan) Highway was finally mapped to follow a series of airfields; its highest point would be a 4,212-foot pass in the Canadian Rockies.

In the far north it was still the dead of winter. Engineer units, including several Negro regiments, marched hundreds of miles in –35° windstorms, carrying tons of equipment on their backs. The 35th Engineers marched 325 miles to their particular station. Within days Sturdevant's 10,000 men were building as much as eighteen miles of pioneer road every twenty-four hours.

BY SPRING BUCKNER HAD MORE than thirty Air Force and CAA fields leveled and paved; he had fourteen military bases, three of them in the Aleutians, all stocked with artillery, ammunition and fuel. He had been

7. FDR did not formally approve the Alcan plan until February 11, and it was March 6 before Canada signed her acceptance. But these were formalities, after the fact.

instrumental in devising a Ferrying Command and an Air Service Command, which delivered new planes and organized civilian airliners to bring personnel and cargo from the States to Alaska. He had a small but well-trained Air Force of five combat squadrons, and a ground Army of nearly 5,000 combat troops backed by 20,000 support personnel.

It was not all he wanted, but Buckner was ready. He told a reporter, "If the Japanese come, they may get a foothold. But it will be their children who'll get as far as Anchorage, and their grandchildren who'll make it to the States. And by then they'll be American citizens."

THE NAVY'S ALASKAN COMMITMENT had grown too. Since Pearl Harbor, Captain Ralph Parker's fleet had grown from its Yippee-boat beginnings. The Coast Guard had turned over its three cutters; Seattle had sent him a handful of 1917-class destroyers to escort convoys into Buckner's beehive; the Royal Canadian Navy had placed its coastal bases at his disposal, and patrolled the southern Alaskan coast with three cruisers, seven corvettes and a variety of smaller craft. The U.S. Navy had commissioned its $75,000,000 fortress at Dutch Harbor; Sitka, Kodiak, and Dutch soon had installations for two squadrons of submarines, and the first two S-boats arrived at Dutch Harbor on January 27 to conduct war patrols. Ten PBY Catalinas of Patrol Wing Four had moved to permanent station in Alaska, but it was not until late April that the new wing commander, big Captain Leslie E. Gehres, moved his headquarters north from Seattle.

Gehres was not a patrol or bomber pilot, although he was rated to fly fighters off carrier decks. He did not take time to qualify in PBYs; he came to Alaska as a passenger in a PBY flown by Lieutenant Commander James S. Russell, skipper of one of the three squadrons in his wing.

Russell, wiry and cool, flew Gehres into Dutch Harbor on a cold April evening and told the new wing commander he could do a great deal for morale by joining a PBY combat patrol. Gehres agreed to do it, but in the morning the weather was so bad that all long-range patrols were canceled. The wind tore piles of lumber from their lashings and scattered them out to sea. The wings of PBYs had iced heavily in the snowstorm.

Nevertheless one pilot, Lieutenant Andy Smith, talked Operations into letting him fly a short patrol to scout the nearby island passes.

Commander Russell, who had warned Andy Smith that he was "one jump ahead of the undertaker," was at breakfast with Gehres when they heard the unmistakable roar of a PBY winding up to take-off power. Knowing what it meant, Russell dashed outside. The sound quit, too abruptly; Russell sprinted toward a second PBY that had started warming up at the dock. He leaped aboard and rode the Cat across Dutch Harbor to the narrow spit of sand that closed off half the harbor mouth. He found Andy Smith's plane nose down on the spit and burning. Ice-heavy, Smith had failed to clear the spit.

Russell rushed into the wreck. Three of Smith's bombs had rolled free, but the fourth was in the fire. Russell threw a line around the bomb and dragged it out of the fire.

Three crewmen had escaped from the tail of the wreck; they followed Russell into the burning Cat to find the flight-deck crew. But up front Smith and four others were charred corpses.

Captain Gehres arrived puffing; he had rounded the spit on foot. Russell, his face smoke-blackened, told Gehres, "You might have been on that plane."

"That's right," Gehres replied evenly. Undaunted, he took off next morning to fly patrol in one of Russell's PBYs.

A man who loved his comforts, Gehres was too distant to earn the love of his subordinates; but his powerful ambitions early propelled him into Alaska's top command councils, where he was able to operate far more effectively with his little air wing than he would have done if he had been more retiring. Whether that was good or bad was open to debate; before long, Gehres' men were calling him the Custer of the Aleutians.

ON MAY 15, 1942, A PRELIMINARY alert flashed from Pearl Harbor to Alaska—the codebreakers' first reports of Japanese attack plans. Overnight, every command mobilized. Buckner and the Navy's Parker acted on long-prepared plans by moving merchant ships and civilians out of Alaska while sending urgent demands to the States for planes, warships and troops.

Buckner's planning had been so smooth that within two days almost all command arrangements had been completed. There was little more to do but follow Japanese movements as Intelligence divined them, and await the impending arrival of Admiral Fuzzy Theobald and his North Pacific Force. But Simon Buckner had already been waiting almost two years, and the prospect of still more weeks bound to his desk was too much for him.

Commander Russell was on his way to the Aleutians with a very important passenger: Commander Paul F. Foster, personal troubleshooter for President Roosevelt, come to assess the defenses of the Aleutians and decide their value as a staging route for a Northern Invasion of Japan.

Foster's visit offered Buckner a chance to "quit sitting on my big fat headquarters" and get out to the front. Commander Russell wrote:

> The General invited himself along. I didn't like to have him go because we were pretty sure the Japanese would pay us a visit soon and I didn't fancy being the agent for delivering our beloved Commanding General into the hands of the enemy. But go he would—as he had several times before—all equipped for the field with eiderdown sleeping bag and rifle.

On May 18, two PBY-5A amphibious flying boats set out from Kodiak with Buckner and Foster aboard. The two ships were flown by two of Alaska's crack Navy pilots—Russell and Lieutenant Samuel E. Coleman, who would soon prove that a lumbering PBY was good enough to sink an enemy submarine. But even these two were no match for the fierce weather that hurtled into Kiska Harbor just after they landed to refuel from the tanks of seaplane tender *Williamson*.

The inspection party took cover while williwaws shrieked through the night and on into Tuesday afternoon. *Williamson's* meteorologist said it looked like a long blow. Russell wrote:

> We held a council of war and after great reluctance on the part of the General we finally argued him into taking the tender back to civilization. Commander Foster and his party went too. Sammy Coleman and I were weather-bound for five days.

Williamson took Buckner back to Kodiak in time to prepare for Admiral Theobald's arrival. Meanwhile, as Coleman and Russell waited out the storm at Kiska, the Navy's seaplane tender *Casco* came pitching into harbor as a replacement for *Williamson*, and to bring supplies to a ten-man weather-observation radio team on the island. Weather invariably moved eastward through the Aleutians and the Navy wanted to know the weather at Kiska, which ordinarily would be Dutch Harbor's weather a few hours later. The radio team kept Dutch advised. Ensign William C. Jones went ashore in a whaleboat and helped the radio crew set up their new gear in huts near an abandoned trapper's shack. Ensign Jones felt deeply for these ten men; he gave his pet brown-and-white mongrel pup, Explosion, as a mascot to Aerographer's Mate William Charles House, who commanded the isolated team. More than fifteen months later, the little dog was to play a surprising role in the last act of an eerie drama at Kiska.

The storm abated. Russell and Coleman flew back to Cold Bay; Ensign Jones stood on *Casco's* fantail and saluted the ten men left behind, as the tender pulled out of the harbor.

Two weeks later, the Japanese bombed Dutch Harbor. Aerographer's Mate House and his team could do nothing but broadcast weather reports now and then, and huddle around their radio listening to the news. When the battle at Dutch Harbor was over, House and his men went outside and stood in the cold rain, watching the gates of Kiska Harbor. Shaped like a C-clamp and guarded by steep mountains, it was by far the best harbor in the western Aleutians, capable of sheltering forty ships at a time. If the enemy landed anywhere, it was likely to be here.

House and his men did not have long to wait.

Eareckson's War

CHAPTER
SEVEN

The Kiska Blitz

WILLIAM HOUSE'S RADIO SHACK ON Kiska was one of three tiny cabins connected by boardwalks, squatting in a muskeg valley beneath the looming snowy volcano. In a clear moment a man could look up and become dizzy from the spectacle. There were few clear moments. Once or twice a day House and his nine men could hear the rumor of heavy aircraft engines as Russell Cone's old B-17 flew its lonely patrol high above the soup; but the low fog ceiling truncated the volcano, and they had no glimpse of the plane.

The Battle of Dutch Harbor had taken place on June 3 and 4, 1942. Through the next two stormy days, House picked up enough radio gossip to know that nobody was sure where the Japanese might strike next. Enemy carriers had been reported in the Bering Sea—Admiral Theobald was up there somewhere, chasing phantoms—but no one really knew.

With one man standing by the radio, House dispersed his crew to bury emergency caches of supplies in nearby canyons, in case the enemy should land and drive them back from their camp. It was about all he could do; House rolled up his crew in sleeping bags, close-crowded inside the little shack. By midnight June 6, they were asleep.

THREE HUNDRED AND FIFTY MILES west of Kiska, Attu Island's village of Aleuts went to sleep that same night. Chichagof village had a population of forty-four persons: forty-two Aleuts (fifteen of them children), a sixty-year-old white teacher named Foster Jones, and his wife.

Word of Japanese atrocities in China had implanted a deep-rooted horror of the Japanese in Foster Jones. He expected the enemy to land on Attu; he was determined not to be captured alive. He had secreted a private radio back in the canyons—he had been sending out daily weather reports—and was ready to take to the hills the minute the enemy appeared. In the night of June 6, convinced the enemy was nearby, Jones packed a pair of knapsacks for himself and his wife.

BEFORE DAWN ON SUNDAY, JUNE 7, 1942, the Imperial Northern Force landed almost 2,500 crack combat troops on the beaches of Kiska and Attu.

Kiska was hit first. At 1:20 in the morning, Captain Takeji Ono, IJN, reached shore with the first platoons of his Special Naval Landing Force. By dawn, 1,250 Japanese soldiers were ashore. Their movements muffled by steady rain, the marines disembarked from their whaleboats and swiftly moved up the canyons. It was 2:15 a.m. when an advance patrol crept up behind the American radio shack.

The ten American sailors awoke with 13-mm machine-gun bullets splintering their cabin. A slug rammed into W. M. Winfrey's leg and lodged there; another ripped through M. L. Courtenay's hand. William House dropped flat on the floor, yanked the door open and ordered his men to run for it. The little dog, Explosion, ran outside yapping. Eight men crawled into the brush on their bellies, seeking concealment in the low fog. House and J. L. Turner stayed behind to burn their vital code books while machine guns cut the walls to ribbons and smashed their radio transmitter; then they crawled outside and squirmed for cover.

Weather separated the ten Americans. Two were captured immediately; a Japanese surgeon on the beach removed the bullet from W. M. Winfrey's leg in a hastily erected tent. Scout patrols found the Americans' buried emergency caches and staked them out. Then they waited for the Americans to give themselves up.

There was little choice; the odds were 125 to 1. Within a few days, all but one of the U.S. sailors had surrendered. William House alone held out. Kiska was 110 square miles of rugged mountains and caves; there was plenty of room to hide. House retreated to the far side of the island and settled in a cave. Stocky and sandy-haired at twenty-nine, he had little fat to feed on; he tried to keep himself alive by eating grass, worms and shellfish he caught during midnight forays to the beach. He kept waiting for the United States to counterattack and reoccupy Kiska. His hope dwindled.

Cold, hunger, and exposure to the madness of Aleutian weather stripped him of strength. Finally he tied a scrap of cloth to a stick of driftwood and walked into the Japanese camp in rags, his long brown beard flowing in the wind. He weighed less than a hundred pounds; his cheeks were sunken, his arms reduced to strings, his thighs no larger than a healthy man's wrists.

When William House made his separate peace on July 28, he had been at large fifty days.[1]

A FEW HOURS AFTER THE first Japanese landings on Kiska, Rear Admiral Sentaro Omori steamed into Massacre Bay, Attu, swept the harbor for mines, and at dawn sent a preinvasion reconnaissance party onto the beaches. Within a few hours he had landed 1,200 troops in Massacre Valley.

Omori's landing battalions, lacking maps of the interior of the big island, got lost in the hills on their way to Chichagof village. Some of them almost starved in the snow-drifted passes before they found their way out. It was embarrassingly clear that even a small party of defenders could have thrown them off the island. But there were no defenders—only the forty-two Aleuts in the village, and Mr. and Mrs. Foster Jones.

When Omori's troops rushed into Chichagof village, Jones made a dash for his secret hideout in the hills. He only made it as far as the edge of the village. The Japanese took him prisoner and confined him to a hut where he died—possibly a suicide, possibly a victim of execution.[2]

Jones was the only man killed during the Japanese invasion of the western Aleutians. Virtually unopposed, the Japanese quickly set up ack-ack and harbor guns to command the approaches. Kiska and Attu harbors teemed with ships, from which materials and men poured onto the beaches.

While Americans scoured the Bering Sea hundreds of miles away, impotently seeking the elusive Japanese task force, Admiral Boshiro Hosogaya's Northern Force secured its positions under the protection of fog and rain, and dug itself in. By nightfall that Sunday, just three days after the Battle of Dutch Harbor, Japan had won the second round of the Campaign: she had taken the western Aleutians.

STILL UNDER RADIO SILENCE, Admiral Theobald prowled the fog-muzzled sea in his flagship while Generals Buckner and Butler studied

1. Treated with respect, House was nursed back to health in the Japanese camp hospital. He survived regular American bombing raids and a naval bombardment. On September 19, 1942, he was taken to Japan and put to work on forced-labor prisoner gangs in shipyards and steel works. At the end of the war he and all nine of his companions from Kiska were released to return home. House retired from the Navy in 1966 as a lieutenant commander.

2. Japanese files and memories bear out this account, but the Aleut survivors insist that Jones committed suicide rather than submit to capture, and that his wife tried to kill herself with him, but recovered under Japanese care. In any event Foster Jones died on June 7, 1942. Mrs. Jones and the thirty-nine Aleuts were sent to an internment camp in Hokkaido, Japan.

maps and radio reports at their headquarters in Anchorage. The only ranking American official in the Aleutians was Governor Ernest Gruening, who went down to Dutch Harbor to inspect the damage.

Rain pelted the Aleutians without mercy. Bomber Command's Colonel Eareckson, red-eyed and chain-smoking, kept growling, "Find the bastards." His weary pilots had been searching for more than a hundred hours without a break. But the fog was "Hirohito's new secret weapon" and his pilots saw nothing beneath the droning Fortresses but a sea of clouds. On through June 7, 8, and 9, while the Japanese secured their gains in the west, Eareckson's pilots and copilots took turns sleeping in flight; but the only result of their efforts was the series of remarks penned at the end of each day's squadron log:

"Mission pursued without success...An unsuccessful search for the Japanesez...Search results negative."

ON THE FIFTH OF JUNE, a day too late to fight at Dutch Harbor, the new 54th Fighter Squadron had droned into Umnak with its shiny long-range P-38 fighter-bombers. They were the first of the twinboomed Lightnings ever to be flown in a combat theater. The fliers were as green as the planes; on their way into Umnak they had earned an ignominious baptism of fire by strafing a hapless Russian merchantman that was flying the Japanese colors because a Japanese submarine had fired across her bows earlier in the week.

Any hopes the new P-38s could help spell the tired bomber crews were quickly dashed. The Lightnings had to be modified, their pilots trained for the Aleutians. And so the handful of PBYs and bombers hunted alone, around the clock, in circumstances recorded by Billy Wheeler in the 36th Squadron diary:

> Ship stuck in the mud at Umnak.... Ground crews tried to light the runways with searchlights but in their ignorance they shot the powerful beams downwind into the eyes of the pilots.... Morale is high but our energy reserve is low. These two days are to be remembered vividly because during this interval we have seen no food. McWilliams felt like offering a half interest in Hell to anyone who could produce a sandwich.

The job, said Colonel Eareckson, was like looking for a needle in Nebraska. The Japanese were somewhere in the North Pacific or the Bering—but where?

Reports from House's Kiska transmitter and Jones' amateur set on Attu had broken off June 7; it began to look as if the islands had fallen; but Kiska and Attu were totally hidden by fog—until June 10, when Captain Robert E. "Pappy" Speer found a hole over Kiska and took his LB-30 Liberator down for a look at the harbor.

No one was quite sure where Admiral Theobald's radio-silent ships were. Speer and his co-pilot, Frederick Ramputi, thought the ships in Kiska Harbor might be American. They circled low to make sure—and the ships opened fire.

Speer heaved the Liberator back into the clouds, unhit but angry because he and Ramputi still believed the ships were Theobald's, and had fired by mistake. In the end the two pilots went back to base to find someone who could tell friendly ships from enemy ones.

At Umnak, Speer and Ramputi described the ships to a black-shoe Navy officer, who told them they had been fired on by a three-stack Natori-class cruiser, not Admiral Theobald's *Nashville*. Startled, excited, and grim by turns, Speer went to the radio and called Colonel Eareckson.

Eareckson received Speer's message on the heels of a broadcast from Lieutenant (jg) James Bowers, whose PBY was at this moment in the air over Kiska, scouting the Japanese fleet in the harbor.

At last, after a week's searching, the patrols had borne fruit. The enemy had been run to ground.

THE UNITED STATES HAD TO make an immediate decision: whether to leave the enemy alone on Kiska and accept an unsteady stalemate while waiting to see what Japan would do next, or to attack Kiska and try to drive the Japanese back out of the Aleutians.

It would not do for American commanders to suggest, even to themselves, that the loss of Kiska was meaningless. The instant and instinctive reaction was to hit back: American territory had been violated and captured.

The word flashed to Washington. All along the chain of command, the reaction was the same. Only the rationalizations for it were different. These varied from headquarters to headquarters.

The Air Force (Eareckson, Davis, Butler, Hap Arnold) wanted to plaster the enemy on Kiska from the air. Beyond patriotic considerations, they wanted to prove the effectiveness of attrition bombardment as a strategic weapon.

The Army (Buckner, DeWitt, Marshall) wanted to push the enemy out of the Aleutians, use the islands for steppingstones, and have a crack at the Japanese on their own soil.

The Navy (Theobald and Nimitz) wanted to contain Japan and convince Tojo and Yamamoto that America could and would defend herself by forcibly rebuffing any attempt at invasion.

The War Department (Secretary Henry L. Stimson) was embarrassed by the loss of Kiska. It wanted to erase that embarrassment by getting Kiska back.

Congress wanted Kiska recaptured, to reassure itself and its constituents that North America was not about to be invaded by a "yellow horde."

And the President wanted to end the war, by defeating the enemy wherever he could. Since Kiska was closer to home than any other Japanese-occupied ground, and since the emotional value of Kiska (as American home territory) was immeasurable, it seemed a good place to start.

Orders flashed from Washington to Hawaii and San Francisco, and thence to Alaska: *Fight back. Push the enemy into the sea. Get Kiska back.*

It was, of course, much easier said than done.

A HOWLING STORM BLEW IN from the west. There wasn't a chance of launching an air strike before morning. Eareckson showed his impatience; he wanted to hit the Japanese before they could get entrenched. But all he could muster by way of heavy bombers were seven B-17s and two LB-30s (scattered from Kodiak to Umnak); his pilots and crews were exhausted beyond belief—for the past two days squadron leaders had had to kick men awake and drive them back into their cockpits; and, always the thorniest obstacle of all, the weather was awful.

Luck was never all bad, not even in the Aleutians. It was at this point that a rare but welcome fortune of war smiled on Eareckson.

The 21st Bombardment Squadron, new in Alaska for what it was told would be two weeks of routine patrol duty, flew its brand-new B-24 Liberators into Cold Bay that evening, June 10. Eareckson strode out to the field to watch them land. The pilots were barely on the ground when he had them assembled for a briefing. The new squadron was to join the veteran 36th, load all its equipment and get ready to fly down to Umnak as soon as the ceiling lifted. At Umnak they would dump equipment, load fuel and bombs, shuffle crews, and take off to bomb the enemy. Eareckson himself would lead the mission.

It would have been out of character for Eareckson to do anything else.[3] He had brought the pioneering 36th Squadron to Alaska; he had

---

3. Born in Baltimore on May 30, 1900, William Olmstead Eareckson enlisted as an Army private at seventeen, fought as a footsoldier in World War I and was appointed from the ranks to West Point. From his commission forward, he devoted his entire service to military

nurtured it, trained it, and flown with it in every capacity from turret gunner to lead pilot. "Wild Bill" to his Navy friends, "Eric" to his bomber comrades, "Colonel E" to his subordinates, Eareckson had brought flair and style and a unique esprit to his command.

Eareckson was a lanky, loose-jointed man. His hair was going silver. He had a cropped thin mustache that always seemed on the verge of twitching—half the bomber pilots in the Aleutians emulated it. He had a keen sense of the ludicrous; in a way he had never outgrown playing hooky, and it often appeared that he never properly understood the mystery of command—he did not resist "The Army Way" but there were times when he virtually ignored it, and superiors like General Butler complained sourly that Eareckson "can't even *spell* discipline."

Months ago, he had flown the first B-17 patrol in the Aleutians. Now Eareckson proposed to lead the first bombing mission against the enemy in the western Aleutians. It was the beginning of Eric Eareckson's fifteen-month private war against Kiska.

THE FIVE FORTRESSES OF THE 36th Squadron, delayed by bomb rack failures and flat tires, were not ready to go. The new 21st Squadron waited, impatient to take off from the Umnak mat runway. It was Thursday, June 11; the weather had cleared back to partial clouds—a good day for bombing. Snappish with the delay, Eareckson went into a huddle with Captain Jack Todd, the new commander of the 36th Squadron, and Lieutenant Clark Hood, a crack Navy navigator on loan to the new squadron to insure they wouldn't get lost in the Aleutians.

It would be hours before the 36th's Fortresses would be ready, and no one knew how soon the weather would sock in again. Regretting the need for it, Eareckson ordered the green 21st Squadron to take off alone.* The B-17s would follow as soon as they could. He gave the new squadron two veteran pilots. Jack Todd would lead, and Pappy Speer—who had

---

aviation, learning to fly everything airworthy—he was rated to fly all classes of bombers, fighters, transports, and scout planes, and in 1928 he won the Gordon-Bennett International Balloon Race for the United States. He had taken over the veteran 36th Squadron in February 1940, and brought it to Alaska a year later. Bush pilot Bob Reeve recalls, "He was a rake hell leader, a good ham actor—all sparkle and fire."

*1995 ADDENDUM: I erred in this account. Jack Todd commanded the 21st Squadron, not the 36th. As veteran Allen McRae recalls in a letter to Ralph Bartholomew, the 21st Squadron with its six B-24 heavies had arrived from the States at Cold Bay only one day previously (June 10, 1942), and had flown down to Umnak very early on the 11th, where the crews dropped off their personal luggage and took off almost immediately after refueling and arming their planes. They left one of their six Liberators behind (mechanical trouble?); its place was taken by Capt. Robert "Pappy" Speer and his LB-30 from 36th

discovered the enemy ships yesterday—would go along, in the veteran LB-30. Eareckson himself would stay behind with the 36th Squadron to lead the second strike.

The colonel said, "Go to war," and watched the five high-wing Liberators splash down the strip and carve a path into the westward sky.

WITH NAVY LIEUTENANT HOOD to chart the course, Captain Todd flew west-by-south, parallel to the Chain. From 15,000 feet it was possible to see a long way. Broken clouds overhung most of the islands; here and there they could see a patch of beach, a volcano cone, a snowy mountainside. The green Bering Sea contrasted sharply with the deeper blue of the Pacific on the far side of the Aleutians. In the channel passes between islands the two seas met and foamed the slots with high white froth. Todd led the B-24s through the unbeaten track of the Aleutian sky to Kiska, and into the first action of what was soon to be called the Kiska Blitz.

The Japanese had had four days. Their big 75-mm antiaircraft guns and smaller wheeled 23-mm Oerlikon-type AAs were dug into heavy revetments on all sides of the horseshoe of Kiska Harbor, on the slopes of Little Kiska and the canyons of the main island. When Japanese spotters saw the American planes above the dotted clouds, the big 75s opened up and found the range quickly.

Jack Todd's bombardier cranked open the bomb-bay doors—and flak exploded on the right wing and detonated the bombs in Todd's bomb bay. Todd's Liberator blew up so violently that it crippled the two bombers flying to his left and right. A wing fell off Todd's plane; the burning wreckage tumbled through the sky, flashed across the Japanese positions and smashed into the side of the mountain pass. On shipboard, a Japanese photographer snapped a picture of the action. Pieces rolled down the slope toward the harbor; Todd, Clark Hood and the entire crew were gone.

Major Edward Miller and Captain Lynn Moore struggled to keep their battered planes airborne. Only Captain Dick Lycan and Pappy Speer were left unhurt by the single shellburst. The two dropped their bombs through flak so thick they could not see the results; their bombs pitched harmlessly into the harbor and exploded underwater.

Squadron. My account implied that Jack Todd was on loan from the 36th; in fact Todd, although a veteran of the theater who had flown with the 36th, had assumed command of the 21st Squadron, and it was entirely appropriate that he lead this mission. For veterans these details are important in confirming that the 21st, with its own leader, was the first Bombardment Squadron (Heavy) to attack the Japanese at Kiska.

Above the volcano, a flight of Navy PBYs arrived and peeled off to join the bombing attack; but for the Air Force Liberators the fight was over. After just twenty seconds over Kiska, the four surviving bombers—two of them crippled—turned and headed home.

THE 36TH SQUADRON WAS AT last ready to go. Captain Russell Cone had five Fortresses available for the second mission. Eareckson outlined the plan he had devised in the few minutes since the remnants of the first mission had limped to ground. High-level bombing was out; formation attack was out. The Japanese obviously had a heavy concentration of flak guns; the small, mountain-ringed harbor was hard to find and hard to hit—but four-engine planes at high altitude were big, slow targets for trained antiaircraft gunners.

Eareckson proposed to go in at 3,000 feet, well beneath the level of the volcano peak—to squirm through the mountain passes and hit before the enemy even knew the attacking planes were there. The Fortresses would bomb individually, to avoid being easy targets.

Eareckson would lead the first three planes; Cone would lead the second element.

With their ball turrets splashing down the muddy runway, the B-17s left rolling wakes as they lifted free with water streaming from wings and tail. Cloud tendrils slipped past the wings. Eareckson led them toward Kiska, 600 miles to the west, reminding his crews that they were flying at maximum gross weight and they had to remember to keep the overloaded ships' noses down on the turns. Gunners' .50-caliber shells lay gleaming dully in cosmolined belts. Tons of explosive squatted like brood embryos in the Forts' bellies. Pilots searched the crowded instrument panels and the wet wings, waiting for them to ice up. But the sky remained clear, the temperatures above freezing, and when they reached Kiska late in the afternoon they found broken clouds low over the island.

Approaching the combat zone, they test-fired their guns over the water; the machine guns cleared their throats and short bursts of tracers arched toward the sea. The B-17s wheeled across Kiska, through the canyons, banking steeply to keep from crashing into peaks. Past the mountains, down in the harbor, ten warships and four transports lay at anchor. If there were shore installations, they were invisible to the fast-moving pilots; the best targets were the ships, and as the Fortresses roared out of the mountains Eareckson called targets—hit the cruisers first.

For the crews with Eareckson, it was a new experience and a frightening one, flashing out over the harbor at less than 3,000-foot altitude.

Billy Wheeler wrote, "The Colonel knows no fear." They thought they were going in too low—the enemy could count the rivets in their bellies; the soldiers down there could hit them with rocks. Neither the crews nor Eareckson himself knew that before the end of summer they would be going in far lower than this—they would be coming home, literally, with mud on their windshields.

There could be no evasive action once they turned onto the bomb runs. But today they did not need evasive action. The attack took the Japanese so completely by surprise that their antiaircraft never found the range. Eareckson's plane banked into the harbor, sideslipped into a level run and released its sticks of 500-pounders. The threestack Japanese cruiser disappeared entirely under tons of water, smoke and shrapnel. Eareckson swung past the outcrop on Kiska's North Head; behind him, Captain Lucian Wernick and the others unloaded on destroyers and cruisers and followed the colonel away.

As the last plane pulled out, at least two cruisers and a destroyer appeared to be inundated by smoke and heaving water. Confirming each other's strikes, the pilots logged hits on three enemy ships, and headed home.

The sense of triumph made them forget their exhaustion. The five planes landed, unscratched, at Umnak; the mission's post-mortem debriefing was eager and happy—until the lab developed the day's strike photos, and the truth was revealed. All the smoke and debris had been thrown up by near-misses. The zealous bombardiers had not made a single hit.

Eareckson sent his crews to bed, to rest for tomorrow's mission. They would go back to Kiska in the morning—at 1,200 feet.

THE ELEVENTH AIR FORCE had been at war nine days. It had not scored a single hit on an enemy ship.

Not the least interested in the Air Force's unhappy record was Navy Patrol Wing Commander Leslie Gehres, who saw an excellent chance to step into the dismal situation. Admiral Theobald was somewhere at sea, out of communication; Gehres had a bold idea, but it needed authorization. On June 10, shortly after the Japanese were reported at Kiska, Captain Gehres took a chance and notified CINCPAC directly of the enemy presence on Kiska—and mentioned that he had a PBY tender at Atka Island in the central Aleutians, halfway to Kiska and within easy striking distance. The tender was mother ship to twenty Catalinas, including a full squadron of brand-new PBY-5As fresh from the States.

In reply to Gehres' broad hint, CINCPAC granted the burly wing commander authority to arm his Catalinas for combat and "bomb the Japanese out of Kiska."

THE NEW PBY SQUADRON, VP-43, equipped with the latest ASV search radar, had just arrived from British Columbia under Lieutenant Commander Carroll B. "Doc" Jones. Gehres had sent them out into the Chain to help relieve the battered remnants of his Patrol Wing, down now from its original twenty-three to fourteen planes. At Nazan Bay, an Aleut fishing village on Atka, the Catalinas moored like a brood of huge chicks around their mother hen, seaplane tender *Gillis*.[4]

Gillis's skipper, Commander Norman Garton, had accepted the new squadron without complaint, though it doubled the size of the air unit he was supposed to accommodate with fuel, oil, parts, food, ammunition and bombs. To serve the extra planes and crews, he had taken over part of the Indian village to house part of his men, and had pressed into service a half dozen willing Aleuts and Mrs. Ethel Oliver, a white teacher who commenced to feed more than fifty PBY crewmen from her tiny kitchen.

All day June 10, while Gehres was exchanging messages with CINCPAC, the planes of Squadron 43 had straggled into Nazan Bay. One of them, flown by Ensign Leland L. Davis, had sighted a Japanese super-submarine off Tanaga and attacked it with bombs and depth charges; sure he had sunk the submarine, Davis had gone on to Atka to join the squadron. (He had damaged the submarine—it was the I-boat that had remained near Akutan for several days, hoping to pick up the Japanese pilot who had crash-landed his Zero intact on the island—but in spite of damage, the submarine got home safely to Japan.)

It had been the squadron's first day in action. When Ensign Davis arrived in Nazan Bay, a message was coming in from Captain Gehres. It ordered the PBYs to arm with full bomb loads and attack Kiska with everything they had, starting first thing in the morning. They were to continue attacking until they either ran the Japanese out of Kiska or ran themselves out of fuel and bombs. And, Gehres finished, they would attack and keep attacking *regardless of weather*.

---

4. The seaplane tender was a frequently overlooked Navy institution. Usually a converted destroyer of great age, the tender provided flying boats with all the services of an aircraft carrier except a 'flight-deck runway. As floating homes for seaplane squadrons, tenders gave the PBYs valuable extensions of range and mobility. Completely self-contained, they only required reasonably calm seas for airplane recovery—waters like those in Atka's sheltered Nazan Bay, which was to become almost a permanent PBY base in the months to come.

Thus was the die cast for the Kiska Blitz. A few of the pilots, fed up with fruitless patrols, applauded Gehres' orders. But most of them did not. The PBY was big, slow, easy to hit from the ground; it was neither well armored nor heavily armed; it had primitive bombsights, exposed fuel tanks, and all the maneuverability of a hippopotamus. It was no attack bomber. The Catalinas would be waddling into a meat grinder.

The pilots' fears were justified. Within seventy-two hours, half the PBYs now moored in Nazan Bay would be destroyed.

THE PBY BLITZ BEGAN, EARLY June 11, on the heels of the First Air Force bombing attack on Kiska Harbor.

The Catalinas of Patrol Wing Four rumbled past Kiska volcano only moments after Captain Jack Todd's B-24 Liberator was shot down by a flak burst inside its open bomb bay. Spray had hardly settled from the bombs of the Air Force attack when the Navy PBYs came beating down through the scattered 1,000-foot overcast in a hearty parody of dive-bombing.

The PBYs had to get in close, to find targets for their seaman's-eye bombsights. They broke through the clouds at 200 miles an hour, diving steeply. It was far more than the Catalina was designed to take. Bombs fell from the wing racks; pilots and co-pilots braced themselves to haul the controls back in four-handed pullouts that took every bit of strength in their arms. Brittle cracks exploded in the air frames; the great square wings flapped like seagulls'. Barely hanging together, the plummeting PBYs leveled off at zero altitude and heaved out of the harbor.

Japanese gunsights, set for the high-level Air Force bombers, shifted to the diving Catalinas; a flak burst blew away part of one plane's wing; the starboard engine erupted in flame. Another shell exploded beside the port gun blister, shattered the glass, killed two men in the plane and injured two others. The stricken PBY growled away on one engine.

In the harbor, concussion from nearby bombs badly damaged the Japanese destroyer *Hibiki*. Antiaircraft bursts followed the PBYs away in rage—and Captain Takeji Ono flashed a panic-stricken signal to Japan. Within hours, Radio Tokyo accused the United States of attacking Kiska with a secret new dive-bomber that looked curiously like a PBY.

The Catalinas pounded back to Atka to fill up with bombs and return to battle. A badly mauled PBY staggered into Nazan Bay, landed in the water and ran up on the beach to keep from sinking. Another ran out of fuel short of base, landed in a sheltered lagoon and ran aground in the shallow water. Ensign Leland Davis, who had attacked an I-boat the day before, returned from Kiska with a dead crewman aboard, refueled and bombed up and went back. Skipper Norman Garton of *Gillis* kept his crew dizzy servicing the twenty PBYs of the combined wing; the Catalinas came in from Kiska and took off again as fast as Garton could get them fueled and armed. They drummed up and down the Chain like a shuttle service, hitting Kiska in hourly avalanches. The Blitz went right on into the night and the next day. A report came in that the Japanese had set up a tent camp on Attu; a few of the PBYs went out to bomb it, but most of them ran the Kiska Express.

At night, when the PBYs could not see well enough to land in the bay, they landed in the open sea and taxied into Nazan Bay. June 11, 12, 13—*Gillis* worked seventy-two hours straight through, the boat crews never leaving their boats. Mrs. Oliver made bunks for the wounded in the schoolhouse; she contributed her entire supply of rags and pencils to plug the bullet holes in the PBYs.

Led by Doc Jones and Aleutian veteran William Theis, the Catalinas put Kiska under continuous bombing siege. The job grew steadily tougher; as aircrews lost energy, enemy flak became more deadly. The Japanese trained their guns on the holes in the 1,000-foot overcast and waited for the PBYs to plummet through; the planes ran into a withering concentration of fire each time they appeared. Before long, the patrol wing's crew had their own name for Kiska: "PBY Elimination Center."

Ensign Leland Davis ran into a fusillade of flak and machine-gun bullets that junked his plane in midair; he manhandled it back to Atka but it was so riddled that it sank in the water beside *Gillis*. Davis piled his crew into another plane and went back again. He had crippled an enemy submarine and lost one PBY in two days; now he dive-bombed Kiska and was hit by flak again, tried to pull out of his dive and felt the battered plane begin to die. The strain of the pullout was too much; the wings came off the big PBY and Davis crashed flaming into the sea, down with all hands. Another PBY lost two crew members; and Lieutenant (jg) Ted Sorenson scored a hit on a destroyer before he zigzagged crazily away through the acrid pollution of sulphur smoke and flak puffs. Sorenson, like several others who flew through the madness of the Blitz, won the Navy Cross.

Colonel Eareckson's Air Force bombers blasted Kiska at the same time; but they had to come the 600 miles from Umnak, and they could not fly more than two missions a day from that distance. The PBYs bombed every hour. Kiska suffered, inevitably, from the combined attacks; ships took hits, three big Mavis seaplane bombers burned and sank at anchor, 75-mm guns were buried under tons of rock. But almost half the PBYs were shot down or crippled in the first three days of battle.

CINCPAC radioed I AM CONFIDENT YOU WILL CONTINUE ACCOMPLISHING THE IMPOSSIBLE, but it was not altogether clear whether Captain Gehres' PBY command was actually accomplishing much. The attacks were not "bombing the enemy out of Kiska," as Admiral Nimitz had hoped; if anything, the Japanese were dug in more solidly than they had been before. Their flak was heavier and more accurate, their ships departed quickly after having unloaded, and now they were beginning to field float-equipped Zeroes against the PBYs. The Catalinas themselves were thinning in number; those that were not shot up or shot down had run their old Twin Wasp engines up past 900 hours since their last overhauls—and there was no major service center closer than Seattle. Then, the final straw, on June 13 *Gillis* ran out of aviation fuel, ammunition, and bombs.

ADMIRAL NIMITZ'S BASEMENT INTELLIGENCE teams were still monitoring Japanese radio traffic; the Japanese, unaware their top naval codes had been cracked, had not changed the ciphers. But the cryptanalysis in Honolulu was not perfect. When Admiral Hosogaya (at Paramushiro) radioed orders to Kiska to field the three remaining float-bombers in Kiska Harbor, Nimitz's codebreakers interpreted the message to mean Hosogaya was sending a large number of four-engine bombers from Japan to attack the American seaplane tender in Nazan Bay.

Alarmed by the possibility of a large-scale bombing attack on the lone seaplane tender, Admiral Nimitz had his signal office code new orders for broadcast to Alaska.

At Kodiak, Admiral Fuzzy Theobald had just come to earth after a week of steaming through fog. He received Nimitz's orders to stop the PBY raids and get *Gillis* away from Nazan Bay—and forwarded the orders to Gehres.

Late in the day (June 13) the word reached Commander Garton at Atka. Garton told Mrs. Oliver and the Aleuts that enemy bombers were coming; he offered to evacuate them with his own men if they wanted to come. A few villagers were at sea fishing; their families chose to stay behind. The rest climbed aboard *Gillis* after burning down the larger buildings in town. Garton promised to send a flying boat to collect those who remained behind; then, just at nightfall, he steamed out of Nazan Bay.

The next day, Sunday, the three lumbering Japanese Mavises lifted off from Kiska Harbor and flew to Atka. They found nothing left to attack.

An American PBY had picked up the last Natives[5] a few hours earlier. The disgusted Japanese pilots cratered the burnt-out village and returned to Kiska, landing just after a bombing attack by a lone PBY.

The PBY headed east, landed in a lagoon at Kanaga, and fired a flare signal. Kanaga was a small island between Atka and Kiska; the last of the U.S. Navy Aleutian weather teams was still operating from it. Now the PBY picked up the five-man radio crew, destroyed the little station, and flew back to Dutch Harbor.

At the end of that mission—the last PBY flight of the Blitz—no American forces were left anywhere in the Aleutians west of Umnak. The western one thousand miles of the Chain had become partly Japanese possession and partly no man's-land. By default, the Japanese had won the third round; the Blitz had ended in an American retreat.

The Aleutian Campaign was eleven days old. It had established its character. At great expense, Japan had captured a pair of islands she did not really want and had precious little use for. At equal expense, the United States had made strenuous but impotent efforts to defend the same unwanted and useless islands. Whether the Aleutians would ever have a strategic use remained to be seen; in the meantime both nations carried on the fight, simply because this was where the fight was.

Japan was afraid of an American invasion; America was afraid of a Japanese invasion. Fear forced the choice of their pathetic battleground.

5. The Native populations of the Aleutians and Pribilofs were evacuated, to keep them out of the line of fire. Most of them were resettled in southern Alaska and on timbered Admiralty Island, where the Aleuts stared in befuddlement at the surroundings—they had never seen trees before—and complained bitterly of the 75° summer heat. After the war many of them moved back to the Aleutians.

CHAPTER EIGHT

Mission to Seek and Destroy Enemy in Alaska

HIS SPIRIT CRUMPLED AND TORN, Admiral Yamamoto questioned his very reason in the shambles that followed the Battle of Midway. On the seventh of June he was retiring toward Kure with his battered fleet when he received word from the Northern Force that Kiska and Attu had been taken.

Though Yamamoto was depressed, common sense told him to salvage whatever advantage he could from the minor victory in the north. When he forwarded the news to Prime Minister Tojo in Tokyo, he added a dispatch of his own which stressed the importance of holding onto the Aleutians. Victory at Midway might embolden the Americans; they might fight back in the north; Japan ought to be ready for it.

Yamamoto's urgings did not impress Tojo nearly as much as the news of success in the Aleutians. It came at the right time. Tojo desperately needed something that would help the high command save face.

On June 8, 1942, he met secretly with top admirals and generals at Imperial Headquarters. No matter how difficult it seemed, Tojo told them, the debacle at Midway must be kept secret from the Japanese people. He passed Yamamoto's dispatch around and pointed out that the Aleutian success could provide good propaganda to help mask the disaster. He ordered elaborate preparations: hospital wings were locked up; massive transfers and reorganizations of naval forces were completed overnight, made deliberately confusing; and the families of the 3,000 Midway dead were fooled into the belief that their loved ones were still carrying on the Emperor's war somewhere in the Pacific.

Tojo's scheme was so successful that the Japanese public did not learn the truth about Midway until after the war. It succeeded because of an old trick of sleight-of-hand: Tojo's press release of June 8 carefully drew attention away from Midway, by directing it toward the Aleutians.

The "diversion" at Midway had assured the devastating success of the "great Aleutian victory," while Japan had "sunk" two U.S. carriers and many other ships, with only the loss of a single carrier.

The public was mollified, but the General Staff did not let its own propaganda mislead it. Yamamoto, particularly, had taken note of submarine reports of General Simon Buckner's frenetic construction work along the Alaska coast. He suspected the Americans were preparing bases from Seattle to Dutch Harbor to support an Aleutian counterattack and a northern invasion of Japan. When he reached Imperial Headquarters, Yamamoto urged again that the northern perimeter be strengthened at Kiska and Attu, to protect the homeland. He pointed out that Japanese patrol planes from the western Aleutians could find any U.S. task force headed for Japan from the north, giving the Japanese fleet time to smash invasion forces while they were still at sea. And there could be no more Doolittle-type air raids from that direction as long as Japan held the Aleutians.

The Army belittled Yamamoto's arguments. The generals still had their eyes on Australia; they did not see how the Americans could fight in the terrible weather reported by the expeditionary force at Kiska and Attu. Tojo and the high command heard the arguments and finally reached a compromise: Japan would hold the western Aleutians until fall, regardless of enemy pressures. When winter came, if the Army still felt as it did, then Japan would withdraw. It was unlikely the Americans would consider a winter campaign in the north.

For the time being, then, Kiska and Attu would be held.

ALREADY OVERREACHED, JAPAN HAD to open yet another long supply line from the Kuriles to the Aleutians—650 miles to Attu, 800 miles to Kiska. It meant taking transports, cargo ships, submarines and warships from other fronts; it meant bringing airplanes up to support them.

Vice Admiral Boshiro Hosogaya had the job of implementing the orders of high command in the North Pacific. He was a lean, craggy-faced man, his slightly cruel mouth bracketed by deep creases. His spartan personality had little in common with Admiral Theobald's, but Hosogaya was Theobald's Japanese counterpart in responsibility and bailiwick, and throughout the next six months Hosogaya's problems and decisions ran strikingly parallel to Theobald's. Hosogaya worked for Yamamoto; Theobald worked for Nimitz. Hosogaya never had enough cold-weather clothing, enough transport vessels, enough escort warships to make his Aleutian forces comfortable; neither did Theobald. Hosogaya's troops got better food; Theobald's got better equipment; but neither had enough of anything, and both had the same enemy—the Aleutian weather.

EARLY IN JUNE, HOSOGAYA HAD readied a composite wing of seaplane fighters and bombers at Paramushiro, to be rushed into the Aleutians as soon as bases could be secured for them. On June 7 his forces took Kiska and Attu; within twenty-four hours the bases were ready. The first of Hosogaya's planes rumbled into Kiska late on June 8—six huge four-engine Kawanishi "Mavis" flying-boat bombers, nearly twice as big as PBYs. They were quickly joined in the foggy harbor by the seaplane carrier *Kimikawa Maru*, which had been in and out of the North Pacific ever since her planes had reconnoitered Adak and Kiska a month ago; she steamed into Kiska Harbor with eighteen fast Zero seaplanes in time to join battle against the PBYs on the last day of the Kiska Blitz.

At sea, Admiral Kakuji Kakuta was still hovering near the western Aleutians with his carriers *Ryujo* and *Junyo* and his sizable fleet of cruisers and destroyers. Admiral Yamamoto, thinking the Americans might counterattack in the Aleutians, reinforced Kakuta with two more aircraft carriers, *Zuiho* and *Zuikaku*—giving Kakuta the strongest naval striking force anywhere in the Pacific Ocean. Cruising south of the Chain, Kakuta sent his air armada winging out over a vast area, all of it fog-covered, trying to find the American fleet.

Japanese Intelligence was just guessing when it suggested the U.S. fleet might be coming north; it was a good guess. On June 8, CINCPAC had sent a coded signal to Admiral Theobald's Kodiak headquarters:

> TASK FORCE 16 ADMIRAL SPRUANCE WITH 2 CARRIERS
> 6 CRUISERS 10 DESTROYERS EN ROUTE TO REPORT....
> MISSION TO SEEK AND DESTROY ENEMY IN ALASKA.

Rear Admiral Raymond A. Spruance's *Enterprise-Hornet* task force had whipped the Japanese at Midway. Now Spruance plowed into the stormy North Pacific, looking for another fight—and once again the enemy was waiting for him with a fleet twice the size of his.

But Spruance was only halfway to the Aleutians on June 10 when American air searches felt out the enemy on Kiska. Spruance's carrier-cruiser force was the only naval force Nimitz had; it had too few planes left, after Midway, to fight off Japanese planes from Kiska, Attu, and Kakuta's four carriers. Besides, a naval assault alone would serve no purpose without a trained Army prepared to defeat the enemy on the ground. Nimitz regretfully decided not to pitch Spruance against the enemy in the western Aleutians; accordingly, on June 11 (during the Kiska Blitz) he recalled Spruance. Task Force Sixteen never reached the Aleutians, and the Japanese Second Mobile Force made no contact with it.

Badly muffled by fog and storms, Admiral Kakuta's imposing battle fleet would mill around the North Pacific for three weeks more, finding nothing that looked like an American task force. Finally on July 6 it would withdraw from the theater, leaving behind a squadron of destroyers, a seaplane carrier, and Japan's last chance of a major decisive naval battle in the North Pacific.

IT WAS WAR, BUT NOT TOTAL WAR. Civilian populations, women and children were not threatened. It pitted men and their machines against the elements in a contest where tactical imagination meant more than brute force. There were no mass dead, no dismal trench battles. The balance of strategic power could be affected at any time by one warship, a few dozen men, a small decisive action; the individual assumed value far beyond what was artificially accorded to returning heroes from the crowded major theaters, and the magnified importance of individual exploits often left room for the sentimental, the comic, and the heroic.

That June Rommel threatened Alexandria; Hitler had his Panzers in Russia; Roosevelt wanted an autumn offensive against Germany; massive convoys were needed for the support of England, Malta and Cairo; the Japanese were pushing down through the Solomons and New Guinea. Alaska was hardly an important theater. It squatted at the bottom of the priority heap and fought a shoestring war.

In San Francisco, Western Defense Command's Lieutenant General John L. DeWitt asked the War Department for a joint expeditionary force to eject the Japanese from the Aleutians. All he received in the next month was a pair of replacement bomber squadrons—hardly enough to keep pace with the attrition of aircraft in the Aleutians. The Royal Canadian Air Force set up "X Wing Hq" at Anchorage to command the several Canadian combat squadrons now stationed in Alaska and the Aleutians, but even so the Eleventh Air Force's total fighting strength was only a few dozen planes—not nearly enough to "bomb the enemy out of Kiska," as Admiral Nimitz had hoped.

"There is considerable conjecture," wrote Billy Wheeler, "about the Japanese need for such a God-forsaken hole. The general consensus seems to be that they need a submarine operating base ... from which easy raids on our lend-lease shipping to the U.S.S.R. can be carried out."

The Japanese had concentrated more and more strength at Kiska. Admiral Nimitz knew his tiny forces could not push the Japanese out; but he was afraid that if he left the Japanese alone, their northern ambitions would grow. Consequently, he ordered General Buckner and Admiral Theobald to keep all possible pressure against the Japanese—keep them off-balance, uncertain, and always on the defensive.

For the next six months, this was the strategy of the Aleutian Campaign: a nerve-racking, corrosive harassment of the enemy on Kiska.

TO MOST OF THEM, DEATH HAD always been faraway and impersonal. Now they found themselves in an arena of survival and the everyday threat of individual extinction. Though afraid to die, they did not want to die afraid; they put on smiles and hard expressions, and manned their ships and planes.

The PBY Blitz had been complemented by a steady series of long-range raids flown by Colonel Eareckson's heavy bombers from Umnak. On June 12 Eareckson took five heavies in at 1,200 feet, the lowest level yet, and inflicted heavy damage on a Japanese cruiser. Eareckson heckled the Japanese by radio—"How'd you like that bomb, Tojo? Give Tojo headache, maybe?" It quickly became a daily trademark and before long Tokyo Rose was airing sarcastic remarks aimed at Eareckson by name. He took his bombers back over Kiska on June 13 and 14, during the end of the PBY Blitz; by the 14th Billy Wheeler was writing, "Another day, another mission—the damned war seems to be getting in a rut."

By now the Japanese were sending up all the float-fighters Eareckson could eat. To neutralize fighter opposition and the worsening weather over Kiska, Eareckson turned to a new bombing technique, devised during the Blitz by PBY pilot William Theis. Eareckson's bombers flew directly over the peak of the volcano, using it as a reference point; made a time-distance run with compass and stopwatch, and dropped bombs through the fog to unseen targets below. Blind calculation bombing—"DR Runs" (for "dead reckoning")—did no crucial damage; it was not expected to. But the orders were to keep the Japanese shaken up, and it did that. It slowed their construction, kept them running for bomb shelters, and occasionally scored a hit on something important.

Whenever he could, Eareckson went in under the fog. On June 14 the six-plane mission bombed at 700 feet, the lowest yet. Billy Wheeler wrote:

> Two cruisers hit. Fifty caliber fire cut our B-17's up quite thoroughly, though no one was injured. Cone's ship, leading the second element, had the Number Two engine shot out and his left tire pierced. [Captain Donald] Dunlap's ship had its hydraulic system punctured and rendered useless. Dunlap made a beautiful landing without brakes. The radio chit-chat will be good for a smile, for it took Dunlap at least twenty minutes to explain to the tower, while he was still in the air, what he meant by "No brakes."

Once in a while the weather permitted precision high-altitude bombardment. On June 18, after a week of missions, Eareckson sent eight heavies in at 14,000 feet. They sank transport *Nissan Maru,* mauled a cargo ship and shot down two Zeroes; but Captain Ira F. Wintermute's B-24 was chopped up by flak and crash-landed in the sea. The plane broke apart and sank immediately; two crew members, including the navigator, were trapped in the wreckage and drowned. Wintermute and the other five men got out in a life raft and were picked up by a PBY. It was not the last time Wintermute would be shot down, lose his navigator, and be rescued in the Aleutians.[1]

Eareckson kept trying new ideas. He devised time-delay fuses to prevent bombs from exploding directly under the low-flying planes that dropped them. He built homemade incendiary bombs out of rubber, filled with gasoline. He started intensive programs to train his pilots to fly at virtually zero altitude—ten feet off the water. His grueling practice runs annoyed newcomers, but never for long; to stay alive they had to learn a hundred tricks they had not been taught at the Muroc Bombing Run in California. The weather was murderous, and even coming home was a peril—the Umnak runway was still "unfinished" and the big four-engine planes had to operate on it as if it were a carrier deck.

Eareckson's experiments drew critical attention from above. Admiral Theobald became curious about the colonel's constant requests to pass the ammunition—Eareckson was using up a lot of bombs, going out with a maximum effort virtually every day regardless of weather. Theobald found out what he was up to—precision bombing on clear days, blind DR

---

1. Young Lieutenant Knute W. Flint earned a chestful of medals flying a one-man Air Force search-and-rescue service in a borrowed Navy PBY. He accompanied dozens of bombing missions throughout the next year, hovering nearby, ready to go down after stricken planes. Colonel Eareckson's Command Flight Surgeon, Major O. P. Moffit Jr., often rode along with Flint as a volunteer passenger. There was no formal air-sea rescue service in the Aleutians, but Flint and many Navy pilots more than made up for the lack of an official unit.

bombing on occluded days. The admiral complained furiously that there was no way to observe results when the target was obscured by fog; he told General Butler he could not justify spending so much costly explosive without a proven record of hits. The blind attacks must be discontinued.

Theobald's order, issued late in June, put an end to the daily bombing missions. Henceforth, the Japanese would only be attacked when they could be seen. In the Aleutians, that meant one day out of every four or five; it meant respite for both the embattled Japanese and the exhausted American bomber crews. It also meant the Aleutian Campaign would slow to a crawl, and give the enemy time to fortify Kiska against a long siege.

BACK IN THE STATES, REACTION was virtually nonexistent, mainly because no one knew much about events in Alaska.

On June 12, 1942—forty-eight hours after the Japanese were discovered on Kiska—the Navy in Washington was still declaring, "We have no information about any Japanese on Alaskan soil." Late that evening, red-faced Navy public-information officers acknowledged the enemy occupation of Attu (but not Kiska). Attu was far away in the Eastern Hemisphere; the loss of Kiska and the full extent of the enemy drive were not officially disclosed until the Navy made a statement to the press on June 21:

> The enemy inflicted minor damage to the Naval Station at Dutch Harbor and the Army post at Fort Mears, but did not seriously impair their military effectiveness.
>
> The enemy has occupied the undefended islands of Attu, Kiska and Agattu[2] in the westernmost tip of the Aleutian chain, and has constructed temporary living facilities ashore.

This was two weeks after the fact. For the most part the American press accepted the delay without complaint, although Time criticized the Navy's "drum-tight censorship" and pointed out caustically that the only news from the Aleutians was coming from Radio Tokyo. Following the same line, *Life* assailed the military for its dribbles of "hints and half-news," and tried unsuccessfully to clear its reporters into the Alaska theater.

The news eclipse was immediate and total. On June 20, the Japanese submarine *I-26* torpedoed a Canadian lumber ship off Cape Flattery and

---

2. Agattu lies about 35 miles southeast of Attu. Japanese ships were using it as an anchorage to avoid American air attacks; a few small Army units had gone ashore, but there was never any real attempt to build bases on the island.

shelled a telegraph station on Vancouver Island; the next day it bombarded the naval base at Astoria, Oregon; three days later it shelled Fort Stevens. Official U.S. sources glossed over all these incidents. Washington tried to put the best possible face on things, even when it meant denying the obvious. War-industry workers by the thousands were threatening to go out on strike (and soon did so), and throughout the nation the civilian populace seemed only half-aware the country was at war; but the government stubbornly kept up a barrage of press releases calculated to reassure the public, rather than instill a realistic sense of crisis and concern. Public information offices released reams of self-aggrandizing puffs about the Battle of Midway, the sinking of two U-boats in the Atlantic, the American capture (unopposed) of Wallis Island, the sinking of two Japanese I-boats in the western Pacific; at the same time, very little was said about the sinking of seven U.S. warships and sundry other setbacks—notably the loss of the western Aleutians.

Corey Ford, Keith Wheeler and several other American journalists in the Aleutians were sent packing soon after Dutch Harbor. Occasionally one of them would slip back to Alaska, sometimes at the risk of arrest, but for the most part the Aleutian Campaign for the next six months was without benefit of press—a policy which the War Department started, but which Admiral Theobald heartily supported. The Campaign was disagreeable to those who fought it and embarrassing to those who commanded it.[3]

The secrecy assumed paranoid proportions. Even servicemen did not know they had been assigned to the Aleutians until they arrived there. Battalions of SeaBees, trained in the Great Lakes, were equipped for the tropics and sent south on troop trains to Texas, informed by deliberately leaked "rumors" that they were going to the South Pacific. Then, from San Diego they were sent to Seattle on sealed trains and shipped out under secret orders which were not opened until they were well at sea: DESTINATION ALASKA.

Alaskans themselves received no magazines or newspapers from which censors had not clipped all references to Alaska. The mimeographed four-page *Military Press*, published more or less daily at Dutch Harbor, gave the isolated troops capsule-news from other fronts, but

3. As far as Theobald was concerned, the less said about the campaign the better. So great was his disgust with the whole Aleutian operation that nowhere in his postwar autobiographical summaries does Theobald so much as mention the ten months he spent in command of the North Pacific Force.

news of their own theater had to be cleared by the Navy in Washington for general release before it could be published at Dutch Harbor. Thus, for example, it was not until August 12 that the *Military Press* reported a July 22 Air Force attack on Kiska.

The news blackout led to speculation and wild rumors. Alaska's Delegate to Congress, Anthony Dimond, told the House there were 25,000 Japanese in the Aleutians (there were about 3,500), and Congressman John M. Coffee supported Dimond on the House floor by saying, "There will be an attack on the Alaskan mainland...before the end of summer." Dimond and Coffee admitted privately that they knew next to nothing about the enemy's strength or plans; they were just trying to light fires. Joining their camp, Kentucky's crusty Senator A. B. "Happy" Chandler threatened to take a congressional investigating party to the Aleutians if the Navy would not take the wraps off the Campaign, but even that threat failed to provoke the censors.

One reason the Navy refused to divulge the facts was that it didn't really *know* the facts. Admiral Theobald maintained twenty-four-hour air and sea patrols, but his tiny forces couldn't hope to cover the entire North Pacific-Bering area; all he knew for certain was that the enemy had garrisoned three Aleutian Islands. He had no knowledge of the disposition of enemy sea forces, supply lines, or plans—not until June 20, when three separate reports told of an enemy task force in the Bering Sea between the Pribilofs and the St. Lawrence Islands.

Two of the reports came from PBY radar; the third came from Pearl Harbor—an Intelligence code-intercept evaluation, indicating the Japanese might be planning a raid or invasion at Alaska's western outpost of Nome.

For weeks Alaska had been bombarded with rumors of enemy invasion. No one questioned the new reports, even though Nome was as militarily useless and isolated a spot as could be found. Even if the reports were not definite, it would be foolhardy not to act on them.

General Buckner had full jurisdiction; Nome was on the mainland. He was not going to make the same mistakes that had been made at Dutch Harbor, where he had allowed the Navy to scatter his Air Force in a hopeless widespread search for the enemy. This time, if the Japanese wanted a fight they could come and get it. Buckner would be waiting for them. Nome would be beefed up; the Air Force would move in and wait for the enemy. If the Navy wanted to chase around through the fog, that was Admiral Theobald's prerogative, but the Army would stand fast by its guns.

Less than twelve hours after the first reports of the enemy threat, "Operation Bingo" was under way—the first mass airlift in American military history.

TO REINFORCE ALASKA AFTER DUTCH Harbor's proof of vulnerability, the War Department had sent Buckner a rush of supplies, men, and equipment. The Ferrying Command had placed eleven scheduled airlines under military orders; overnight, United, Northwest, and other airlines canceled their commercial schedules, dropped passengers at the handiest airports, and sent all their available planes to the railhead at Edmonton, Canada.

By June 17, forty-six commercial airliners had been gathered at Edmonton; by the time the enemy threat against Nome was reported on June 20, almost all of them were in Alaska, having delivered their cargo, getting ready to return to the States. Buckner immediately grabbed them.

Theater commanders enjoyed almost limitless emergency powers inside their own jurisdictions. In the early months of the war it was common for generals to divert occasional airplanes and use them for tactical purposes. But when Simon Buckner hijacked the entire Northwest Ferrying Command, it was by far the biggest coup of all.

Buckner ordered an Army take-over of every aircraft that crossed the border into Alaska, no matter who owned it.[4] Within a few hours on the night of June 20, he suddenly had a huge fleet of planes. The job of organizing them took all night; at dawn the Nome airlift began.

If the Japanese were in the Bering Sea, they might hit Nome at any time. If it was going to be defended at all, it would have to be done fast. Buckner's G-3 officer, Colonel Thomas M. Crawford, used fifty-five airplanes—Lodestars, gooneybirds, Army C-53s, even old Ford tri-motors and bush planes. In less than twenty-four hours they made 179 trips, executing a mass movement of 2,272 men, twenty antiaircraft guns, and tons of equipment up the 600-mile air corridor from Anchorage to Nome.

Thirty-six hours after the first warning flash from the Bering Sea, Nome was garrisoned. The battalions dug in their flak guns and shore positions, and waited for the enemy to appear. In the meantime the airlift continued, day after day, bringing in still more might. The civilian

4. The War Department was incensed. It issued a letter-order prohibiting theater commanders from interfering with the Ferrying Command. Buckner's barracks-lawyers found enough loopholes in the directive (particularly a clause referring to "occasions of specific emergency") to allow him to disobey it without running the risk of court-martial. It was almost a month later when he finally relinquished the planes.

pilots, most of them new to the region, roared through savage storms on instruments—knowing their maps were inaccurate, their route without emergency facilities, and their area without a search-and-rescue system. To give them a better chance, Buckner sent out Major Charles F. Felstead of the Signal Corps with scribbled authority to commandeer any radio equipment he could find—military, commercial, even amateur. Felstead set out to build six emergency radio stations for the airlift, and within three days, using planes, trucks, and even sleds, Felstead had five of them built and operating.

During those three days, the haggard pilots roared back and forth to Nome without a break. Captain Philip T. Durfee of the 42nd Transport Squadron[5] wrote:

> Over half the time we landed and took off in cross winds, and in these parts a cross wind is not a zephyr but a gale, and it always blows. Sometimes we got lost and landed on frozen lakes. We slept in sleeping bags inside the planes or (if weather was clear) under a wing.

Sergeant R. C. Hampton wrote:

> We tied our plane so the wind wouldn't blow it away. But it started blowing 90 miles an hour and tore the tail surface loose, and the inner bracing and riveting were shearing fast. We spent the next two hours driving 4 x 4's in the mud to tie the plane to, and then returning to sleep, we found the wind had blown down our tent.*

TO GUARD AGAINST SURPRISE, Buckner hand-picked the best pilots from Navy and Air Force to keep a reconnaissance umbrella over the seas off Nome. Navy's James S. Russell and Marshall Freerks, Air Force's Cone, Marks, and Lucian Wernick were among them. Starting the first day of

5. Durfee's squadron provided the Aleutian bases with most of their supplies. One of the 42nd's pilots, Lieutenant Miles A. Werner, became a legend, barnstorming his C-53 up and down the chain regardless of weather, flying a one-man war. On June 16 he was unloading at Umnak when he heard a distress radio call from a young P-38 pilot, Lieutenant L. B. Stockard, overhead in the fog and unable to find the island. Werner borrowed a plane, found Stockard above the soup, and after five tries and an hour's hair-raising flying, finally led Stockard down to a safe landing. Werner met his death months later in a P-38 he had borrowed to take a crack at the enemy; he was shot down by Japanese flak over Attu.

*1995 ADDENDUM: Things don't change much in the Aleutians. In 1987 the National Climactic Data Center listed Cold Bay's average annual wind speed at 16.9 mph—among the highest in the world.

the airlift, they cruised offshore and tried to pick up sign of the rumored Japanese task force. The weather out at sea was not too bad, and it became certain there was no such force in the immediate waters; the patrols expanded to cover wider and wider arcs, until by the third day the long-range bombers were regularly flying all the way to the coast of Siberia. All they found was a Russian ship that had strayed into the Pribilofs. If there was a Japanese task force in the area, it was well hidden if not invisible.

In fact, the Japanese had never had designs on Nome. Nimitz's codebreakers, for once, had misinterpreted their clues. PBY radar had indeed detected a force in the Bering Sea on June 20—it was Admiral Kakuta's big four-carrier fleet; but Kakuta had merely been cruising around in search of the American Navy, and when he did not find it he went back across the Chain to the Pacific.

It had been a false alarm; that became slowly evident. The airlift tapered off into early July, having brought almost 900,000 pounds of men and equipment into the little gold-rush camp. As usual in the Aleutians, the big build-up led to naught, and so military historians paid little attention to it, even though it had been America's first large-scale military movement ever performed by air. Merrill Field, at Anchorage, had been busier than New York's La Guardia Airport; the principles like those Simon Buckner devised for the Bingo Operation would be hauled out of the files, many years later, in Berlin and the Congo.

LIFE FOR THE NEW NOME residents was considerably different from life in the Aleutians. Billy Wheeler wrote:

> At Nome the crews are settled in tents. A few of them tried to dig foxholes but were stopped at a depth of eighteen inches by rock-like frozen ground [permafrost]...Wernick's crew went into the town of Nome to see the natives in action. They report steak dinners for a nominal $2.50 served in the quiet and restful atmosphere of the Polar Bar Grill. Good whisky is very reasonable and the assortment could be considered a minor miracle considering the difficulty of shipping such items from the States. Nome is proud of its boast that a greater tonnage of liquor is shipped in each year than food.

Living was less pleasant for the four Signal Corpsmen who had been sent into the Pribilofs to set up two outpost radio warning stations.

The four privates kept a twenty-four-hour watch from June to October, saw nothing worth reporting, and had to suffer the loneliness of total isolation without so much as a tree to break up the view. Early in July, Wernick and the other veterans were relieved at Nome and sent back into the Aleutians. The new outfit that relieved them, the 404th Bombardment Squadron, came sheepishly into Nome with eight B-24D Liberators which the Air Force in its wisdom had painted with desert-camouflage colors. The "Pink Elephants" took over the Bering Sea patrols, suffering more from catcalls and insults than from combat; they survived thirty-nine missions without a single mishap.[6]

By the Fourth of July—a month after the Battle of Dutch Harbor—the Nome airlift was ended. It had provided Simon Buckner with a valuable new base within easy distance of the Pribilofs and Siberia; though major forces were gradually withdrawn, the new Nome air field became an important staging base for Lend-Lease aircraft deliveries to the Soviet Union. For the next three years the little ghost camp throbbed with the hum of airplane engines and the tramp of Russian jackboots. For the first time since the 1900 gold rush, Nome was on the map.

The same was not true of the Aleutian Campaign itself. The news blackout continued; neither the American public nor the Allied high commands displayed much interest in the struggles of their tiny northern armies. The few veterans who came home to the States were perplexed, angered, and finally awed by the seeming apathy of America. They began to wonder about the war from which they had returned. When they launched into their war stories, half their listeners refused to believe them. After a while some of them began to doubt their own memories. Was there really a war in the Aleutians—or had they only dreamed it?

---

6. The 404th Squadron performed altogether too well to suit some of its members. Its record in Alaska and the Aleutians soon became outstanding; its dubious reward was that, when the other squadrons were rotated home, the 404th stayed in the Aleutians. It did not go back to the States until September 23, 1947.

CHAPTER
NINE

"When You Could See a Hundred Feet, That Was a Clear Day"

THE AMERICAN COUNTEROFFENSIVE IN the Aleutians was slow to get started and equally slow to gain momentum. Nevertheless it was the United States' first retaliatory campaign in the Pacific. (It preceded Guadalcanal by sixty days.) It was weak, uncertain, and plagued with misfortune and mistakes; but it was a start. More than that, it was a rehearsal.

Army and Navy air arms had warmed up with "search and destroy" missions, the Kiska Blitz, and subsequent attack operations against Japanese bases and shipping. By experiment and error the fliers learned about war, the hard way. But the Campaign had already begun to take shape as a replica, compact and prophetic, of the Pacific war to come. And airmen were not the only members of the cast to take part in the dress rehearsal.

It would be another ten months before infantrymen would see bloody ground fighting in the Aleutians (Buckner kept his 4th Infantry Regiment hard at training), but almost all the other Alaskan forces had already gone to war. Signal Corps, Medical Department, Engineers, SeaBees, Transportation (air and sea), Quartermaster, Supply, Ordnance and all the other supporting groups worked and suffered and learned their way around the Aleutians. The conditions were war conditions—war with the enemy, war with the perpetual enemies of weather, water, and terrain. Antiaircraft and shore-defense batteries were manned around the clock. Navy ships prowled in search of action.

And underneath, the submarines went to war.

Servicemen in the Aleutians were as ignorant as the Stateside public of the doings of Alaska's Silent Service—Captain Oswald S. Colclough's tough North Pacific Submarine Division. Its undersea campaign, like everything else in the Aleutians, started badly but soon made progress by virtue of the theater's unique on-the-job-training program.

It was the middle of June, just after the discovery of the enemy on Kiska, when Lieutenant Herbert L. Jukes, skipper of the submarine S-27, took his old pigboat out of Dutch Harbor with orders to find out if the enemy had occupied Amchitka, a narrow island just east of Kiska. S-27 cruised west 500 miles through heaving maelstroms that mauled half her crewmen. On June 19, Jukes finally surfaced off Amchitka to recharge his batteries and scout the coast. At 10:40 that evening, inching through the fog without fathometer or radar, S-27 rammed a reef.

Driven onto the rocks by the fifteen-foot surf, she rolled over; the crew pitched and carmomed off bulkheads and valve wheels. The antique submarine started to flood. Sea water hit her batteries and the chemical reaction sent deadly chlorine gas billowing through the hull.

Lieutenant Jukes clambered through the submarine, drove all his men topside and shepherded them into rubber rafts. When he was certain everyone was out, Jukes climbed into a raft and paddled to shore on Amchitka with all hands, a supply of food, and all the side arms available on board. The submarine tipped up awash behind them, a derelict.

There were no Japanese on the island. They set up camp in the church of the abandoned Aleut village in Constantine Harbor and spent six days there until a patrolling PBY found them and took thirteen of the men off. Next day, June 26, three Catalinas sortied out of Dutch Harbor in a bad storm, picked up the rest of the crew, and flew the 500 miles back to Dutch at 50-foot altitude.

Lieutenant Jukes and his crew came through without injury. The skipper's main concern, wrote the PBY pilot who rescued him, "was the loss of his new blue service uniform, which he felt would be absolutely necessary for wearing at his general court-martial."

An inquiry cleared Jukes; the Navy sent him back to sea with a new command. But the loss of S-27 had been the first submarine action of the Aleutian Campaign. It was a bad omen; the Chain's monstrous seas made it likely the same kind of thing would happen again.

S-27 and the other five World War I pigboats in Colclough's division were about as well designed for Aleutian duty as a pup tent for hurricane protection. The odds were high against survival for sailors on S-boat war patrols. For that reason, Captain Colclough was deeply pleased that American shipyards were rapidly turning out big new fleet-class submarines equipped to withstand heavy beatings. Through Theobald and Nimitz, Colclough prevailed on the Navy to give him early priority in the assignment of the new boats.

It was only June 28 when the modern fleet boat *Growler* steamed into Dutch; she was soon followed by *Tuna, Triton, Grunion*, and four others.

Action in the North Pacific picked up swiftly for the underwater fleet. *Nautilus,* one of America's three 2,700-ton super-submarines, was operating out of Pearl Harbor on June 25 when she sank the Japanese destroyer *Yamakaze* off northern Japan; *Nautilus'* Aleutian colleagues soon had their own victories to boast, with an impressive string of kills racked up on July Fourth.

The fireworks started early in the morning. *Growler,* under Lieutenant Commander Howard W. Gilmore, slipped silently into Kiska Harbor at periscope depth. It was the first war patrol for both the young skipper and the brand-new submarine, but Gilmore tooled *Growler* through the pinnacle reefs like a veteran. He brought her dead-center into Reynard Cove and found himself staring at three anchored Japanese destroyers.

Gilmore fired one-two-three. The first torpedo struck destroyer *Arare* dead amidship; her boilers blew up and the 1,850-ton ship sank within minutes. Destroyer *Kasumi's* bow was smashed; *Shiranuhi's* hull broke in half. Both destroyers were settling in the water, *Arare* already sunk, when Gilmore down-periscoped, slipped to the bottom and crept out of harbor, rigged for silent running.[1] He zigzagged away from Kiska pursued by Japanese ships that shook up *Growler* with furious depth-charge attacks. It took Gilmore three days to shake the enemy; he finally returned to Dutch Harbor without injury.

Also on July 4, *Triton,* under Lieutenant Commander C. C. Kirkpatrick, pursued a phantom silhouette for ten hours in the fog off Attu until it was positively identified as an enemy destroyer. Kirkpatrick then fired two fish which took the 1,600-ton *Nenohi* amidship and sank her with a loss of two hundred men

Eleven days later, *Grunion,* under Lieutenant Commander Mannert L. Abele, sank Japanese subchasers SC-25 and SC-27 off Kiska and crippled a third ship. On her first war patrol, fresh from the construction yard, *Grunion* chalked up her victories and continued on patrol toward the southwest, where a week later two Japanese I-boats torpedoed and sank the U.S. Army Transport *Arcata.* Only twelve Americans survived the sinking; every PBY and submarine in the North Pacific headed out to find the raiders. The Japanese I-boats were next seen when they shelled the *Felix Dzerjinsky,* a Russian freighter on her way to Petropavlovsk on a Lend-Lease run. Commander Abele took *Grunion* after the two enemy

---

1. Kasumi and Shiranuhi were refloated, towed back to Japan, and rebuilt. Arare was a total loss.

submarines, and on July 30 he evidently found them. He made a routine radio report early that morning—and was never heard from again. *Grunion* disappeared without a trace.

COLCLOUGH'S SUBMARINE DIVISION WORKED, suffered, and did its job. But it did not draw much attention from higher commands. The same could not be said of Captain Leslie E. Gehres' air wing of PBYs.

At forty-six, Gehres was a huge, rock-jawed man with level gray eyes and a stern mouth. He had come up fast the hard way, serving in World War I battleships as an enlisted seaman and then taking a mustang commission. He had led the Navy's aerobatic team in the National Air Races, and developed such a reputation as a hot carrier pilot that it had seemed natural to high command to put him in command of the Navy's combat air patrol in the Aleutians. But he had never bothered to check out in PBYs, and the tough Kiska Blitz had given CINCPAC another view of Gehres; when matters began to settle down later in June, Admiral Nimitz decided a steadying hand was called for—he had already had to caution Gehres, more than once, that when he wanted PBYs to fight like B-17s he would let Gehres know.[2]

Patrol Wing Four had been acting as an independent arm under the informal aegis of Admiral Theobald's North Pacific Force. Now Nimitz curtailed Gehres' freewheeling independence by placing the Navy air wing directly under the command of General Butler of the Eleventh Air Force. Nimitz hoped the steady, cautious Butler would help tone down Gehres' wilder ambitions—though Butler had hardly succeeded, in that respect, with Bomber Command's impetuous Colonel Eareckson.

Nimitz's well-intentioned decision added further discord to the Alaskan command structure. The Navy (Theobald) and the Army (Buckner) were hardly speaking to each other, yet they shared control of the Air Force (Butler). Butler in turn was not on the best of terms with Eareckson and his other staffers, let alone his new subordinate, Gehres. But in spite of the strained command structure, the fleet air wing kept operating at capacity. Throughout June the PBYs kept regular missions in

---

2. Gehres' impatience with "necessary" limitations sometimes worked in his favor. For his bold work in the Aleutians he was awarded the Legion of Merit and the Army's DFC. Later, he took command of the big carrier Franklin just before she was bombed near Honshu in March 1945. Gehres' was credited with saving the ship, which most observers had given up for lost; he brought her all the way to the Brooklyn Navy Yard under her own power, and earned both the Navy Cross and the nation's accolades, though many officers insist his "childish immaturity" hurt morale and caused him to make costly mistakes in handling the Franklin disaster.

the air, to Kiska and out to sea, and it was on one of those patrols that Lieutenant Jack Litsey was attacked by a new, unfamiliar, and terrifyingly fast Japanese float-fighter. Litsey, whose mail plane had been shot down on June 3 at Dutch Harbor, limped back to Dutch with one dead man aboard, a badly shaken crew, and a description of the plane that had attacked him.

It was a new type of Zero—the Nakajima "Rufe," a 300-mph fighter with four heavy machine guns and maneuverability enough to do everything but fly backwards. Litsey was lucky to get back alive. His encounter with the Rufe had been the war's first contact with the rumored new Japanese plane.

General Butler asked Gehres to cancel his PBY missions over Kiska. Gehres replied that he wasn't afraid of the new Japanese planes; he disregarded the request, and during the next six weeks lost four PBYs (killing nineteen of the thirty-two men on board) in repeated bombing and depth-charging attacks on the enemy.

At the same time williwaws and high seas kept pounding the PBYs at anchor; by the end of July, despite the arrival of two new squadrons and additional replacements, Gehres had lost more than a third of his planes and had only thirty-one PBYs left flying.

Gehres wanted his Catalinas in the air all the time, regardless of weather. Every flight was a perilous adventure. William S. Webster recalls:

> I remember my first patrol. I was green, just out of flight school, and it scared me to be flying at 50 feet not knowing where we were. On the way home after half a day over the Pacific we flew back and forth along the Chain, trying to recognize something, trying to tell one fog-decapitated island from another. It took us four hours to find Priest Rock. The PBY could stay in the air around the clock if it had to, but that didn't make me any less nervous. We took a bearing on Priest Rock, the pilot punched his stopwatch and pulled up into the soup, and we trundled along for quite a while and let down. Lo and behold there was Cold Bay, dead center. But I was all ready to pack and go back home, right then.

On July 19, to extend the range of his air patrols, Gehres sent seaplane tenders *Casco* and *Gillis* out the Chain, to Adak and back to Atka, abandoned a month earlier. Enemy response was quick; the next day, three four-engine Mavis bombers from Kiska made a bombing attack on *Gillis* in Kuluk Bay, Adak.

It was PBY pilot Frank S. Caughey's birthday. Caughey was aboard *Gillis*, which had one ancient 3-inch gun astern. "If we ever have to fire that gun," Caughey recalls saying, "the whole ship will fall apart." But skipper Norman Garton ordered the gun manned, and got *Gillis* under way. There were no PBYs here yet, *Gillis* was alone. By zigzagging, Garton dodged all eighteen bombs dropped by the enemy flying boats. The old 3-incher banged away steadily, making the ship's boiler-plate armor ring with a fearful clanging. And finally the Japanese ran out of bombs and circled away.

CAPTAIN SUKEMITSU ITO, IJN, HAD brought his six Mavis bombers in from Paramushiro six weeks earlier. He had lost three of the planes in the Blitz. Since then he had been training his pilots to fly in the Aleutians. Because a cargo ship had sunk on a reef and another had been bombed, Ito's stockpile of bombs was pitifully small; and to compound that handicap, he found that Japanese navigational charts were dangerously inaccurate, despite prewar surveys made by Japanese "fishing" boats. Ito's chart placed Nazan Bay three miles from its actual location (and at Kiska no one was sure whether the harbor would freeze over in winter). Ito had spent the past month scouting the Chain, to correct his charts and prepare his pilots. Now, he felt, they were ready to go to war.

The attack on *Gillis* was the opening action of what Ito hoped would be a strong retaliatory bombardment campaign against the American PBY tenders. After a new shipment of bombs arrived, he gathered his crews for a predawn briefing and sent them to their planes. On August 3, Ito droned out of Kiska Harbor in the lead bomber of his three-plane formation; over Kuluk Bay they lined up their targets—*Gillis* and the nearby destroyer *Kane*. But once again the U.S. ships maneuvered evasively and sent up flak, and while Ito's bombs chewed up the harbor bottom and spewed mud on the beaches, they failed to score a single hit.

Disappointed but determined, Ito resolved to go back the next day and knock out the American ships for good.

IT WAS EARECKSON WHO SET UP the ambush.

Combating the Japanese air raids had been hard, because American fighters lacked the fuel capacity to circle Atka all day waiting for the enemy to attack; it was a long way back to Umnak. Besides, enemy planes were impossible to find in the fog, especially for American fighters which had maneuverability and firepower, but no radar.

Eareckson solved the problem with typical inventiveness. No one had ever heard of using bombers to escort fighters; traditional air tactics worked the other way around. But traditional tactics had not been devised with the Aleutians in mind. Eareckson's new P-38 "Peashooter Patrol" sent five radar-equipped B-17 bombers out, as mother ships to a pack of Lightning fighters.

On August 4, Eareckson's patrol was orbiting Nazan Bay at 5,000 feet inside the solid cloud overcast, when a B-17's radar flushed the three oncoming enemy bombers. Fed range and direction by radio, the P-38 fighters dived straight into the soup and broke through shooting. The loud whine of their superchargers, the chatter of their cannon and machine guns caught the big Kawanishi 97s totally by surprise; Captain Ito only had time to shout a brief warning and wrench his bomber aside before the P-38s were flashing through the V of the Japanese formation, cutting the big bombers apart. Ito zigzagged desperately into the clouds, barely escaping; his two companions were not quick enough. The fighters shot them both down into the sea.

It was the first P-38 victory of the war.

Eareckson kept his Peashooter Patrols in the air for about a week until it became certain the Japanese weren't coming back. The Americans believed they had frightened the enemy off; actually, Captain Ito had no planes left. Within ten days he flew his last surviving Mavis back to Japan.

CONTEMPTUOUS OF USELESS HIGH-ALTITUDE bombardment, which he described as "trying to kill ants with a pogo stick," Colonel Eareckson put his crews through the daily hurdles of deck-level practice missions at altitudes as low as 75 feet. He relied heavily on the planes and crews of his *alma mater*, the 36th Squadron, while other squadrons for the time being followed more traditional procedures. Once, when the 36th was grounded at Umnak, one of its pilots, Pappy Speer, hitchhiked over to Cold Bay and tagged along on a Kiska bombing mission with another squadron. Billy Wheeler reported, "They dropped in a formation through overcast at a calibrated altitude of 17,000 feet," and added sarcastically, "Bombardier on Speer's crew doubts they hit the right island."[3]

While he worked out new tactical schemes and led many of his own missions, Eareckson had the continuing responsibility to keep pressure

3. Wheeler's war diary includes many names, military abbreviations and technical terms. Rather than fill quotations with brackets and ellipses, I have in a few cases abridged and revised his remarks. I hope the sense of them remains intact, but if there are small inaccuracies they are more likely the author's fault than Wheeler's.

on the enemy. To determine Kiska's weather he had established the routine of sending a single bomber on dawn patrol; often as not the weather plane reported back, "Weather unflyable"—and then, somehow, had to find its way home. To avoid heavy losses on weather missions, Eareckson regularly assigned the best veteran crews to them; frequently he lent them his own navigator, Captain Philip Sevilla, whom Frederick Ramputi recalls as an uncanny pathfinder: "I could depend on Phil making a landfall within fifteen seconds after a 600-mile over-water leg in the worst storms."

At Kiska, Japanese defenses were concentrated around the harbor, where in a small area the Japanese had grouped almost one hundred rapid-fire antiaircraft guns—the heaviest flak concentration of any forward Japanese base in the Pacific. But Eareckson seldom lost a plane to enemy flak: he made it a point to brief every outgoing mission on the exact location of every antiaircraft gun, as determined by weather planes' photoreconnaissance.

The lean, wisecracking colonel became a legend in both camps. At Kiska the Japanese order came down: "Get Eareckson." And at Umnak, Billy Wheeler wrote:

> 24 July 1942: The entire bomber command was assembled in the first mass military formation the Air Forces have seen since reaching this island of Umnak. Colonel Eareckson was presented the Distinguished Service Cross for bravery beyond the call of duty. He has earned it.

Eareckson's DSC Citation states in part:

> INSTEAD OF REMAINING IN COMPARATIVE SAFETY AT HIS HEADQUARTERS, HE REPEATEDLY TOOK TO THE AIR IN DIRECT PERSONAL ATTACKS AGAINST THE ENEMY, AND PERSONALLY FILLED GAPS ON NUMEROUS FLIGHTS BY ACTING IN EVERY CAPACITY FROM FIRST PILOT TO GUNNER.

It should be mentioned that Lieutenant Billy J. Wheeler was not only the 36th Bombardment Squadron's assigned unit historian, but also one of its regular officers. He flew scores of missions as pilot and co-pilot. It is impossible to read the whole of his vibrant diary (on file in the National Archives) without feeling warm affection for its zestful author; it was with a shock of personal sadness that I learned of his death in an aircraft accident in South Dakota on September 28, 1944.

GENERAL BUTLER'S STAFF INCLUDED a number of paperwork addicts who demanded "certificates of airworthiness" before releasing grounded planes, condemned beat-up engines and tires as "unfit for use," and tried to ensnarl Eareckson's Bomber Command in the kind of red tape loved by all military organizations. Eareckson bulldozed his way through it all. In the process he became known as "Commander in Chief, Junkman's Air Corps," because every plane in his command was composed of the cannibalized parts of at least three wrecked bombers.

He got maximum use out of his handful of Fortresses and Liberators. During the Campaign's first sixty days his raiders dropped more than 125,000 pounds of high explosives on Kiska. The results gratified higher commands; Eareckson's pressure, abetted by the stings of PBY raids and occasional belly-tank missions flown by medium bombers and P-38s,[4] slowed Japanese construction to a standstill and drove the enemy into cramped tunnel warrens from which the Japanese could not conduct any offensive operations at all.

The Air Force's hard-crusted, improbably tender warriors lived a spartan existence leavened by the pretended arrogance of hollow jokes—"They gave me a choice between this world, the next world, and the Aleutians." The constant threat of sudden death was laughed off with cracks about "flying into a stuffed cloud." Umnak pilots dry-cleaned their clothes with gasoline and hung them near stoves to dry—and several tents burned to the ground. It was all food for laughter. Everyone waited with wry retort for the next "canned mission"—there were so few targets that Eareckson often began his briefings with a simple, "Mission Number D-2, take off as soon as you can."

Laughter was a defense, but it often faded—on night missions, when pilots feared vertigo and couldn't tell up from down; in tense moments of landing, mushing down through the weather while ears measured the steady beat of the engines; on bright clear days when outbound pilots could see parts of planes scattered on the sides of volcanoes—planes that had tried to find home in the soup; on evenings in the Ops shack, waiting with muted sobriety for news of a fellow pilot who was twenty minutes late, then forty minutes, then an hour.

---

4. Only in optimum weather (perhaps once in three weeks) could the B-25 and B-26 mediums reach Kiska. As for the twin-engine P-38 Lightnings, their 1,200-mile missions were flown, recalls Major General Norman D. Sillin, "carrying two belly tanks and cruising at 1,400 rpm. After the belly tanks and bombs had been dropped and ammo expended, they returned single-engine."

From May to late August on the 52nd Parallel there were eighteen to twenty hours of daylight, but dense fog was the rule. Lieutenant William Johnson wrote: "Weather hangs over life like the curtain of the legitimate stage—the actors walk around in the dim backstage light, studying their lines and wondering when the curtain will rise."

"When you could see a hundred feet," Lucian Wernick recalls, "that was a clear day." Taking off, a pilot would radio the plane ahead to make sure it was clear of the runway before he started to taxi. Wernick described the take-off:

> My co-pilot would stick his head out the window and look straight down at the runway stripe, which I couldn't see straight ahead in the fog. The co-pilot would call "One degree right" or "two degrees left" and that's the way we took off, day in and day out.

At Kiska the Japanese had strung cables across the passes to snare American bombers coming in on the deck. The flak—"You could get out and walk on it." Every pilot feared getting lost in the muck on the way back; and when they did find their way home, Marshall Freerks recalls, "You could land, and the tower didn't even know you were there."

OLD SEVENTY, THE ANTIQUE B-17E, had developed a reputation for willfulness. Nothing could touch her; she seemed invulnerable. When she was not part of a bombing mission she flew the morning weather patrol over Kiska; she was in the air every day. Billy Wheeler wrote, "The old crate is a light ship and capable of greater range than the new type." But Old Seventy, treated with the warm affection of a mascot, ran out of luck on July 17, 1942.*

---

*1995 ADDENDUM: Like so many incidents in the Aleutian theater, this one—the death of Old Seventy—is not remembered identically by all parties. Some years ago, after having read this book, Capt. Richard Ragle wrote, "Balderdash! Marks had a new B-17E and was shot down over Kiska by a Rufe. Walseth [sic] hit a mountainside at Umnak with 'Old 70' returning from a recon flight." Ragle's "Walseth" probably refers to Lieutenant Albert Wilsey, who with his Fortress was lost about six weeks after Marks's death… Aircraft expert and author-historian Steve Birdsall wrote me (March 1, 1995), "It seems to me that fourteen B-17Es served with 36th Bomb Squadron, and four were lost in action: 41-2586 with Lt. Major H. McWilliams collided in midair with 41-9094 and crashed into a mountain on January 21, 1943… 41-9084 with Lt. Thomas F. Mansfield disappeared after attacking Japanese warships on June 4, 1942… 41-9126 was lost with Lt. Albert Wilsey and his crew on August 28, 1942… 41-9146 was shot down over Kiska with Captain Jack Marks on July 17, 1942. Over the years there have been variations of a day or two either way on some of these loss dates, and in these cases I follow John Cloe's latest research. Also, some sources indicate 41-9126 was the Marks plane [i.e., "Old

The Aleutian Campaign was just seven weeks old, but both Old Seventy and her pilot, Major Jack Marks, were blooded veterans. Then squadron leader Russell Cone recalls, "Jack Marks kept begging me for weeks to let him handle a mission. I relented and let him lead a flight of three B-17s on a Kiska mission." Marks was jumped over Kiska by a pack of Rufe fighters; they shot up Old Seventy but it looked as if she could get home. She didn't make it; she ran into a mountain in the fog. Cone took the news bitterly. "It always bothered me awfully that I had let him go."

It had been a heavy day for the Rufes. One pilot on the mission estimated that more than fifty individual fighter attacks were made on his ship during the short period he was locked into his bomb run. Of the eight bombers in the day's missions to Kiska, seven returned to Umnak—every one riddled.

During the next two weeks the Rufes waged a determined contest with Eareckson's bombers. They suffered heavy losses against the thirteen machine guns carried by each Flying Fortress; but they inflicted so much damage that by the end of July, Eareckson's command had diminished to a total strength of eleven heavy bombers. The number dropped to ten on August 4, when Captain Ira F. Wintermute (who had already lost a navigator and ditched a plane a month earlier) had his B-24 Liberator chewed up by flak and Rufes. With two engines on fire, Wintermute lost altitude but determined to stay in the air. His navigator, Lieutenant Paul A. Perkins, kept saying, "We'll make it—we'll make it." But Wintermute rehearsed ditching procedures with the crew. The ship had crabbed about 150 miles toward home when one engine fell off. Wintermute felt the plane going out of control, and gave the order to bail out.

Lieutenant Perkins jumped with the first group. His chute was caught in a crosscurrent; Perkins landed in the water 300 yards off the shore of barren Semisopochnoi volcano, and was swept under and drowned, unable to reach shore. In the air, the sergeant ahead of Wintermute got his shroud lines tangled in one of the dead propellers as the plane flipped over; Wintermute, kicking away from the floundering plane, hung from his chute and watched with horror while the plane dragged the gunner into a spiral dive and exploded against the cone of the volcano.

The six survivors gathered on the steep ocean bank and rigged improvised shelter from parachute silks and muskeg. Three days later a

---

Seventy"],41-9146 the Wilsey plane. This is only possible if 36th Bomb Squadron originated a transposition error… the numbers are very similar, but this still seems unlikely unless paperwork was completed well after actual events… Perhaps surprisingly, most of the 36th Squadron B-17Es survived to return to the ZI [Zone of the Interior, or 'lower fortyeight']."

PBY found them and picked them up. At Dutch Harbor, Eareckson took one look at the battered Wintermute and ordered him back to the States, where Wintermute became a pilot instructor. "Two to a customer," Eareckson said, "is enough." But Wintermute was among a select handful of Aleutian pilots to get home in 1942. There was no policy of rotation for crews in the Eleventh Air Force: "The only way to get home is in a box," pilots observed. Eareckson and Simon Buckner asked Washington for replacements and authority to establish a rotation program, but Washington had no replacements available. Brigadier General Lawrence S. Kuter, Deputy Chief of the Air Staff from Washington, told Buckner that the Aleutians were a minor theater of operations, priority calls were higher in other theaters, and Alaska had to keep the Japanese "on the defensive with no further air reinforcements."

ATTRITION HAD DEPLETED JAPANESE air forces just as savagely. Seaplane carrier *Kimikawa Maru* had brought eighteen float planes to Kiska in June. American attacks had forced the carrier to take refuge at Agattu, whence she made frequent refueling and supply runs to Kiska by night. At Agattu, American raids shook up her crew; after a while she stood out to sea near Kiska. By the day after Wintermute's crash, only two of her eighteen Rufes were still operational—six had been shot down in dogfights, two or three bombed on the water, and the rest destroyed by surf and weather.

Early in July, Admiral Hosogaya had brought a formidable supply convoy to Kiska with 1,200 new troops and six midget submarines. (The four destroyers sunk and crippled by U.S. submarines on July 4 had been escorts to that convoy.) That same week, with heavy commitments in the south, Admiral Yamamoto had withdrawn most of Hosogaya's ships, including Admiral Kakuta's four-carrier task force. It left Hosogaya with a weak skeleton force, which was further crippled when *Kimikawa Maru* withdrew to Japan; with all but two of her fighters destroyed, there was no point in her staying in the Aleutians.

To consolidate his remaining strength, Hosogaya abandoned the tent camp on Agattu and used the troops to bolster the defenses of Kiska. He still had a garrison on the far western island of Attu, but it was seldom attacked by the Americans, and Hosogaya began to toy with the idea of moving the Attu force as well to Kiska.

In the meantime, the largest naval unit he had intact was his fleet of a dozen I-class submarines. Instead of using them to attack Allied shipping, Hosogaya was forced to put the big submarines (and his few destroyers) to use carrying cargo to the Aleutians, to keep his forces from starving.

At the same time, he ordered the troops on Kiska and Attu to come out of their underground shelters and start leveling ground for air fields. Local commanders objected immediately: they could not build air fields without heavy construction equipment, and heavy equipment could not be transported by submarines and destroyers. In fact, Hosogaya not only lacked shipping, he lacked construction machinery as well; Japan's industry lagged far behind her needs throughout the Pacific, and Imperial Headquarters had the same feeling toward the Aleutians as the American command had: they were a minor, backwater theater. Tojo still planned to abandon the Aleutians as soon as winter set in. Consequently he refused to give Hosogaya construction equipment.

But without air fields, Hosogaya could not guarantee the security of Kiska and Attu. In a quandary, he did the only thing he could do. He ordered his soldiers to start leveling air fields—by the slow brute force of manpower and hand shovels.

CHAPTER
TEN

The Navy's Spring Plowing

THE *COMMAND HISTORY, NORTH PACIFIC FORCE* for July 1942 admits modestly, "Some differences of opinion [have] developed between the Army and Navy Alaskan commands."

"Heaven cannot use two suns," went an old Japanese proverb, "nor a house two masters."

Simon Buckner's Intelligence Officer, Major Joe E. Golden, was leaving for the States for reassignment. As a parting shot, Golden sent a memorandum to General DeWitt in San Francisco:

> 21 JUNE 1942
> FROM: G-2, ADC
> TO: CG, WDC
>
> ...THE COMMANDING GENERAL, ALASKA DEFENSE COMMAND, HAS NOT BEEN CONSULTED ON CONDUCT OF OPERATIONS TO DATE.... [I RECOMMEND] THAT HE BE GIVEN MORE AUTHORITY UNDER THE PRESENT COMMAND SET-UP THAN HE NOW HOLDS...[SINCE] HE IS OMITTED FROM THE PICTURE, SO TO SPEAK, UNTIL A STATE OF GROUND-OPPOSED INVASION IS DECLARED.

Three weeks later, Simon Buckner, a formidable frowning Buddha, sat looking at a carbon of Golden's memo and feeling as if he had been talking into a dead phone. He had received no response at all.

Meanwhile, down at Kodiak, Admiral Theobald sat at his desk and scowled at a signal from CINCPAC. It told him, in essence, to get a move on.

The buck had been passed—up, down, and around full circle.

BUCKNER WANTED THEOBALD TO BESTIR his striking force of ships, to go west into the Aleutians and pound Kiska with naval bombardments that would soften up the enemy and perhaps drive him out.

DeWitt, on receipt of the Golden memo, had needled the Joint Chiefs of Staff. General Marshall needled Admiral Ernest J. King; Admiral King passed the baton to Admiral Nimitz; Nimitz passed it back to Theobald, in the form of a message urging Theobald to do what Buckner wanted (partly as a diversion to distract the Japanese from Guadalcanal).

Theobald objected. Taking a task force close inshore to shell Kiska would imperil the warships. Fathometers would not show a pinnacle rock until the hull was impaled on it. Besides, what good would naval bombardments do that Air Force bombing attacks could not?

Buckner was no cartoon martinet, but his Patton-leather character made it hard for him to understand how the Navy could go on, just letting the Japanese sit there.

The stalemate hardly made Theobald any happier than it made Buckner. "Fuzzy Theobald," recalls Colonel William Alexander, "felt that he had been marooned. He hated the Aleutians, the Navy, the Air Force, the Army, the SeaBees, the weather, Jakie Reeves,[1] and the seagulls."

JULY 18, 1942: THEOBALD RAN UP HIS flag on heavy cruiser *Indianapolis* at Kodiak and steamed west at the head of a column made up of cruisers *Louisville, Honolulu, St. Louis* and *Nashville,* and nine destroyers. They set course for Kiska, intending—with some misgivings—to submit the enemy to a punishing bombardment.

One day out, a sailor fell overboard. Rescue teams recovered him almost immediately; but the icy waters had already taken his life.

Scuttlebutt traveled from watch to watch: "Jonah patrol"—it would be a jinxed voyage. The midsummer fog hid everything beyond the few yards of water around each hull. With alarming frequency, sister ships curtsied past each other, threatening collision. Westward the seas climbed—so rough they dumped water down the air intakes of rolling destroyers. Salt water and vomit clung to every surface.

(At the same time, in the churning waters of Unimak Pass, the YP-74, carrying a crew of SeaBees, crashed head-on with a freighter in the fog. The boat sank in ninety seconds; four men were lost.)

---

1. On June 26, 1942, Rear Admiral John W. Reeves replaced Captain Ralph C. Parker as commander of shore-based naval operations and patrol craft in the Alaskan Sector. The Sector, separate from Theobald's command, took its orders from the Seattle Naval District. Essentially, the difference was that Theobald's was a striking force, Reeves' a geographical jurisdiction.

The attack fleet kept moving. On July 22 Theobald was edging gingerly toward Kiska, but fog hung stubborn and thick and the island was never in sight. Weathermen could promise nothing. In the Aleutians, if the weather was bad it would probably get worse. Theobald withdrew to a safe distance and waited—and waited. Finally on July 27 he tried again, but the fog gave no break. He withdrew for the night. Hoping the weather would lift in the morning, he ordered an air strike by Air Force and Navy bombers to coincide with the shelling planned for the next afternoon.

Commander James S. Russell led his squadron of PBYs over Kiska, and Eareckson's bombers sortied from Umnak. Wheeler wrote, "Ceiling zero and visibility less than fifty feet." The planes waited for the Navy ships to start shelling, but Theobald didn't show up and at dusk the Air Force heavies turned back. Russell and the PBYs orbited half the night and finally headed home in thick fog; they landed at Atka, Umnak, and Dutch Harbor—some as late as 6:30 in the morning.

Theobald had been trying to skirt the reefs. As his fourteen ships moved blindly through the fog, two of the destroyers collided. Then a third destroyer rammed a fourth.

With nearly a third of his ships damaged, the admiral disgustedly took the task force back to Kodiak. He had not fired a shot.

THERE WAS, RECALLS COLONEL William Alexander, "a snarl from CINCPAC regarding NORPACFOR Commander going to sea when he should be at his headquarters to make frequent reports as to what was going on." So Theobald went back into the enforced imprisonment of his office. On August 3, under orders from CINCPAC, he turned over his ten undamaged ships to Rear Admiral William W. "Poco" Smith and ordered Smith to have another go at Kiska.

Navigating through the fog by radar and dead reckoning, Smith headed west through four days of risky voyaging, plunged into clear weather at 7:30 on the evening of August 7, and heard a lookout shout "Land Ho!"

Smith had found Kiska—no mean feat. As he moved into position, he called in an air strike from the bombers waiting overhead; Eareckson's planes plastered the harbor, and a few minutes later Admiral Smith launched six observation planes from the catapults of his cruisers. Admiral Theobald had ordered him not to go in close to the island; reefs were too plentiful and the waters were not well charted. The task force stood out, five miles offshore, hidden from its targets by high ridges. Gun crews waited for the observation planes to signal target coordinates.

Kiska's two remaining Rufe float-fighters had taken off valiantly to chase Eareckson's bombers. They were still in the air when the American catapult observation planes appeared. Kiska's deadly nests of flak guns filled the sky with black orchid bursts so heavy that the American SOCs could not get a clear view of the targets; harassed by the two fast Rufes, the clumsy old SOCs had to take refuge in the clouds. A Rufe shot one of them down; another came chugging down onto the water beside *Indianapolis*, splintered by 167 bullet holes (one of them in the pilot's foot). The four other observation planes got shot up and chased into the clouds.

With his aerial eyes blinded, Admiral Smith was ready to abandon the effort when the two Rufes slithered into sight overhead and started calling target fire for Kiska's batteries. In a ludicrous reversal, Japanese shore guns began to bombard the American ships.

Incensed, Admiral Smith put his ships into line astern and steamed back and forth, five miles offshore, loosing enormous salvos in the general direction of the Japanese base. More enraged than worried by the long-range Japanese gunnery, he pounded Kiska with every ton of high explosives in his magazines. The barrage was so heavy that he ran out of ammunition in seven minutes. Thereupon he recovered two of his catapult planes (the others flew to Umnak) and retired into the fog. None of his ships was damaged except for chipped paint here and there.

The Air Force immediately dubbed it "The Navy's Spring Plowing." Admiral Smith's huge broadsides had dug a spectacular great hole in the muskeg half a mile from the nearest targets of any importance. A few stray shells had done small damage—two Japanese soldiers were killed, holes were blown in a barracks and two landing barges and three beached, previously wrecked flying boats. The only real harm was done to a small freighter, hit by a wild, random four-inch shell that set her on fire and made her an easy target for a PBY which sank her later in the evening.

Poco Smith's bombardment of Kiska—the first and last such operation in 1942—had been a valiant effort. But like so many other incidents in the Aleutian war, it was more notable for what it missed than for what it achieved.

A BOMBARDMENT OF INVISIBLE TARGETS from five miles offshore, Simon Buckner bellowed, was worse than no bombardment at all. No reasoned arguments swayed him; he refused to admit that it would have been folly to drive a heavy cruiser right up on the beach; and from that moment forward, Buckner gave Admiral Theobald few moments of peace.

Throughout the Pacific, it had been a bad week. In the worst Allied naval disaster since Pearl Harbor, the U.S. and Australia lost four cruisers and two destroyers, with more than a thousand men killed and 709 wounded, at the Battle of Savo Island. Another destroyer struck a mine and sank off Espiritu Santo. On August 7, the day Poco Smith bombarded Kiska, the U.S. Marines invaded Guadalcanal. Three U.S. ships were crippled, a fourth sank, and the Marines found their thin beachhead quickly surrounded.

Guadalcanal immediately shaped up as a pivotal strategic contest, and Admiral Nimitz reached out for every available ship to feed the precarious lifeline supporting the embattled Marines. Within weeks, CINCPAC had drained Admiral Theobald's force of most of its strength—nine warships, four fleet submarines, and a squadron of PBYs. It left Theobald with only two light cruisers, four old destroyers, and an assortment of small craft.[2]

Reduced to impotence, Theobald sent in an icy memorandum that amounted to a resignation: he recommended that the North Pacific Force be withdrawn and disbanded at once. Nimitz refused the request. To sweeten the pot slightly, he prevailed on the Royal Canadian Navy to send two corvettes and three merchant cruisers to Theobald's aid. The reinforcement still did not make Theobald's force anything more than an escort unit; for the duration of his tenure in the Aleutians, Theobald was forced to limit his operations to convoy duties and a minor harassment of enemy shipping.

Meanwhile Simon Buckner assumed a greater role in the continuing Air Force campaign against Kiska. Trading lives for time, because he knew no other way, Buckner held on, waiting for the United States to send him enough men and enough muscle to do the job for which he had spent more than two years preparing.

EARLY IN AUGUST THE WAR Department belatedly released a newsreel movie of the bombing of Dutch Harbor. By this time, censorship of Alaskan operations had so infuriated the Senate Military Affairs

---

2. Both sides rushed reinforcements to Guadalcanal. Two weeks after the battle started, one of the war's frequent eerie coincidences took place at the Battle of the Eastern Solomons, when Admiral Kakuta's *Ryujo* (the carrier that had begun the Aleutian Campaign) was sunk by a task group commanded by Rear Admiral Thomas C. Kinkaid, who would presently relieve Theobald and bring the Aleutian Campaign to its close.

Committee that Senator A. B. "Happy" Chandler had carried out his threat to organize a congressional scouting party and lead a fact-finding expedition to the blacked-out Territory.

The legislators and their entourage arrived in Alaska a few days after the naval bombardment of Kiska. On August 17 they flew down to Dutch Harbor. It was the first sunny day in weeks. Billy Wheeler wrote, "The committee landed at Umnak this afternoon and interviewed Speer and other commanders. Happy Chandler set foot in Umnak's mud but pulled it out again quickly."

The visitors flew back to Kodiak that same day. They had spent less than half a day in the Aleutians, and all that time the sun had shone magnificently. From then on, on the rare occasions when the sun came out, soldiers called it "Senatorial weather."

Chandler and his party went back to Washington scoffing at the "rumors" of fog in the Aleutians. They reported they had been dismayed by the use of "PBY Patrol-observation planes for bombing expeditions on enemy beachheads in the Aleutians," and Chandler urged that Simon Buckner be given more authority over the Navy.* Chandler implied that he had not been favorably impressed by Admiral Theobald and Captain Gehres. He produced a table of statistics showing that there was less fog in the Aleutians than in the North Atlantic—a statement that must have come as wonderful news to the men in the Aleutians.

Chandler denied that fog was a serious threat to bombers. He therefore urged the Joint Chiefs to give Buckner a strong increase in air strength. Thus, for all the wrong reasons, the Senators came out foursquare in favor of exactly what Simon Buckner wanted.

IN 1897 MEN HAD CROWDED INTO miserable little steamships to get to the Klondike. The only difference now was that the voyage was not voluntary. The 2,000 miles from Seattle to Umnak had to be traveled by every man, bullet, and can of Spam—and shipping was scarce. Crowded to the gunwales, old ships like the Army's St. Mihiel[3] carried reinforcements and cargo up the open-sea run or the Inside Passage, ten days or more at 8 knots; the convoys were full of rumors that the

---

*1995 ADDENDUM: Ironically, the Chandler committee recommended that Alaska be designated a separate theater of operations, but General DeWitt balked at that, evidently because he didn't want to give up his authority.

3. Built in 1920, the redoubtable and legendary St. *Mihiel* had spent twenty years in Army Transport service between San Francisco and Manila before she had been transferred to the Alaska run. She had brought Buckner's first troops to Alaska. A 7,555-ton troop ship designed to carry 1,247 passengers, she usually carried half again that number. She had

ships just ahead had been bombed or torpedoed. Once the dazed newcomers reached Anchorage to be staged through, they found the city as overcrowded as the ships. Anchorage was so packed with war workers and agencies that the Signal Corps had to station a sentry in the Federal Building basement to prevent some other agency from invading and occupying its office.

From Anchorage, the new arrivals were trundled up to the forward bases: Cold Bay, where William Johnson wrote, "No one remembers having seen the sun"; Dutch, where Broadway was a wooden footwalk three planks wide; Umnak, where Billy Wheeler wrote, "From here even Kodiak looks like Los Angeles."

William S. Webster recalls, "You couldn't tell a General from a Seaman Second. Everybody was wearing Army clothes, no insignia. They were the only warm clothes around." Fuel was so short that men burned their summer clothes in their tent stoves; even candles were worth their weight in coin—for their heat, not their light.

Tired, ill-supplied, ill-fed, they lived on their nerves. The contrast was striking between the clean-shaven faces of the new replacements and the haggard, lined faces of the young veterans. Dr. Benjamin Davis recalls, "There was a terrific shortage of proper food. We never had any but powdered milk and eggs in the twenty-nine months I was up there. Bad food ruined the men's teeth.... When I finally got back to Anchorage I had my mouth X-rayed and found that every tooth in my mouth was abscessed. I left all my teeth in Alaska. Not only that, but for months I was without a set of replacements. That could have been worse, though—at the time it didn't matter much because we didn't have any meat to eat anyway."

Airmen at Umnak caught their own fish to supplement the tinned rations. A quick way to defeat the Japanese was proposed—"Feed them the same food we have to eat." Pilots after endless breakfasts of fatty tinned Vienna sausages quipped that they were "going from bed to wurst."

And: "All this and Attu."

At Cold Bay, Ensign William S. Webster was waiting on the chow line just outside the mess tent when a bulky figure in parka and hood

---

curious tendencies to roll and pitch even on glass calm water. Somehow she survived nearly every major operation in the Aleutians, and afterward served in the Mediterranean, at Saipan and at Okinawa, as a hospital ship. At war's end she was at Yokohama for the Japanese surrender. Unsinkable (to many veterans' chagrin), she continued in service long after the war, transporting military dependents.

appeared. Men began to murmur, "That's General Buckner," and Webster backed away to give the general a place at the front of the line. But Buckner waved him back. "There are three places where there is no rank—a poker game, a whore house, and a chow line. Keep your places." Buckner fell in at the back of the line.

At Blackie's Unalaska Bar, the only saloon in the Aleutian Islands, the queue of Dutch Harbor servicemen often extended all the way around the outside of the building. Whisky was 50¢ a shot (an Army private earned $50 a month), and one veteran wrote, "Regardless of how drunk we got, there was never enough room in the place to fall down." The other bases had no bars; enterprising enlisted men set up bootleg potato distilleries in their tents. Some died from drinking methyl alcohol, torpedo juice, and other concoctions. Air Force planes returning from overhauls at Anchorage carried bomb-bay loads of cased whisky.

The only diversion other than alcohol was gambling. Poker games were monumental, classic, and established in perpetuity. At Umnak the enlisted men's poker banker, Mess Sergeant Clifford Hunter, never carried less than $1,000 cash in his pockets.

Very occasionally, there were moments of beauty. Lucian Wernick recalls, "On Umnak I walked over the hill and saw the valley ablaze with wildflowers. The contrast between that and the total muddy drabness of our base made a poet out of this completely non-poetic soul."

For company, men brought a vast number of pet dogs into the Aleutians. Colonel Eareckson's pilots flew a solitary little tree down to Umnak, a gift for the use of the colonel's pet sled dog, Skootch. They planted it inside a wooden fence and put up a sign, "Umnak National Forest." It was the only tree in the Aleutians.

Seldom was tedium appeased. The *Kodiak Bear*, with the largest circulation of any newspaper in Alaska, ran an advice column, "What to Do in Case the Sun Shines." But the occasion rarely came up. Billy Wheeler wrote, "Bad weather follows the squadron the way Skootch, the husky, follows Colonel Eareckson." The long days were like perpetual misty sunsets, pastel-gray when storm clouds did not turn them black-on-black.

It was dreary but seldom calm. Corporal Dashiell Hammett wrote: "There was a gauge to measure the wind, but it only measured up to 110 miles an hour, and that was not always enough." Only a tenderfoot would spit into a williwaw. There were several brown bears which became nuisances rooting for scraps at Cold Bay; it was said one of the bears had the same baby three times.

Finally Captain Roy Craft, editor of the *Kodiak Bear*, announced in a page-one black box, "Weather reports suspended for the duration."

At Cold Bay, soldiers of the 260th Transportation Battalion built a hut for their day room (with 6 x 6 studs and joists stolen on a moonlight requisitioning sortie from Navy ships). Wind rolled the building away. The soldiers set it right-side-up and anchored it down with steel cables imbedded in concrete. After that the hut stayed put, but it was the only permanent above-ground structure in the area. Throughout the Aleutians in the next two years, the rule was dugout architecture.

The weather, "Made in Japan," lent truth to standard jokes: "It's too thick to fly if you can't see your co-pilot."

"Stick your hand out. If it touches a ship's mast, you're flying too low."

One pilot claimed he followed a duck because he knew it wouldn't fly into a cliff. Umnak used "a 500-pound bomb for a windsock." A PBY pilot claimed a seagull landed on his wing; convinced that weather too thick for Hannibal the Hitch-Hiking Gull was too thick for a PBY, the pilot landed his seaplane on the water, and watched the gull jump off and go away—swimming.

The stories were not always apocryphal. It wasn't unusual for flights of B-17s to fly at 25-foot altitudes, so that pilots could follow the sea wake of the airblast from the leading plane's propellers. On a socked-in July day, three bombers landed at Cold Bay at six-minute intervals: the first found the runway fogged in, the second found a clear 5,000-foot ceiling and landed easily, and the third couldn't find the field in the fog. "The weather," wrote Wheeler, "goes up and down like a whore's drawers."

Headwinds sometimes made it six hours to target and two hours back. The noisy wind often blew west at one end of the runway and east at the other. In a single cloud front, a bomber could pick up a ton of ice.

At Umnak, PFC Edward O. Stephens invented a wind-driven washing machine. Others boiled their laundry in discarded metal drums. When they hung clothes out, they took three days or more to dry. Ground crews burned oil-sump fires in open fifty-gallon drums near waiting planes, where crews could warm their hands before take-off—in midsummer. Pilots went around in white scarves and World War I open-cockpit flying helmets with earflaps. At mainland bases, as the early fall came in, oil became lumpy as caramel and canned juice on a tent floor had to be placed on the stove to melt. Ice formed on men's clothes and froze to their skin. They changed shoes every fifteen minutes and kept the second pair on the stove. Men returned from latrines with frost-bitten buttocks.

From Cold Bay and Umnak the air warriors saddled the weather and rode it out to Kiska and, usually, back home. It was a hell unlike any other. Constant turbulence tossed airplanes like kites. Ground crew mechanics learned to hate the unstable Aleutian air. It twisted airframes, wracked fuselages, stretched and loosened rivets, bent wings. It shook up cockpit instruments and threw them out of whack. It clogged carburetors. It loosened window seals, rusted landing-gear oleos, ruined fuel lines, shook engine mounts loose, gummed guns, froze bomb-bay rack releases, and fouled hydraulic systems. It killed.

The groundling grease monkeys seemed to keep the planes flying with nothing but skyhooks, rolling their own spare parts with hand-bellows forges and hammers, maintaining aircraft outdoors in williwaws with only flashlights and truck headlamps for illumination. The chief stockpile of repair parts was wrecked planes. There were no inspectors, but the ground crews never failed to make a repairable plane airworthy within twenty-four hours. It sometimes took four back-breaking hours in gale winds to refuel a B-17 by hand, pouring gas through a chamois filter. Colonel Everett S. Davis wrote to Hap Arnold, "Don't figure on getting any serviceable planes back from us. We have been hard on them."

The early fall blew in blizzard-cold. Emergencies kept the shop open around the clock at the Cold Weather Test Lab in Fairbanks, where mechanics had to thaw engines with firepots and find ways to keep rubber from shattering, keep planes from freezing solid, and keep overdressed pilots from freezing in their own sweat. Even in moderate Alaskan weather, the inside cabin temperature of a B-17 at 35,000 feet reached 85° below zero—and if a bare finger touched the plane's aluminum skin, the flesh turned instantly to white, dead ice.

Hydraulic fluid wouldn't flow below –25°. Spark plugs wouldn't heat; moisture congealed in engine sumps; grease in the control cables froze like concrete. Under Colonel Dale V. Gaffney, the Fairbanks laboratory fought to find solutions. The worst difficulty, to which no real solution was found, was the problem of expansion differential—with changing temperatures, steel and copper and aluminum contracted and expanded at different rates. Parts fitted to close tolerances became loose; highly tuned, supercharged engines rated at thousands of horsepower began to make noises like asthmatic outboard boat motors.

Everett Davis made frequent trips back from the front to the lab; engineering research was his first love. It was Davis who developed the quilty down-filled flying jacket still used in Alaska. He devised the loud Chinese red paint that was splashed on wingtips and tail surfaces to make downed planes show up in the snow. He charted the wilderness and developed compass-correction cards for use over the big magnetic deposits of Atka and other islands.

A strip of oil spilled on the ground could be picked up like a board. Before take-off it took four men with brooms to whack the ice off the wings of planes parked inland. As a result, they soon adopted old bush-pilot techniques, spreading canvas over engines and wings, and draining engine oil into cans which could be taken inside and set near stoves. Before morning take-offs they had to light plumbers' firepots under the engines and thaw them, sometimes for hours; they went over their planes for oil leaks and ice damage, which were often repaired with wadded rags or whittled twigs; then they brought out the cans of oil and poured it back into the engines.

Out in the Aleutians, though high wind drove the chill factor down to painful levels, extreme cold was not a problem on the ground, where the temperature seldom dropped below zero. But in the air, every added 1,000 feet of altitude was like moving 500 miles closer to the North Pole. The standard aviator's rule—if the weather is bad, climb out of it—did not apply in the Aleutians. "Our essential problem," Lucian Wernick says, "was not to find room above the weather, but to find room underneath it. The pilots who tried to get above the stuff were the pilots who iced up, got lost, and went into the drink."

Mathematically, the lift of an airplane wing depended on its eccentric shape. Ice, forming on the wing, changed its shape. Pilots lived with a vivid terror of this quiet substance that rendered their airfoils inviable.

Next to ice, getting lost was the greatest fear. Winds in the fog could blow a plane a hundred miles off course, or change its relative ground speed by a hundred miles an hour. There were almost no radio navigation beams in the Aleutians, but even if there had been more, they would not always have worked. Countless charges and discharges were suspended in the heavy air. They had the same effect on a radio as a powerful neon light. The frenzied electrical activity inhabited every weather front—and almost every foot of sky over the Aleutians could be described as a weather front. The static was impenetrable, earsplitting; it sizzled like bacon in a hot frying pan. Often it drowned out all signals from the ground in a pilot's headset.

Wind made the 1,200-mile round trip to Kiska far longer than that sometimes. Late in August the B-24 weather plane flew out to Kiska in a little more than two hours—and took nine hours to find its way back;

it had just ten gallons of fuel left when it landed. To give pilots the greatest safety margin, Eareckson loaded all his heavy bombers with extra bomb-bay tanks (at the expense of 1-1/2 tons of bombs); with 3,250 gallons of fuel aboard, the heavies needed at least one mile of runway to take off. Pushed to the wall and beyond, at 65,000 pounds gross weight, the big planes responded slowly, their wings cutting through the fog like shovels. Some of them did not get into the air at all. They ground-looped and crashed at the end of the runway. Others managed to take off but never returned. There were nights like August 28, when Eareckson returned to Umnak from a Kiska bombing strike. Half an hour later one of his wingmen landed. The other wingman did not get home at all. A fourth B-24 cracked up, landing on the slippery runway; a P-38 overshot the field and cracked up; two B-26s of the 73rd Squadron crashed at Naknek. Five planes lost in two hours—and not one of them scratched by combat.

The weather, like a Chinese water torture, abraded men and airplanes alike; it wore down men's spirits and health. Rickety and weak, they succumbed easily to disease. Yellow jaundice reached epidemic proportions—2,000 cases were checked into the Elmendorf hospital. Every time a supply ship landed at Umnak, a bad head cold made the rounds, and for some it became pneumonia.

Life ran a gamut from tedium to boredom to madness. There was no way to channel rage and frustration into action. There was nothing for them to do but wait out their time until they could escape. Umnak became "Alcatraz." For a time they sat coiled like taut-wound watchsprings; and then, in the penetrating damp air, they became loose and untidy. Their expressions faded; their stoic fortitude became the bland apathy of boneless sprawls and glazed, opaque eyes—the Aleutian stare. They looked like veteran commuters waiting for a train that would never come.

In the end, some of them reached the worst kind of desperation—a total unfeeling calm. By ones and twos, they began to disappear, sent back to the States under sedation.

"Hurry up and wait."

ALEUTIAN LIFE FOR THE JAPANESE was no better. The theater commanders—Admiral Hosogaya (Navy) and Lieutenant General Hideichiro Higuchi (Army)—did all they could to send food, clothing and recreation equipment to Kiska and Attu. It was never enough. American planes were always searching for convoys, American submarines and picket boats cut the supply lines regularly, and by August Hosogaya was having trouble finding enough ships to keep his forces alive.

PBYs flew 15-degree sector patrols with a 600-mile radius from their tenders at Atka. Japanese sea captains knew that. They monitored PBY radios to find out their positions, then followed in through the search sectors, right behind the scouting PBYs. The transports timed their arrivals for darkness, discharged cargoes at top speed, and tried to get away before the first American bombing attacks of the morning.

Even outlying anchorages were under American air surveillance. No longer able to keep seaplane carriers in the area, the Japanese flew Rufe fighters from carriers far out at sea, to land on the water at Kiska and survive as long as they could by climbing into the air every time American planes appeared. Often there wasn't enough warning time; the Americans would swoop in beneath the clouds, strafe and sink the anchored Rufes. The wrecks would be dredged up with great effort, their parts used to repair other planes.

Sometimes the Rufe pilots had to take to the air six times in a day. Hollow-eyed, underfed and unnerved, even the best aviators couldn't respond with the speedy coordination that combat flying required. In the face of the bristling machine guns of the American bombers they hung back with bone-weary reluctance and closed for combat less and less frequently.[4]

On the ground, soldiers scratched at the springy muskeg with hand shovels and picks in a valiant but foredoomed effort to level runways for land-based combat planes. It was like trying to dig a deep hole with toy shovels in soft beach sand. No sooner was an area leveled than it filled slowly with oozing mud and water. In the first six weeks they made virtually no progress.

Bombarded daily, Kiska's soldiers had moved steadily farther underground into timber-shored tunnels. Moisture that seeped through the muskeg made the living quarters even worse than tents above ground. The rabbit-warren life bred foot rot and nervous tremors that echoed the periodic rumblings of the volcano. Never quite dry in their clothes, men huddled around small radios and listened to Tokyo and wished they were home. Badly drafting flues brought stove smoke back into the tunnels; it was hard to breathe, hard to sleep.

---

4. After the war in an interview with Captain James S. Russell in Tokyo, Aleutian air-combat veteran Commander Shigefuso Hashimoto said he "respected greatly that the Americans flew and attacked in weather which the Japanese considered impossible for air operations."

Work crews began to make a little progress on the runway surface—and American bombs made a muddy lake of it. Navy engineers built a shore pen for midget submarines—and an American thousand-pounder smashed it to rubble. The first mail in weeks arrived aboard a small freighter from Honshu—and a PBY attack sank her with the mail sacks aboard. An I-class submarine arrived with food and medical supplies—struck a reef, foundered, and sank inside Kiska Harbor.

It was nobody's favorite war.

CHAPTER
ELEVEN

Forward to Adak

THE ORDERS FROM WASHINGTON WERE to harass the enemy. It was being done, but the cost was brutal. For months, Generals Buckner and DeWitt had been pressing the Joint Chiefs for authority to move farther out into the Chain and establish bases within shorter striking distances of the Japanese.

Late in August 1942, General Marshall authorized the move into the Andreanof island group of the central Aleutians, less than 250 miles east of Kiska.

Two islands were under consideration. Butler of the Air Force wanted to build the new air base on Tanaga, about 190 miles from Kiska. But Tanaga had a very poor harbor; Admiral Theobald preferred Adak, 50 miles farther from Kiska. Butler retorted that the Adak terrain was a nightmare—it would take at least four months to build an air field there. Tanaga at least had some flat places.

By now interservice bickering seemed prerequisite to all Alaskan command decisions. But this time, Simon Buckner did not take sides in the argument. For one thing, he did not particularly like either Theobald or Butler. For another, he wanted to get the new base built as quickly as possible. In any case there was a board of arbitration whose decision would be final: the Joint Chiefs of Staff. Once their decision had been rendered, Buckner would need all the Army-Navy cooperation he could get to see that the new base was built without delays.

Rawboned Lieutenant Colonel William Alexander, forty-nine, reported to Buckner in mid-August and was immediately sent out to mediate the Air-Navy quarrel. Alexander had a unique asset: though an Army officer, he was a graduate of the Naval Academy at Annapolis. Equally at home with Navy and Army, he had known Colonel Eareckson since school days in 1910, and had been General Butler's commanding officer in the 6th Field Artillery in France during World War I.

A caustic professional with a mind like a computer, Alexander made his appearance at Kodiak late in August, just when Admiral Theobald received a formal directive from the JCS that named Adak as the final site for the new base—and fixed August 30, just one week hence, as D-day.

The JCS decision favored Theobald's request; it seemed a rebuff to General Butler. Colonel Alexander had to move fast to mend bridges—a job hampered by the fact that he had soldiered with Butler in 1918 and had never got along with him. But it was no time for personal differences. A big operation had to be planned, equipped, and executed within seven days.

At Kodiak, with Alexander gadflying about like a juggler, the joint commands worked out a bold scheme for the invasion and occupation of Adak.

The island was code named Fireplace. Alaska Sector's Rear Admiral John W. Reeves, small and peppery, would command the Navy's force of scrounged warships and transports; the occupation troops would be commanded by stocky Brigadier General Eugene M. Landrum of Buckner's staff. It would be Reeves' and Landrum's job, together, to put 4,000 men on Adak—overnight, so that they would be well dug in if the Japanese counterattacked.

Adak was almost 300 square miles of mountains and muskeg, populated mainly by bald eagles and grotesque scavenger ravens. It lay within 250 miles of the main Japanese base at Kiska, and more than 350 miles west of the present American front-line base at Umnak.

The Japanese had periodically landed small units on various islands to the west. They had landed more than once on Adak; whether any of them were still there was uncertain. It would be better if they were not, obviously; the best chance for an American success was to slip in by night, unload in the fog, and get as much construction work done as possible before the enemy could discover what was going on.

Since before Pearl Harbor, Simon Buckner had been training a small but deadly unit of commando rangers, the Alaska Scouts. Up to now they had had no test in combat. The Scouts would slip into Adak at night, silently, a day or two ahead of the planned troop landings. They would creep across the island, root out any enemy soldiers and silence them before they could send radio messages back to Kiska.

THE PREVIOUS NOVEMBER, BUCKNER had authorized two of his top intelligence men to form the Scouts. Boyish Colonel Lawrence V. Castner and tall anvil-jawed Major William J. Verbeck were both Alaska veterans; with four tough sergeants from Chilkoot Barracks, they had hand-picked a platoon of volunteers and put them through an intensive, irregular commando combat course. Castner's father, General Joseph C. Castner, had organized the Philippine Scouts, and Castner knew how to go about his job. He quickly formed a hard-bitten outfit, each member a specialist. Collectively they owned an intimate firsthand knowledge of every part of Alaska and the Aleutians. Anthropologists, doctors, engineers, fishermen, hunters, prospectors, trappers, Aleuts, Eskimos, Indians, the Scouts were long on special skills and short on military discipline; with their rustic parkas, gleaming knives, loose-slung rifles and bearded faces, they were soon known throughout the Territory as "Castner's Cutthroats."[1]

IN THE HEAVING DARKNESS OF the night of August 28, 1942, fleet submarines *Triton* and *Tuna* surfaced a mile off the Adak coast. Without lights or sound, Colonel Castner and thirty-seven commandos slipped into rubber boats, pushed away from the pitching submarines, and rowed toward the dim coastline.

Crossing the reefs, they paddled into Kuluk Bay, dragged their rafts up on the beach and fanned out inland. They covered ground thoroughly, taking all night to sweep the island. They found no Japanese; there were not even any ashes to indicate recent enemy presence on the island code-named Fireplace. In the cold morning fog, Castner set out an "All clear" cloth-strip signal for a PBY overhead, which radioed the news once it had flown away from the island.

---

1. At the same time, a less publicized unit, the Eskimo Scouts (formally, the Alaska Territorial Guard) was organized in part by a colorful Arctic veteran, Major Marvin "Muktuk" Marston. As Buckner's Special Services officer, Marston had built the huge log Kashim—the base enlisted men's club—at Fort Richardson, with funds raised by slot machines he installed. "Regulations," Muktuk Marston insisted, "are of best use in the absence of brains." On a trip to the Pribilofs in 1942 with entertainer Joe E. Brown, Marston had been forced down in a PBY on a frozen lake. When wind threatened to destroy the plane, local Eskimos drilled a hole in the ice, ran a line down from the plane, and urinated in the hole to fill it, so that it would freeze fast around the line and anchor the plane.

Marston was so impressed by the Eskimos' resourceful ingenuity that he decided to enlist them as minutemen. He traveled a thousand miles, much of it by dog team, to recruit Eskimos, and organized them into an advance warning network that kept watch for enemy activity along the Arctic coasts and islands. Though the Eskimo Scouts saw no combat—they had no connection with Castner's Alaska Scouts—they served well; Marston fought bureaucrats for years to preserve the Eskimo organization, and today [1969] they maintain their association as a National Guard unit.

TWO DAYS EARLIER, SIMON BUCKNER had come down to Kodiak to see them off—Castner's Scouts aboard the submarines, General Landrum's big invasion force aboard two transports, and an Engineer force aboard a weird collection of tugs, power barges, fishing schooners and private yachts. It was all Alaska had. Perhaps not since Dunkirk had such a motley litter of vessels been used in a military operation.

Canadian and American cruisers and destroyers covered the task force as it moved west into the Chain. The convoy was still well short of Adak on August 29, when two radio messages came into Admiral Reeves' flag cabin. The first, from the PBY with Castner, confirmed there were no enemy troops on Adak. The second, from Kodiak, reported a strong enemy task force nearby.

At Cold Bay, Bomber Command was alerted. General Butler, who had come down to take part in the air-cover phase of the Adak operation, joined Colonel Eareckson in addressing a briefing of keyed-up flight crews. During the briefing, Wheeler reported, "A message was received that the task force was our own fleet and not the enemy as had been reported."

"The alert," Wheeler added dryly, "was canceled."

When the confusion was straightened out, Theobald signaled Admiral Reeves to proceed.

That afternoon the west wind brought a heavy storm that almost scattered the fleet. One patrol boat, carrying a gang of SeaBees, tried to put into Otter Point for shelter, but heaving seas drove them away, and the men aboard the boat were forced to land by dinghy around the side of Umnak Island, where steep cliffs cut right down to the water line. Rescue crews from the Umnak base hauled them up the wave-battered cliff with ropes; the patrol boat behind them was dashed to pieces.

The next day, Sunday, was D-day. Buckner sent his senior engineer, Colonel Benjamin B. Talley (who had built the Umnak air field), to Dutch Harbor. There Talley boarded a PBY that would take him to Adak to join the landing force. Also aboard were Talley's second-in-command, Lieutenant Colonel Leon B. deLong, and the PBY wing commander, Captain Leslie Gehres, who wanted to be in on the invasion too.

That morning a storm blew in from the west. When the PBY reached Adak, General Landrum's troops were starting toward shore in their landing boats, but the seas were furious and Captain Gehres refused to take the chance of wrecking the PBY by trying to land in the frothy breakers. So the PBY turned back to Atka, where seaplane tender *Casco* stood at her usual anchorage in Nazan Bay.

Talley recalls: "We landed about midmorning, but the sea was so rough we were able to board *Casco* only via our inflated life rafts and whaleboats whose crews dragged us out of the rafts at the end of a line."

Destroyer *Reid* pitched back and forth across the mouth of Nazan Bay, stationed there to protect *Casco* from enemy submarines. Talley continues:

> Captain Gehres decided that because of the storm, which by this time was intense, there was little likelihood of enemy submarine action in the bay. He asked the destroyer to carry Colonel deLong and me to Adak, after which it would return to station at Atka. After considerable difficulty due to the storm, Colonel deLong and I boarded the destroyer and left immediately for Adak.

Destroyer *Reid* pushed away pitching. She was hardly hull-down over the horizon when Nazan Bay erupted in action.

COMMANDER TOKUTOMI HAD BROUGHT submarine RO-61 into Nazan Bay early the previous morning, making his way gingerly through the rocks, intending to torpedo the seaplane tender. But the American destroyer had appeared behind him and sealed off the only exit from the bay. Tokutomi had settled quietly to the bottom of Nazan Bay and had lain there all day, all night, and all Sunday morning. By noon the submarine's batteries were exhausted and the air was almost unbreathable.

There were only two choices for Tokutomi. He could surface and surrender; or he could try to sink both the tender and the destroyer with the only two torpedoes he had. He was making his final decision when his executive officer called him to the sound-gear station. The American destroyer, for some serendipitous reason, was departing.

Quickly, Tokutomi readied his torpedo crews, lifted RO-61 clear of the bottom and swung her around to take dead aim on *Casco*. As soon as the destroyer disappeared over the horizon, he gave the order to fire both fish.

The first torpedo wobbled erratically, slipped past *Casco* and ran up on the beach without exploding. In the smash and heave of the storm waves, no one aboard *Casco* saw it go by.

In the meantime the second fish ran straight and true. It took *Casco* amidship on her port side, penetrated the hull and blew up inside Engine Room Number One. The explosion killed five men, injured twenty, destroyed the diesel and made a shambles of the engine room. Sheets of fuel oil and gasoline from ruptured tanks splashed overboard and blanketed the roaring waves—and one of the life buoys in the water was tripped and ignited its own automatic flare.

The combination of fire and floating fuel was deadly. The burning phosphor torch bobbed violently on the oil-covered surf, flame heaving and dipping toward the incendiary fuel that surrounded the ship. If it caught fire, *Casco* would be inundated in flames.

At the port rail, young Aviation Ordnanceman J. Cobean hardly seemed to stop to think: he dived over the side, swam strongly through the greasy slick, yanked the flare from the buoy and held the fire under water until it finally choked, sputtered, and went out.

Deck crews were too paralyzed to cheer. Gagging on oil fumes, Cobean splashed to the ship and was hauled aboard, drenched in black grease. When he got his breath he tested himself for injuries, and found he was unhurt.

(There was one noteworthy case of injury: knocked off his chair in the captain's cabin by the explosion, Captain Gehres, after the excitement had died down, found enough scratches and bruises about his body to qualify for the Purple Heart.)

The storm soon broke up the floating slick. Listing badly, *Casco* lost power in her second diesel; her skipper, Commander Willis Everett Cleaves, drifted her up onto the beach. (Presently the crew discovered the unexploded torpedo on the beach; a demolition crew later coiled a rope around the warhead, ran out to the end of the line, took cover and unscrewed the warhead fuse without exploding it. The torpedo was sent back to the States, intact, for study.)

Casco would soon be repaired and refloated. In the meantime, two PBYs roared out from Dutch Harbor, bent on revenge. They found the Japanese submarine. Lieutenants Samuel Coleman and C. H. "Bon" Amme attacked with everything they had. Commander Tokutomi desperately dived his boat, but his decks were still awash when the depth bombs started raining on him. The bombs opened seams in *RO-61's* hull; she submerged, leaving a thick oil slick. Destroyer *Reid*, in the meantime, had delivered her passengers and was on her way back; she came in sight at flank speed, relentlessly pursued the telltale oil slick and depth-charged the stricken submarine. When RO-61 finally bobbed to the surface, *Reid* shelled her dead on the water and sent a triumphant radio signal to *Casco:*

> GOT SUB THAT GOT YOU. HAVE FIVE PRISONERS FOR PROOF.

Tokutomi was not one of the five. He had gone down with his ship.

For the Navy air wing, the *Casco* incident was a tumultuous climax to a harrowing week that had cost the damaging or loss of six PBYs in storms and dogfights, and the damaging of two tenders—one striking a reef, the other blown up by its own depth charges. Sammy Coleman, when he was awarded the DFC for helping sink *RO-61*, said he deserved the medal—not for sinking the submarine, but for surviving routine patrol duty in the Aleutians.

THE AUGUST 30 STORM PINNED down the American planes which were supposed to cover General Landrum's invasion of Adak. Not even Eareckson's weather ship got off the ground. Kodiak radio advised Admiral Reeves that his air support was grounded, but Reeves and Landrum decided the bad weather would ground the Japanese as well; they decided to proceed on schedule.

That Sunday morning the deceptively mild and pudgy Brigadier General Landrum hit the beaches with the 4,500 men of Buckner's 4th Infantry Regiment. Roaring storm wind piled barges on the beach, smashed lighters in the water and spilled tons of cargo to the bottom*; but within eighteen hours Landrum had his regiment ashore, had set

*1995 ADDENDUM: I do not know whether there has been any official confirmation or denial regarding veterans' reports that several soldiers drowned during these Adak landings on August 30, 1942, and that the services imposed a cover-up of their deaths. One account, in a letter from a Navy man who was there, gives particularly harrowing images: "Waves were crashing.... Coxswains had trouble keeping their landing craft from broaching. Fully loaded craft on the way in slammed into empty craft trying to back off. Other craft hit rocks offshore. One landing craft hit something and the coxswain, apparently thinking he was on the beach, dropped the front door, flooding the vessel....The Adak storm was so bad that the barge carrying the Marsden mats sunk. This happened at sea, while approaching the island. I don't know if the crew was rescued or went down with the barge.... [A sailor] told me he saw one landing craft with many men aboard go down. Some were rescued but he saw others sink out of sight. We both helped drag soldiers out of the surf and up on dryer land. All up the beach were soldiers, wet and exhausted. Many were getting artificial respiration. I don't know how many died. I never found a single fact or loss figure, except [that] Squeaky Anderson, the beach master, told me two days later that 23 of the first 25 landing craft were destroyed, wrecked or sunk....This operation always disturbed me, and still does. Three weeks later when my boss, [the] Commander, came ashore from [a] seaplane tender...I asked him pointedly, 'Did you receive all the weather reports prior to the landing?' 'Yes' was his one-word answer. Again I asked, 'Were any of them garbled?' 'No' was his one-word answer. He then gave me a penetrating look that clearly meant the topic was not open to discussion. These were the only answers I would ever get from him. He must have known it was extremely hazardous to proceed with the landing under those terrible condition. I believe his recommendation for a postponement must have been cast aside. Again it must have been a case of 'all dressed up for the party.'"

up his antiaircraft and coastal guns, and had manhandled a muscular collection of heavy construction machines onto Adak with several units of the crack 807th Aviation Engineer Battalion.

Landrum established his headquarters on top of a packing crate and held a fast conference with beachmaster Carl "Squeaky" Anderson, who had the tough job of organizing the storm-scattered boatloads of men and machinery and putting everything where it was needed. Squeaky's loud piping voice cut through the howl of wind in thick-accented bursts of profanity; in a miraculously short time he had the flotsam-littered beach—"Squeakyville"—as organized as a supermarket. (Asked how he did it, Squeaky said, "Hell, by damn, it's easy. The admirals and generals give me hell, and I just pass it on.")[2]

With barges still bucking ashore, Engineers and Scouts fanned out in search of a site where they could build their air field. Half in jest, a Scout suggested the flattest place was the long narrow lagoon in Sweeper Cove—a basin that flooded every time the tide came in. The joke stirred Colonel deLong's interest, and he discussed it seriously with the Engineer unit commander, Colonel Carlin Whitesell.

Talley, deLong, and Whitesell were a trio of mesomorphic men of action. The crazy idea was no sooner voiced than they put their gangs to work.

In storm winds fierce enough to make men walk bent over, the Engineers sounded the lagoon and learned within an hour that it was as flat as it looked. The next step was to dry it up. The Engineers beefed up the spit separating the lagoon from Sweeper Cove; they built a dam, a series of dikes, and a tide gate, constructed (Talley recalls) "from materials at hand: lumber, scrap, and ship's dunnage. We weighed speed of construction against the bare minimum standards acceptable to the Air Force—and they were not finicky."

On August 31, the day after the landings, the Engineers were ready to drain the lagoon. They left the gate open until the tide emptied out of the lagoon. At dead low tide the gate was slammed shut and sealed. Before morning, the Engineers had rolled their weasels and graders into the muddy lagoon. The steel mat designed for the runway had sunk with a capsizing barge; Colonel Whitesell's Engineers did without, by bulldozing a flat airstrip of hard-packed sand.

---

2. Destined to become a beachmaster of great legend throughout the Pacific in World War II, Squeaky Anderson had a peculiar attitude toward regulations and government property. He once traded an expensive coil of Navy manila line to the Unalaska store keeper in exchange for a case of whisky, which he regarded as a vital necessity for his crew's Christmas celebration. Accused of disobeying regulations by selling Navy property, Squeaky drew himself up and piped, "By damn, around here I make the regulations."

The storm quit four days after the landings. Fighters from Umnak flew relays of air-cover umbrellas over Adak, but the Japanese did not come; they were too busy at Kiska, where Eareckson was using every hour of flyable weather to pin them down and keep them from flying search missions eastward. Pilots took extraordinary risks to stay over Kiska as long as possible and keep the Japanese busy; one P-38 strafed a mess line of Japanese soldiers, beat up several Rufes on the water, and stayed over Kiska for four hours. It returned to Umnak after nearly nine hours in the air, with a teaspoon of fuel remaining. A few days later, Captain Fred M. Smith flew the weather mission to Kiska, and did his bit to keep the enemy occupied: he had no bombs aboard, but his machine guns were loaded, and when he saw a Japanese destroyer-minelayer at Kiska, he went in shooting.

Captain Smith then radioed Eareckson:

> SAW STEAMER, STRAFED SAME, SANK SAME, SOME SIGHT, SIGNED SMITH.[3]

In the meantime there were no Japanese attacks on Adak. Uninhibited by enemy discovery, the Engineers rushed ahead. General Butler had feared it would take four months to build the air field. In the end, it took Talley's Engineers a flat ten days.

It was September 10, 1942, when Colonel Eareckson landed the first plane on the new Adak runway. Within the next two days, the 36th Squadron brought its B-17s to "Longview," as the new base was coded; eighteen other planes came too, including a squadron of P-38s and a Lodestar carrying General Butler, his face red. A new shipment of steel matting arrived, and the Engineers laid it out—overnight. For the speed of its construction, Longview was an incredible triumph; but in other ways it left one or two things to be desired. Talley recalls: "Many was the time I stood beside the runway with my heart in my mouth watching a friend take off or land a heavily loaded aircraft. I kept remembering I had told the Air Force it was the best we could do in the time allowed."

It was September 13, exactly two weeks after the Adak landings, when the Air Force flew its last long-range 1,200-mile Umnak-to-Kiska flight of the war. Lucian Wernick flew the photorecon mission, in one of the old

3. Pilots in the Aleutians were "old or bold, never both." Captain Fred M. Smith was killed on March 31, 1943, when his B-24 was shot down over Kiska.

LB-30 Liberators escorted by two Lightnings. It proved a stirring climax to the Umnak phase of the Aleutian Campaign. Wheeler wrote:

> Two Zeroes* were laying for us at the base of the overcast. They were flushed out and engaged by our escort. [A P-38 shot one Zero down in flames.] Coming out of our bomb-photography run, one Zero paralleled our course until a few bursts of our waist gun dissuaded his attempts to cut in on us. Shortly after, we saw two fighters flying under a cloud base at 3 o'clock. Captain Wernick turned to a head-on course to them, thinking they were our escort.
>
> It turned out they were Zeroes. One Zero, completely surprised, pulled up and fled into the overcast. The other attacked, put one explosive 20mm shell through our left bomb-bay door, cutting a fuel line and just missing the nose fuses of our 500 lb. bombs.

Wernick's turret guns had jammed. When the Zero circled wide to make another pass, Wernick turned toward it, to give the Zero the smallest target and the shortest possible time-on-target. Wernick was flying a collision course toward the enemy plane. "He didn't know what kind of secret weapon I had," Wernick recalls. "He fired one more burst and ran for home."

Newspapers[4] later picked up the story and dubbed Wernick "the only four-engine pursuit pilot in the Air Force."

Wernick's mission took place on Sunday the 13th. The Navy's Lieutenant Commander Russell put up his tent at Adak that day, and the Eleventh Air Force moved up to the new base in strength.

In less than two weeks, the United States had pushed her front lines nearly 400 miles closer to Japan. Adak was ready for war. On September 14, the new base launched a combined maximum effort—a deck-level attack by two squadrons of heavy bombers and twenty-eight fighters. It was the first combined zero altitude strike of World War II.

EARECKSON LED. ESCORTED BY FOURTEEN P-38 Lightnings and fourteen P-39 Aircobras (going into their Aleutian baptism of fire), his twelve Liberators droned across the 240 miles to Kiska at wave-top level,

---

*1995 ADDENDUM: During the war many Americans referred informally to all single-engine Japanese warplanes as Zeroes. There were no Zeroes at Kiska at this time; the float planes to which Wheeler refers were Rufes.

4. Typically, it was not until October 8 that the Navy revealed to the press the August 30 occupation of "an island somewhere in the Andreanofs."

hoping to take Kiska by surprise. But visibility was good and the Japanese observation post on Little Kiska picked up the approaching airplanes far out at sea. Kiska's antiaircraft opened up at ten miles and rode the mission all the way in.

At fifty feet, risking dunking in the waves, Eareckson took evasive action. The heavies banked and sideslipped through the enemy flak with only a few minor hits. They roared in like meteors, too fast and too low for the 75-mm flak guns to follow, but big targets for Kiska's machine-gun bunkers. Splattered with bullets, Eareckson's twelve B-24s dropped an avalanche of explosive in the space of three minutes which caused more damage than all previous raids combined (not excluding the Navy's bombardment of the previous month). They sank two Japanese ships, set three others afire, destroyed three midget submarines and their pens, collapsed half a dozen antiaircraft guns, smashed several buildings to junk and set fire to a dozen shore installations. More than two hundred Japanese soldiers were killed or wounded.[5]

One flight of P-38s came in low, strafed the harbor, destroyed a flying boat and chewed up seven anchored Rufes. Overhead, the P-39 Aircobras swirled into wheeling dogfights with the five Rufes that had managed to take off.

The five Japanese pilots were weatherbeaten, fatigued, and outnumbered. Their reactions were slow; they flew badly. One by one, the American pursuit planes cut them out. All five Rufes went down flaming. None of them had hit any American planes, but two P-38s, chasing the same Rufe down, collided in midair and crashed; one had been flown by Major W. M. Jackson, commander of the 54th Fighter Squadron.

In the context of the Aleutian Campaign, it had been a historic mission. It had hurt the enemy; it had proved at once the value of the new striking base at Adak. The first three months of the Campaign had consisted of "seek and destroy" missions with the emphasis on "seek"—seek the island of Kiska, seek the enemy there, and seek the long way home to Umnak, from which all the Kiska missions had been flown.

5. Eareckson's delay-fuse deck-level bombing technique made its way into the tactics of Air Forces in other theaters. It proved most brutally effective in March 1943, when Air Force bombers attacked a Japanese convoy of the Tokyo Express in the Bismarck Sea. Using Eareckson's methods, the bombers sank all eight transports and four of the eight escorting destroyers. They destroyed twenty-five Japanese planes and killed at least 3,600 Japanese sailors and soldiers. The furious attack frightened the Japanese into canceling all further New Guinea convoys; as a result the Fifth Air Force gained uncontested control of the sky in the Southwest Pacific, and Japanese forces in New Guinea-underfed, unsupplied, and quickly outnumbered when their reinforcements were canceled—were inexorably driven out.

But the move up to Adak changed the emphasis; with this advance, the Aleutian war went into a new phase.

IN HIGH-GEAR OPERATION, THE BASE at Adak handled four million pounds of incoming supplies every day. Simon Buckner intended to make the island impregnable—and, perhaps, to make it his own forward headquarters for the offensive he hoped would soon take him into Japan itself. (About this time, Buckner's favorite toast, drunk in bourbon and branch, was, "May you walk in the ashes of Tokyo.")

But in the early weeks, life for the men at Adak was misery. Wheeler wrote:

> For an island completely uninhabited eighteen days ago, Longview is a marvelous scene of industry and ingenuity. Living conditions, however, are terrible. Where motor vehicles have moved for any length of time, there is a quagmire. Our tents are pitched on low hills about two feet in height. The constant fog and rain make life wet and miserable.
>
> The rain is accompanied by winds in excess of 60 mph. To be abroad means to be soaked to the skin regardless of the type of clothing one wears. The weather is so disagreeable that many of us prefer to remain in our tents rather than face the elements during a dash to the mess tent. Fortunately some of us had the foresight to provide ourselves with canned delicacies—soup, chili, preserved meats, jams, crackers, fruit juices—and with these we prepare meals in our tents, thereby obviating the need to wade the half mile to the mess. Type C ration is the only food available at the mess anyway.
>
> Our pyramidal tents are pitched on excavations cut into embankments that overlook the perpetual marsh. The construction engineer forgot to include drainage in his plans, and consequently the tents were erected in an excellent reservoir some four or five feet deep. There is no flooring except a few pieces of heavy paper that we scavenged and placed near our canvas cots. The tents are heated by tiny metal stoves, the fires fed with coal because there is no natural fuel on the island. In the downpour the floors become damp and now there is nothing but mud.
>
> The rolled flaps are excellent traps for collecting gallons of water that drain in a steady stream into the tents. Several men have delved into their bags to retrieve their life vests; the floor is covered with three inches of water and it is rising. We are going out into the

> rain armed with shovels to dig trenches. Sgt. Paul Ruebush is bellowing heartily, "Well, boys, when the going gets too God-damned tough for the rest of 'em, it's just getting good for us."

Umnak and Cold Bay had just begun to be habitable; only recently had Quonset huts, permanent showers, and GI movie theaters been built there. Now the warriors had to start from scratch all over again.

This time, to avoid agony and delay, Buckner committed a huge complement of Engineers and naval construction battalions to Adak. He had the forces by now: there were more SeaBees in the Aleutians than in any other theater of the war.

The SeaBees moved into Adak to build an entire city: housing, hangars, warehouses, offices, recreation buildings, kitchens, baths, power lines, roads. During the next four months they would average one day off per month. They ate from mess kits and slept wherever they could—on packing cases, on the ground, in Air Force pilots' tents, in the musty holds of emptied cargo ships in the harbor.

"All I can remember," says Frank Cale, "is we built a hell of a lot. Rating badges didn't mean much—we stevedored, we built docks and huts and roads and warehouses. Today you'd be the gang leader, tomorrow you'd be an ordinary laborer." They carved down mountains, leveled lava badlands, filled marshes, connected islets together. SeaBee commander Earl Kelly wrote:

> Where even Jeeps cannot travel, material and tools were carried on human backs. The crying need was for new speed records. Without time to study soil conditions, it was inevitable that a foundation or two began to crack; because we could not estimate the destructive force of the Bering Sea in a williwaw, big fills were washed away. We had to be tied down to rafters so that the wind couldn't blow us off a roof; we had to spend days rebuilding what williwaws blew down in a few minutes.

On treeless Adak, the 8th SeaBee Battalion was assigned to rig power lines. SeaBee lumberjacks brought in log rafts and erected poles and high lines. Williwaws regularly scattered the hundred-foot logs, forcing crews to comb the beaches for weeks to recover strays. Men on the log crews averaged two dunkings in the sea every week. Quickly, the city took shape.

THE FIRST DOCKS WERE HARDLY built when a tough new outfit sailed in to make its base at Adak—Motor Torpedo Boat Division One, four hotrod PT-boats under young Lieutenant Clinton McKellar Jr. The PT-boats had been sent into the Aleutians in the misbegotten hope they could get close to enemy ships in the fog and torpedo them left and right.

Life in the Aleutians was catastrophic for McKellar's unit. The only heat in the PT-boats came from the two burner gasoline cookstoves in the galleys. The 77-foot motorboats were beaten so savagely by the Aleutian sea that none of them got anywhere near the enemy's shipping lanes. Within three months all four PT-boats had to go back to the mainland for major overhauls that amounted to being rebuilt from the keel up. But their adventures were not over; the coming year promised, if anything, to be even worse.

CAPTAIN OSWALD COLCLOUGH'S PLUCKY submarine division had been stripped of its big fleet boats for Guadalcanal. All Colclough had left were five little old S-boats, but with these he had stepped up the pressure on Japanese shipping, sinking four enemy ships that fall, including the 2,800-ton transport *Keizan Maru*. The little transport was no great prize, but the circumstances of her sinking were important: *S-31* sank her far inside Japanese home waters, just off Paramushiro in the Kuriles. It was the first time American undersea raiders had ventured so close to home in the north, and the incident badly shook up the big Kuriles fishing fleet.

No one envied the submariners. Duty was terrible. On every S-boat voyage men were pitched around so violently that hardly a patrol escaped without several sets of broken ribs, smashed faces and severe contusions. On December 21 the most awful voyage of all began when Lieutenant H. S. Monroe, surely a great unsung hero of the sea, plowed his antique *S-35* into a smashing storm off Amchitka, about 45 miles from Kiska.

Running on the surface, *S-35* caromed through a heaving twenty-foot sea trying to charge her batteries and freshen her air supply. A monumental wave dashed Monroe against the hatch cover, the salt water inundated the control room below. Badly bruised, his arm and leg sprained, Monroe was taken to his bunk—and had not even closed his eyes when he was yanked up, as if by the arm, by the dread cry, *"Fire in the control room!"*

In great pain, Monroe dragged himself to the control room, where the seawater had shorted out electric wiring and set fire to the insulation. Seams had sprung; water was rising below decks in the bilges.

Hardly able to stand, Monroe instantly took charge. He ordered fire extinguishers into the control room; they put out the fires but by then arcing sparks had burst into the forward battery compartment, where choking fumes and smoke mushroomed, driving the crew out.

Monroe disconnected all forward electricity by opening the master switches. The bow compartments were abandoned and sealed—and fire, smoldering all the while, broke out again in the control room.

The crew exhausted its extinguishers but the electrical fire kept sizzling. Its poison smoke drove everyone aft. Monroe, last to leave, secured the engines and sealed off the deserted control room. The crew crowded aft.

A chain reaction of short circuits leaped through the boat, knocking out almost every electric circuit, including those which operated the steering, power, and bow and stern planes. *S-35* was done for. Every man knew it, but Monroe refused to accept it; he did not look kindly upon the thought of being set adrift in the gale-tossed North Pacific in a raft.

Men put on smoke lungs, charged them with oxygen, and rammed into the wall of fumes in the control room. They flooded the magazines, blew a ballast tank and slowly fought the fires out with blankets. All night the fight continued, with *S-35* dead in the water, blizzard-lashed.

Early in the morning the mechanics finally got the motors started but at seven o'clock new fires flared up, and Monroe ordered the crew topside into breathable air. On the open deck, wind and icy water flayed them mercilessly. Monroe closed all hatches, hoping to smother the fires below. For almost two hours the entire crew clung to the few cables and handholds of the slippery deck while *S-35* tossed like a toothpick on 50-foot swells.

At nine, a crew went below and got the diesels going. Slowly the boat got way on and headed for Adak. That afternoon the fires erupted again; once again Monroe sent everyone topside and sealed the boat to smother the fires. The entire terrible performance had to be repeated again the next morning, and yet twice more the following day.

Finally, on Christmas Eve, after four days of hell, Monroe brought *S-35* into Adak's harbor without a single loss of life.

HEROISM WAS EVERYWHERE ONE LOOKED for it. On September 20, at an awards presentation, one small unit—the 36th Bombardment Squadron—garnered twenty-two Purple Hearts and seventy-eight Air Medals for its activities of the past three months. The recipients included Captain Robert "Pappy" Speer, Major Jack Marks (posthumous), Captain

Frederick Ramputi, Captain Lucian K. Wernick, and Lieutenant Billy Wheeler.

From its Adak base, Eareckson's Bomber Command stepped up its Kiska missions. Canada's 111th Fighter Squadron came down to join in, and by late September regular missions were going out with a dozen heavy bombers, a dozen mediums, and thirty fighters. They would rendezvous off Little Kiska. The fighters had three minutes to knock out flak guns before the bombers made their run. Fighter strafing helped keep Japanese heads down while the bombers attacked. A flight of fighters flew top cover, close to the photorecon plane. One flight of bombers would go for the ships in harbor; the other flight would paste ground facilities—particularly the air field the Japanese were trying to build.

Eareckson sometimes came in as low as ten feet off the water, to stay under the field of fire of the ships' flak guns. One fighter was assigned to scout for submarine nets, another to search Gertrude Cove and other bays for hidden submarines. Pilots were warned not to be fooled by dummy float planes. Kiska had a Japanese radio operator who knew just about every American pilot by name; he would call in, trying to confuse the pilots: "Jim, where's Red at?" American pilots cursed him, tried to find his radio shack and bomb it, but never succeeded; the radio room was underground.

Raids in September and on into October brought real all-out war to Kiska for the first time. They destroyed dozens of Rufes, sank several ships, killed more than a hundred soldiers. It was not altogether one-sided.* Major Wilbur Miller—who wore a fedora hat with his leaf

---

*1995 ADDENDUM: Wartime foul-ups could be maddening and murderous. Take, for instance, the notorious unreliability of U.S. torpedoes. Col. Lawrence Reineke says, of outspoken Aleutian veteran Navy weather officer Paul Carrigan, "One C.O. said he had three enemies: Weather, Japanese, and Carrigan." The latter has developed a widespread reputation based on his ability to blow away the fogs of self-serving pencil-pushers' obfuscation with refreshing gusts of Carriganesque candor. In a letter to Reineke from the 1980s, Carrigan recalls "a fiasco when B-26s from Adak batted zero on a torpedo attack against heavy concentration of ships at Kiska. This was Oct. '42." (Reineke adds, "Kiska—what a farce. Torpedoes didn't work but the blame was put on the Sub commanders.") Carrigan continues: "Torpedoes. This was a disgrace. During the first 18 months of war our torpedoes ran not only low but high, sometimes porpoised, ran erratic, often failed to explode, and even ran in circles. This last problem is believed to have caused loss of two U.S. subs and several close calls. Admiral Monroe told me the SOP for early fleet boats was to take boat [down] to 60 feet. This gave safety margin [overhead] in case torpedo ran circular course. Crux of problems with design flaws in gyro, firing pins, testing etc., can be traced to naval torpedo factory in New London. This was epitome of bureaucratic 'closed shop'. The wasted effort, cost, imperilment of sub crews, lives lost-incalculable. Those responsible should have been shot. None were even court-martialed. Stiffest penalty during shakeup in mid-1943 was a few reassignments."

insignia pinned to the crown—was shot down just after sinking submarine *RO-65.* Captain Arthur T. Rice, one of Jack Chennault's P-40 jockeys, shot down the two Rufes that had killed Miller, but Chennault himself, after shooting down a Rufe, ran into devastating enemy fighter fire and barely limped home. Chennault, by then a lieutenant colonel—three promotions in seven months—was commanding the 343rd Fighter Group, his Warhawk snouts painted with snarling Bengal tiger jaws. The Japanese made a particular effort to single him out, as they did Eareckson, but neither man was ever shot down.

The United States lost only nine planes in combat that fall—but lost sixty-three others to weather and mechanical trouble. And as winter crept in, with no sign that the Japanese on Kiska were being softened up at all, American airmen found themselves asking more and more often if there was any point to it all. Was it really worth it?

CHAPTER TWELVE

"I Had a Sheep-Lined Fur Parka–And Then I Had One to Wear Outdoors"

KISKA WAS TAKING A BEATING. To the Japanese command it was urgent that they find the new American base. But every time their pilots tried to tail the American bombers home, weather defeated them. Finally a Rufe pilot discovered the base on Adak on September 30—a month to the day since the Americans had landed there.

During the next five days Adak was bombed every day. The Japanese had so few planes left that the biggest air strike they could mass was an October 4 mission flown by three planes. The rest of the time the raids were flown by just one plane ("Good Time Charlie"). American fighters neutralized every raid; the attacks achieved nothing. The U.S. base was so dispersed that nothing short of mass bombardment would hurt it. Wheeler wrote, "No damage except to nerves and sleep." After the fifth fruitless day the Japanese gave it up.

Elsewhere, Japan's war was going badly. The tough Guadalcanal battle was eating up resources, demanding more and more strength in the air, on the ground and at sea. The Imperial Army had been defeated at Milne Bay in New Guinea. Naval battles in the Eastern Solomons and at Cape Esperance had cost several ships. Allied submarines and airplanes were attacking the Empire's shipping everywhere in the Pacific, and Japan's industry couldn't keep up with the losses. Imperial Headquarters pretended all these things were temporary setbacks, but at least for the moment there was no strength to be spared for the Aleutian garrisons. At any rate, as long as the ultimate plan was to give up the western Aleutians when winter came, there didn't seem to be any point in trying to counterattack. All they had to do was dig in and hold on—keep the enemy at bay until winter, when Japan's Aleutian forces would fall back on the northern Kuriles.

Defending Kiska was strictly a sacrifice maneuver. Bearing that in mind, Admiral Hosogaya decided to abandon the Attu garrison; it seemed clear the enemy lacked the forces to attack, occupy and hold the far western island, and it would be wasteful to keep up the garrison there. The Attu force would be transferred to Kiska.

Hosogaya ordered it done. The move took place in September, while the Americans were stepping up their aerial bombardment of Kiska. By the time the Americans discovered the withdrawal from Attu, the 1,500 troops had already reappeared at Kiska. As Hosogaya expected, the Americans continued to concentrate their attacks on Kiska, and did nothing about the abandonment of Attu. (The wretched irony of this became apparent eight months later, when the Americans—who could have taken Attu without a shot in October 1942—had to fight one of the most costly man-for-man battles of World War II to get Attu back after Japanese reoccupation.)

Hosogaya's new reinforcements increased Kiska's already massive antiaircraft concentration, and beefed up its network of underground bunkers. By early October the fortress was virtually impervious: the only vulnerable points were transient ships and flak gun emplacements. The Allies were wasting men, planes, bombs, and great effort in a campaign that could not possibly do much harm; and the status quo was maintained, which was all Japan wanted. Blocked by Kiska, the Americans could not move forward to attack Japan.

For a few weeks the situation seemed to satisfy Imperial Headquarters. But soon after the Americans secured Adak, General Buckner landed small forces on Atka, Sequam, Tanaga, and St. Paul Island in the Pribilofs. All this activity persuaded some uneasy officers of the Japanese General Staff that the American advances were a prelude to a northern invasion of the homeland. As a result, after a subtle series of shifts in opinion (of the kind that often preceded new decisions), Imperial Headquarters changed its North Pacific policy. It was hard to say who had swayed the balance of opinion—probably Yamamoto had a hand in it—or exactly when it had taken place; but by early October the new feeling pervaded the entire staff. It was decided: the Aleutians would not be abandoned for the winter. They would be held—forever, if need be.

In a broadcast speech, Premier Tojo admitted that the troops at Kiska were in a desperate plight. But, he said, the worst was nearly over. Help was on the way.

At Paramushiro, a mixed force of Infantry, Engineers, antiaircraft batteries and support units was assembled under Lieutenant Colonel Hiroshi Yanekawa, with orders to reoccupy Attu and try to build an air field there. The 303rd Independent Infantry Battalion, 1,100 troops, was readied for shipment to Shemya, a small flat atoll not far from Attu. Yet another battalion was outfitted for landings on Amchitka, a long narrow island about forty miles east of Kiska. Hosogaya chose Amchitka because it might be easier to build a runway there than to continue trying to hack one out of the mountains of Kiska.

On October 29 the Attu force landed in Holtz Bay and re-established the Japanese base there. The Americans offered no opposition; they did not even discover the development until almost two weeks later. Hosogaya's convoy moved on toward Shemya, getting ready to set the 303rd Battalion ashore; but the troops had not yet left their ships when an American B-24 flew by overhead and, as if in punctuation, a signal from Japan warned Hosogaya that Intelligence believed a strong U.S. Navy task force had recently moved into the Aleutians and was on the prowl in Hosogaya's vicinity.

Hosogaya's few escort cruisers and destroyers would be no match for an enemy fleet. Now that he had been located (he thought) by the American B-24, it wouldn't be long before the enemy task force ran him down. Reluctantly he postponed the Shemya landings, turned back and took his force home to Paramushiro.

THERE WAS NO AMERICAN TASK force in the North Pacific. What Japanese Intelligence had intercepted were a few fragmentary clues from American radio dialogues; the apparent orders to a new American task force were actually portions of messages in which CINCPAC, knowing the Japanese planned to occupy Shemya and Amchitka, had ordered Admiral Theobald to reorganize his meager North Pacific Force and stand by to repel the enemy advances. Since most of his ships had been taken away for the invasion of North Africa, Theobald had a "task force" that was less than half the size of Hosogaya's tiny fleet.

Admiral Nimitz had studied reports on the island of Amchitka. The Alaska Scouts had reconnoitered the island on September 23, and their reports showed that the island was long, narrow—and flat, except for the inevitable volcano at one end. It was a marshy quagmire, but by now it was taken for granted that Colonel Benjamin Talley and his runway-building geniuses could make an operating air base out of any flat space overnight.

Nimitz decided it would be a shame to let Hosogaya get there first. Generals DeWitt and Buckner agreed heartily, and the Joint Chiefs authorized the occupation of Amchitka as soon as it could be done.

Admiral Theobald, however, was acerbically reluctant to try to establish a base under the enemy's nose—Amchitka was only forty miles from Kiska.

On November 7 (the day of the North African invasion), one of Eareckson's pilots discovered the enemy on Attu. The information temporarily gave Theobald and other commanders something other than Amchitka to think about. During the next few weeks the admiral increased his scout perimeter of picket boats, submarines and PBYs, with special attention to Amchitka, hoping to intercept any enemy advances in that direction; but in the meantime, combat emphasis shifted to Attu.

During the Umnak days, Attu had been far beyond the range of bombers based at the eastern island. But now that Adak was the main American operating base, Attu was no farther away than Kiska had been—600 miles. Eareckson lost no interest in Kiska, but the new logistics meant he had an important alternate target: when weather prohibited attacks at one Japanese base, it might still permit them over the other. The addition of the secondary target made it possible for Eareckson to send out missions more frequently. His attacks destroyed several beach installations at Attu, sank a cargo ship and scrapped nine Zeroes that had landed in Holtz Bay to refuel before going on to Kiska.

Eareckson's stepped-up pressure against Kiska and Attu caused a significant change in Japanese plans. On November 28 Admiral Hosogaya once again came into the Aleutians with a task force, to have another try at occupying Shemya and Amchitka. But the ferocity of Eareckson's constant raids convinced Hosogaya that he couldn't afford to divide his forces as he had intended. Instead, he took the entire convoy to Kiska, to help reinforce the fortress. He landed the troops under cover of darkness on the night of December 2, and made good use of the next day's roaring storm to get his ships well away before the Americans could take to the air against him.

ON DECEMBER 17, SIMON BUCKNER sent an order down through channels to Colonel Eareckson. It called for an exploratory air raid against Amchitka, to find out if Japanese troops were on the island. Eareckson was to demolish every building of the deserted Aleut village, including the church. If all went well, the Alaska Scouts would land the next day to survey the island.

Eareckson decided one bomber would be sufficient. He flew the mission himself, carrying several sticks of 250-pound HE bombs which he released one at a time over the village. His bombardier's accuracy was so great that virtually every bomb hit a different hut. Soon nothing was left standing but the little Russian Orthodox Church. The idea of bombing it did not appeal to Eareckson at all; he made several halfhearted passes, pulling away before the bombardier could drop. Finally, reassured by his crew, he bombed the church flat.

That night, unable to sleep, Eareckson spent the night playing poker. By morning he had lost $640. Without having slept, he climbed back into his plane to lead a flight of bombers and fighters to provide air cover for the Scout landings on Amchitka.

The scouting expedition was headed by Engineer Colonel Benjamin Talley and Lieutenant Colonel Alvin Hebert, who would command the proposed Amchitka air base if the survey proved a base could be built. They went over the island with the Alaska Scouts, studying the terrain. One of the Scouts, an American Sioux Indian, found signs that the Japanese had been there recently, evidently doing the same thing—surveying for an airstrip. It seemed the race was on.

IT WOULD TAKE AT LEAST a few weeks to assemble the forces and ships to launch an invasion of Amchitka; nothing less than a full-scale occupation would do, with the island so close to Kiska.

Meanwhile Major General Simon Buckner's Alaska Defense Command had assumed the size and stature of a real combat army. In time, Buckner was sure, he would reach his goal of driving the enemy from the Aleutians and invading Japan. By December he had 150,000 troops in the theater. Dutch Harbor, gateway to the Aleutians, handled nearly 400,000 tons of shipping a month. Alaskan coal production had multiplied tenfold during the year, and the oil industry was burgeoning: Colonel Theodore Wyman's Task Force 2600, acting on an idea of Benjamin Talley's, had built an oil pipeline to Whittier and was now building the Canol Pipeline. The population had mushroomed. Under Navy and Coast Guard protection, Alaskan fleets hauled in record fish catches—much of it for export back to the States.[1]

A large part of the credit was Buckner's. Alaska was not yet self-sufficient, but no longer was it totally helpless. It was on the map.

---

1. Prices had boomed as they had in the gold rush. In Anchorage, even ice cost $80 a ton. The Office of Price Administration had no visible anti-inflationary effect on Alaska, where nickels and dimes were useless and the smallest coin in general circulation was the 25¢ piece. At Kodiak, cheap whisky was $5.50 a quart; at Adak it sometimes brought $50. At Dutch Harbor, ham and eggs cost $1.50; at the South Seas, Anchorage's raciest dive, whisky was 25¢ a shot—and Coca-Cola 75¢. Alaska was so overcrowded with war workers and military transients that travelers slept on cots in hotel corridors; at Sitka the town jail charged $3 for a night's lodging.

The biggest breakthrough came with the completion of the Alaska ("Alcan") Highway on November 20, 1942. Brigadier General William M. Hoge's civilian and Army Engineers had achieved a miracle of construction, reflected in its staggering statistics: It was 1,671 miles long. It had cost $138,000,000. It bridged 200 streams and had more than 8,000 culverts. It had taken 16,000 workers to build it. And it had been completed, from scratch, in just eight months and eleven days.

The crews had fought summer mosquitoes and –70° winter temperatures to bring in the "Oil Can Highway" (so-called because of the thousands of empty oil drums discarded along the right of way in the rush for completion), and at its completion, even though it was only an unpaved military road, it connected Alaska by land with the States for the first time.

It was little more than a pioneer trail, subject to frequent landslides and floods. Nonetheless it was a triumph. By December, weasels and tough Army trucks were crawling north to Alaska in convoys packed with vital materiel for Simon Buckner's command—and for the Soviet Union. ALSIB—the Alaska-Siberia Lend-Lease route—was open for business.

THE HISTORY OF ALSIB WENT back to the spring of 1941; from the beginning, Buckner had played a key role in it.

The Lend-Lease bill had been signed into law on March 11, 1941; six weeks later, Hitler's troops had marched across the Russian border, and the United States suddenly had a new and hungry ally. Red scares were forgotten; President Roosevelt's top adviser and personal representative, Harry Hopkins, had flown to Moscow to promise Stalin that war supplies would start flowing into the U.S.S.R. at once. On July 7, 1941, Soviet Brigadier Mikhail Gromov and a party of eighty-seven commissars and aides had flown into Nome on the first leg of a top-secret air trip from Vladivostok.

Eleventh Air Force bomber pilot Frederick R. Ramputi had flown General Buckner and his party to Nome, where Buckner welcomed the Russians with a dinner in the Nevada Cafe. Buckner, a proud man himself, resented the visitors' arrogance—and so he encouraged Ramputi to enter into a drinking contest with a braggadocio Russian subaltern. The officers traded vodka and bourbon across the roughhewn plank table. Ramputi was a huge young athlete; when he and Buckner got up to leave, the Russian subaltern was passed out under the table with his boots protruding.

Thus began the Alaska-Siberia Lend-Lease program.

The Soviet visitors' next stop had been at Kodiak. They had brought their two crowded Soviet-built PBY flying boats down to a precise landing in Woman's Bay. The Navy's air squadron commander James S. Russell had greeted them with suitable diplomacy; but he had been glad to see them go on their way next morning. They had run him ragged all night with complaints about their quarters and the "stupid" lay-out of the base, then only half-built.

The Russians went on to Seattle, where they met for secret discussions with U.S. officials at the Olympic Hotel. The decisions made at these and subsequent meetings led to the accelerated construction of the Alaska Highway, the strategic rationale behind the vigorous prosecution of the Aleutian Campaign, and the development of the Alaskan route to Siberia for the delivery of monster shipments of airplanes and equipment.

ALSIB cut the travel distance from 13,000 miles via the Middle East to 1,900 miles—from Great Falls (Montana) to the U.S.S.R. When it opened for business in September 1942, Buckner was prepared: he had spent months exchanging liaison officers with Siberian commands, and as early as the Battle of Dutch Harbor he had already gathered forty-one radio operators trained in Russian code and radio procedures, as well as scores of interpreters.

The Russians took on Lend-Lease destroyers and other ships at Cold Bay. Cargo was shipped by sea from West Coast ports, escorted through the Aleutians by U.S. and Canadian Navy ships to Vladivostok. Staple supplies came up the Alaska Highway by truck. Lend-Lease planes were flown up from Great Falls to Fairbanks, where Buckner turned them over to the Russians; from there, Russian pilots flew them to Nome for refueling, and on into Siberia.

By the end of 1942, America's frantically expanded aircraft industry had rolled 40,000 airplanes off the production lines. Of these, not much more than three hundred had reached Alaska—and 148 of them were turned over to the U.S.S.R., all in the last two months of the year.

When one Russian pilot was reported missing in a Lend-Lease fighter somewhere between Fairbanks and Nome, Brigadier General Dale V. Gaffney of the Alaska Transport Command offered American search-and-rescue help to the Russians. The Soviet commander at Fairbanks refused the help; through his interpreter he conveyed a shrug—"He wasn't a very good pilot anyway."

Such attitudes were incomprehensible to the American pilots who daily risked their lives over Alaska. The reassuring presence of Gaffney's search-and-rescue planes became steadily more important as the months passed: the winter of 1942–1943 was the worst in thirty-four years.

"I HAD A SHEEP-LINED FUR PARKA," recalls Dr. Benjamin Davis. "And then I had one to wear outdoors."

On practice maneuvers that winter, 143 men were frostbitten. At Fairbanks temperatures went to –67° in December. Even out in the Aleutians, it took crews two hours to get the ice off airplane wings, and planes had to have their engines thawed with blowtorches before they could be started. When the PBYs took off from the water, frozen spray turned their windshields to frosted glass.

Breath turned to icicles. Eyelids froze together and mechanics' fingers were eaten as if by leprosy. Flesh that touched metal could not be separated from it without cutting. A drop of high-octane gas on the skin would raise a blister the size of a golf ball.

Inland, snow drifted deep in the passes. One crew in an iced-up plane bailed out within sight of an air field; their plane was never found. General Gaffney's search planes sought circles of brush on the snow—the standard SOS signal—and sent caterpillar-treaded weasels into the wilderness to pick up stranded airmen. The vicious winter set records for remarkable heroism and endurance—Lieutenant Leon Crane crashed in the mountains and walked out after eighty-four days—but on November 28 something happened that numbed every pilot in Alaska. Colonel Everett S. Davis, pioneer genius of Alaskan military aviation, Chief of Staff of the Eleventh Air Force, was blown off course by a storm on his way to the Aleutians, and crashed his C-47 into a mountain near Naknek. The wreck was not found until the summer thaw.

Davis's disappearance was proof of mortality. What happened to Ev Davis could happen to any one of them.

Out along the Chain, November had blown in with an 80-knot wind. Engineers and SeaBees at Adak worked into the perpetual night under floodlights, building accommodations for 15,000 men and all the facilities that went with them. The Mexican-American workmen of the 176th Engineers from Texas had never seen snow before. Williwaws kept blowing them off their feet—the same williwaws that wrecked or disabled nine PBYs at Dutch Harbor and Adak during the month.

Unforgiving, the seas swept madly through island passes. They caught the destroyer-minesweeper U.S.S. *Wasmuth* off Umnak; two of her depth charges broke loose and exploded under her keel, breaking her in two. All hands were saved by a tanker, but *Wasmuth* went to the bottom in two pieces. A few weeks later, the salvage vessel *Rescuer* ran aground and sank in the same waters.

"Flying," Billy Wheeler wrote that winter, "has been limited to that necessary to give flying time and pay to flight personnel." On November 10 and 12 the total entry in the 36th Squadron log is, "No fly." Wheeler wrote:

> Contract bridge has become the reigning passion. Three tables are running at any hour of the day and most of the night. Terrific winds have fanned the 10-inch snowfall into a continual blizzard. The average wind velocity has been over 40 mph. Walking requires as much energy as climbing a steep hill.
>
> No single factor has as bad an effect on morale as being grounded and at the same time kept on continual alert status. Patience is a virtue rarely present in the makeup of a flier.

The Air Force flew whenever it could. Eareckson's B-17s, B-24s, B-25s, and B-26s kept up the harassment of the enemy by bombing Kiska's sub base and seaplane hangars, plastering flak batteries, attacking Japanese ships—in one raid alone, supply-carrying destroyer *Oboro* was sunk and escort destroyer *Hatsuharu* took a direct hit which destroyed her rudder and forced her to limp home to the Kuriles. By the end of the year, the Eleventh Air Force had destroyed at least fifty enemy planes in combat, and lost only a dozen of its own in battle; but it had lost almost eighty planes to "other causes." (Japanese losses to weather were equally high.)

Several influential Stateside commanders still believed Senatorial complaints that the Air Force had exaggerated the brutality of Aleutian weather. Early in December, a visiting Inspector General, Major General William E. Lynd, gave Alaskan pilots a bad time until, riding as passenger on a bombing mission, he found himself trapped by wall-to-wall fog. With both Umnak and Adak socked in, the B-24 ran out of fuel and crash-landed on Atka Island. All hands were rescued immediately by a PBY, but General Lynd had suffered a broken collarbone in the crash, and after that there were no more complaints from Stateside desk pilots about exaggerated weather reports from up north.*

---

*1995 ADDENDUM: John Cloe remarks that General Lynd was in the theater to investigate "sloppy administration practices in the Bomber Command—probably one of the reasons Eareckson did not get his star."

Twice in a week, in a pair of eerily similar accidents, parked B-24s at Adak were hit by fighters landing in the fog. All four planes were totally demolished; one P-38 pilot burned to death in his plane.

On a typical mission, Lieutenant Irving Wadlington of the 21st Squadron went out to bomb Attu. Wadlington's clean-shaven "Glamour Crew" reached Attu, ran into a williwaw, got knocked down a thousand feet, and had the ammunition jarred out of the ammo cans and the bombs out of their racks. Wadlington jettisoned them with great care and headed home. En route he saw a P-38 ditch in the surf off Tanaga. The fighter sank; the pilot, in his Mae West, splashed to shore. Wadlington stripped his crew of parkas, matches, gloves, cigarettes and chocolate bars; he circled down to fifty feet, dropped the wadded package to the fighter pilot and flew on home, directing a PBY to the site to pick up the downed pilot. Wadlington had spent a day on a harrowing "combat mission" during which he had neither seen the enemy nor dropped a bomb nor fired a shot.

IN SPITE OF THE WEATHER, EARECKSON'S handful of bombers managed to drop more than half a million pounds of explosives on the enemy bases during the last three months of 1942. Wheeler wrote:

> Col. Eareckson's Bomber Command is determined to make use of all available daylight. Eight missions were scheduled to take off at one-hour intervals today. Nearly all crews were scheduled for two sorties—one in the morning and another as soon as bombs could be reloaded, men fed, and aircraft serviced.
>
> The first two missions were accompanied by P-38's and P-39's to protect them from fighter opposition. Further protection for ensuing flights was unnecessary, for no Japanese peashooters came aloft during the day. 36th Squadron, with only six B-17's in commission, flew four of the eight missions.
>
> Col. E. led twice. Two of our ships were damaged by AA fire in the first mission. The Col. knows no fear and passed over the camp on Kiska two or three times at low altitude to take photos.

To overcome the shortness of daylight, Eareckson bombed at night. Missions bombed by the light of burning incendiary bombs, dropped by a single plane that preceded the main flight by one minute. On December 30, a night mission of thirty-one planes dropped 42,000 pounds of bombs on Kiska—but most of them were wasted because of a marvelous Japanese trick. For weeks a bomb-wrecked Japanese freighter hulk had stood beached in Kiska Harbor. On December 30 a fully loaded transport, identical to the beached wreck, had arrived. The Japanese floated the wreck, anchored her out in the harbor, and beached the sound sister ship where the wreck had been. Eareckson's raid finished off the wreck but left the beached ship untouched and ready for unloading.

The night raid did a little damage to ships, beat up a few midget submarines and demolished a Rufe; but the cost was high. Two P-38s were shot down. Lieutenant Jules Constantine's Liberator was shot down on the water; a PBY landed to meet the raft; diving Rufes strafed the raft and the PBY, and killed all the men on both crews. Meanwhile Lieutenant C. E. Rodebaugh, USN, ran into a pack of four Zeroes; with his nose gun jammed, Rodebaugh flew his PBY in a tight circle around conical Segula Island while his turret gunners successfully kept the four fighters at bay. The Zero (like any other single-seat fighter) was a weapon which had to be pointed in the direction in which it was shooting; its guns were fixed. Rodebaugh's clever maneuver prevented the Zeroes from lining up on his PBY without crashing into the mountain or the sea. He finally ducked into a bay and climbed safely into the clouds.

THE NEW YEAR OF 1943 CAME in without fanfare. Alaska had been at war more than six months, and one man in particular had been in the thick of it: with the exception of one brief October mission to the States, Colonel William O. Eareckson had been in the air, and in combat, on virtually every flyable day of the Aleutian Campaign.

Ernest Gruening recalls, "Eareckson was an excellent man. A splendid person, popular and dashing." A compelling figure of violent heroics and warm compassion, Eareckson was nonetheless his own enemy in one sense: if ambition burned any holes in his pockets, they only smoldered unseen. In the European theater, a Bomber Command boss rated the two stars of a major general. It did not seem to trouble Eareckson that he was still a colonel. Simon Buckner had recommended to the Air Force that Eareckson deserved star rank, but no promotions came through for the iconoclastic pilot. The Army did not like lone wolves; and Eareckson, in Colonel Lawrence Reineke's words, was "the honest sergeant on the police force. He bucked the system, and suffered for it." Lucian Wernick recalls, "Eric was absolutely incapable of bowing and scraping. He refused to show respect for superiors unless he felt it, and up there he didn't have very many opportunities to feel it."

He had only one friend at court—Simon Buckner, himself frequently out of favor with higher echelons. By the first day of 1943 Buckner had received a drawer full of communications from General Butler suggesting that Eareckson had too many missions under his belt, that he was flak-happy, that he had been warned to stop trying to be both commander and crew, and that he needed a rest. Butler said Eareckson had ignored his warnings; consequently, Butler was now sending him home to the States.

Buckner was not willing to see Eareckson go home to a training command (the usual fate of combat air officers rotated home). Eareckson was too valuable to him.* Buckner took the chance of breaking into the Air Force chain-of-command. He transferred Eareckson to his own staff—thus pushing Butler out of the picture—and allowed Eareckson to have a deserved rest, by sending him to the States on a sensitive mission for the Alaska Defense Command. He told Eareckson that when he returned to Alaska it would be as Deputy Chief of Staff for the Eleventh Air Force.

Just after the first of the year, Eareckson flew home to California. When he reported at San Diego, and his taunts were no longer being heard over the radio on Kiska bomb runs, Tokyo Rose announced with grim satisfaction, "Our very good friend, Colonel Eareckson, is no more. He was shot down in the sea on January 13."

"When Eric learned of this," recalls Colonel William Alexander, "he said, 'Why, the little bitch, wait till I get back up there!'"

Kiska had not seen the last of Eric Eareckson. Within a few months, with yet another important tactical innovation, he would be back.

ON DECEMBER 31, 1942, AFTER a day in Dutch Harbor, Vice Admiral Frank Jack Fletcher flew into Adak. Fletcher, Commander of the Northwestern Sea Frontier and the 13th Naval District, was on a sensitive mission for CINCPAC.

No one could have missed the fact that Admiral Theobald and General Buckner were not getting along with each other. Theobald had been asking for months to be relieved and given a new assignment. Buckner had complained for months that Theobald had balked at sending his ships out to pound the enemy—"He's as tender of his

---

*1995 ADDENDUM: Eareckson's raids on Kiska achieved significant effects on Japanese strength and morale. Karl Kaoru Kasukabe's records show that from June 1942 through July 1943, Japan's anti-aircraft batteries on Kiska lost 40% of their personnel to Allied air raids and naval bombardments.

bottoms as a teen-age girl," were Buckner's words. Frank Jack Fletcher had come to Alaska to appraise the situation and submit a confidential report to Admiral Nimitz.* The report reached CINCPAC on New Year's Day.

On January 4, a gruff naval hero with fierce bushy eyebrows landed on Kodiak: Rear Admiral Thomas C. Kinkaid, protagonist of half a dozen major Pacific naval battles, had arrived to take Fuzzy Theobald's place.[2] The Navy piped Admiral Kinkaid aboard the landlocked flagship of the North Pacific Force that same day—and the Aleutian Campaign went into high gear.

*1995 ADDENDUM: John Cloe adds, "Interestingly, General George Marshall was planning to relieve General Buckner of command because of his carping about Theobald's performance and his open insults. Theobald, however, asked for a reconsideration." It isn't clear whether Theobald's request was motivated by respect for Buckner's achievements or by a feeling that he, Theobald, rather than Buckner, should be the one allowed to take leave of this God-forsaken theater.

2. Rear Admiral Robert A. Theobald became Commandant, First Naval District (Boston). In October 1944 he was relieved of all active duty; he retired in February 1945. After the war he wrote two books—The Final Secrets of Pearl Harbor (1954) and Death of a Navy (1957)—in which he charged President Franklin Roosevelt with deliberately inviting the Japanese attack on Pearl Harbor. Theobald died in Boston in 1957 at seventy-three and was buried at Arlington National Cemetery. Official Navy biographical summaries, prepared by Admiral Theobald, identify him during his Pacific tenure of 1942 only as "a member of Admiral Nimitz's staff."

PART THREE

Kinkaid's War

CHAPTER
THIRTEEN

Kinkaid's Blockade

KINKAID WAS FIFTY-FOUR YEARS OLD. He had spent more than half his life tramping steel decks. His service record described a man six feet tall, 180 pounds, brown eyes, brown hair, ruddy complexion. It did not add that he had a pleasant bulldog face, that his hair was shot with gray, or that he liked to play golf, fish, and read detective stories. The Annapolis Yearbook, Class of 1908, described him:

Thomas Cassin Kinkaid: "A black-eyed, rosy-cheeked, noisy Irishman who loves a rough-house." The combative impulse was such a deep-rooted part of his nature—"I've had to fight my temper all my life"—that he had willfully courted the painful art of self-control, and succeeded: soft-spoken and suave, he made himself so easy to get along with that he came to be known as a reliable plodder.

In many respects he was Admiral Theobald's antithesis. Theobald had been caustic, brainy, inclined to be bitter because his pessimistic side always saw the possible perils of any undertaking. Kinkaid was the opposite. Far from contemplative (he had ranked near the bottom of his Naval Academy class), he made quick decisions, boldly committed everything he had, and bulled ahead tenaciously, letting chips fall where they might.

A remark attributed to his friend and mentor, Admiral William F. Halsey (to whom Kinkaid bore a distinct resemblance), summed up Kinkaid's own attitudes: "There are few great men. There are only great challenges, which ordinary men are forced by circumstances to meet." The challenge was there; if Kinkaid was that man, then he would make the decisions. It was that simple.

Rear Admiral Kinkaid came to his new Aleutian command with an extraordinary record of decisiveness and heroism at Coral Sea, at Midway, at the eastern Solomons, Guadalcanal, and the Battle of the

Santa Cruz Islands. He had seen action in more big naval battles than any other American admiral. By nature he had always shot from the hip—often a distinct virtue in the fast sway of battle, where cautious contemplative pauses could lose a tactical advantage. So far, he had made no mistakes.

It was said you could tell where the action was by looking for Kinkaid. Now Kinkaid had steamed into the Aleutians. And the action began instantly.

THE JOINT CHIEFS HAD ORDERED NORPACFOR to occupy Amchitka Island. Eareckson had bombed the village flat and the Alaska Scouts had landed there in December. Now, on January 5—the morning after his arrival—Kinkaid ordered the full troop landings to be executed.

That afternoon the Air Force launched recon flights to make photo strips of Amchitka and bomber strikes to pin down the enemy at Kiska and Attu. Three Mitchell bombers sank the 6,577-ton freighter *Montreal Maru* approaching Kiska; a B-24 sank the 6,100-ton *Kotohiro Maru* off Attu. Both ships went down with full loads of soldiers and supplies. At Kiska, American planes went in determined to keep the Rufes down—Amchitka was so close (40 miles) that it could be seen from a plane only a few hundred feet above Kiska.

Within hours, Kinkaid had assembled a taut little combat force of three battle-hardened cruisers and four destroyers under scholarly Rear Admiral Charles H. "Soc" McMorris (who had replaced Rear Admiral W. W. "Poco" Smith). Kinkaid grouped the McMorris force around the four transport ships which would deliver to Amchitka 2,100 Engineers and Army troops under Brigadier General Lloyd E. Jones, a Buckner protégé.

On January 6, forty-eight hours after Kinkaid had stepped ashore, Captain Walter Feinstein, M.D., wrote in his diary: "Got word today that there was going to be some activity down the line. We are all keeping our fingers crossed." Kinkaid was moving fast. But the weather closed in solid, and within two days—with the naval landing force already at sea—Kinkaid learned how impossible it was to complete any naval operation in the Aleutians without delays. The weather had to be obliged.

Only one Air Force plane got off the ground on January 8—Lieutenant R. W. Travin's B-24 weather ship. Travin bucked a raging blizzard from Adak to Kiska and then all the way out to Attu, where he dumped his bombs on a Japanese transport ship in the Bering Sea, and sank it. His radio report elicited an immediate reply from General Buckner:

CONGRATULATIONS TO THE CREW OF THE WEATHER SHIP FOR TURNING IN THE BEST WEATHER REPORT SO FAR RENDERED IN ALASKA.

But real weather reports were not good at all. The naval invasion fleet slammed around off Amchitka until the night of January 11, when the storm slacked just a bit; impatient with passivity and afraid of time, which was eating up his supplies, Admiral McMorris ordered the Army to go ashore in the morning regardless of weather. It was a bold decision, but if it worked it would prove that amphibious landings could succeed under tougher circumstances than had ever been tried before.

Rear Admiral Charles Horatio McMorris' middle name seemed particularly apt at the moment. Shortly after midnight he brusquely ordered destroyer *Worden* to move into Amchitka's Constantine Harbor and land her spearhead detachment of Alaska Scouts. At that time the surf was running bridge-high on a destroyer.

Worden blasted through the surf at the harbor mouth shortly before dawn. Brawling Lieutenant Colonel William J. Verbeck, Lawrence Castner's second-in-command, shepherded his Scouts into whaleboats and led them ashore through the driving blizzard. Castner's Cutthroats made the beach, but when *Worden* steamed back out of the harbor, the brutal current dashed her onto a pinnacle rock. It came through her hull like a torpedo, punctured the steel plates and ripped open her engine room.

Destroyer *Dewey* raced to her assistance, rigged a cable and tried to pull *Worden* off the rock. But she was impaled. The cable broke; *Worden* pivoted and capsized. Her crew abandoned ship and *Dewey* circled to pick them up, but even inside the harbor the sea was running to twenty-foot crests and the water temperature stood at 36° Fahrenheit. Fourteen sailors drowned in the few minutes before *Dewey's* help could reach them. *Worden*, on her side, lifted on the waves and smashed against the rocks, and plunged to the harbor bottom, a total wreck.

Transports eased past the wreckage and disgorged their troops onto the beaches of Constantine Harbor. By late in the day the 2,100 men were ashore—soaked, swamped, and oil-drenched. They ate cold rations and faced a night in a blizzard without shelter. Meanwhile one of the transports, unloaded and turning about, presented her beam to the 80-knot wind and hurtled onto the reef like a toy sailboat. She lodged there, solid aground, and was only refloated weeks later.

Amchitka Island was secured within twenty hours of Admiral McMorris' order to land. The storm did not abate, but on the morning of

January 13 a squad of Alaska Scouts struck out along the 30-mile length of the island on foot. At the end of the trek they established an observation post at the northwest tip of the island. From here, through breaks in the weather, they would be able to see the peaks of Kiska. Within a few days, when the Japanese began to launch air strikes, the Scouts were able to spot the Rufe fighters as they took off.

It was "Pontoon Joe," a Rufe seaplane familiar to troops from Adak, who flew over Amchitka on January 23 and spotted the American activity. The enemy's Amchitka Express started that day, and came calling at intervals for several weeks. It started as a series of two-plane raids. The Japanese float planes inflicted moderate damage on Squeaky Anderson's beach facilities; on January 24, Wheeler wrote, "It has been deemed wise to establish a peashooter patrol to prevent recurrence of the Japanese bomber attacks."

Eareckson's device of using a B-17 to fly mother-ship to the fighters was employed again. "But the Japs simply wait until our fighters have left the scene and then fly over in leisurely fashion to drop a few bombs." On January 26 a pair of Rufes bombed the half-built American runway; they killed three Engineers, and encouraged the rest to work faster. The next day six Rufes made a concerted attack; they cratered the runway in three places. In spite of the bombings, Buckner's Engineers once again performed their tidy miracle, and on January 28 Jack Chennault brought a P-40 squadron in to land on the new air field. Though the weather had been terrible and there had been no ready-made flat lagoon-bottom, Colonel Benjamin Talley had finished the Marsden mat job in less than two weeks.

When two Rufes attacked again on January 29, the Scouts at Aleut Point saw them take off from Kiska, and flashed warnings to Chennault. The Flying Tigers were in the air, waiting, when the Japanese arrived. Both Rufes went down in flaming spirals.

After that the Amchitka Express became more sporadic; it quit altogether on February 18. The Japanese had too few planes left to keep it up. There was only one more air-raid alarm at Amchitka, when a sentry spotted thirty fliers in V-formation advancing from the direction of Kiska. Alarms had spread across the entire island base before a Navy pilot scornfully observed it was the first time he had ever seen Japanese airplanes flapping their wings. It was a formation of geese.

Soon ten P-38 fighter-bombers joined the Warhawks on station at Amchitka and began daily raids against Kiska. Seaplane tender *Avocet* anchored in Constantine Harbor to provide a new base for the persistent

PBYs of Captain Gehres' command. Mitchell and Marauder medium bombers roosted on the new runway and subjected Kiska to daily—sometimes hourly—punishment. But it was late March before the runway was extended enough for the first heavy bombers to move up.

The 36th Bombardment Squadron, weary veteran of two years' Alaskan flying, had at last received a month of recuperation and training—at Umnak. "All this Paradise needs," Wheeler grouched, "is an Eve—and an apple tree." The squadron's administrative headquarters was still back at Kodiak, though the 36th had not flown a mission from there in almost a year. Now the squadron, headquarters and all, was ordered to move up to what Wheeler called, incredulously, "the permanent base of the 36th—Amchitka!"

> Ours is the first heavy bomber formation to land topship on the new strip at Amchitka. We flew over our new, tent-studded area and buzzed it in the best peashooter fashion as dogfaces gaped wide-eyed and slack-jawed below.
>
> These same Air Corps Glamor Boys cursed and fumed shortly after landing, as we struggled through mud and water to reach the tent area. No roads; the most direct route to the tents leads through numerous small lakes, and so do most of the indirect routes. We packed our barracks bags, B-4 bags, and foot lockers on our backs, and settled down to life in tents again.

CINCPAC HAD POSTED KINKAID TO the North Pacific with orders to clear the enemy out of the Aleutians. Amchitka was the first step. The next moves were to hit the enemy harder than ever before, and to starve him out by establishing an unbreakable naval blockade.

Kinkaid had only the ships Admiral Theobald had left behind. To Theobald, this handful of vessels had been too small to be of any use at all. To Kinkaid, it was all he had, so he put it to work without questions or complaints. He assembled a tough little striking force—cruisers *Indianapolis* and *Richmond* and four destroyers. Not since Poco Smith's attempt to bombard Kiska six months ago had the North Pacific Force's ships been gathered into a single aggressor pack. Now, early in February, Kinkaid sent Rear Admiral "Soc" McMorris to blockade the enemy's approaches to Kiska and Attu and take any other offensive action that might seem appropriate.

McMorris, a gentle warrior whose kindliness was exceeded only by his mental pyrotechnics, steamed west into action that almost turned into a minor disaster. Off Attu, on February 18, he picked up a submarine report of several enemy ships in Attu's Holtz Bay. The same signal reached Adak, where the Air Force launched a bomber strike to \“attack shipping in Holtz Bay prior to sunset.” The Air Force did not expect McMorris to reach Attu until after dark. But as usual the Aleutian weather played a trick of its own. McMorris' deck officers logged “Ceiling and Visibility Unlimited,” and instead of feeling its way slowly through fog, the fleet roared toward Attu at full speed. And so, neither expecting the other, the Navy and the Air Force reached Attu at the same time.

McMorris formed his six ships in column, with Attu to starboard. He did not see the reported enemy ships anywhere. Overhead, seeking the same ships, Captain Frederick Ramputi appeared at 10,000 feet in his Flying Fortress. Ramputi recalls:

> I had a Chief Petty Officer, veteran of eighteen years in the Navy in my plane to verify naval identifications. I reconfirmed three times with him on target identification. He confirmed the ships were Japanese—six wakes. I made two bomb runs but the normal, emergency, and manual rack releases all failed to function.

McMorris, in flagship *Richmond,* watched the B-17 make bomb runs with its bomb-bay doors wide open. Unable to reach the bomber by radio, McMorris bleaky ordered *Richmond* to open fire. Her flak batteries opened up instantly.

Billy Wheeler innocently reported, “Antiaircraft fire was sparse but the bursts were unusually large, indicating very heavy caliber guns.”

Ramputi recalls, “I aborted and went back to Adak. I was met by General Butler's staff car at the end of the runway. Admiral Kinkaid had a few wry remarks to make.” And Wheeler added, “Bomber Command is insisting that all flying officers be thoroughly briefed in surface ship identification henceforth.”

ON THE MOUNTAINS OF ATTU, a few Japanese skiers watched the near-battle take place between the American bomber and the six-ship fleet. The skiers did not realize the ships were American until McMorris opened fire at 2:30 in the afternoon, shelling Chicagof village and Holtz Bay from several miles offshore.

McMorris marched his salvos through a checkerboard pattern, firing for two hours while his ships paraded back and forth. He stayed well out,

Major General Simon Bolivar Buckner, Jr.

U.S. Army photograph.

Kodiak crews thaw a PBY Catalina before starting engines.

U.S. Navy photograph.

B-25 Mitchell bombers in their Umnak revetments. Note the steel mat runway perforations visible in the lower portion of the picture.

Photograph from the author's collection.

Colonel Benjamin Talley's Army Engineers lay perforated steel-mat runway sections.

U.S. Air Force photograph.

Flying past Kiska volcano a B-24 makes a DR bomb-run above the soup.

U.S. Air Force photograph.

July 1942: General Butler emerges from his headquarters office – one of the first Quonset huts erected in the Aleutians.

U.S. Army photograph.

The only tree in the Aleutians: A gift from the enlisted men to Colonel Eareckson's dog.

U.S. Army photograph.

Crippled by flak over Kiska, a B-24 crash-lands on the way home.

U.S. Army photograph.

Adak in the fall of 1942: A few weeks earlier this airfield was the bottom of a lagoon.

U.S. Army photograph.

Japanese seaplane pilots at Kiska, November 1942.

Photograph from Bob Reeve's collection.

This PBY caught in a williwaw at Dutch Harbor in November 1942 flipped over a moment after the picture was taken.

U.S. Navy photograph.

Vice Admiral Thomas C. Kinkaid (center) talks with soldiers at Adak.

U.S. Army photograph.

Amchitka, April 1943:
Lockheed P-38 Lightnings come in to refuel before returning to the flak-scarred skies above Attu.

Photograph from the author's collection.

Amchitka, April 1943: A P-40 revs up to try and achieve lift-off despite the sucking mud.

U.S. Army photograph.

Supplies pile up in Constantine Harbor, Amchitka; soldiers call the muddy road "Buckner Drive".

U.S. Army photograph.

Beaching a PBY at Kodiak.

U.S. Navy photograph.

Adak 1943: Admiral Kinkaid prepares to award medals. Looking on at the door by the end of the hut are General Butler, Lieutenant Reinecke, and Commodore Gehres.

U.S. Navy photograph.

Soldiers dig out a storm-buried Quonset hut at Adak in January 1943.

U.S. Army photograph.

The first wave gropes toward Massacre Beach.

U.S. Army photograph.

How to ski on shovels: Sergeant W.P. Wheeler demonstrates at Kiska, September 1943.

U.S. Army photograph.

Southern Force moves up Massacre Valley.

U.S. Navy photograph.

Ankle deep in muck, Sergeant George F. Cova hauls supplies to the front line.

U.S. Army photograph.

Attu, May 1943: Supplies continued to back up on the beaches.

U.S. Army photograph.

Patrols (left and center) move forward on May 19, 1943, while fog conceals Japanese defenses on the heights east of Jarmin Pass.

U.S. Army photograph.

After the last Banzai five hundred Japanese soldiers commited mass suicide with grenades at the foot of Engineer Hill.

U.S. Army photograph.

July 1943:
Bombardier's view of the bombs striking Kiska.

U.S. Air Force photograph.

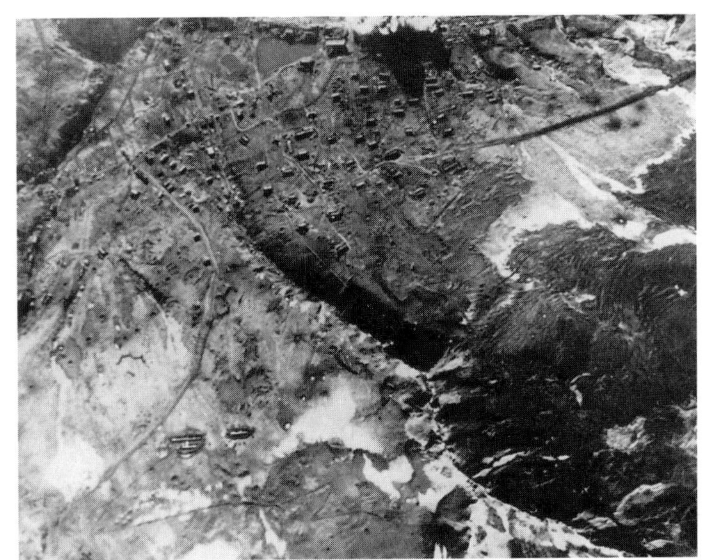

Adak,
August 1943:
35,000 men aboard these transports await the order to invade Kiska.

Photograph from Admiral James S. Russell's collection.

All they found was abandoned wreckage.

U.S. Air Force photograph.

Having found no enemy troops on Kiska, disgusted troops of the American-Canadian invasion force climb back into a landing craft to return to their transport.

U.S. Army photograph.

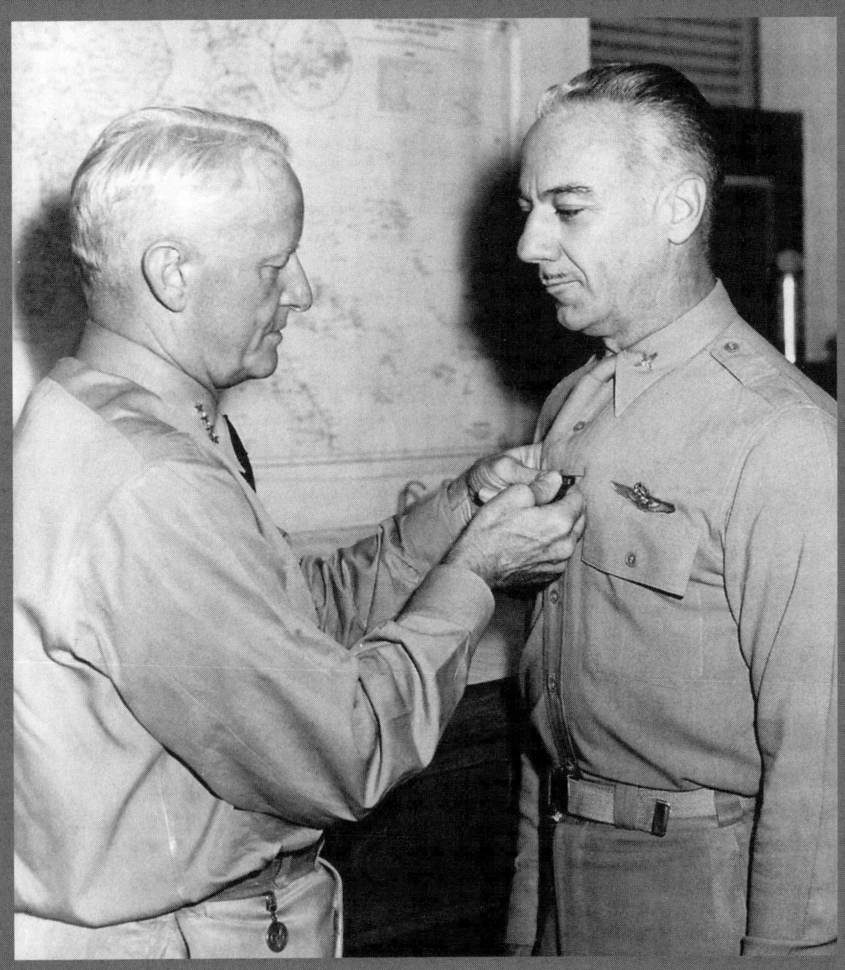

The Campaign over, Fleet Admiral Chester W. Nimitz pins the Navy Cross on Colonel William O. Eareckson for outstanding heroism and leadership.

U.S. Navy photograph.

By war's end things were getting downright civilized: even the Umnak National Forest had been transplanted to Attu. (Later it was replicated at Adak.)

U.S. Air Force photograph.

Ghost of a fallen P-38 begins to disappear under drifting snow.

Photograph from the collection of Art Kidder.

too far to do very much damage; the bombardment killed twenty-three, wounded one, and demolished a building. Originally McMorris had not intended to shell Attu at all, but it seemed a reasonable response to Admiral Kinkaid's order to "take any appropriate offensive action."

After he had shaken up the defenders of Attu McMorris continued west into the ocean between the Aleutians and the Kuriles. His orders were to blockade both Kiska and Attu. Since he had only six vessels, and Kiska was hundreds of miles from Attu, he could not keep watch on both harbors at once. He reasoned that the best way to enforce the blockade was to cruise just outside Japanese home waters and intercept any outbound convoys.

It worked. East of the Kuriles he encountered the 3,100-ton *Akagane Maru*, en route to Attu with an infantry platoon, air field construction materials, munitions and stores. *Indianapolis'* big guns crippled the transport; McMorris' destroyers fired six torpedoes, all of which malfunctioned, and finally sank the Japanese cargo ship with gunfire. Two other enemy ships, on their way out from the Kuriles, were not detected by McMorris' force, but the sinking of *Akagane Maru* and the shelling of Attu persuaded them both to turn back without delivering their cargoes to the Aleutians.

McMorris' venture into the western ocean brought American sea power to that area of the world for the first time since Pearl Harbor. And once he got there, McMorris stayed. To Admiral Theobald, who had seen every plan in terms of what might go wrong with it, such a tiny token effort would have seemed fruitless and absurd. To Kinkaid, a dedicated exponent of the calculated risk, the blockade, whatever its weaknesses, seemed to offer the best chance to force the Japanese to abandon the western Aleutians.

LIEUTENANT GENERAL HIDEICHIRO HIGUCHI, Japanese commander of ground forces in the North Pacific, was beaten on paper without yet firing a shot. As soon as the Americans advanced to Amchitka, Higuchi knew his only options were to withdraw from the Aleutians or beef them up immediately with strong reinforcements, finish the runways on Attu and Kiska, and persuade the Navy to attack the American supply lines that supported the Adak and Amchitka striking bases.

Admiral Hosogaya vetoed the latter request. His only vessels capable of cutting enemy supply lines were submarines—and Imperial Headquarters had restricted the duties of the I-class pigboats to supply runs to beleaguered outposts and torpedo attacks on enemy capital warships. Though Germany kept trying to persuade Japan to make submarine attacks against Allied merchant shipping (as the U-boats did in the Atlantic), the Japanese command never came around to that way of thinking: it was still in the grip of the more honorable but less practical Yamamoto idea to sink men-of-war only. Consequently Japan posed no serious undersea threat to Allied shipping.

As for the unfinished air fields on Attu and Kiska, General Higuchi's troops kept up their frenzied efforts, but they had poor materials and no construction machinery—and no sooner was a yard of ground leveled than it was cratered by American bombs.

Yet Imperial Headquarters denied Higuchi's request to abandon the Aleutians. Evacuation would leave the Kuriles, and all of northern Japan, wide open to attack from America or Russia. So, on February 5, 1943, Imperial Headquarters ordered Admiral Hosogaya and General Higuchi "to hold the western Aleutians at all costs."

Higuchi exhorted his officers to redouble their runway-building efforts and "Carry out preparations for war.... The principal task is to secure the western Aleutians, to break up the enemy's united attack, check the bond between the United States and Russia, and make plans for future assault operations."

The dictum had a hollow ring. He had fewer than 8,000 troops on Kiska and only about 1,000 on Attu, and they were not first-line soldiers. They were retreads and recruits under a small cadre of Regular Army officers and noncoms. The total mechanized strength on Kiska amounted to sixty trucks, twenty motorcycles, fourteen passenger cars, and two small tractors. The beaches were defended sparsely, with mines and barbed wire. The troops had mortars, machine guns, rifles, and grenades, but virtually no mountain artillery.

Only the antiaircraft strength was impressive. Kiska and Attu had everything from six-inch naval guns to 120-mm, 75-mm, 23-mm and 13-mm flak guns. The Eleventh Air Force's General Butler remarked that if there were 8,000 Japanese on Kiska, "it looks like half of them are busy throwing up AA fire." Wheeler wrote of one early spring mission, "The targets were plainly visible, but so were we. It was a question of who's synchronizing on whom. Certainly they synchronized on us, for five of our six planes were hit repeatedly."

But hit or not, the American planes dropped their bombs, and a good many of them exploded on the half-built runway near Salmon Lagoon. By the middle of spring the Japanese had surrendered the air entirely to the Americans—they had no seaplanes left, and no hope of replacements, for by March the Guadalcanal campaign had cost Japan more than a thousand airplanes.

At Attu, troops were hard at work on a 3,500-foot airstrip. Superior to the Kiska runway, it would be capable of handling bombers as well as Zeroes—if it could be completed. General Higuchi knew his only chance to push the Americans back was to get his air fields into operation (Wheeler wrote, "Target again the runway—we are really sweating out those land-based Zeroes!"), and he pulled men off all projects except flak batteries to pitch in on the construction job.

But nothing helped. *Chieribou Maru* brought three bulldozers to Attu but an American plane bombed it in Holtz Bay, and the ship sank in thirty fathoms with the bulldozers still on board. Lance Corporal Nogi Tanaka wrote in his diary, "Seven planes came over without showing themselves. There is nothing more terrifying than not being able to see them. You never know where the bombs will fall." By early March, the American Air Force had sunk or crippled at least forty Japanese ships in the Aleutians, and Japan's North Pacific commands recorded a casualty list in the Aleutians that had mounted to 3,477. Kiska coded a signal to General Higuchi:

> BOMBING IS GETTING MORE VIOLENT MONTH AFTER MONTH. THE BOMBING TECHNIQUE USED IS MEDIOCRE, BUT WHEN ENOUGH BOMBS ARE DROPPED THERE IS BOUND TO BE DAMAGE. WE ARE LOSING PERSONNEL, INSTALLATIONS, AIR DEFENSE ARMS, FUEL AND FIREARMS. EVEN THE ANTI-AIRCRAFT GUN GRADUALLY LOSES ITS AIMING EFFICIENCY.

The Americans bombed constantly, often six or seven times a day. Higuchi's garrisons were running low on food and ammunition; the last supply convoy had come in December. Small convoys had attempted the northern run since then, but all of them had been spotted by American ships or PBYs and sunk or driven back. Only occasional lone ships had made it through. Then, at last, a big convoy slipped past Admiral McMorris' blockade in a soupy fog on March 9 and arrived undiscovered at Attu, where it landed a huge shipment of supplies and reinforcements, some of which were soon transshipped to Kiska. The beleaguered soldiers took it not only as a physical reinforcement but as a good omen; their diaries became more cheerful.

Japanese troops in the Aleutians had improved their living conditions since the Campaign's early days. They lived in uncrowded quarters, underground at Kiska and above ground at Attu. They drank tea, sake, cider and gin; they ate clams, seaweed, fish, rice, plums, greens, and bamboo sprouts. They worked hard, but received regular days off. They kept diaries and did a good deal of fishing. One skiing enthusiast spent so much time on the snow-covered Attu peaks that he wondered whether he had "joined the Army or a wealthy winter lodge. How the members of my old ski club would envy my life on Attu!"

They wished they had something to smoke—cigarettes were scarce, parceled out according to military rank. They built Shinto shrines: the largest, on Kiska, was guarded by a polished cedar arch and two rows of 5-inch U.S. Navy duds, collected after Poco Smith's Spring Plowing. They spent hours polishing the huge British railroad gun which had been captured at Singapore and lugged all the way to Kiska.* They studied English, the better to insult their attackers. They pretended to believe the old Japanese proverb, "Adversity is the source of strength." But all they really wanted was to go home.

On March 10, a transport ship brought supplies to Attu. It was to be the last. In the next week half a dozen ships were turned back by the American blockade force. Finally Admiral Hosogaya decided the only way to run the blockade was to do it with all the assembled power at his command. At Paramushiro, he filled three big transports to the gunwales and loaded an overflow of supplies onto the decks of four destroyers. Then he gathered the pride of his Northern Force—four heavy cruisers—to escort the convoy to the Aleutians. This time, Hosogaya would personally take command of the expedition. He ran up his flag on heavy cruiser *Nachi* and steamed out of the Kuriles in battle order on March 22, 1943, resolved to blast his way through.

The result, in four days' time, would be the major sea action of the Aleutian Campaign—and the last and longest classic daylight naval battle in the history of fleet warfare.

---

*1995 ADDENDUM: The existence of this railroad gun from Singapore has been questioned by veterans and scholars. Described in one of the Japanese soldiers' diaries from the Reineke/Russell collections, the gun may have been kept in a tunnel where it couldn't be seen from the air. It wasn't found on Kiska. If it existed at all, it could be under water or may have been removed from Kiska prior to the Allied invasion in 1943.

CHAPTER FOURTEEN

The Battle of the Komandorskis

BUNDLED IN HIS THICK BLUE bridge coat, Admiral "Soc" McMorris searched the wide ocean from the bridge of his flagship, the old (1918) light cruiser *Richmond.* It was 7:30 in the morning, March 26, 1943—an hour before sunrise. Strung out ahead and behind him in a six-mile column were his four destroyers and the newcomer, thirteen-year-old heavy cruiser *Salt Lake City*, a 600-foot seagoing teakettle better known as "Old Swayback Maru." She had completed six months' repairs after the Battle of Cape Esperance and had just arrived to take the place of Indianapolis, which was en route back to Pearl Harbor.

McMorris had pressed far to the west in his attempt to cut Japan's Aleutian supply lines. This morning he was almost two hundred miles west of Attu, crossing an ocean deep about a hundred miles south of the Russian Komandorski Islands. The temperature stood at 34°; the air was crystal clear—in the gray dawn lookouts could see jumping fish several miles away. In the flag cabin, the admiral studied reports from PBYs of a fleet of several ships that had kept appearing and disappearing somewhere to the west. It sounded like a supply convoy, a big one; McMorris was anxious to find it.

A fifty-three-year-old Alabaman who had taught English and history at Annapolis, McMorris was best known for his ability to leaf through a thick sheaf of reports and memorize them all verbatim, while carrying on a conversation at the same time. He had ranked fifth in the USNA Class of 1912, where his purported Socratic wisdom had earned him the nickname "Soc." Only once had he been known to blunder: On December 3, 1941, he had stated flatly that Pearl Harbor would never be attacked from the air.

In the South Pacific, with Halsey and his friend Kinkaid, he had already earned the Navy Cross, his country's second-highest military honor. Today he had no visions of glory; he anticipated only a routine interception of an enemy cargo convoy, perhaps a few destroyer-escorts to fend off before sinking the transports. Victory in the Aleutians, he was certain, would be won not by big decisive battles but by attrition—the steady erosion of the enemy's power and will.

It was routine in contested waters to call General Quarters each day at dawn. Right after breakfast McMorris' six old ships sounded GQ and went to battle stations. The Klaxons still echoed when a message was piped to the flag bridge from Radar Plot: the flagship, and leading destroyer *Coghlan*, were in radar contact with several unidentified ships about ten miles north.

McMorris made a code signal to Admiral Kinkaid at Headquarters:

> CONTACT GROUP OF SHIPS EASTERLY COURSE LAT 53-00 LONG 168-40 X CONCENTRATING TO ATTACK.

He gathered his ships, strung out at one-mile intervals, into a close pack around *Richmond*, and made a stately fleet-turn toward the northeast to intercept the enemy. Galley cooks prepared sandwiches and readied coffee; sentries released prisoners from the brigs; lookouts searched the horizon with keen alertness.

Ten miles distant, a Japanese sailor in *Nachi's* crow's nest made out the approaching American vessels in the dawn. Admiral Hosogaya immediately ordered his three transports to fall behind while he maneuvered his nine fast warships between the cargo ships and the Americans. McMorris' lookouts recognized one Japanese ship as a heavy cruiser—then two; two light cruisers as well, all of them moving fast toward *Richmond's* starboard bow, while the Japanese destroyers swung to bear down on the port bow.

The odds suddenly looked terrible. McMorris had two cruisers. Each of them was smaller, older, and several knots slower than the four Japanese leviathans bearing down on him. He was outgunned, outsped, and outnumbered by two-to-one.

He had obviously run into Japan's entire Northern fleet.

But if he refused to accept battle, the enemy convoy would reach the Aleutians, resupply Attu and Kiska, and possibly lengthen the campaign by months.

McMorris made up his mind in the half-dozen seconds after the enemy ships had been identified. He decided to make a fight of it. His main objective would be the Japanese transports; he would try to feint, draw the enemy cruisers away, and dash in behind them to sink the cargo ships. Then he would retire; he was not bloodthirsty enough to want a duel for its own sake.

He notified Kinkaid and requested air support from Adak and Amchitka; he signaled Captain Bertram Rodgers, skipper of *Salt Lake City,* that *Richmond* would follow the more powerful *Salt Lake City's* movements.

Richmond was already swinging into a westward turn, as if she intended to retire. She had only started at 8:38 a.m., when the Japanese cruisers opened fire on her.

The range was twelve miles. The second enemy salvo straddled *Richmond,* close enough to splash her decks. Then the Japanese shifted their fire toward *Salt Lake City*—Admiral Hosogaya had decided not to waste ammunition on the smaller ships whose guns could not reach him at long range.

At 8:42, Old Swayback's forward turrets opened fire. The Battle of the Komandorskis was on.

FRIDAY MORNING, MARCH 26, 1943: 8:45 A.M. *Salt Lake City's* eight- and five-inch batteries thundered full salvos; the concussion made her decks jump. More than twenty thousand yards away, Admiral Hosogaya's flagship *Nachi* stood in faint silhouette against a gray horizon, her guns erupting in hard orange lances of flame.

Old Swayback's fourth salvo whistled across the sky, deadly accurate—flames mushroomed at the base of *Nachi's* bridge and enveloped her superstructure. Japanese crews swarmed in from fore and aft, hosed the fire and brought it under quick control; but during the interval a faulty generator failed. The break, which would go unrepaired for almost a half hour, turned off forward electric power and put the flagship's main battery out of action. It forced *Nachi* to zigzag so that she could bring other batteries into play—a maneuver that slowed her forward speed, made her movements clumsy, and canceled the five-knot advantage she had held over *Salt Lake City*. But in the meantime Hosogaya had changed course and swung into closer range.

Hosogaya's sharp move cut McMorris off from the Japanese transports. Like a chess player, McMorris responded with a new maneuver—a 40-degree turn to port, to confuse the enemy's gunners. At 25 knots, Richmond and Old Swayback heeled precariously in response to maximum rudder. The four Japanese cruisers were still closing, their speed in excess of 30 knots; Old Swayback went to emergency flank speed and kept turning away to the southwest, with *Nachi* now on her port quarter, still closing the distance. The range was less than nine miles.

Hosogaya launched eight torpedoes from *Nachi;* Captain Rodgers wheeled Old Swayback through a quick series of shuddering turns and evaded all eight fish. Hosogaya's salvos crashed close enough to drench Old Swayback's open bridge; Rodgers, soaked to the skin, made fast guesses where the enemy would throw his next salvo, and threw Old Swayback into still more turns. As a rule he headed toward the point where the last salvo had hit, assuming the Japanese spotters would correct their aim each time.

In that manner, Rodgers chased salvos with skill and aplomb; several times he grinned at his bridge officers and shouted, "Fooled 'em again!" With uncanny timing, Old Swayback pitched and careened through the slalom course of enemy big-inch explosions. Gunnery Officer Commander James T. Brewer dashed back and forth, trailing a tangle of interphone wires, blurting corrections and fire orders to his batteries. Gunners rammed loading trays home, shoved heavy shells into the breeches, dumped powder bags inside, shouldered the breech blocks shut and ducked, holding their ears. Firing buzzers clacked; the guns roared and skidded back in thunderous recoil.

Sixteenth salvo: with superb marksmanship at eight and one half miles, Old Swayback made three solid hits on *Nachi.* The eight-inchers exploded against *Nachi's* mainmast, torpedo tubes, and bridge. The last shell mangled bridge platings and killed three officers within a few yards of Admiral Hosogaya, but Hosogaya escaped unhurt. Thick black oil smoke enveloped the forward stack; and at the main battery, where electric power had only just been restored, explosions wrecked the wires that connected flag gunnery control with the main battery. Once again *Nachi's* forward turret was stilled. The big cruiser had to continue zigzagging to keep her secondary batteries in the fight; once again she lost her speed advantage. It was another quarter of an hour before the crew rigged a new circuit and Hosogaya was able to salvo his main battery.

McMorris managed to stretch the range to 24,500 yards; then a Japanese shell exploded starboard amidship on *Salt Lake City,* the first hit. It was 9:10 A.M. Two men were killed, but the damage was not severe. Astern, *Nachi* had slowed down, smoking heavily. It began to look as if McMorris might make his end run after all: he still wanted to get around the enemy warships and attack the transports.

NACHI HAD TWO CATAPULT SEAPLANES. One had taken off quickly and buzzed over *Salt Lake City* to spot for the Japanese guns. McMorris' flak guns drove it into the clouds. *Nachi's* second launch plane was still on the starboard catapult when one of *Nachi's* own salvos destroyed it; Hosogaya jettisoned the plane.[1]

Hosogaya sent one of his light cruisers out, to cut across the arc of McMorris' westerly turn, get within 18,000 yards of the Americans, and spot for the heavy cruisers while she harassed Old Swayback with extreme-range shellfire. At the same time McMorris' destroyers circled toward the enemy to get their five-inch guns in range. Now one of *Coghlan's* shells burst above *Nachi's* deck. The explosion killed all the men in the trouble-plagued Number One turret.

So far, *Nachi* had taken the brunt of the battle's punishment. McMorris had been running in luck; now it changed, when the shock of Old Swayback's gunfire damaged her own hydraulic steering system. It meant the rudder had to be worked by hand. Rudder-angles were limited to ten-degree changes. Old Swayback was in trouble, but Captain Rodgers kept chasing salvos, his turns less precise than before.

By now more than two hundred Japanese shells had exploded within fifty yards of Old Swayback. Several times McMorris, on *Richmond's* bridge, had seen Old Swayback disappear under mountains of water and thought she had blown up, but each time *Salt Lake City* came battling through the cataracts.

The duel had raged more than an hour. During the interval, both opposing admirals had requested air support; each expected planes to show up at any time. But at 9:50 Hosogaya received a wireless from Japan, telling him there were no planes available. And at Adak, the Eleventh Air Force's bombers had been loaded for an attack against Kiska; they had to be unloaded and rearmed with torpedoes and AP bombs—and Adak's bomb dumps were dispersed all over the island. As a result, at ten o'clock the bomber strike was not nearly ready to take off. The few airborne PBYs, armed only with antisubmarine depth charges, were too slow to reach the battle in time. And so, through no intent of its participants, the Battle of the Komandorskis shaped up as the last slug-out gunnery duel ever to take place between opposing surface fleets without the use of combat airplanes.

---

1. The first Japanese catapult plane, driven off by American flak, flew to Attu but crashed in the harbor when it landed. Spotters on Salt Lake City saw the floating wreckage of the second Japanese plane, the one Nachi's own gunfire had wrecked; the Americans claimed a kill. The error was perpetuated by Samuel Eliot Morison and other historians who maintained that the American ships had shot down a Japanese plane during the Battle of the Komandorskis.

At 10:10, an hour and a half after the battle had started, a high-trajectory Japanese shell plunged through *Salt Lake City's* main deck and smashed straight down through the hull below the waterline. The ragged huge hole half-flooded an engine room.

McMorris' luck had changed. Old Swayback was already steering badly; now she slowed, taking water. Captain Rodgers asked for a smoke-screen to conceal him—he could no longer chase salvos. In instant response, McMorris ordered his destroyers to lay smoke, and turned the fleet with the wind to stay inside the thick cover. On Old Swayback's fantail, sailors manned the smoke-tank valves and the old cruiser vomited a slow-rolling pall. While engineers worked with frantic haste to patch the below-decks hole, the ship lost headway and the enemy closed in hot pursuit, blazing away with full salvos every time an American ship appeared in a hole in the smoke.

Retiring with the east wind, McMorris was getting into even more dangerous water. By 10:45 he was more than five hundred miles from the U.S. Air Base at Adak—but only four hundred miles from Paramushiro, the Japanese Gibraltar in the Kuriles. Japanese bombers might appear momentarily; the American planes, he knew, still had not taken off from Adak.

And Hosogaya was closing the gap by a steady two and one half knots. Another hour—assuming Old Swayback could maintain speed—and McMorris would be in point-blank range of the enemy's big guns.

The Japanese had McMorris on the run; there was no pretending otherwise. Their machinery had him outclassed in every respect; his biggest ship was half-crippled. And now the Japanese had him in a wide pincer, between Hosogaya's fleet and the Kurile air bases. If McMorris kept retreating with the east wind, Hosogaya would soon pin him against a Japanese shore.

McMorris ordered a wide turn to the south. The smoke screen fooled the enemy until a gust dispelled it momentarily; Hosogaya made an immediate sharp turn to port to cut across the arc of McMorris' circle. The Japanese gained distance quickly, shooting all the time.

At 11:03 Old Swayback took a second brutal hit, below the waterline. Exploding aft, it flooded her after gyro room, burst oil tanks, bulged and twisted steel bulkheads, and poured a flood of water and fuel oil into the portside compartments. Icy water rose fast in the bilges; cold congealed the floating oil into heavy clinging sheets of tar. *Salt Lake City* lost headway and stumbled blindly through the smokescreen. Men below decks stood up to their chests in freezing water and tar, braced against the fantastic shapes of steam lines and weird-shadowed machinery, and caulked leaks with their own shirts.

Pumps, working at maximum capacity, were not enough to keep Old Swayback from tipping over, taking a five-degree list. Her engineers fought to stem the flooding; their efforts accidentally dumped salt water into a fuel line.

Old Swayback's batteries never stopped firing, but her speed went down to 20 knots—and then, at 11:50, salt water in the main fuel line flowed into her burners and extinguished them. Steam pressure dropped; the big engines slowed to a halt. *Salt Lake City* drifted a few more yards; and then Captain Rodgers signaled the flagship:

> MY SPEED ZERO.

SHE WAS DEAD IN THE WATER. The Japanese fleet was now at 19,000 yards and closing rapidly. Old Swayback's after batteries kept shooting, but she was down to the last 15 percent of her ammunition.

McMorris edged *Richmond* in close, ready to take off Old Swayback's crew. Both ships were still concealed from the enemy by smoke, but it might be only a matter of seconds.

McMorris asked Rodgers if he wanted to abandon ship. Rodgers refused. There was still a chance to get steam up; he needed time. He asked McMorris to order a diversionary torpedo attack.

McMorris obliged. He detached one destroyer, to make tight circles around the stricken cruiser and lay as much smoke as possible. Then he sent a terse message to Admiral Kinkaid:

> SALT LAKE CITY STOPPED REPEAT STOPPED X DALE STANDING BY X OUR DESTROYERS ATTACKING,

It was a suicide attack, to hold the enemy at bay, to buy time: three tin cans against an enemy task force; 5,000 tons against 50,000. Captain R. S. Riggs, commanding Destroyer Squadron Fourteen, wheeled his three destroyers out of the smokescreen. The fast little ships heeled over in a rushing turn, took formation together and made emergency flank speed.

Riggs signaled TARGETS ARE THE HEAVIES. He had a long way to go, to reach torpedo range—and every foot of the way he was under the enemy's big guns. A single direct hit from an eight-incher could blow an entire destroyer out of the water.

The three high, narrow destroyers roared boldly into the blaze of gunfire. Ten thousand yards out, destroyer *Bailey* took a hit on her starboard side. It cut off her electric power. *Bailey* launched a spread of five torpedoes, lost headway and began to turn aside, smothered by the splashes of enemy near-misses.

At 12:03 the two remaining destroyers, *Monaghan* and *Coghlan,* were within 9,000 yards of *Nachi*—and then the enemy heeled into an abrupt westward turn.

Unaccountably, the enemy was breaking off the action!

Captain Riggs stared at them in astonishment before he reduced speed and flashed a signal to McMorris:

> THE ENEMY IS RETIRING TO THE WEST. SHALL I FOLLOW THEM?

WHY DID THE JAPANESE BREAK OFF the battle?

Admiral Hosogaya did not know *Salt Lake City* had stopped. She was invisible behind smoke. Hosogaya's radio men had monitored American broadcasts that seemed to indicate a bomber strike was on the way from Adak, and then an odd coincidence had convinced Hosogaya that he was actually under air attack: at 12:00, *Salt Lake City* ran out of armor-piercing shells and started shooting high explosives, whose white phosphor splashes looked exactly like bombs being dropped through the overcast. Hosogaya's antiaircraft batteries started shooting into the clouds.

Besides, the fleet's fuel had been reduced drastically by the hours of high-speed maneuvering, and ammunition was low as well (though not nearly as low as the Americans'—a fact Hosogaya didn't possess). And so, believing he was under air attack and had pushed his luck far enough, Hosogaya left the field of battle.

"The Japanese could have sunk *Salt Lake City* with a baseball," Admiral Kinkaid recalls. "She was dead in the water." But McMorris' luck had returned. Hosogaya fled, chased by salvos from all the American ships, including the final shells from Old Swayback's magazines. Captain Riggs turned his destroyers back, profoundly relieved. At 12:12 the enemy had steamed out of range; McMorris ordered the guns to cease fire.

The Battle of the Komandorskis had lasted three and one half hours; it had been the longest continuous gunnery duel in modern naval history.

Salt Lake City's fast-working crew got steam up in her boilers and had her under way at more than 25 knots before the Japanese disappeared over the horizon. McMorris set course for Dutch Harbor, gathering damage and casualty reports. Only seven men had been killed. There were seven hospital cases and thirteen minor injuries.

Admiral Kinkaid signaled:

> YOUR ACTION APPROVED.... YOUR TASK GROUP HAS SCORED SIGNAL VICTORY. WELL DONE!

Hosogaya's casualties were also low: fourteen killed, twenty-seven injured. No ships on either side had been sunk or permanently damaged; but the Battle of the Komandorskis had been without historical parallel—and it had been decisive. After Hosogaya turned back, no further Japanese convoys would reach the Aleutians. Admiral Kinkaid's ridiculous little blockade had achieved complete success: Soc McMorris' victory at the Komandorskis ended Japanese naval supremacy in the North Pacific, and brought the end of the Aleutian Campaign in sight.[2]

2. Admiral Hosogaya's displeased superiors told him he should have sunk *Salt Lake City* and proceeded into the Aleutians. They put him on the beach, took away his command, and sent him into the ignominy of the Reserve. An American officer received a similar tongue-lashing, but kept his command: Major General William O. Butler was blistered by Kinkaid, Buckner, and Hap Arnold because his bombers had not reached the scene until three hours after the fight had ended.

CHAPTER FIFTEEN

"The Hunger Was Maddening..."

THE SUCCESS OF KINKAID'S DARING blockade sealed the fate of Japan's Aleutian garrisons: now it was a matter of when, not whether, the Americans would recapture the western islands.

The Allies had already begun to lay plans to take back the Aleutians and use them as staging bases for a Northern Invasion of Japan.* But in the meantime the Buckner-Kinkaid forces had to secure their advanced bases and work the remaining bugs out of their war machinery.

In the first months of Admiral Kinkaid's command, the North Pacific submarine force healed its wounds, gathered its strength for the final push, and ran routine patrols, but it recorded no memorable adventures—partly because the hideous weather cramped operations, partly because the hard-hitting commander of submarines, Captain Oswald Colclough, had been drafted by Kinkaid as his new Chief of Staff. But if the submariners enjoyed a few months without victory or disaster, the same was not true for the unfortunate mariners of Lieutenant Clinton McKellar's PT-boat division.

Early in January the four torpedo boats had set out from King Cove on a voyage to Dutch Harbor. They plowed through a squall, coated with four inches of ice. Two of the boats collided in the murk; the crash holed one boat in the side and tore away its steering control. All four boats made it to the nearest sheltered harbor—Dora Harbor, on Unimak. Here for nearly a week, during the American invasion of Amchitka, they fought dragging anchors in a howling 80-knot wind. Anchor lines parted; jagged rocks holed PT-27's bottom in three places; PT-28, with McKellar aboard, went aground and sank; PT-22 crashed on a reef and sank.

*See next chapter.

Somehow the dogged young McKellar kept his crews intact. No one was killed. Finally, after six days, cannery tender *Virginia E.* arrived. She broke several towlines but finally pulled both surviving boats free. McKellar, with half the fleet he had started with, reached Dutch Harbor two weeks late.

Two months later McKellar and most of his bleary crewmen finally went back to the States,[1] telling anyone who would listen that it was folly to sail PT-boats in the North Pacific. Yet in March the Navy sent Lieutenant Commander James B. Denny into the Aleutians with a new squadron of Higgins boats. Denny brought them all the way from Florida to Adak under their own power (mainly as a trial run to test the new design). The Higgins torpedo boats, fitted with hot-air heaters, were at least more habitable than McKellar's old 77-footers but they tended to nose down and plow through seas the hard way: Denny remarked, "We made most of our runs at periscope depth."

Denny tried to add McKellar's two surviving boats to his squadron, but the old PTs sprang seams and swamped, had to be towed into port, and were finally shipped back to the States to be rebuilt. Meanwhile Denny endured endless practice maneuvers while he waited for orders that would take him into action.

PILOTS OF THE ELEVENTH AIR FORCE had begun to learn their way around in the Aleutian sky. But the January weather was so bad that only a handful of missions got off the ground; all month, the bombers dropped only 10-1/2 tons of explosives on Kiska and Attu.

On January 18 two Liberators disappeared on a routine flight. A third cracked up, landing on Great Sitkin. A fourth overshot the flare-lit Umnak runway and tangled with two parked P-38s. Later that week two midair collisions in the fog claimed pairs of B-17s and Mitchells. All told, the Air Force lost eleven planes in January—none to enemy action.

In February they managed to outwit the weather often enough to plaster Kiska and Attu with 150 tons of bombs, a total that would have been far higher but for constant crippling failures of bomb-bay rack mechanisms, which froze when caked with corrosion and ice. Nearly half the February missions made impotent runs over Kiska. "Enough to break

1. Son of a Tennessee postmaster, Clinton J. McKellar Jr. was twenty-nine years old when he left the Aleutians. In the course of the war—at Midway, in the Aleutians, and later in the island-hopping campaigns of the Central Pacific—he won the Bronze Star, the Legion of Merit, and seven other medals. Yet in his own summary, the lean, mustached sailor only said, "Spent most of the war in Motor Torpedo Boats in Pacific."

a conscientious bombardier's heart," Wheeler wailed. "Some days the visiting team doesn't even bother to bang away at us. The bombardiers are practically in tears."

One day he wrote despondently:

> Speer made three dry runs over the target, his racks failing him. He picked up several holes in the fuselage and consequently did not attempt a fourth run. All three planes in the flight had rack trouble. It isn't enough that the bombardier has to beat his hips black and blue crawling into the nose of these Baker Two Four Dogs—apparently he's expected to crawl back to the bomb-bay to kick the bombs out with his feet during the run.... [In fact today we] flew over the camp again and bombed by having the radio operator salvo the bombs manually from the catwalk.

Because of their clumsy rack machinery the B-24D Liberators were particularly susceptible to failures. For that and other reasons, pilots and bombardiers regarded the B-24s as "heavies" in every sense of the word, and vied for assignment to the dwindling number of tired B-17 Flying Fortresses that remained in service. Seven of them belonged to the veteran 36th Squadron, until February 13, 1943, when Wheeler wrote:

> On this sad day the 36th flew its B-17Es into combat for the last time. Tomorrow we are to become, by order of Bomber Command, a B-24D outfit. Many an eye was moist as the Big Boeings settled in their revetments for a well-deserved rest. Someone even proposed a mad dash to Paramushiro in our remaining Seventeens—an heroic gesture in the manner of Old Ironsides.

The Forts' last mission was led by Major Robert D. "Pappy" Speer, who now commanded the 36th Squadron. With them flew several noncombatant passengers: Lieutenant John Huston and a professional motion-picture crew, cameras grinding.

Hollywood had come to the Aleutians. The past August, Colonel Darryl F. Zanuck and John Huston had flown to Umnak under military orders. Huston, colorful director of *The Maltese Falcon* and other cinema classics, had joined the Signal Corps and picked the toughest theater of the war for his first combat documentary. To make the film, he and his cameramen spent six months at Umnak and Adak, riding the attack bombers on fifteen combat missions. (Huston's stunning, stark forty-seven-minute Technicolor film, narrated by Walter Huston, was titled *Report from the Aleutians*. It was not released by military censors until the Campaign was over in August 1943. The first of the War Department's series of documentary feature films, it splendidly caught the texture of the Aleutian war.)[2*]

At Adak the aircrews gave their Fortresses friendly handpats before they chinned themselves into the hatches. Dressed in heavy coveralls beneath their electric flying suits, the pilots moved, hunched over, into the austere cockpits. Engines belched white smoke. The five B-17s, one million dollars worth of flying machines,[3] roared down the runway with cries of power and lifted, steeply banking.

At military speed, 165 miles per hour, it was less than two hours from Adak to Kiska, barring headwinds. The wind was 20 knots, with gusts; fog hung almost down to the water. Speer stayed on the deck. The huge winged machines beat thunder across the water while the thin needles of outside-temperature gauges stood just above freezing. Pilots judged wind direction and speed by watching ocean crests, and made course corrections swiftly. Every few minutes they reset their altimeters to compensate for strange variations in sea-level atmospheric pressure.

They reached the enemy; Wheeler wrote:

> Weather: broken cumulus from 2,000 feet to 7,500 feet. The attack was made at 7,000 feet from the volcano... [It] apparently confused the North Head Pinochle and Athletic Association, for the AA fire indicated that an attack from [the opposite direction] had been expected.

Six Rufes came up to intercept. They hung just outside the flak and waited for the bombers to come out. Speer led the flight across the main camp; the bombers behind him dumped more than 40,000 pounds of explosives and scored several hits. But Speer's racks failed.

He made a 360-degree turn past the volcano and made another bomb run. Altogether, Wheeler wrote, "Speer made three runs over the target. Stinson, though he had dropped his bombs on the first run, stayed with

---

2. *1995 ADDENDUM: In the 1960s when The Thousand-Mile War was written, I had a difficult time tracking down a Technicolor print of John Huston's movie. Today the documentary is readily available on videotape.

3. It is of rueful interest to compare the $200,000 cost of a B-17 Flying Fortress, the greatest plane of its era, with the price of 1969's fragile two-man, 1,650-mph warplane, the F-111A: six million dollars each.

Speer during the subsequent trips through the AA fire." Huston's cameras ground away steadily. Escorting fighters kept the Rufes at bay; Speer's bombardier kicked the bombs out one at a time while Speer exchanged taunts with a Japanese radio operator who spoke English with a Harvard accent.

Flak ripped up a B-25 ahead of Speer (it crashed on the way home) but the B-17s came through their last mission without losses. At Adak, bundled-up ground crews played desultory baseball on the air field, waiting for the mission to come home. When they heard the first distant drone they tensed up, the game forgotten, awaiting the count of returning planes.

The Forts rumbled down and stopped; several men wept. To the airmen, the dowager Fortress was a craft that would bring them home—they accorded it an anthropomorphic will to survive that they found in no other airplane. Shattered and shredded, gutted and smashed, the B-17 could be depended on to claw the air, struggle, heave, gasp, and remain aloft.

For the 36th Squadron, it was the end of an era.[4]

"WHEN I FIRST ARRIVED IN KODIAK," Admiral Kinkaid recalls, "I took a walk to look the place over, walked up through the town, and decided I didn't want to do it again."

Kodiak was the Navy's Alaskan headquarters. All the other major commands had their official seats elsewhere, mainly in Anchorage. Practical needs had gradually shifted their operations, *de facto,* to the Navy's Alaska Sector Building at the Kodiak base. General Buckner and Admiral John W. Reeves had offices on the ground floor; General Butler and Admiral Kinkaid were on the second floor. ("Occasionally from my office window," Kinkaid recalls, "I'd see a bear on the side of the hill.")

The rivalry between Buckner and Admiral Theobald in 1942 had affected all joint operations, often bringing the American effort close to paralysis. Now that Theobald was gone, CINCPAC at last reached his goal of a "command relationship based on mutual cooperation." Buckner found that the new admiral shared his view of ends and means.

From the moment of Kinkaid's arrival, neither commander was to make a single important decision without first consulting the other. It made for a tight relationship with almost awesome "mutual cooperation"

4. After the 36th Squadron switched to B-24s, two other squadrons retained a handful of B-17s. The old Fortresses flew combat, in the Aleutians and later from Aleutian bases against the Kuriles, right up to the end of the war in 1945.

which far exceeded Admiral Nimitz's wildest hopes. It remained to be seen, however, whether Buckner or Kinkaid would benefit from the absence of critical opponents with rank high enough to force effective examination of their hip-shooting schemes.

The first major joint decision was a sensible one: Buckner and Kinkaid ordered Army, Navy, and Air Force to move their headquarters out to Adak, a thousand miles nearer the enemy. By late March, on the eve of the Battle of the Komandorskis, the advance was completed. Kinkaid, Buckner, Butler, and Gehres all moved into quarters within a few yards of one another on an Adak hillside. The flag officers' mess set a single two plate table for Buckner and Kinkaid. At the same time, a fusillade of promotions came through from Washington—Buckner to lieutenant general, Kinkaid to vice admiral, Butler to major general, Gehres to commodore.[5]

For the first time, the Aleutian command was located in the Aleutians. The move soon brought new comforts to Adak's inhabitants; Billy Wheeler wrote:

> Adak is practically a garrison post at this writing, no longer the quagmire of which I wrote so piteously September 18. The entire Bomber Command has now moved from the haunts of pleasure and the marts of sin at Elmendorf to this barren and desolate island. We're now living comfortably in Quonset huts and bathing daily in the luxurious Navy shower located next to Major General Butler's quarters. The food has improved with the transfer of mess personnel from Elmendorf. Somewhat outdated Grade B films are screened nightly in four or five different theaters to which we have access. The new Post PX even peddled Cokes recently—we all sweated out a Coca-Cola line a block long. Cultural note: the installation of electric lights in our snug new latrine has materially strengthened our reading habits.

Centralization of the major headquarters at Adak's forward field base accented the differences among the various eccentrics in flag country.

5. Periodically the U.S. Navy reinstates the rank of commodore. It is equivalent to "Rear Admiral of the Lower Half." The one-star rank parallels the Army's brigadier general. Rear admiral is equivalent to major general; vice admiral is equivalent to lieutenant general, the three-star rank. Two Aleutian Campaign veterans ultimately reached the rank of four-star admiral—Kinkaid and James S. Russell. No Army or Air Force officer from the campaign achieved the four stars of a general, although it seems likely Buckner would have, had he survived the Okinawa campaign in 1945.

At close range, both Kinkaid and Buckner found General Butler even harder to get along with than before; Butler appeared placid and stuffy alongside the other officers, and soon had Kinkaid wondering aloud about his qualifications for leadership. Brigadier General Norman D. Sillin, then head of Butler's Fighter Command, recalls, "Bruce Butler...was a former lighter-than-air pilot and had little command experience in tactical units," and several subordinate air commanders found their problems doubled now that Butler was up front, personally running the show. Several times flight leaders had to scrub missions which Butler had conceived, when they discovered that the ordered mission would have left their planes out of fuel hundreds of miles from base.

There was nothing placid or slow about Navy Air's tough Commodore Gehres, but he also stimulated Kinkaid's anxiety. Once Gehres mistook a group of civilian engineers for military personnel, and put them on report for being out of uniform. He and his staff enjoyed a large dinner table with amenities like plug-in telephones and a ready supply of brandy. When Gehres angrily called Captain Oswald Colclough at Amchitka to find out why his PBY pilots weren't flying on schedule, Colclough looked out at the 100-knot williwaw and answered, "Nothing around here flying but a few Quonset huts."

But the greatest trouble was caused by an officer who was not even present—Colonel William O. Eareckson.

Eareckson had gone to San Diego on temporary assignment, but he had left the imprint of his personality stamped so firmly on his men that they could not but resent the man who took his place as chief of Bomber Command. That resentment, in this case, bordered on hatred, because the new man was Eareckson's direct antithesis.

Colonel Earl H. DeFord had an impossible act to follow. Eareckson could be succeeded, but never replaced. It didn't matter that the handsome fifty-three-year-old DeFord had a long and unimpeachable record as a pilot and group commander, or that like Eareckson he had served with distinction in the Infantry in the First World War.

Wheeler wrote coolly, "This was the day of the party. Col. DeFord, our new Bomber Command C.O., gave a party. Col. DeFord believes in friendly get-togethers among the officers of his command."

With his strong character and precise habits, DeFord soon became known as the "Mayor of Rat Island."[6] Courteous but distant, he insisted

6. The Aleutians are grouped into several sub-categories—the Sanaks, Krenitzins, Foxes, Shumagins, Andreanofs, Rats, and Nears. Rat Island, specifically, is a tiny islet midway between Amchitka and Kiska, recognized by its 1,319-foot volcano. The epithet "Mayor of

on his exact prerogatives, which included a table at the front of the air-officers' mess where his staff cook laid a tablecloth and served steaks and other meals unavailable to the junior officers who had to walk past on their way to and from dinner. Frederick Ramputi recalls, "Early in 1943, DeFord selected me to command the 21st Bomber Squadron and that automatically made me a member of the poker games. DeFord liked to play poker and I was a contributor."

Conscientious, cautious and determined, DeFord was neither spitfire nor martinet; but his only defense against the Eareckson mystique was to assert himself rigidly. Inevitably, he soon developed an abiding dislike for Eareckson, a man he had never met. (He still maintains, "Colonel Eareckson was, in my opinion, more reckless than efficient.") He soon came to regard any "Eareckson idea" as automatically suspect; Ramputi recalls, "I had to sell DeFord on our radar bombing tactics, and until we had accurate photographic proof of our success, he wasn't easy to sell."

DeFord believed it was his job to coordinate plans, devise missions, give orders, handle disciplinary and administrative problems, and be available at headquarters at all times. Consequently he seldom took to the air, particularly in his early weeks when he was unfamiliar with the theater. When he did fly missions, he usually rode as "command pilot"—a passenger-observer function designed for officers who didn't want to push another pilot off his plane, or who wanted to get airtime for flight pay, or who (like DeFord) were candid enough to admit they were not highly schooled in the special skills needed to fly combat in such a new, violently strange theater.

Fresh from the States and unaccustomed to Aleutian warfare, DeFord made natural mistakes which in other circumstances might have been understood and forgiven. Lucian Wernick recalls:

> DeFord rode along on my plane once. We were five miles short of Kiska and he said, "Circle here. I want to observe the action when they go over." I just looked at him—I had bombs in the airplane. He said. "Keep circling, I want to watch." So we circled. We couldn't see anything going on at all, of course.

It was an error, and DeFord did not make it again, but it was added to the grudge list against him. A song about him, "The Man Behind the Armor-Plated Desk," made the rounds, and Colonel Lawrence Reineke

---

Rat Island" was applied to DeFord after the incident when DeFord circled the island while his air group went in to attack Kiska.

recalls, "We all got drunk one night and sang the song to DeFord. He was less than pleased."

LADD FIELD (FAIRBANKS) AND ELMENDORF Air Base (Anchorage) were "the country clubs," with coffee breaks, lawns, bars, sports, clubs, women, and real beds. From there the quality of life deteriorated in geometric ratio to the westward distance.

Kodiak was a permanent base, substantial and comfortable, though it was common for pilots to be told to circle the field before landing while ground crews chased bears off the runways.

Dutch Harbor was more primitive, and badly overcrowded: it was the funnel through which supplies staged into the chain.

At Umnak, where westward advances had reduced the population, comforts were reasonable by Aleutian standards. But the war had bypassed the former front-line air base, and supplies did not arrive often enough to prevent men from eating Spam three times a day, sometimes for weeks on end.

At Atka—"Atkatraz"—the Army had built a dugout Quonset village for antiaircraft crews who guarded the Navy's PBY base. There were magazines and laundry service, but there was virtually nothing to do.

Adak had become the center of frenzy. The harbor teemed with Liberty ships manned by bearded merchant sailors. Ravens croaked above construction sites, where Engineer Colonel Carlin Whitesell had invented a method of floating roads on top of 20-foot-deep tundra. Originally an air base, Adak had assumed a naval flavor—the Air Force had moved on to Amchitka. Office walls in Adak's headquarters were hung with posters that warned against imperfect camouflage and venereal disease, with the official portraits of FDR and several admirals and generals, and with spectacular calendar nudes. (The latter were taken down for inspections.)

Amchitka, farthest west, was the end of the line. The base owned one frayed nudie magazine. Men slept in sleeping bags on the mud floors of their tents, and ate C-rations on their feet. Sergeant George R. McBride wrote:

> It was the usual sight to see several pairs of shoes atop the oil stove: we changed our shoes about every fifteen minutes, to keep our feet from numbing.
>
> I had to walk about a mile across the open tundra to get to my weather station...with that wind, a parka was little better than a

> T-shirt. In the station, with oil stoves going, there was a 100-degree difference in temperature between floor and ceiling.
>
> At the outside latrine, it was the usual procedure to remove gloves, wipe, and get the gloves on as fast as possible to avoid frostbite. Our diet was constant—soggy corn-willy, Vienna sausage, coffee. Our so-called pancakes were popularly referred to as manhole covers. How is it possible to describe the misery of that mess hall? The hunger was maddening....

All along the chain, supply was still the outstanding problem. The modest increase in shipping, provided by the besieged War Department, had not kept pace with the Aleutian population boom. A year ago there had been 5,000 people on the islands; by early 1943 there were nearly 40,000. The bottleneck was so severe that the States could hardly keep Buckner's ground forces supplied with ten rounds of ammunition per weapon. Food shipments, aside from a handful of high-ranking officers' allotments, were limited to concentrated rations, canned vegetables, and occasional shiploads of foul-smelling mutton from New Zealand. Mail came by slow ship—packages marked "Do not open until Christmas" arrived in April—and some men hadn't been paid in six months. (A planeload of fertilizer reached Adak, ordered by a high Navy officer whose flower garden had refused to bloom; an Army sergeant observed, "The war must be over. We're getting horse manure by air mail.")

Inevitably, the shortage lifted ingenuity to new heights. Dr. Nathan Davis recalls:

> I had two crafty soldiers in my outfit. No matter what we wantd—tractors, paint, lumber—they could get it. I never asked them where it came from. But the coin had two sides. Half the supplies intended for us got sidetracked and we never saw the stuff. It was a constant fight for supplies. And then of course there were snafus—once I received an enormous shipment of obstetric forceps, and another time we received cases of antisnake venom; there were no pregnant women, babies, or snakes within a thousand miles.

And, of course, Dutch Harbor had a pair of SeaBee Supply noncoms named Ketchum and Cheatham.

THE MAIN ENTERTAINMENTS WERE RADIOS, scratchy phonograph records (*The Warsaw Concerto* and *Don't Sit Under the Apple Tree With Anyone Else But Me* were popular), and movies (*The Man Who Came to Dinner, The Fighting SeaBees, Destry Rides Again,* and newsreels of the bombing of Dutch Harbor). For six months soldiers on Adak had crowded around John Huston's film crews. A former movie star, SeaBee Lieutenant Commander George O'Brien moonlighted from his regular duties as Squeaky Anderson's assistant to entertain Adak troops. And several Hollywood personalities had trekked into the Aleutians to amuse the inmates: Joe E. Brown, Al Jolson, Bob Hope, Edgar Bergen, Errol Flynn, Marjorie Reynolds, Olivia de Havilland, Jerry Colonna, Ingrid Bergman, and singer Frances Langford, who was reputedly the first white woman ever to set foot on Umnak (where she had to wash her lingerie in a soldier's steel helmet).*

The actor troupes found their audiences unique. They had volunteered to divert "our fighting boys overseas," but these troops were suffering not from combat fatigue but from pathological boredom. Except for a handful of flying crews and pale bearded submariners, the thousands of men were in no real danger of attack and had no fighting to do. (The 203rd Anti-Aircraft Regiment, a Missouri National Guard outfit, had spent a year in the theater and would be there another two years, and would never fire a shot in combat.)

They grasped at every distraction. Hundreds participated in the Aleutian bone-hunt boom when a handful of Stateside archaeologists came to comb bulldozed areas on Adak and Amchitka for relics of prehistoric Aleut villages, hoping to unearth treasures quickly in case the Japanese came back and started bombing. Photography became a widespread hobby. One officer maintained his sanity for a year by compiling an atlas of all the plants and flowers on Amchitka (it is now in a Chicago museum). But that sort of singleminded ingenuity was rare. Most men regarded their plight as unjust penal servitude; they became petty and cranky, turned inward to feed on their own acids, and retired from reality. They asked one another what day it was—sometimes what month.

Alcohol was scarce and obtaining it became an obsession. Wheeler wrote, "A rumor filtered through that beer was to be had at Atka.

---

*1995 ADDENDUM: In 1994, Lt. Col. Royal A. Sorenson (USAF Ret), who flew C-47 transports during the war, wrote to the newsletter of the 11th Air Force Association: "Aside from the bad weather, the cold and long hours of flying, we had some good times. I flew Bob Hope, Frances Langford, Jerry Colonna, Margie Reynolds and Joe E. Brown down the islands to entertain the troops."

We raised two hundred dollars and I flew down to investigate. I returned sadly empty-handed." SeaBees liberated twenty-five cases of beer from a freighter in Dutch Harbor. Real bottled whisky could be had for about $50 a fifth, but drinkers accepted almost any substitute—"Sneaky Pete" cocktails of apple juice and pure grain alcohol, "Torpedo Juice," and one other desperate imitation: the Adak Post Exchange had to stop selling shaving lotion because men were drinking it.

Captain Frank L. Orth wrote, in the daily Operations Report of the 11th Fighter Squadron at Adak:

> Five pilots got back from Elmendorf after a harrowing rest leave. One man was noticed playing ping pong with himself. On this day of pink elephants the Lord favored us with unfavorable flying weather, while His medical disciple spread the gospel with bromo and aspirin. Blessed are the meek.

Men pointed out, with dismal accuracy, that there was a woman behind every tree in the Aleutians. The only human females on view were the distaff sailors on Russian ships which put into Aleutian harbors now and then on Lend-Lease runs. Soldiers whose huts were wallpapered with thousands of Hollywood pinups found the Russian ladies unsatisfactory; Dr. Walter Feinstein recalls, "When I left the ship I could readily understand why Leningrad, Stalingrad and Moscow could never be taken [by the Germans]."

To the theater commanders, the problem was one of "morale" and it had to be met with recreation programs, better housing and food, and organized athletic competitions. But baseball games only added to frustration in the wind and mud, and a half-buried Quonset hut on Umnak or Adak was no one's preference in luxury living. The real problem was medical, and headquarters could do nothing about that, short of shipping the men home.

Every morning, Air Force crews trudged to briefings. Wound up, they had to wind back down, day after day while fog sat implacably on their runways. They were like condemned men receiving daily twenty-four-hour stays of execution. After a while, reprieves lost all quality of relief. Crews ran out of defenses; tension pushed them toward madness.

Malingering and irritability led to deliberate infringements of regulations by flying crews who wanted to get grounded. In the jargon of medical reports, they "rejected their environment" by inventing illnesses which soon became real. Lingering head colds were so tenacious they were called "Aleutian malaria." Self-inflicted wounds, anemia, ear infections and various forms of psychosomatic pain and withdrawal took scores of men out of the lists. The number of suicides increased each month. There were reports of widespread homosexuality.[7*] Men lost initiative, sleep, and supper; they became argumentative, inattentive, or apathetic. Refusing to work, they sat quietly for hours and did not even read their mail. They neglected their appearance, even basic hygiene. The Surgeon General's reports underscored a unique Aleutian syndrome—"group depression." Men wouldn't even joke about sex. Pilots overshot fields on clear days; men repeated themselves endlessly; when the sun shone for even a few minutes, crowds became ecstatic. Dr. Benjamin Davis recalls:

> Meeting men for the first time, I could pick out the ones who'd been six months or more on the chain. They looked through things. They had a peculiar stare, you couldn't mistake it. We called it the Aleutian stare. Once I was in a plane with six GIs in straitjackets, and they all had it, the Aleutian stare. They'd been on those islands too long.

AFTER ALMOST A YEAR'S CAMPAIGNING, the basic strategic picture hadn't changed: the Japanese still had Kiska and Attu. For the American servicemen in the Aleutians it would have been a great help to morale to know what was going to happen next. But high command was not in the habit of revealing its plans to the ordinary footsoldier; and unlike the British Tommy or Russian peasant, the American GI did not have an overwhelming sense of purpose to keep him going during the bleak months of bad weather and inactivity. Visiting War Department propagandists like Major Kermit Roosevelt tried to convince them that "Japs are Beasts," but none of the dogfaces had even seen a single Japanese soldier, and few expected they ever would. They remained

---

7. Homosexual behavior in the Aleutians was a topic so sensitive that even the Surgeon General's reports skirted it gingerly with euphemisms and apologies. It was a major problem. Gore Vidal's hit Broadway play of presidential politics, The Best Man, throws as much light on the subject as any official work; the play's Joe Cantwell, a presidential candidate, is threatened with a political smear based on his reputed "degeneracy" in connection with a wholesale roundup of "deviates" in the Aleutians in 1943.

*1995 ADDENDUM: In the 1940s, gay behavior hardly ever was mentioned, let alone discussed. Reports tended not to be made at all, and those that did make their way above local-unit levels tended to be purged from the official record. Their existence has been challenged and frequently denied, but was confirmed for me in a conversation a few years ago at the Santa Barbara Writers' Conference with Gore Vidal, who served in the Aleutians in an Army transport ship.

unconvinced that their imprisonment on worthless Aleutian real estate did any good; they couldn't see how their noncombatant presence helped the war effort at all. They believed the bosses in Washington had no interest in prosecuting the Aleutian war; they inhabited, as correspondent Corey Ford put it, "Our Forgotten Front."

Like any entrenched human institution, war creates a vested interest in its own perpetuation. The United States had almost 200,000 troops in the Alaska-Aleutian theater, and staff officers on every level argued seriously that the Allies must press on in the Aleutians, to protect those men's morale and give them a reason for being where they were.

It was a specious argument; it was advanced by officers who felt the Campaign's real strategic value had run down and stopped: the enemy was incapable of any real threat in the North Pacific, and Alaskan staff officers knew of no immediate plans for an Allied offensive toward northern Japan.

Neither Kinkaid nor Buckner wanted to fight just for the sake of the troops' morale; nevertheless, they did want to fight: they knew things their staff officers didn't know.

By January 1943, the Japanese Navy had stopped and searched a hundred Soviet ships in the North Pacific. Japanese submarines, presumably by mistake, had sunk three Russian cargo ships. Washington pointed out that Moscow could repay American aid and Lend-Lease help by joining the war against Japan, especially since Japan was making war on Russia anyway. But Stalin saw no profit in opening a new battle front. Gratitude was seldom a guiding principle of international relations.

As long as Russia maintained neutrality in the Pacific, it was unlikely the Allies could invade Japan from the north. Yet the western Allies still hoped to persuade Stalin to get into the war. Acting on these thin hopes, the United States had supported Admiral Kinkaid's successful campaign to isolate the enemy on his Aleutian bases. The next step was to clear the enemy out of the Aleutians so that, just in case Stalin should change his mind, the chain could be used as a staging route into Siberia and the Kuriles.

CHAPTER
SIXTEEN

Operation Landcrab

IN JANUARY 1943, AS SOON as he had taken stock of the Aleutian situation, Admiral Kinkaid submitted to CINCPAC and the Western Defense Command a general plan to invade Kiska with amphibious forces. Nimitz and DeWitt approved the plan and sent it upstairs.

A copy went to the Allied Combined Chiefs of Staff, who met with President Roosevelt and Prime Minister Churchill at Casablanca the third week in January. The Combined Chiefs accepted Kinkaid's proposal, and directed the Joint Chiefs in Washington to execute the operation.

The Joint Chiefs in turn asked San Francisco's General John L. DeWitt to recommend forces and methods. DeWitt's first thought was to use the Army troops already in Alaska—Buckner had the regulars of the 4th Infantry Regiment and a variety of activated National Guard units. But the troops were scattered over hundreds of thousands of square miles; the largest single concentration of combat infantry was at Adak, numbering less than 3,000 soldiers. Morale was poor, the troops were not trained in amphibious operations, and it would be impossible to strip Alaska's outposts of enough men to make up a full combat division—the smallest force capable of doing the job.

Buckner regretted that he could not furnish enough forces for the job—the Campaign had been his from the first—but he had to agree with DeWitt that it would be better to bring in a trained combat division from outside.

To the War Department, DeWitt recommended the 35th Infantry Division, commanded by Major General Charles H. Corlett, with Brigadier General Eugene M. Landrum as assistant commander. Both generals had served in the Aleutians—Landrum had commanded the occupation of Adak last fall.

The War Department worked in mysterious ways its blunders to perform. It rejected DeWitt's advice, and instead assigned the 7th Motorized Division to the job. Since the beginning of the war, the "Hourglass Division" had been training in the California desert as a mechanized division for use against Rommel in North Africa. Since neither tanks, trucks, nor armored tactics would be of the slightest use in the Aleutians, both DeWitt and Simon Buckner protested vehemently. Their protests were turned aside; Rommel was no longer a threat, so the War Department did not need the 7th Division in Africa. Besides, the 7th was "in a more advanced state of readiness and training" than the 35th Division (the one DeWitt had asked for). When DeWitt and Buckner protested again, the War Department told them, in essence, to be glad they could get any division—the cries for manpower clamored on every front. If DeWitt refused to accept the 7th Division then he would get no division at all.

The Hourglass Division had a tough combat record dating back to 1918, when it had lost 1,700 men in France. Between wars it had languished, a tiny cadre of regulars. In 1941 it had reformed by calling up National Guard units from southwestern states. Its men were Mexican-Americans, Utah Mormons, New Mexico and Arizona Indians, and Texas cowboys. Its commander, Major General Albert E. Brown, was a handsome gray-haired fifty-three-year-old South Carolinian whose last combat action had been the Meuse-Argonne offensive in 1918, where he had served as an infantry major.

American soldiers had made amphibious landings in North Africa, and the U.S. Marines had landed on Guadalcanal, but the Army had no experience with amphibious fighting on islands, let alone Aleutian islands. To make over a desert-warfare tank division into an Arctic infantry amphib-force promised to be a maddening exercise in futility. What made it even more lunatic was the War Department's timetable, which called for invasion of Kiska in the spring—three months away.

Nimitz, Kinkaid, and Buckner helped as much as they could, by sending experienced advisers. CINCPAC supplied Commander James S. Russell and an amphibious assault specialist, a rock-hard U.S. Marine who would conduct landing and beachhead exercises—Major General Holland M. "Howlin' Mad" Smith, former commander of the First Marine Division. Admiral Kinkaid supplied Captain Colclough and other valued members of his staff. General Buckner sent four of his best colonels—Castner, Eareckson, Alexander, and Carl Jones.

The Joint Alaskan Staff went to San Diego, where the Kiska push would be mapped out under the over-all command of Vice Admiral Francis W. "Skinny" Rockwell, fifty-six, a lanky sailor with blond wavy hair who had been the senior naval officer evacuated from the Philippines with MacArthur. Castner, Eareckson and the others found quarters at the U.S. Grant Hotel in San Diego and went right to work in Rockwell's headquarters on the Broadway Pier.

It was hard work with long hours. Colonel William Alexander recalls:

> I pointed out that none of the needs of man (fuel, food, water) were available [on Attu and Kiska] and therefore we had an unusual set of conditions to deal with, not to mention the cold temperatures and the muskeg—muskeg that quakes, shivers, and gives way under the weight of a man, let alone wheeled vehicles. I emphasized the utter futility of trying to conduct an operation along conventional lines.
>
> Two factors were important: fire support and supply. Artillery, I assumed, had to be of sufficient caliber to reach the high peaks from the beaches on which it was landed—moving it forward would be ridiculous because of the muskeg. The 105-mm howitzer filled these requirements but it took me quite a bit of desk pounding to convince the artillery officers that the 75-mm pack howitzer, which they offered, was as good as no artillery at all....
>
> As for supply, I kept in mind that an infantryman equipped for combat could, with luck, make 1-1/2 miles an hour, unopposed, over terrain of that sort. And for every soldier engaged in combat there must be two to carry supplies—one going and one coming from the front line. We could not do it with wheels or tracks, so we would have to do it with manpower, the quantity of which would be determined by the distance from the beach to the front lines.
>
> Alexander's was excellent advice. Unhappily a good part of it was soon to be rejected or ignored.

THE BATTLE OF GUADALCANAL STILL raged, wicked and bloody; Allied troops rolled across North Africa; the Allies were preparing to invade Sicily and the Solomon Islands. All these operations required huge numbers of men, supplies, and particularly ships. When the Navy told Admiral Rockwell what ships would be available to him for the Kiska invasion, he was forced to conclude there were not enough of them to guarantee the success of the attack.

At the end of February, Admiral Kinkaid made a flying visit to California, where he suggested to General DeWitt that the available shipping strength would still be enough if they hit Attu instead of Kiska. Kinkaid's appraisal stated, "Japanese force on Attu estimated to be 500.... Estimate one reinforced infantry regiment...could effect landing and occupation of Attu."

Attu was more than 200 miles beyond Kiska. By bypassing Kiska and going for Attu, Kinkaid hoped to leave Kiska high and dry, surrounded by American forces; the enemy might even evacuate Kiska without a fight, once it was cut off.[1]

The unprecedented leapfrog plan appeared sound. CINCPAC and the JCS approved it, and the 10,000-man 7th Division was broken up into regimental combat teams for training at Fort Ord and San Diego.

Attu was code-named Jackboot, the operation Landcrab. The battle plans drawn up at San Diego were based on Kinkaid's inaccurately low estimate of Attu's strength, but other factors compensated for that: Kinkaid overestimated Kiska's strength (he believed the Japanese had 9,600 troops there when in fact they had 6,000), and pointed out that Kiska might reinforce Attu by sea within twenty-four hours of the American landings. Also, enemy planes from Kiska and Paramushiro might try to obstruct the invasion, and it would take only a day or two for the Japanese to get aircraft carriers in strike position from Paramushiro.

Still, Kinkaid stuck to the belief that a single regimental combat team could handle the job. He convinced General DeWitt, who espoused the same idea at a top-level conference at San Diego on April 1. DeWitt, Admiral Rockwell, Simon Buckner, 7th Division's General Brown and various staff officers gathered there to work out the final plans for the invasion of Attu; CINCPAC, informed that the Aleutian season of worst fog would set in by June, had assigned a target well in advance of that. D-day was to be May 7—five weeks hence.

The San Diego conference quickly deteriorated into a series of disruptive arguments which several times threatened to scuttle the whole operation, and finally left it half-crippled by dissent. DeWitt said Japanese strength on Attu was so slight that a regiment could take Attu in three days flat. General Brown retorted that the terrain alone would keep his men from crossing the island in less than a week, even without opposition. ("It is my opinion," Brown recalls, "that General DeWitt

1. Admiral Kinkaid's idea to go for the more distant Attu, while bypassing the fortress of Kiska, set a precedent that led to the eminently successful leapfrogging campaign in the Solomons and the western Pacific.

sold a reluctant War Department on this operation by assurance of a quick victory.")

DeWitt stuck to his guns, and privately told both Kinkaid and Buckner that he was not happy with the choice of Brown as commander of the infantry force. DeWitt did not like Brown's pessimism. Arguing that the commanding general ought to be intimate with Aleutian conditions, DeWitt pressed to have Brown relieved so that an Alaskan general (Landrum) could take command.

But the War Department insisted it could not arbitrarily relieve General Brown of command of his own division. DeWitt then recommended that Brown at least employ Landrum as his second-in-command. But Brown chose Brigadier General Archibald V. Arnold, a 7th Division artilleryman.

Stung by the rebuff, DeWitt made no bones of his displeasure. He kept it no secret from Kinkaid and Buckner. Kinkaid had never met Brown; Buckner had met him once, at this present conference. Influenced by DeWitt, both Alaskans turned cool toward Brown.

The incident strained relations between Brown's officers and the visiting Alaskan advisers; as a result, warnings from Eareckson and the other "outsiders" about Aleutian terrain and climate were accepted with reservations and suspicion. Colonel Castner, the Alaska Scout, urged Brown to make a personal reconnaissance of the western Aleutians. Brown did not go. Colonel Alexander, of Buckner's staff, pointed out that Navy, Army and Air had four different sets of map coordinates; but the confusion was not corrected. Colonel Eareckson pointed out that in his experience, Japanese airplanes would offer little if any resistance, and in view of the shortage of shipping, flak defenses could safely be limited to naval ships' batteries; yet a 90-mm antiaircraft regiment was assigned to the overburdened force. Lieutenant Colonel Carl Jones of the Alaska staff was the only visitor whose recommendations were acted upon; but Jones had never been west of Kodiak, where the ground was firm and the climate far drier than in the Aleutians. The clothing and equipment he recommended would not have been adequate in the Aleutians even in midsummer. Unhappily, the 7th Division requisitioned its clothing and boots on the basis of such misleading advice.

The bickering went on. Buckner said his troops had been a long time in Alaska; their morale, already low, would be destroyed if they were not included. He hoped General Brown would find an opportunity to use the Alaskan troops. (And, he added, "You'll need them. The Infantry will have to go in there with corkscrews to dig out the Japanese.")

But Admiral Rockwell's limited shipping capacity was already strained. There was no room for more troops. DeWitt snapped that he would assign at least one of Buckner's battalions, regardless of what Rockwell had to say about the lack of ships. DeWitt made good his argument by chartering the commercial ship *Perida* to carry Buckner's soldiers into the battle.

Rockwell complained he couldn't land the extra soldiers quickly enough to protect them if the enemy resisted—the beaches would be too overcrowded. DeWitt refused to budge; Rockwell threatened to cancel the whole operation. But Admiral Kinkaid (who was in fact his junior) superseded Rockwell in the command structure, and Kinkaid ordered him to go ahead with the operation as planned.

Then General Brown cut in. He had a close-knit division, its officers and men accustomed to working together; he said the addition of strangers would disrupt the well-fitted machinery.

Finally they reached a compromise. Buckner would provide logistical support, and his 4th Infantry Regiment would be held in combat-ready reserve at Adak, prepared to ship out and hit Attu on less than twenty-four hours' notice.

The parties reached a *modus vivendi,* but their differences did not augur well for an easy success at Attu. The problems became more acute when Kinkaid's intelligence staff, studying Air Force recon photos, submitted a revised estimate of Japanese strength on Attu—up from 500 to 1,600. Aerial photos showed few big guns, but photography was uncertain in the foggy Aleutians and no one could promise that the enemy didn't have guns hidden in tunnels and caves overlooking the beaches.

The new estimates put Admiral Rockwell in a bind. He did not think 2,500 Americans could defeat 1,600 Japanese dug in on their own ground; it was axiomatic that an invasion force had to be overwhelmingly stronger than the defending force. Yet the operation had been ordered by the Combined Chiefs, the JCS, CINCPAC, Kinkaid's NORPACFOR, and DeWitt's WDC. Rockwell could not cancel it. On April 18, with just nineteen days left to D-day, he decided to commit the entire 7th Division and its reinforcements to Operation Landcrab—10,000 men in all. He would find shipping for them somewhere.

THE COMMANDERS' DISPUTES WERE AGGRAVATED by several handicaps. One was geography—Rockwell was in San Diego while Brown's headquarters was more than four hundred miles distant at Fort Ord.

A second was supply: it was up to DeWitt to furnish the 7th Division with whatever it needed, but the San Francisco G-4 depot was woefully unequipped for the job. The Army's winter equipment had been concentrated in England and Africa for the impending Italian campaign; no one had expected to need cold-weather gear in the Pacific, where Guadalcanal had established a tropical stereotype. With D-day Attu only weeks away, there was no time to order special gear manufactured, or have it shipped back from England. Thus, even when the Californians got good advice from the Alaskans, they could not act on it; items like waterproof "shoepac" boots simply were not to be had.

A third handicap was the lack of time for training; a fourth was topography: under Brown and General "Howlin' Mad" Smith, the division piled out of landing craft in the surf and charged up and down the beaches of Monterey Bay and San Diego's San Clemente Island, but the California coast had almost nothing in common with Attu, and there was no way to simulate Aleutian terrain, or even explain it to anyone who had not actually walked on muskeg.

These problems were tackled just as Rockwell had tackled the shipping problem when it became necessary to commit the full division: arguments and "It can't be done" fell by the wayside in the face of necessity. Kinkaid, faced with constant objections to one proposal after another, finally snapped, "Do it—ask me how later." And in that manner, most of what was needed was obtained. They would do without the rest.

Meanwhile the combined staff had worked out half a dozen possible plans for the actual landings. The final choice would be made just before D-day after the latest intelligence photos had been studied. Most of the alternate plans called for one or two massed landings on northeastern beaches, with a smaller landing on the opposite side of the island, to be executed by a small crack team of combat specialists who would come up behind the Japanese. Success might hinge on this small team, for its orders were to keep the Japanese from falling back into the mountains where they might hold out for weeks or months.

To lead this "Provisional Scout Battalion," General Brown tapped one of his regular battalion commanders, Captain William H. Willoughby, thirty-four, an athletic six-foot California dairy farmer who had been Brown's ace troubleshooter for the past year. Willoughby was given *carte blanche* to raid every platoon in the division for top soldiers. He also recruited men from the Coast Artillery, the Fourth Army replacement pool, even the Fort Ord guardhouse. They were picked for special skills and tough physical condition—they had to be able to march four miles an hour over mountains under full combat packs.

Willoughby's Scout Battalion, 410 officers and men, trained vigorously in the short time they had. Willoughby got rid of half his rifles and all sub-machine guns and other small weapons; he replaced them with automatic rifles, machine guns, mortars and demolition equipment. He exchanged soft-lead ammunition for tracers and armor-piercing bullets, because these would penetrate ice without ricocheting. He filled his men's packs with grenades. By the time it was ready for action, Willoughby's outfit had the highest per-man firepower of any battalion in the Allied armies.

Like the rest of the division, the Scout Battalion received short-sleeve fatigues and lectures on tropical diseases; every effort was made to keep their destination secret, and only a handful of the division's top officers knew they were going to the Aleutians. In mid-April the division rendezvoused at San Francisco to ship out. Cargoes of clothing and equipment were loaded onto ships in sealed crates, not to be opened until the force was well out at sea. The soldiers marched up the boarding ramps convinced they were headed for the Solomons.

At 1:00 p.m. on April 24, 1943, the Landcrab assault force set sail in five terribly overcrowded transports (including the chartered *Perida*) with strong naval escort. The 7th Infantry Division was on its way to war.

WHILE THE CALIFORNIANS TRAINED AND shipped out for the invasion of Attu, Kinkaid prepared for it in the Aleutians. His orders from CINCPAC were to "take vigorous offensive measures within the framework of calculated risk." Kinkaid ordered General Butler to saturate the enemy's Aleutian islands with bombs.

The orders came down at a time when Butler's Air Force was grounded by a paroxysm of Aleutian weather. For a full week in early April, stinging 100-knot winds and heavy snow bashed the Chain. While Frederick Ramputi wrote with magnificent understatement in the 36th Squadron's daily journal, "No flying this station due to inclement weather," the greatest storm in recorded Aleutian history destroyed the 110-knot anemometer at Adak.

Finally the storm passed. Butler ordered everything with wings into the air. During the rest of April the Eleventh Air Force flew 1,175 combat sorties. Once, in a single twelve-hour period on April 15, it made 112 sorties and dropped 184,000 pounds of bombs.

But only 4,000 pounds fell on Attu; the rest were dumped on the alternate target, Kiska, because Attu was socked in. That was usually the case. Attu had the worst weather of all the Aleutian Islands. In any event, Kinkaid did not want the enemy to suspect that Attu was the target for invasion. While for two straight weeks sixty planes a day bombed Kiska, bombers over Attu spent most of their time seeking holes in the fog through which they could take pictures. Then, on May 1, the emphasis shifted at last to Attu. Admiral McMorris bombarded the island with naval gunfire, and in the next week the Air Force sought every opening in the maddening cloud cover, to soften up the island for the impending invasion. In seven days they dumped almost 200,000 pounds of bombs on Attu.

Colonel DeFord's recon planes brought home an impressively sharp series of photographs. Japanese strength was greater than Kinkaid had thought; the photos showed about 2,600 Japanese soldiers on Attu. When General Brown learned this, he sought to have his force substantially increased; but Kinkaid and Rockwell had no more men, equipment, or ships to give him.

Brown's division had steamed into Cold Bay on the last day of April, painfully cramped aboard the five transports. (Colonel Alexander recalls: "The ships had been built with accommodations for men and women. The ladies' toilets and showers were the stowage space for 105-mm ammo, shell powder charges, fuses and caps, loaded and packed in indiscriminately.") For the desert warriors, Cold Bay was wet and miserably cold. There were no accommodations ashore; the soldiers had to stay on their ships, where it was virtually SRO with men sleeping in shifts.

D-day was still a week away. There was little chance for exercise; many of the soldiers, jammed together like sardines, did not even get to break in the stiff new leather boots they had been issued at sea.

Captain Willoughby's Scout Battalion, the only outfit to escape the cramped shipboard inactivity, had gone on to Dutch Harbor and embarked on a week's last-minute training in the snow and muskeg. Willoughby had his men refitted by the supply depot with jackets, socks, and carefully chosen boots. (When the base supply officer demanded a "shipping number," Willoughby asked how many digits such a number should have. The answer was four; Willoughby shot back "7744" off the top of his head, and hauled away his loot.)

He subjected his men to harrowing lectures on the dangers of trenchfoot and frostbite, and led them out to practice beach exercises on the sand spit where Navy Lieutenant Andy Smith had cracked up his PBY a year earlier.

The Scout Battalion was scheduled to land from two giant fleet submarines, *Narwhal* and *Nautilus* (each displaced 2,700 tons; they were the largest subs in the U.S. fleet, though only half the size of Japanese I-boats) and from a destroyer which would carry the second wave of 165 men. The landings were to take place at night, in complete silence, so that Willoughby could get ashore secretly and surprise the enemy from behind. To achieve the necessary silence, Willoughby rehearsed a tricky and unprecedented operation.

It wouldn't do to have 250 men jump from the decks of surfaced submarines into rubber rafts. Their equipment would clank and the heavy weapons would rip holes in the fragile rafts. Instead, the soldiers came topside, inflated their rubber boats on the afterdecks, and crowded quietly into the boats while they were still high and dry. Then the submarines submerged under them, and the boats floated off without a ripple. It was an adventurous scheme in the cloak-and-dagger tradition—but it required reasonably calm seas to work. Whether such conditions would be found off Attu was highly dubious.

Willoughby and his men at least kept warm by moving around. There was no such opportunity for the rest of the 7th Division. Cold Bay was windswept and blanketed with snow. Captain John Elliott, a ship's Marine guard, wrote: "On one watch I wore an ordinary suit of underwear, two woollen suits (long handles), khaki trousers, flannel shirt, windbreaker (lined), muffler, massive sheepskin coat with waterproof outside, two pair woollen socks, field boots, galoshes and woollen cap."

THE ASSAULT FORCE ASSEMBLED IN the beginning of May 1943. The division had its three regiments of infantry, four battalions of artillery, and a variety of supporting arms (combat engineers, medics, flak batteries and others). The Alaska Scouts scattered their members among the various regiments. Army and Navy fire-control parties would go ashore with portable radios, to call down naval gunfire on enemy positions.

The gunfire would come from the three colossal old battleships which now steamed into Cold Bay to join up: *Nevada, Idaho* and *Pennsylvania,* repaired and put back in action after being damaged at Pearl Harbor. With the battlewagons came six cruisers, nineteen lean high destroyers, and the escort aircraft carrier *Nassau,* which would be the first of the new CVE carriers to see action in the Pacific Theater of Operations. All together, it was the largest American force to be assembled in the Pacific since the invasion of Guadalcanal eight months before.

At Adak, Buckner's 4th Infantry Regiment marched on board ship to await orders. In the western ocean, Admiral Soc McMorris kept up his vigorous blockade patrol, beefed up to a strength of three cruisers and six destroyers (battered *Salt Lake City* had been relieved by the new cruiser *Santa Fe*). A handful of American submarines and picket boats deployed wide of the Chain, hoping to intercept any enemy forces that might try to get through to Attu. At Amchitka and Adak, the Eleventh Air Force moved up in maximum strength to support the invasion: with reinforcement by four Royal Canadian Air Force squadrons, air strength was up to 222 Army and Navy planes, plus the twenty-four fighters aboard carrier *Nassau*.

At Cold Bay, the principal commanders spent May 1 and 2 aboard *Pennsylvania,* discussing the five alternate landing plans. Admiral Rockwell wanted to land the entire division at Sarana Bay, on the southern side of Attu, but General Brown rejected that idea. He said it would require a long, protracted fight—Attu was 40 miles long, 17 miles wide—and would leave the northern harbor and submarine base in Holtz Bay free for enemy use. Brown preferred "Plan E," drawn up by Colonel William Alexander of the Alaska staff. It called for two landings, one in Holtz Bay on the north side of the island, the other in Massacre Bay on the east side. Chichagof Harbor, where the main Japanese camp was, lay to the northeast, between Holtz and Massacre. Brown proposed to land a regiment on each beach; he would hold the third regiment in reserve until it became needed at one place or the other. Meanwhile Willoughby's Scout Battalion would land at Scarlet Beach on the west side of the island and press eastward. The key to the plan was to have all three forces join up in the mountain pass between Holtz and Massacre Valleys. That would trap the Japanese in Chichagof Valley on the northeast corner of the island; there the enemy would be open to naval bombardment, air attack, and the 7th Division's massed advance from the high ground.

Rockwell's intelligence of Holtz Bay indicated that it was littered with shoals and reefs. It might mean heavy losses of landing craft there. Besides, he warned, he could not keep up full-scale supply activities on two beaches as far apart as Holtz and Massacre. He continued to press for a single massed landing. Brown held out for the divided landing. Like political candidates in search of delegate votes, each sought support from as many high-ranking officers as they could entice into their corners. The trouble was, neither Rockwell nor Brown had any experience with amphibious operations; nor did Kinkaid or Buckner or any of the others.

They all relied on judgment, whether instinctual or the textbook variety; none of them really knew what was likely to happen.

Buckner and Kinkaid were out at Adak. They signaled that they would support Brown's plan, since he was the one who was going to have to do the fighting on the ground. Outflanked, Admiral Rockwell reluctantly agreed to the divided operation.

Accordingly, the Division was reorganized into four segments: Northern Force, to hit Holtz Bay; Southern Force, to hit Massacre Bay; a reserve regiment, to wait on shipboard; and the Scout Battalion, to hit Scarlet Beach. Rockwell sent out mimeographed copies of the two-inch-thick Plan E to all interested commanders, including Air Force and naval gunnery officers who ought to know where the Americans would be so they wouldn't get bombed or shelled by mistake.

One of the Air Force officers who took his copy of the plan to Adak to explain it to the eager pilots was met by an avalanche of friendly abuse. Eric Eareckson was back.

It would be Eareckson's job to coordinate air strikes with ground operations—a tricky job recommended by Buckner, and endorsed by Kinkaid after just one meeting with the lean gray pilot. In effect, the order would muzzle General Butler by putting Eareckson in direct control of air operations at Attu.

Eareckson had been privy to the high-level quarreling that had led up to the pending operation. He made no bones of his opinion that it would be a great deal tougher than the admirals and generals thought. By the day after his arrival, one of Eareckson's doggerel compositions had been mimeographed by a devoted follower and distributed in officer country:

In viewing Attu's rocky shores
    While planning how to take it,
This thought impresses more and more:
    The Nips should first forsake it.
Since Attu ain't worth a hoot
    For raising crops or cattle,
Let's load with booze and take a cruise
    And just call off the battle.

Colonel Alexander recalls, "Eric gathered no kudos for that effort. My copy has the official SECRET stamp on it but it got to General Brown, and Eric got in the dog house."

On May 3, 1943, as the assault force was about to steam out of Cold Bay en route to war, CINCPAC's Intelligence reported that the Japanese knew about the planned invasion.

Somewhere there had been a leak. As the news sank in, Adak monitored a Japanese broadcast from Radio Kiska, warning Attu that the Americans were coming. Radio Attu replied, in codes which the Americans had broken, that Attu was going on twenty-four-hour-a-day invasion alert.

There was still time to cancel Landcrab. In view of the Japanese alert, that might be wise. But the Allied Combined Chiefs had just met at the Washington Conference and dictated an over-all war plan for a strategic offensive to converge toward Japan from Burma, the Celebes Sea, the Marshalls and Carolines, and the Aleutians. Postponement of the Attu invasion could wreck the entire timetable. So advised, CINCPAC ordered Kinkaid to "execute Landcrab as planned."

With great misgivings, Admiral Rockwell gave the order that sent Task Force 51 to sea. The thirty-four ships steamed out of Cold Bay, Colonel Alexander[2] recalls, "in a majestic procession moving west in double column. A Russian tramp came steaming on the opposite heading directly down the middle of the formation."

It was May 4. The seas south of the Chain were so high the plunging battleships had to elevate the muzzles of their forward guns to protect them. The task force cut across the Chain at Amukta Pass and made a wide circle north of Kiska to avoid detection. Past Kiska, it headed for its launch point a hundred miles north of Attu. It got there on May 6, D-day-minus-one. Meanwhile twelve Air Force bombers attacked Attu, and Wheeler reported, "The afternoon mission found ceiling and visibility unlimited, and [photo] strips were taken by five camera ships. This time seventy-two 500-pounders were dropped to convince the heathen of our serious intentions." But a storm blew in that evening, and the sunset WX plane reported high winds blowing snow off the Attu mountains. By morning the surf would be far too hazardous for troop landings.

Rockwell steamed his transports in circles, and dispatched the battleships to the west in case Japanese reinforcements were on the way from the Kuriles. From May 7 through 10, the storm broiled the sea, lifted it high above the ships and swept it over the battlewagons' guns and the

---

2. Alexander was aboard *Nevada* at his own request; worried about the differences between Navy and Army charts, he had volunteered to help translate gunnery spotters' instructions for Task Force Gunnery Control. It has already been mentioned that Colonel Alexander was a Naval Academy graduate, uniquely qualified for interservice liaison.

high flight deck of carrier *Nassau*. All land-based planes were grounded during those four days. Rockwell ordered one postponement after the other; D-day crept back by stages from May 7 to May 11.

The prowling battleships found no enemy ships in the west, and returned at sundown May 10. The storm ended. But in its aftermath a soupy fog blanketed the western ocean. Destroyer *Macdonough*, one of the bold tin cans from the Komandorski torpedo attack, accidentally cut across destroyer *Sicard's* course, and *Sicard* rammed her. No one was hurt, but the collision holed *Macdonough* and sprung her hull. *Sicard* had to take her in tow and make for Adak. *Sicard* had been control ship for the landings, and *Macdonough* had had a tricky fire-control assignment; without them, the invasion would be even more difficult than before.

A few hours after the destroyers collided, submarine *Nautilus*, with part of Willoughby's Scout Battalion aboard, made a 4,000-yard radar contact on an unidentified vessel. She turned toward it; Lieutenant Commander Brockman maneuvered into position to launch torpedoes. He was about to fire when he recognized the target—*Narwhal*, half a mile ahead, carrying another contingent of Willoughby's soldiers.

At that point radio receivers aboard *Nautilus, Pennsylvania* and other ships picked up an Alaskan commercial rebroadcast of the previous Sunday night's Walter Winchell broadcast "To Mr. and Mrs. America and all the ships at sea." Winchell said bluntly, "Keep your eye on the Aleutian Islands."

Whoever the security leak was, he had done an expert job. At the one time in the Aleutian Campaign when censorship made sense, the whole world seemed to know what was happening.

ON ATTU, COLONEL YASUYO YAMASAKI took stock of the information he had at hand. Yamasaki had arrived by submarine a month ago to take command of the troops on Attu. On May 4, he had been warned by radio to expect an American invasion. For a week after that he had kept his men in combat-alert positions. Now, on the 10th, the men were exhausted. It looked as if the radio warning had been a false alarm. Yamasaki sent his men back to their regular duties, leaving the beaches unguarded.

He knew he was taking a risk; that evening his suspicions were confirmed when his signal team monitored American ship transmissions near Attu. But he did not send his tired men back to the beaches. To do so would be useless; his force was small and he did not want to divide it to cover every possible landing beach—although cliffs made up 95 percent of the shoreline, there were dozens of little beaches around the ragged 135-mile circumference.

Yamasaki had received word from Vice Admiral Shiro Kawase (who had taken the place of the disgraced Admiral Hosogaya) that Japanese forces were weak after the long bloody siege at Guadalcanal; Imperial Headquarters[3] had sent all available reinforcements into the New Guinea-Solomons area to counter Allied offensive preparations there. At the moment, major forces were unavailable in the north. Admiral Kawase promised to send reinforcements to Attu, but not until late May, after the season of constant fog began, and after Japan's transport ships had radar installed. Meanwhile, Admiral Kawase ordered Colonel Yamasaki to hold his ground without outside help.

Yamasaki had 2,650 men, twelve flak guns and a handful of coast-artillery pieces. Most of his firepower was vested in mortars and machine guns. He could not halt any determined invasion force on the beaches; his only chance was to occupy the high ground, draw the enemy back into the mountains far from supplies, and fight a delaying action in the high passes. So deciding, he pulled out of the low areas (except for his headquarters camp in Chichagof Valley) and built bunkers and trenches along the snowy ridges above Massacre and Holtz Valleys.

The Japanese soldiers had few illusions about what was coming. But the Samurai code demanded victory or death. Decades of indoctrination had ensnared them in a net of authority based on Samurai and the Bushido code of honor. Since the 1890s Sino-Japanese War, the Emperor's troops had been regimented under a system of Prussian militarism which emphasized patriotic self-sacrifice. Compulsory military training pervaded Japan's schools, and by 1940 the indoctrination had done its work, abetted by propaganda which stressed the American's alleged bestial brutality toward prisoners. As far as Yamasaki's soldiers were concerned, a dead man was a god but a prisoner was disgraced by permanent excommunication from his home and ancestors.

The proverb said, "It is simpler to die than to live." A man was only a candle burning in the wind; and where an Occidental would use the word "fear," a Japanese might use the word "shame." Now, as Attu made ready

3. On April 18, 1943, one year to the day after the Doolittle raid, U.S. Air Force Captain Tom Lanphier had shot down Admiral Isoroku Yamamoto's plane, killing everyone on board. With Yamamoto dead at fifty-nine, the Imperial Navy shattered into bickering factions which the new Commander in Chief Combined Fleet, Admiral Koga, was not forceful enough to crush until months later. Much of the Japanese indecisiveness during the Battle of Attu must be laid to this confusion.

for battle, its soldiers prepared to match their spiritual strength against American brute force and machinery.

THE ALEUTIAN CAMPAIGN HAD COME west to climax. In a few hours the United States Infantry would execute the first amphibious island landing since the Cuban campaign of 1898. The American and Allied high commands expected it to be a routine ground action, neither noteworthy nor particularly bloody; after all, there weren't many enemy troops on Attu. It would probably be over within a few days.

That kind of careless optimism would be dashed very quickly. Before it ended, the Battle of Attu would become, in proportion to the numbers of opposing troops, the second most costly battle of the war in the Pacific.

CHAPTER SEVENTEEN

The Battle of Attu

TUESDAY, MAY 11, 1943.

At 1:00 a.m., three miles off the western shore of Attu Island, black water splashed around the emerging hulls of submarines *Nautilus* and *Narwhal.* When they broke surface their hatch-cover wheels were already turning.

Captain William H. Willoughby and 244 men of his Scout Battalion squeezed through the narrow hatches and assembled on the afterdecks. They inflated their rubber boats and climbed in; there was no sound but the gentle lap of waves against the submarine hulls.

Willoughby, a strapping broad-shouldered man, had had to shed almost all his food supplies in order to fit through the 25-inch submarine hatch; most of his men had been forced to do the same. They carried rations for only a day and a half.

They moved swiftly: *Narwhal's* Commander Latta had warned Willoughby that if enemy ships appeared the submarines would dive instantly, no matter what stage the debarkation might be in. With his men packed into the rubber boats, Willoughby made a quiet signal to the conning tower. Hatches eased shut and the submarines submerged; the rubber boats floated free. A few bubbles, and the big pigboats were gone. The soldiers slipped paddles into the water and rowed toward Attu, 5,000 yards away through the fog-thick night.

Two hours later they bumped to ground on Beach Scarlet in Austin Cove. Mountains lifted steeply from the sand. Thick snow extended right down to the waterline, where gentle green-white crests broke on the lee shore in the dawn. Willoughby, his shoulders laden with crossed belts of machine-gun ammunition, rounded up his men, posted flankers, sent a signal-light flash to the submarine periscopes, and dragged his boats inland above the tide line. The temperature hung at 27° Fahrenheit.

The rising sun burned off the mist. Willoughby found an icy little creek and took his men up its precipitous ravine, expecting to meet the enemy at any moment. On this westward side of Attu it was a bright clear morning; the clean snow was blue in the sunlight. As they climbed toward the ridges, the wind rose and the temperatures dipped toward 20°.

The buzz of airplanes drew Willoughby's wary attention toward the beach behind him. Carrier fighters from CVE *Nassau* came zooming down; bitterly, Willoughby watched the F4F Wildcats strafe and destroy the rubber boats he had left behind. It cut off his only possibility of retreat. The three men he had posted on the beach had to scurry for cover, shaking their fists at the Navy planes.

With only thirty-six hours' food in their packs, the soldiers put their backs to the sea and climbed through snow and sucking muskeg toward the white 4,000-foot heights ahead. There was no sign of the enemy.

THE LANDING AREA FOR 7TH Division's Northern Force had been designated "Beach Red." It was a few miles north of Holtz Bay. The offshore water was thick with perilous shoals, as Admiral Rockwell had anticipated. Here the fog squatted thick and unmoving. At 9:00 in the morning, visibility was down to a ship's length. Aboard transport *J. Franklin Bell*, the men of the 32nd Infantry Regiment had been ready to go over the side for hours, but there hadn't been a single break in the fog.

Their commander, Colonel Frank L. Culin, fifty-one, was a mining engineer from Tucson who knew his Southwesterners were anxious to set foot on solid ground. Culin decided to take off with a scouting detachment in two landing craft, to explore the route to shore and feel out the beach.[1] He rounded up Squeaky Anderson, Captain Robert Thompson of the Alaska Defense Command, and Thompson's unit of Alaska Scouts, some of them Aleuts who were familiar with Attu. They all piled into the LCs and set out for shore, towing empty plastic dories and guided by the radar-equipped destroyer *Phelps*. They had to zigzag slowly between half-submerged rocks; half a mile offshore, *Phelps* had come as far as she could. Culin and the Aleuts transferred to the plastic dories to negotiate the shallows, and rowed in to Beach Red.

1. "Shortly before I was to leave the ship," Culin recalls, "positive orders were received forbidding [any reporters to accompany] me on my reconnaissance of Beach Red in advancement of the assault." The reporters who wanted to go were Howard Handelman and Sherman Montrose. All told, nine correspondents were on hand for the Battle of Attu. It was virtually the first break in the "strict and stupid censorship," as Senator Gruening describes it, "imposed variously by the military services and by the Office of Censorship headed at that time by Byron Price."

It proved to be a narrow strip only a hundred yards long, surrounded by steep 250-foot heights. It was so unlikely a landing area that the Japanese had no defenses anywhere nearby. Culin sent the Aleuts forward to check out the surrounding hills, and signaled *Phelps* to send ahead the six boatloads of troops who had followed the destroyer in. These men, the Assault Company of the 1st Battalion Combat Team, emerged slowly from the fog and splashed onto the beach; Culin immediately sent them up the cliffs, to avoid being trapped on the tiny beach. Meanwhile beachmaster Squeaky Anderson organized the pile of equipment from the boats.

Culin still had to decide whether to land his main Northern Force here. To do that would be bold if not reckless; a small handful of Japanese on the heights could pin down his entire regiment in a crossfire. He sent the Aleut Scouts higher in the hills, trying to prevent that, and decided to go ahead; he cranked up a walkie-talkie radio and signaled the main force.

In Culin's absence, shipboard command of Northern Force rested with Lieutenant Colonel Albert V. Hartl, a former civilian accountant. Like several other young officers of the division, Hartl was entering his first combat as a battalion commander; at the moment, in fact, the entire regiment lay in his hands. Hartl was not empowered, however, to commit the Northern Force without authorization by the landing force commander, General Brown; and now Brown appeared reluctant to grant permission.

Part of the regiment—more than a company—was already committed ashore. Hartl uneasily radioed Brown again. By now it was 1:15 in the afternoon. But Aleutian static was having its way; the signals never reached Brown. Finally the reply came—not from Brown, but from Navy Captain Pat Buchanan, who commanded the attack transports. LAND WHEN READY, Buchanan signaled, and Hartl, who had already moved the regiment into their LCs, gave the order to cast off.

Soldiers had to be lowered over the sides by their heels; fingertips trailing the water, they guided the landing force through the foggy shoals at dead-slow speed. As they reached shore and began to unload, Lieutenant Commander Squeaky Anderson roared up and down Beach Red like a cyclone, driving men furiously with the earsplitting squeal of his loud voice.

By midafternoon Culin and Hartl had 1,500 men ashore and climbing. The loudest sound had been Squeaky's voice. So far, there was not a peep out of the enemy—no sign at all of opposition.

THE LARGEST OF THE THREE assault bodies had arrived on transports in Massacre Bay early in the morning—Southern Force, under General Brown's direct command. H-hour had been set for 7:40 a.m., but fog had forced postponements—first to 10:40, then into the afternoon. Soldiers waited aboard ship in growing irritation, spooked by the foreboding name of Massacre Bay (named after the annihilation of native Aleuts there by Russians in the late eighteenth century).

During the morning, battleships *Pennsylvania* and *Idaho* had bombarded Chichagof Harbor by radar for an hour,[2] with no observable effect; if the Japanese were there, radar picked up no movement to indicate it. Offshore, Admiral Soc McMorris cruised around in light cruiser *Raleigh* with a covering group of warships, ready to intercept any enemy ships that might show up.

Aboard battleship *Nevada,* Admiral Rockwell had decided to delay the landing until visibility improved, but by noon there was no sign the fog would ever lift. General Brown said they had better go ahead regardless of fog. Rockwell agreed; at 12:20 the order went down: the boats would launch at half past three. From his armored stance high on the battleship's bridge, Rockwell tried to get a glimpse of Attu while he watched the ship's clock.

Back at Adak, General Buckner and Admiral Kinkaid waited for news; and Billy Wheeler wrote:

> The air is electric with anticipation. The 36th is scheduled not only for bombing attacks directed by Col. Eareckson, but for all sorts of possibilities incident to ground support as well as strafing at need. The weather was rotten this morning, but a nine-ship mission took off, Major Speer commanding. At Attu there is ground fog to 1,500 feet and target areas are 9/10ths cloud-covered to high altitudes. After milling around for an hour two ships dropped their bombs at Holtz Bay. No AA, what a disappointment. We could see the landings under way at the beaches above Holtz Bay, with landing craft, destroyers, and the aircraft carrier *Nassau* standing off.

As the sun moved west it began to filter through the overcast and thin the fog. At Massacre Bay the bullhorns bellowed, "Assault wave man your boats!" and troops spilled down rope nets into their LCs.

"Lower boats...Away all boats!"

---

2. Battleship *Pennsylvania* was twenty-six years old; this was the first time she had ever fired her main batteries in offensive action.

At 3:30 the first wave started for shore. The LCs followed the toots of radar-equipped minelayer *Pruitt's* whistle. They crept slowly through the surf. One LC capsized; another lodged on a rock. It was 4:20 before the first troops hit Massacre Beach.

Rifles lifted, they fanned out across the muskeg. The enemy did not show himself; the landings were unopposed.

The second wave followed quickly. The bow ramp of one LC flapped open and the boat swamped; a dozen men of an artillery Fire Direction Center were carried down by the weight of their equipment and drowned.

Silence greeted the infantry in Massacre Valley. The first sound came from a raven which erupted into startling croaks, and flapped away.

Lieutenant Hubert Long and his platoon, advancing up the valley, "captured" an officer in the fog; the prisoner turned out to be Colonel William Verbeck, who had come ashore with his Alaska Scouts and gone ahead of the infantry. (His superior, Colonel Lawrence Castner, had stayed aboard *Nevada*, already ill with the cancer that would take his life.)

Lieutenant Long moved quickly toward his objective, named on the map "Artillery Hill." The name was fitting: at the top were a pair of Japanese 20-mm pompom guns, which crews now turned toward the advancing Americans. But unaccountably they did not fire. The four Japanese soldiers abandoned their guns and stacks of ammunition, and ran up into the fog.

By five o'clock all the beaches were secured. American troops had been on Attu more than twelve hours; yet, except for naval shelling and a few bombs, not a shot had been fired. The silence was eerie.

TWO COMPANIES OF THE JAPANESE 303rd Infantry Battalion, under Lieutenants Honna and Goto,[3*] lay in their trenches on the ridge above Massacre Valley. During the afternoon the fog lifted slowly; it was not

---

3. These officers are without first names in this book because the difficulty of obtaining details on Japan's side of the Battle of Attu has been extreme. Colonel Yamasaki ordered all documents burned as early as May 16, when he also ordered his field hospital to prepare to "destroy the patients" in case they were overrun. The Japanese defenders of Attu suffered virtual annihilation before the long, bloody battle was over. As a result, few particulars of Yamasaki's story have come to light. Most of what we have comes from Japanese soldiers' diaries found by Americans after the battle, a handful of unburnt captured records, and copies of Radio Attu's transmissions taken down by Admiral Kawase's signal personnel at sea and in Paramushiro. Since the Japanese high command ordered all official documents destroyed on August 15, 1945, and many were in fact destroyed before the order was rescinded, there are obviously gaps in the Japanese side of this story. *1995 ADDENDUM: A degree of additional information has come to light in the years

possible for the Americans to see up into the fog, but the Japanese could see down out of it. They had seen the Americans land, had watched them move inland from their beachhead in Massacre Bay. On the ridge, two machine-gun platoons and two mortar platoons loaded and checked their weapons, and waited for the enemy to come within range.

While they waited, a runner came up with copies of a message from Northern Imperial Army Headquarters (Paramushiro): DESTORY THE ENEMY. WE PRAY AND HOPE FOR YOUR SUCCESSFUL BATTLE.

AT 5:30 P.M. ON D-DAY, the two pronged Southern Force, under Colonel Edward P. Earle, was moving steadily inland from the beach. It was slow going in the muck of snow, mud, and muskeg. One battalion struggled up the valley floor, another up a parallel ridge. The advance party of artillery observers, under Lieutenant James West, disappeared upward into the fog. Beyond the left flank, one company of soldiers got lost in the fog and had to turn southwest and stumble over the hills to reach its objective on a farther ridge.

The first American guns landed on Massacre Beach: Lieutenant William Kimball's Battery C of the 48th Field Artillery Battalion. Cat tractors began to tow the four 105-mm howitzers forward, but none of them advanced more than 75 yards: their treads broke through the muskeg and spun uselessly in the loose black mud beneath.

Brigadier General Archibald V. Arnold, who wore the two hats of Assistant Landing Force Commander and Commander of Artillery, had built heavy sleds for his artillery pieces; but they did no good when the tractors themselves broke through. It was as Colonel Alexander had predicted in San Diego: the big guns were stuck on the beach.

Artillerymen swung the guns around by sheer human brawn, until they had them pointed toward the fog-concealed ridges. Lieutenant Kimball set up his fire-direction center and tuned his radio to the frequency of forward observer Lieutenant James West, who was somewhere up in the fog. Beside Kimball's guns, the tractors' wallowing treads quit after they had mired hopelessly in the mud.

Just after six o'clock word came on the radio from Lieutenant West. He had spotted an enemy mortar position on the ridge.

A gun crew poised its howitzer on the springy muskeg; Kimball spoke into the radio—"One on the way, Jimmy"—and barked at the gun crew: *"Fire."*

---

since *The Thousand-Mile War* was first published. The two lieutenants' full names were Hitoshi Honna and Yutake Goto.

The big gun roared and slammed back in recoil that jammed its sled 18 inches into the muskeg. The echo rolled back from the hills.

The opening round of the Battle of Attu had been fired.

It missed its target by more than half a mile; but after two radio-guided corrections Kimball was on target, ripping into the Japanese mortar position. He ordered fire for effect; Battery C's guns began to growl steadily. Forty-one days after the command decision had been made to invade Attu, the battle was on.

CAPTAIN WILLOUGHBY HAD LANDED 244 men of his Scout Battalion. Behind him Captain James Austin brought 165 more men ashore—the 7th Cavalry Recon Troop. Landing at Beach Scarlet from a destroyer, Austin picked up the three men Willoughby had left behind to guide him, and secured positions in the rear as Willoughby continued to advance.

On the high ridges, blasted by windblown snow, Willoughby reached a crest late in the D-day afternoon. About five miles below he could see Holtz Bay, presumably the enemy's rear. He went back to lead the battalion forward.

Overhead, two bombers circled down. One was Eareckson's. It appeared to Eareckson that the Scout Battalion was turning in too soon, heading for a deep fog-filled cul-de-sac. Eareckson penciled a crude map with appropriate directions and dropped it out the window; unhappily the map caught in the B-24's tail structure and was still there hours later when Eareckson went home. Meanwhile, behind Eareckson, Lieutenant Anthony Brannen dropped parachute loads of food, medicines, and ammunition to Willoughby.

Wind picked up the chutes and drove them past the cliffs; they fell, out of reach, into a crevasse. Willoughby, who knew where he was and where he was going, waved angrily at the two bombers. Circling like buzzards, they might give away his position to the Japanese. He wanted them to go away.

In time they did. Willoughby worked his way forward through the snow, meeting no opposition. The pace was agonizingly slow. Even for his hand-picked men, all in top physical condition, the muskeg and snow made a taffy floor on which walking was agony.

Darkness caught them on a mountaintop in an icy, gale-blasting fog. Willoughby could not move on, for fear of being blown over an unseen cliff. The battalion would have to wait for daylight. Shivering in the ten-degree cold, they posted sentries and ate meager cold rations.

IN MASSACRE VALLEY, the spongy muskeg had restricted Southern Force's advance to a crawl. In the growing darkness, enemy snipers fired sporadically at the slow-moving troops (though some independent flanking platoons would not come under fire until the next day). By 7:00 p.m., the two battalions of the 17th Infantry Regiment had advanced a mile and a half from the beach. Here enemy fire from high ground to the right forced Colonel Earle and his men to take cover. An hour later they were still there.

Earle gathered his companies for a forward push, and launched the strike straight toward the pass ahead. Spotters called down a ragged barrage from the beached artillery. It made a lot of noise but the long-range overhead fire was too spotty to have much effect. Earle's men, several hundred strong, charged uphill.

The Japanese lay in lines along the brow of the pass and the enfilading ridges. They laid down heavy and accurate fire from mortars and machine guns. The American troops were green: confusion, more dangerous than shellfire, spread a contagion of bewildered fear. They shrank back from the firing; the advance ground to a halt, half a mile below the pass. Earle sent them up once more, and the second assault broke down under the same heavy fire from the fog-hidden heights. At nightfall, Earle regrouped behind a defensive perimeter.

During the next five grueling days, these men would batter the high pass with constant frontal attacks—and gain no ground. Japanese entrenchments dominated all approaches; the Americans had to cross open slopes with no cover at all. The Japanese guns were linked along the summits, at the military crest a few feet below the skyline. Fog hid the Japanese, while it revealed the American lines; and even when the fog thinned, the Japanese used smokeless powder which couldn't be seen.

In the cold snow, the slippery muskeg, the loose wet mud, the howling wind, Southern Force dug in for a deadly trench war.

In the meantime Northern Force had made its first contact with the enemy. An infantry platoon at Beach Red had killed two enemy scouts, but two others had escaped. Within a half hour, Japanese artillery was pounding the little beach, but by that time Colonel Hartl had his main force on higher ground. The enemy's artillery failed to find him. By ten o'clock in the evening, though some cliffs were so steep the men had to rope-haul machine guns up their faces, the force was two miles inland and less than half a mile short of its goal, a hilltop dominating Holtz Valley. But here Colonel Hartl (Culin, suffering from exposure, had gone back aboard ship) called a halt. Night had come. He couldn't see, and his maps were inaccurate.

He stayed put until daybreak, by which time the Japanese had taken up strong defensive positions on the hill he had meant to take. The unavoidable delay was to cost two days and severe casualties.

BY TEN THAT FIRST NIGHT, 2,000 men had secured the beachhead in Massacre Bay; another 1,500 were with Hartl north of Holtz Bay; Willoughby had another 400 in the mountains.[4] In Massacre Valley, communications and command posts extended more than a mile in from the beach. At 11:00 p.m., D-day, General Brown and his staff landed and set up an advanced headquarters.

Now, at nightfall of the first day of battle, all the major striking forces had landed and made headway. But they were all stalled in their tracks—by the enemy, terrain, weather, and the impossibility of getting supplies.

The supply problem was worst for the troops who had advanced farthest. Confusion on Massacre Beach (as opposed to Beach Red, where Squeaky Anderson held sway) had piled up immovable obstacles in the form of useless vehicles. Combat troops had to be withdrawn from the lines and sent back in long queues, as Colonel Alexander had forecast. They hand-carried supplies like coolies—everything from ammunition to sleeping bags. It would be twenty-four hours before some forward units would receive their first ammunition or food.

That night artillery's General Arnold found space on a dry gun sled to get some sleep. In the mountains, Willoughby's men chattered with cold while their commander urged them to keep moving around—but some of them found places to hide and lie down, and awoke with severe cases

---

4. Actual disposition of Landing Force Attu on May 11, 1943, was as follows:

Southern Force, at Massacre Bay: Colonel Edward Palmer Earle, Commander, 17th Infantry Regiment; force included 2nd and 3rd Battalions of 17th Infantry, and 2nd Battalion of 32nd Infantry, plus three batteries of 105-mm field artillery and auxiliary troops.

Northern Force, at Beach Red: Colonel Frank L. Culin, CO 32nd Infantry Regiment, and Lieutenant Colonel Albert V. Hartl; force included 1st Battalion of 17th Infantry, one battery of field artillery and auxiliaries.

Provisional Scout Battalion, at Beach Scarlet: Captain William H. Willoughby, Battalion CO; forces included 7th Scout Company and 7th Cavalry Reconnaissance Troop (under Captain James Austin), less one platoon.

The detached platoon of the 7th Cavalry Reconnaissance Troop made a separate landing at Alexai Point, east of Massacre Bay, and linked up with Southern Force after three days' reconnaissance on the right flank.

Shipboard reserve: 2 battalions of 32nd Infantry (Colonel Culin), several medical and auxiliary units. 4th Infantry Regiment was on shipboard at Adak.

Total available strength was about 16,000 men.

of frostbite. Runners dashed to and from General Brown's command post. Medics struggled up to the front to evacuate wounded. Men cleaned their rifles and rolled up in sleeping bags. The Japanese fired sporadic shots to keep them awake.

Fog came down and squatted, thicker than before.

WEDNESDAY, MAY 12, 1943.

D-day-plus-one: dawn brought a bombardment of the ridges above Massacre Valley from the huge guns of battleship *Nevada*. Her great 14-inch projectiles[5] thundered, crashed, and chewed great brutal hunks out of the mountains. Lieutenant Hubert Long, at the front, watched the shelling take effect and wrote soon afterward, "Dead Japanese, hunks of artillery, pieces of guns, and arms and legs rolled down out of the fog on the mountain." All day long the naval guns would growl in response to target calls by observers in the fog.

Meanwhile, far back in the snow of the high country, Captain Willoughby got his men on their feet at 4:00 a.m. and pushed forward against the muskeg's cold, wet resistance. Moving generally southeastward, the Scout Battalion crossed the summit of the western mountains early in the morning; Willoughby wormed forward to overlook the enemy's positions west of Holtz Bay. During the night the Japanese had reinforced those ridgetop lines to repel the main American forces, but so far they had not discovered Willoughby at their rear.

By 8:00 Willoughby's half-frozen men had come down within range of the enemy's rear. They had covered ground quickly in the last hour, sliding down the steep snow-covered slopes like human toboggans.

Inevitably the enemy spotted their movements; Japanese light artillery turned around and shot at Willoughby at long range, while enemy troops wheeled back from the ridges and climbed toward him. The Scout Battalion took cover behind ice boulders and rocks, and returned the fire with machine guns while Willoughby brought his 81-mm mortar up from the rear. The big mortar drove back the advancing Japanese, and Willoughby dug in on the windy slope.

For the rest of the day, and most of the next three days, Willoughby would hold fast in a stalemate. It would injure and kill dozens of men on both sides; but it forced the Japanese to face west, rather than turn to attack Northern Force from the rear.

---

5. The size of a shell, measured in inches or millimeters or caliber, refers not to the length but to the diameter of the projectile's cross-section. Thus a .50-caliber bullet is half an inch in diameter, a 105-mm shell about 4-1/2 inches in diameter, and a 14-inch battleship projectile more than a foot wide (and weighs 1,400 pounds).

In a ravine behind Willoughby's lines Captain David Klein set up a makeshift field clinic. The bantam forty-four-year-old doctor, whom Willoughby had recruited only the day before the battalion left San Diego, was brand-new to the Army and a stranger to combat; still, he operated his open-air clinic as if it were a complete field hospital, and in the next forty-eight hours he would save at least fifteen lives. Another member of Willoughby's party was Lieutenant Jakie Mann, advance spotter for naval gunfire. Mann later reported:

> Capt. Willoughby deployed his platoons for an attack, and the attack was made....
>
> The first target I observed was 5 anti-aircraft guns located near the beach, which fired at our planes as they came over to strafe and bomb. My radio operator...was able to get the *Idaho,* which fired on the anti-aircraft battery as I spotted it.
>
> My observation was not too good, so I informed the *Idaho* to stand by on the assigned frequency while I moved forward. After setting up my new observation post, I was unable to contact the ship. The *Idaho* did not stand by.
>
> Finally I was able to give the co-ordinates to the Air Corps, and they bombed the positions. I think their bombing was quite effective.

In the air, Billy Wheeler took up the account:

> Six heavies attacked target areas with 240 100-pound bombs. Bombing seemed effective, as several batteries quit firing. Plenty of AA and two planes received some damage. Brannen buzzed Holtz Bay after his mission was completed. It was a needlessly risky thing to do at 3,000 feet—the S-2 called him down for it—but the fact that he drew no fire showed that the batteries had been well plastered.

Lieutenant Anthony Brannen was the pilot who had tried to drop supplies to Willoughby a day earlier. Now, after buzzing the enemy flak positions, Brannen decided to try and find Willoughby again. He went back over the mountains, nosed down through the overcast, and plowed into a fog-hidden peak to his death.

IN THE MAIN BATTLE AREAS, the fog started to lift at 9:00 in the morning. It stopped and sat part way up the slopes, concealing the Japanese who had brought up reinforcements to repel Colonel Hartl, to the north, and Colonel Earle, to the southeast.

When the fog seemed to have lifted as far as it was going to, Earle ordered one of his battalions to attack. The soldiers hurled themselves against the Jarmin Pass defenses, made a few yards and were stopped cold by withering fire from the fog above. Japanese shells and bullets laced across the snow valley, sewing tight stitches that hardly failed to penetrate a single foot of exposed earth. Belly-flat, Earle's soldiers crawled back to their foxholes.

At the same time, in the north, one of Hartl's companies attacked the right flank toward the pass, but it too came under a fusillade from mortars, machine guns, and rifles. The company took cover, pinned down in a deep ravine, unable to move forward or back.

THE JAPANESE EFFECTIVELY COMMANDED the southern U.S. positions from three sides. All morning the battalions were stalled in their tracks—and no food had yet reached them.

At Earle's regimental command post the radio went dead. Earle went forward, early in the afternoon, to find out where his own front lines were. He made a tour of the front, and somewhere in the mist between two company areas became the target of a Japanese sniper.

A few hours later a patrol found Colonel Earle. He was dead; the Alaska Scout with him was unconscious, badly wounded.

It was a serious loss. When the news reached the beach, General Brown ordered his Chief of Staff, Colonel Wayne C. Zimmerman, to take Earle's place as Southern Force commander. Zimmerman, a tough forty-six-year-old West Pointer, went up to Earle's headquarters and found that the battalions had not moved all day; in fact they were only then beginning to get supplies.

In the north, Colonel Hartl still had a single infantry company pinned down. He had to rescue it. He called for a barrage to soften up the Japanese and keep their heads down long enough to extricate his isolated company. His batteries were back near the beach, 105-mm howitzers on sleds; they opened up, found the range, and were quickly supported by gunfire from destroyer *Phelps* and strafing attacks from carrier *Nassau's* Wildcats.

At five o'clock, covered by barrages, Hartl pushed his battalion forward and linked up with the isolated infantry company.

They went on from there, moving uphill through heavy shooting. A steel helmet saved the life of Pfc Wilbur W. Cross: it deflected five mortar fragments, which fell down the back of his neck, hot enough to scald him. Others had less luck.

By 6:30 p.m. the battalion had overrun the enemy's first line of defense, but the Japanese regrouped and launched a heavy counterattack. It set Hartl's men back on their heels—killed fourteen men and wounded fifteen. Hartl sent back twelve others suffering from exposure, and drove the enemy back just before dark.

LATE IN THE AFTERNOON OF THAT second day, *Pennsylvania* and *Idaho* worked over Holtz Bay at 14,000 yards; and Major General Albert Brown made a personal reconnaissance of the front lines in Massacre Valley.

Brown had sent three messages to Rockwell during the day, asking what had happened to the two battalions from *Grant* and *Chirikoff* that were supposed to have arrived at seven in the morning. He received no replies; Aleutian static was having its customary effect. While Brown vainly awaited information, the chartered *Perida* was edging toward Massacre Beach to land her reinforcements and supplies. But Perida rammed a pinnacle rock; water gushed into the forward hold and destroyed valuable radio equipment needed ashore. *Perida* backed off, listing, and staggered back toward the mouth of the bay, where she was beached to make repairs.

The combat forces were stalled. At 7:30 p.m. Hartl of Northern Force signaled Brown, "Have captured last high ground before West Arm of Holtz Bay. Now fighting hand to hand to hold it." Half an hour later he added, "Struggle continues for high ground. Casualties very heavy. Enemy infiltration through high mountains on my right."

At nightfall there had been no change in positions. Fifty-six Americans, including Colonel Edward P. Earle, were dead on Attu.

THURSDAY, MAY 13, 1943.

At nine in the morning Eareckson indignantly disregarded Amchitka's socked-in weather, took off blind, and headed for Attu. He would spend eight hours in the air over the battlefield without getting a single glimpse of the ground. On this day and most others of the battle, his bombers were grounded; Eareckson himself would not miss a day.

While Eareckson fruitlessly cruised the overcast at 20,000 feet, nineteen Japanese attack bombers flew the 350 miles from Paramushiro to Attu, laden with bombs. But the weather chose no sides. They found the weather too thick to bomb through; they turned back. There was no contact.

Underneath the fog, the third day of battle began like the others. The fog did not lift until midmorning, when Colonel Zimmerman—now commanding Southern Force—threw his battalions into Jarmin Pass once again. The soldiers flapped uphill through the snow, blazing at the Japanese guns above, and got within 200 yards of the summit before the triple-crossfire threw them back. Nursing their wounds, they rolled back into their old foxholes.

Alaska Scout Sergeant Joe Kelly went forward to reconnoiter the pass, but he could not get any closer than the infantrymen had gone. The Japanese had a perfect view of the whole expanse. Kelly turned back toward his own lines—and the Americans opened fire on him. He dropped into the rocks, waved a white handkerchief, yelled at the top of his lungs, and came cautiously through the lines.

General Brown had moved up to a forward observation post within a few hundred yards of the pass. His assistant, General Arnold, was with him; so were several staffers. Brown sent a fourth message to Rockwell, again requesting the two promised reserve battalions; Brown said flatly that the troops on hand could not budge the enemy. Rockwell replied that he had no idea where transports *Grant* and *Chirikoff* might be. He would check.

An hour later Rockwell was back on the radio with word that the two ships would arrive early in the afternoon—one at Massacre, the other at Beach Red. They had been standing out beyond range of coastal guns.

At Massacre, *Grant* landed a fresh battalion and a field hospital. The battalion moved up to fill in the front lines, and by midafternoon Brown had fully committed all his strength at the front; he had nothing left in the rear. The guns kept firing but the front line stayed where it was.

At Beach Red, *Chirikoff* stood ready to land her reserve battalion, but Japanese antiaircraft guns had been turned against Beach Red and were laying down a steady accurate fire. Aboard the ship, Colonel Frank Culin, the regimental commander, decided to wait for nightfall to land the battalion on the bombarded beach. In the meantime, still suffering from the chills that had sent him back from the beach forty-eight hours earlier, Culin went ashore to take command of Northern Force.

To cross the beach he had to dodge the whistle and crash of enemy projectiles. From there it was a weary trek to find Hartl, who had moved his battalions well up into the hills and was now signaling Brown, "Ack ack fire…seems to be getting range on first line companies on ridge." In response, Brown called for naval support.

Rockwell moved close to shore in flagship *Nevada* and steamed back and forth in the dangerous waters to hurl 14-inch salvos against the Japanese flak positions that had Hartl in range. Colonel Alexander, in gunnery control, wrote in his log: "Fired on call target.... Visibility nil. Cannot contact spotter on radio. May have hit him instead of target."

Rockwell zigzagged slowly back and forth, very close to shore; an officer on the bridge expressed alarm—enemy submarines were known to be in the area, not to mention shoals and pinnacles. When the officer repeated his query, Rockwell snapped the classic line for which the Navy has remembered him ever since:

"Screw the torpedoes, slow speed ahead."

It was not precisely the way *Farragut* had said it. On the heels of Rockwell's remark, destroyers *Edwards* and *Farragut* flushed Japanese submarine *I-31*, which had lined up for a shot at *Nevada*. The submarine fired a brace of torpedoes; *Nevada* dodged them narrowly; the destroyers trapped the submarine and sank it, and Rockwell, unruffled, resumed his slow-speed salvo runs along the coast.

IN THE WESTERN MOUNTAINS, Japanese guns had kept Captain Willoughby pinned down well into the third morning. He could not get through to anybody on the radio. His haggard men listened to the drone of Eareckson's plane overhead. The soup was thick. The plane's sound faded beyond the peaks. It was the Scout Battalion's second day without food.

In the afternoon Willoughby led an attack on the enemy's high ground. The fighting was savage; men slithered across ice, hurled grenades, vibrated with their chattering machine guns, and ran from cover to cover.

After several hours Willoughby drove the Japanese off the top. The battalion secured the summit and settled down just before nightfall.

The cold was extreme. Beyond the parapets, Japanese officers with megaphones shouted taunts in English. In a snow cave his men had dug, Willoughby's tiny fire—fed by ration boxes and anything else that would burn—warmed the stiff fingers of his men. Willoughby called for an ammunition count. His scheduled link-up at Jarmin Pass was only two miles away, but the enemy stood between him and the pass.

AT BEACH RED, COLONEL CULIN had taken command of Northern Force. Late in the afternoon, after *Nevada* had silenced the enemy's flak guns for the moment, Culin's battalion drove the Japanese from their hilltop trenches. *Nassau's* Wildcats came in low under the clouds, wheeled over the Americans' heads and strafed the enemy with staccato bursts. The whining planes drove the Japanese back still farther, and chewed up the flak guns some more.

When flak had quit falling on Beach Red, Culin signaled *Chirikoff* to land her infantry battalion. The reserve troops started ashore before dark; they went straight up, platoon by platoon, to reinforce the exhausted battalion at the front.

Culin and Hartl prepared to launch a full-scale assault toward the mountain pass and the enemy camp in Holtz Bay, to their left; it would jump off not later than thirty-six hours hence.

When General Brown received that information by radio from Culin, he told Colonel Zimmerman to postpone further southern attacks against the pass until Culin could get into position on the far side. Zimmerman pulled his front lines back after nightfall and the third day ended with Southern Force some distance behind its original starting position, a hundred men weaker than before.

FRIDAY, MAY 14, 1943.

Eareckson circled Attu all morning. He was still there when Admiral Kinkaid got on the radio and asked Eareckson his opinion of weather conditions—Kinkaid, at Adak, had received several messages from Rockwell saying Brown's attacks had been delayed by poor visibility, and Kinkaid wanted to know just how poor it was.[6]

When Eareckson replied candidly—Attu was socked in solid—Kinkaid ordered him to return to base; there was no point wasting fuel in futile circles above the clouds.

In spite of the weather, Brown decided to feel out enemy defenses with one more assault; it was possible the Japanese might have fallen back during the night. He requested air support from *Nassau;* the carrier launched a strike, and her Wildcats sizzled up the valleys underneath the overcast. But just as they approached the target, a williwaw roared through Jarmin Pass. It caught three of the Wildcats only a few hundred feet above the ground and smashed them into the mountainside.

---

6. Major General Archibald V. Arnold, then Brown's second-in-command, recalls, "Attu was the first Army-Navy operation for almost all of us. We had little understanding of successful cooperation. The Navy had no conception of the effect of terrain and weather on the combat efficiency of the troops on Attu. It had no conception of how ground troops fought, and therefore Admiral Kinkaid could not evaluate the prospects for the outcome."

At the same time a PBY waddled across Holtz Bay, returned ground fire with its waist guns and dispersed the Japanese in the small camp. There was no other air action that day.

At eleven o'clock in the morning Brown threw Zimmerman's 3rd Battalion against Jarmin Pass. It ran into a holocaust of shrapnel and bullets. All four company commanders were put out of action—two killed, two wounded and evacuated—and casualties down through the ranks were cruelly heavy. The battalion fell back at a gallop, disordered and disorganized; it took Zimmerman hours to regroup it—in the same trenches it had started from. Zimmerman sorted things out at the front and then asked Brown to replace the shattered battalion with the battalion that had been carrying supplies from the rear for the past two days.

Brown went up to the front with Zimmerman, toured the lines, and agreed the battalion ought to be relieved. But he could not take his supply carriers off their jobs without starving the front lines. He ordered Zimmerman to keep pressure against Jarmin Pass until he could bring up fresh troops; he hoped to take the high ground on both sides above the pass with flanking movements, but that couldn't be done without reinforcements.

Below the pass, the wounded had been lying in the wet at aid stations, some of them forty-eight hours or more. Major Robert J. Kamish brought his portable field medical unit forward in the fog; his men distributed morphine and dressings up and down the line. Evacuees had to be strapped to their litters and rope-hauled over the slick cliffs. Under machine-gun and sniper fire, Kamish brought dozens of wounded men back to the field headquarters, from which they joined the growing stream of casualties awaiting transportation to the next echelon rearward.

On the far side of the pass, where Colonel Culin was consolidating in the face of heavy artillery and rifle fire, Northern Force prepared to jump off the next (fifth) morning; there was no movement of front lines. Squeaky Anderson kept the flow of supplies moving smoothly across Beach Red and up to the front—an accomplishment not equaled at Massacre Beach, where at General Brown's urgent demand a new battalion of the floating reserve came ashore—only to be bogged down on the overcrowded beach.

Reluctantly, Brown surveyed his unenviable situation and radioed a request to Rockwell that Simon Buckner's 4th Infantry Regiment be brought to Attu from Adak. He explained:

> EVIDENCE OF GREATER ENEMY STRENGTH THAN ANTICIPATED. INDICATION OF LACK OF SUFFICIENT FORCE TO ACCOMPLISH MISSION... RECENT CAPTURED ENEMY DOCUMENTS SHOW ENEMY STRENGTH CONSIDERABLY ABOVE THAT ANTICIPATED... REQUEST CONFERENCE WITH YOU IF BOAT IS AVAILABLE. WILL AWAIT REPLY.

COMMUNICATIONS HAD BEEN FOULED by static and a critical lack of radios, most of which had been ruined when *Perida* had rammed the reef. By the fourth morning of battle, Rockwell had no clear picture of Brown's situation. He did, however, have strong indications from CINCPAC's intelligence that big Japanese naval forces were on the way to Attu. He signaled Brown:

> EVERY EFFORT MUST BE MADE TO EXPEDITE CLEARING OF BEACH AND UNLOADING OF TRANSPORTS IN ORDER THAT THEY MAY BE WITHDRAWN AS SOON AS POSSIBLE. REINFORCEMENT BY FOURTH REGIMENT NOT POSSIBLE UNTIL COMPLETION OF ABOVE.

A copy of the message went to Kinkaid, who supported him:

> NO MORE TROOPS SHOULD BE PUT ASHORE UNTIL THE CONGESTION THERE IS RELIEVED. OBTAIN FROM GENERAL BROWN INFORMATION AS TO WHY MORE TROOPS ARE NEEDED.

Brown reacted bitterly; he told a staff officer he didn't believe the Navy cared about the Army's needs. Rockwell seemed interested only in getting his ships away from Attu as fast as he could—indeed, Brown pointed out, that morning the battleships had used up all their high-capacity 14-inch ammunition in a 2 1/2-hour bombardment from 15,000 yards' range. Shortly afterward *Pennsylvania* hammered the concealed hills with six hundred 5-inch armor-piercing shells. By early afternoon all the capital ships had exhausted their bombardment ammunition. "I suspected," recalls General Arnold, "the Navy vessels emptied their magazines rapid fire into the thick fog with no targets available so they could go back to Adak to rearm."

It left Brown with a crucial lack of bombardment support. His own guns were mired down on the beaches, where their fields of fire were restricted; ammunition was low—the transports offshore still had holds bulging with it, but there was no room on the beaches to land it, and besides, Brown feared the Navy would take the transports along (loaded or unloaded) when it left.

Army and Navy: each side thought the other had fallen down on the job. Since Brown was subordinate in the chain of command, the burden of proof lay upon him; and Brown's fate was sealed that afternoon by an untimely accident: his written summaries, explaining his plight and addressed to Rockwell and Kinkaid, were lost when a PBY carrying them from the beach to the flagship dropped them into the sea.

Word of the accident did not reach Rockwell. He assumed Brown had not sent any reports. Rockwell and Kinkaid, already unhappy with what they knew of events on shore, grew angry with the silence from Brown. Kinkaid sent Rockwell a stern demand that he find out "the present intentions of CG Landing Force," and added, "Prevail upon General Brown to send this information to the beach by runner."

Brown had already done that, but the information was at the bottom of Massacre Bay. In the meantime, Brown had gone up to the front again, where he visited his troops and saw that losses from exposure were mounting rapidly: the clothing that had been issued in San Francisco was not nearly warm enough for Attu's trenches. Men were frostbitten, feverish, unconscious.

Brown drew a company out of the line and had them set up a camp of heated tents; he told his staff to set up a system of rotation to give each battalion at least one day in three in the heated tents. But this could be done only if he could get reinforcements.

He went back to headquarters and found a stack of angry signals awaiting him—demands from Rockwell and Kinkaid for information—assuming that the morning attack was not made, advise if the 1500 attack was made. But then the intelligence office back at Adak clamped the lid down with a coded signal to both Rockwell and Brown:

> YOUR VOICE TRANSMISSIONS ARE GIVING THE ENEMY INTELLIGENCE OF OUR PLANS AND DIFFICULTIES. THIS CONDITION MUST BE CORRECTED IMMEDIATELY.

That closed down the few channels of communication that had remained open. From here on, Brown's fate was in the hands of men who had no information at all about his situation on the ground.

WHILE GENERAL BROWN CROSSED SWORDS with the Navy on this fourth day of battle, blood continued to stain the Attu snow. Zimmerman's point, in continuous contact with the enemy, exchanged fire all day; Culin fired, and withstood, mortar and artillery barrages; and in the mountains, forward units of Willoughby's Scout Battalion fought an all-day series of grim firefights with Japanese troops who shouted in English, "Damn American dogs, we massacre you!"

During the morning Willoughby had used the last of his mortar ammunition to repulse an enemy counterattack. His rifle ammunition was low—and his men had no food for the third straight day.

The cold was intense. Men limped on frozen feet and vomited silently. In training, Willoughby had lectured them on health measures; but, Willoughby recalls, "The ones who suffered were the ones who didn't keep moving. I tried to keep everyone on the move, but I didn't catch some of them. They stayed in their holes with wet feet. They didn't rub their feet or change socks when they needed to."

By evening nearly half his men were casualties—wounded, sick, or frostbitten. They kept crawling forward, sometimes with their fingernails, because there was no place to retreat to. Their only hope of survival was to break through the enemy lines and link up with the American forces beyond the ridges.

They fought with the fanaticism of desperation. Ahead of them, Japanese medical Lieutenant Nebu Tatsuguchi could hear the fighting as Willoughby made his inch-by-inch advance; Tatsuguchi wrote in his diary, "Enemy strength must be a division."

"There is a continuous flow of wounded," Tatsuguchi went on, "to the field hospital. In the evening, the U.S. forces used gas, but no damage was done on account of the strong wind."[7]

Willoughby's "division" fought on till sundown, after which sporadic

---

7. The propaganda about gas was untrue, of course, but lies and news management were not one-sided. On May 14, this fourth day of hard fighting on Attu, the Navy in Washington finally announced the American troops had landed on an enemy-held island in the Aleutians. No details were given. Three days later the Navy added only that "Operations against the Japanese on Attu Island are continuing." It was May 18, the eighth day, before the Navy began to release specific information. Meanwhile Radio Tokyo's daily English-language broadcasts (beamed at the States) kept up a detailed, if highly colored, account of the battle.

harassing fire volleyed raggedly across the high peaks. Willoughby collected his exhausted men; Dr. Klein ministered to their wounds and frozen extremities. One uninjured man sank into catatonia and died quietly in the night. The rest stamped their feet in the cold dark ravines and waited for sunrise.

GENERAL DEWITT HAD PROMISED THE War Department they would have Attu within three days after the beachhead landings. The battle now was four days old and the goal of joining all three forces at Jarmin Pass was not measurably closer than it had been seventy-two hours earlier. Willoughby was stalled; Culin had advanced only a mile or two; Zimmerman had not moved at all. Clearly it had hardly begun.

Men with trenchfoot and frostbite streamed to the rear by the score, then by the hundreds. Artillery squatted in the muskeg, immovable by the shore. Supplies on the beaches sprawled in great clogged heaps from which men carried bits and pieces forward on their backs, sinking up to the knees as they walked. Transport *Perida*, her holds bulging with vital supplies, stood beached on a spit of land too far away to be unloaded. LCs carrying supplies in and wounded out were crashing and swamping, and going to the bottom. The Air Force, grounded at Adak and Amchitka, listened miserably to urgent radio calls from ground troops who needed air drops of socks, sleeping bags, and food. The Navy's battlewagons and cruisers had used up their ammunition and now cruised impotently off-shore, their officers badgering Rockwell to get away before enemy naval forces could arrive and destroy them all. If Japan should counterattack from the Kuriles now, it would be a massacre.

SATURDAY, MAY 15, 1943.

Attu did not give the soldier much time in which to learn the rules of survival. Like a high-speed grindstone it polished men up, or ground them down, according to their toughness of body and spirit. Those who endured became hardened veterans almost overnight.

Lieutenant Charles K. Paulson's infantry platoon had been cut off from Southern Force for four days and nights; all that time they had held off the surrounding enemy. Their radios were broken; they had no food. Three days earlier, Paulson had sent his two Alaska Scouts to try and break through and bring help. There had been no word from the Scouts. If the army traveled on its stomach, Paulson bitterly told a squad leader, then his platoon was "traveling on sheer guts"—and not much of those left: they were vomiting green bile.

They stumbled through deep snow, trying to find friendly lines. Paulson found a lost field pack and first-aid kit on a snowbank; he patched a few men's wounds. The soldiers' feet perspired freely in their high leather blucher boots, and when the perspiration froze, frostbite immediately attacked their toes.

The fog began to lift early Saturday morning. An enemy machine-gun nest zeroed in on Paulson's platoon and pinned it down. And then American guns on the beach started to shell Paulson's area.

Desperate to get out from under the shelling, Paulson ordered a detail forward to wipe out the machine-gun nest that had them pinned down. But the men, mentally frozen, did not move. Paulson himself dashed forward, crouching. He flanked a Japanese rifleman in a horizontal trench and shot him; he ordered his men forward again, and again no one moved. American 105-mm shells chewed up the hillside all around them.

The third time Paulson called for an advance, a squad leader broke out of his trance and forced his squad forward; he said to Paulson, "This is our job, not yours," and rushed the enemy machine-gun nest. The squad wiped out the nest with grenades and appropriated the Japanese gun.

In such ways, the green troops of Attu became veterans. Later in the morning one of Paulson's men got through to the American lines, brought a party of Military Police up and guided Paulson and his survivors back to the beach, where a field kitchen fed them hot soup—their first hot meal since they had hit the beach.

LATE THAT MORNING ZIMMERMAN led yet another frontal assault against Jarmin Pass. Like the others, it fell back under a cruel fusillade from three directions. Zimmerman regrouped once again in the original trenches.

But Northern Force was on the move. Colonel Frank Culin's battalions were advancing downhill toward the enemy base in the valley above Holtz Bay. By noon the lack of opposition made it clear that the Japanese had fallen back during the night. They had withdrawn to the ridge on the far side of Holtz Valley.

It was a break—the first since the battle had begun. The Japanese had left behind large stores of ammunition, food, field pieces, mortars, and machine guns. They had retreated, evidently, to avoid being caught between Culin and Willoughby.

Culin marched into Holtz Valley immediately and spent the afternoon securing the area and getting his strike battalions ready to move east during the night. They would cross the bend of Holtz Bay in darkness; at daybreak they would be in position to attack the enemy-held ridge.

It had been the first important forward movement in three days, but Culin's right flank was still hard against the Japanese at Jarmin Pass, and none of the American forces had made any headway in that direction. Culin decided to let that flank alone for the moment. He would press east, pushing the Japanese from the heights east of Holtz Bay back toward Chichagof Valley. That would cut the contact between the main Japanese force and the defenders above Jarmin Pass; by driving a wedge between the enemy forces, Culin would either isolate the small force above Jarmin Pass and starve it out, or persuade the Japanese to give up the pass and fall back from there into Chichagof to join the main body. Either way Jarmin Pass would open up to the planned American rendezvous, and the Japanese could be bottled up in Chichagof, as General Brown had planned from the start.

WHEN THE JAPANESE EVACUATED Holtz Valley on the fourth night of the battle, they took with them troops that had stood against Willoughby's front. The path was now open between Willoughby and Culin. Willoughby recalls:

> Since we couldn't sleep at night, we weren't about to let the enemy sleep. We kept up a din around the clock so that they wouldn't divert any forces away from us against Culin. Finally, when the time looked right, I told Colonel Culin by radio that we were moving down, and we headed down toward Holtz Bay. The enemy was pulling out fast.

Willoughby's straggling men limped across the ridges, slipped and stumbled down into Holtz Bay. Willoughby dropped off two or three men at each abandoned Japanese position to guard it against souvenir hunting and looting; he was alert to the importance of capturing Japanese records and codes intact.

He left about eighty men behind on various rear-guard and mop-up details; he arrived in Culin's area with 320 men, only forty of whom were still able to walk without pain. Somehow, only eleven men (including Captain Austin) had been killed in the four days' fighting across the mountains. Twenty others had been wounded. Most of the rest had bad foot injuries. Some had gangrene; several eventually required amputation of both feet. A number had bleeding, ulcerated lesions on their knees (from crawling, because they could no longer walk).

By the time all the hospital cases had been evacuated Willoughby's strength—originally 420 men—was down to 165, most of them bandaged at feet and knees.

For them the battle was far from over. They would eat, rest, and recuperate for a day or so; then they would go back to war. Attu was not yet done with the Scout Battalion.

THAT NOON, FOR THE SECOND TIME in three days, battleship *Pennsylvania* made a high-speed turn to dodge a spread of torpedoes. A few minutes later the same submarine fired four torpedoes at transport *J. Franklin Bell.*

The torpedoes missed; the enemy submarine was driven off by American destroyers; but Admiral Rockwell was no longer in a mood to disregard enemy torpedoes with a coarse joke. The battle had dragged on far beyond expectations, there was no end in sight, and at any moment the enemy might appear over the horizon with bombers or a carrier-cruiser fleet. With its big ships out of main battery ammunition, the North Pacific Force—still more than forty ships at Attu—was a sitting duck.

In the morning a signal had come from General Brown on shore:

> REPEAT REQUEST FOR 4TH INF AS THIS IS CONSIDERED VITAL NECESSITY. REQUEST REPLY CONCERNING OUR RECOMMENDATIONS…THESE TROOPS MIGHT STILL MEAN THE DIFFERENCE BETWEEN SUCCESS AND FAILURE THE OPERATION.

Rockwell replied that he was still against it. Massacre Beach was jammed, and the ships carrying the reinforcements would only add to the number of floating targets.

Both commanders were merely repeating what they had said a day earlier. Exasperated by the impasse, Brown chose to go over Rockwell's head.

General DeWitt had flown up from San Francisco to find out why the battle was lagging behind the schedule he had given the War Department. He had arrived at Adak and gone into conference with General Buckner, Admiral Kinkaid, and Marine General "Howlin' Mad" Smith, at Kinkaid's headquarters. Word of DeWitt's arrival had reached Brown; now Brown asked DeWitt to intercede:

> HAVE MADE FREQUENT ATTEMPTS TO HAVE [ROCKWELL] PROCURE ADDITIONAL TROOPS BUT WITHOUT

> SUCCESS. REQUEST YOUR ASSISTANCE IN THEIR DISPATCH....

The message bewildered DeWitt and Kinkaid, who had just noted in his fleet war diary, "Communications with General Brown very bad. One memorandum by plane drop has been received.... Am trying to arrange conference with [Brown] for today."

No one had a clear picture of the whole. The obvious solution was to get everyone together and thrash out the problems face-to-face. Kinkaid radioed Rockwell to set up a conference with Brown.

Kinkaid was unaware of it, but Brown himself had asked for such a meeting the previous day. Now Brown heard that Rockwell was planning to pull out of Attu, with the Navy ships, within twenty-four hours; it became imperative that Brown talk to Rockwell personally. And so, without any knowledge of Kinkaid's orders, Brown left General Arnold in temporary command ashore and set out for the flagship in Massacre Bay.

By the time he arrived aboard the battleship at two o'clock in the afternoon, Brown was fighting mad. He was prepared to remind Rockwell of Article 99 of the Uniform Code of Military Justice, which made it a court-martial offense to fail to afford all practicable relief and assistance to forces engaged in battle.

But Brown got no chance to bring that up. Rockwell disarmed him by listening courteously to his arguments—and then agreeing with them.

Culin's advance into Holtz Bay that morning had persuaded Rockwell there was still a good chance for success under Brown's plans and leadership. Half an hour before Brown's arrival on the flagship, Rockwell had sent a message to Kinkaid endorsing Brown's request for the 4th Infantry.

Together, Rockwell and Brown prepared a joint dispatch to Kinkaid. It repeated the request for reinforcements, stated that the outlook was encouraging, and added parenthetically that Colonel Benjamin Talley of the Engineers (who was at Brown's headquarters on Attu) wanted road-building equipment sent forward from Adak. The equipment Talley wanted was already aboard Navy freighters at Adak; it included enough fuel and construction supplies to last sixty days. Talley wanted to start building roads so he could clear up the jam on the beach, move the artillery forward, and get load-carrying infantrymen back into the fighting lines.

Brown and Rockwell did not foresee that the hastily worded message to Kinkaid left itself open to misinterpretations that would cause personal disaster for Brown and embarrassment for everyone concerned.

Kinkaid saw the Engineer's request as an indication that Brown expected the battle to last sixty days. Brown was forever asking for more troops; the message made it appear he had gone on the defensive and proposed to sit still until he got his reinforcements.

Kinkaid signaled Rockwell:

> IF BROWN LACKS AGGRESSIVENESS HE SHOULD BE RELIEVED.

Rockwell shot back an immediate reply:

> RECOMMEND SUCH ACTION NOT BE TAKEN WITHOUT ACQUAINTING YOURSELF WITH BROWN'S DIFFICULTIES.

Kinkaid, who had never met General Brown, consulted with Buckner and DeWitt. DeWitt had never liked Brown; he took this opportunity to suggest that if Brown could not get the job done, then Brown was not the man for the job.

Buckner, who had no more information than Kinkaid had, said Brown's weakness was probably his inexperience with the Aleutians. He put forward the name of Major General Eugene M. Landrum as a possible replacement. Landrum knew the territory; he had led the Adak landings nine months earlier.

Kinkaid had always respected Buckner's judgment, but this was a case of one Alaskan's putting forth another Alaskan for a job now held by an outsider. As for DeWitt, his motives were equally clouded—by his friendship with Buckner, his dislike for Brown, and his failure to make good on his promise to the War Department that Attu would fall in three days.

To take Brown off the field in mid-battle would injure the troops' morale and cause confusion ashore; yet the difference between the right general and the wrong general could be a difference measured not only in days but in lives. Kinkaid retired to make his solitary decision. He was in charge: it was up to him. The loneliness of command isolated him completely. He studied the information he had, and made his decision; at midnight he sent a cipher to CINCPAC:

> [IN VIEW OF] THE UNSATISFACTORY SITUATION ASHORE AT ATTU...IT IS WITH REGRET THAT THE TASK FORCE COMMANDER HAS DECIDED THAT THE COMMANDING GENERAL LANDING FORCE MUST BE

SUPERSEDED. THEREFORE GENERAL LANDRUM WILL PROCEED TODAY BY PLANE AND RELIEVE GENERAL BROWN.

SUNDAY, MAY 16, 1943.

Admiral Nimitz replied:

CONCUR YOUR DECISION TO REPLACE GENERAL BROWN.

Kinkaid signaled Admiral Rockwell, who lost his temper, regained it, and radioed General Brown:

REGRET TO INFORM YOU, AS DIRECTED BY COMNORPAC, THAT BECAUSE OF TACTICAL SITUATION HE HAS ORDERED GENERAL LANDRUM AS RELIEF AS CDR LF.

Shocked, Brown replied that the battle was well under control; he added a demand which Rockwell passed on to Kinkaid:

GENERAL BROWN REQUESTS THAT AN IMMEDIATE INVESTIGATION ON THE GROUND BE MADE IF GENERAL LANDRUM IS RELIEVING HIM BECAUSE OF ANY FAILURES.

Kinkaid answered:

REGRET THAT TIME DOES NOT PERMIT THE INVESTIGATION GENERAL BROWN REQUESTS. INFORM HIM THAT GENERAL LANDRUM IS EN ROUTE.

In Massacre Valley, Brown's officers rallied around him until the general sent them back to work: until his successor should arrive, Brown was still in command, and there was still a battle to be fought.

Brown now ordered yet another head-on assault by Zimmerman's regiment, against Jarmin Pass. It was like butting a cliff; the attack fell back without making a dent in the enemy's defenses.

While Southern Force, with the largest body of troops (American or Japanese) on Attu, was at a standstill, Culin in the north pressed his attack. He had crossed Holtz Valley under cover of night; now he put pressure on the ridge east of the valley. Heavy Japanese fire from the rim pinned his main battalions to the valley floor, but Culin sent platoons out along the beach to his left. These flankers worked around the enemy's right and began to climb the steep seaside ends of the ridges. Against tough opposition, they advanced from hump to hump and charged into several hours' savage hand-to-hand fighting.[8] By evening they had driven the enemy back and secured the high ground. Culin then occupied the length of the ridge with his battalions.

Word of the advance had not yet reached carrier *Nassau*, which launched a bombing-strafing attack against the ridge Culin had just taken. American troops dived for cover while radio men blistered *Nassau* with oaths; the strike was recalled, but not before several men had been wounded.

By sundown the advance was complete; Culin, with troops on all the heights surrounding Holtz Valley, had full control of the area. That was important, because it meant he could now move ships into the west arm of Holtz Bay and use the good harbor facilities there instead of the tight little strip at Beach Red.

Culin's capture of Holtz Valley had been accomplished by men who did not know General Brown had been relieved. When Culin radioed a report to Brown, it was the only good news Brown had received all day. He sent a "Well done" to Culin. A few minutes later he heard that General Landrum had arrived in the harbor.

EUGENE LANDRUM, STOCKY AND CHERUBIC, was recovering from a broken leg he had suffered in an accident. With some difficulty, he came across from Amchitka by PBY and destroyer, transferred from *Dewey* to *Pennsylvania* in a breeches buoy, and reported himself to Admiral Rockwell.

Shortly afterward, Brown came out to meet them. The conference was subdued and awkward. Landrum listened to Brown's summary of the situation on Attu, and made it clear he found no fault with what Brown had done. He said he would make no changes in Brown's tactical plans.

At dusk on the sixth day of battle, Brown had his last look at Attu. By nightfall he was on his way east.

---

8. Its brave attack on Davis Hill, one of the ridges Culin overran on May 16, earned a Presidential Unit Citation for Company B of the 17th Infantry—the fourth such citation awarded units of Brown's command for their performances during his tenure. Brown's supporters later held these up as evidence of Brown's achievements in training and leadership.

IT DID NOT TAKE LONG FOR Admiral Kinkaid to get word of the strafing of American troops by carrier *Nassau's* planes on the ridge above Holtz Valley. Late in the afternoon Kinkaid radioed Colonel Eareckson, who was circling Attu's overcast for the eighth straight hour, with orders to report to General Landrum and take direct control of all air operations. Eareckson was to coordinate air strikes with ground operations. Kinkaid hoped it would prevent further mistakes.

At 7:00 p.m. Eareckson reached Attu in a PBY and reported to Landrum, who was then aboard *Pennsylvania* waiting for Brown. Shortly afterward Eareckson commandeered a Navy Kingfisher (a two-seat, single-engine observation seaplane) and was flying it off tender *Casco,* amused by a message Kinkaid had relayed to him: Kinkaid had ordered General Butler to "Hold flights until further instructions from Colonel Eareckson." Butler, as usual, had been shunted aside.

MONDAY, MAY 17, 1943.

Colonel Frank Culin hoped to reduce the danger of enemy machine-gun fire by fighting at night. Just after midnight his men synchronized their watches, loaded their weapons, and passed signals along the front lines. All the troops of both Northern Force battalions would make a massed attack on the Japanese positions on the second ridge east of Holtz Bay.

At 12:10 a.m., Northern Force began its uphill charge. Voices called hoarsely across the fog-black ridge, muzzle flames lanced forward through the cold. Artillery, fired from the beach by radio instructions, marched its explosions ahead of the advancing American line. The gunfire was intense. Soldiers with teeth chattering from cold climbed by the light of exploding shells; to one observer the eerie scene looked like an old movie film projected in jerky stop-motion.

Within three hours, Culin had taken the ridge without a single casualty. The Japanese had withdrawn before him, retreating toward Chichagof Harbor.

WHEN GENERAL BROWN REACHED ADAK in the morning, he went directly to headquarters for a meeting with Kinkaid and DeWitt. Kinkaid had never met the general before; he recalls:

> He seemed a very nice chap, very well put together. I had to relieve him, that was all.... When I saw him, I told him that what had touched me off was his request for tremendous supplies. I asked him what he'd expected to build there—a stadium, or a

city? He'd asked for supplies that he couldn't have used over a period of months.

The meeting was cool and formal. Old accusations were resurrected; DeWitt admitted he had never wanted Brown to command the Attu force, and Brown accused DeWitt of making him a scapegoat when he did not stick to the impossible three-day victory schedule which DeWitt had promised the War Department. Brown said Kinkaid must have misinterpreted the situation (and, according to Brown, Kinkaid then admitted he would not have relieved Brown had he been more completely informed).

But it was done, and Kinkaid could not reverse himself now. The meeting resolved nothing. Later in the day General Brown boarded a plane and headed for Kodiak, on his way back to the States. For him, the Aleutian war was over.[9]

---

9. Lieutenant General John L. DeWitt wrote, in Albert E. Brown's efficiency report for the period of the Battle of Attu: "Personality and temperament not conducive to command joint operations. Impulsive." It was a damning comment, since an officer's efficiency report was used as the basis for promotions and assignments.

Major General Brown did not learn of DeWitt's condemnation until years later. Meanwhile he had been given command of the 5th Infantry Division, which he led into combat in Europe. After the war he took over the 6th Division in Korea. It was only in 1947, after his return to the States, that he saw DeWitt's statement.

He drew up a detailed rebuttal on May 4, 1948, asking the Chief of Staff to review his case. "I am of the firm opinion," Brown wrote, "that [my] relief...was without cause." He said Admiral Kinkaid should have made a more thorough investigation before relieving him on false assumptions. He included testimonials and letters from many officers whose loyalty to him had not flagged. Major General Archibald Arnold wrote, "General DeWitt, who felt it would be a short affair, had so informed the War Department. When progress was slow there was an embarrassing question which called for an answer in action. Relief of the commander seems to have been the answer... The Division certainly did a job up there, something you can well be proud of. The big regret is that they didn't let you finish it."

General Landrum, who had taken Brown's place, promised to be the star witness on Brown's behalf. Landrum wrote him, "The fight rolled along just as you had planned it ...Your strategy paid big dividends." (Ironically, Landrum himself was relieved of command of the 87th Infantry Division at the Normandy landings in 1944.)

DeWitt and others lined up against Brown. They insisted he should have gone for the high ground west of Jarmin Pass instead of massing useless frontal assaults up the floor of the pass. They scored him for not having listened to the advice of Alaskan officers in San Diego. They said he should have equipped his men with proper footgear and clothes, and anticipated the impossibility of using vehicles on Attu. (Brown replied that he had tried to get adequate clothing and equipment but DeWitt's supply people hadn't furnished it.)

Clearly no one was wholly free of responsibility for the mistakes at Attu; equally clearly, Brown was not entirely to blame for the circumstances that conspired against him. In 1949 the Chief of Staff endorsed Brown's claim, thereby officially clearing his name and record.

IT WAS THE SEVENTH DAY of the Battle of Attu. According to the command count, which was not complete, the American force had suffered 1,100 casualties, 500 of them exposure cases. By now there were 12,500 American troops on the island, about 3,500 of them in the front lines. Facing them was a Japanese force that now numbered fewer than 2,000 men.

The Japanese had done what Colonel Frank Culin had expected them to do. By withdrawing his main forces from Holtz Bay to the vicinity of Chichagof Harbor in the northeast, Colonel Yasuyo Yamasaki had left unguarded the rear of his positions overlooking Jarmin Pass. Culin's eastward advance along the northern coast would soon isolate Jarmin Pass completely. It left Yamasaki with no choice but to pull his men out of Jarmin Pass, even though they had kept the Americans from gaining a foot of ground there for an entire week.

Above the pass, under cover of predawn darkness and fog, Lieutenants Honna and Goto gathered their men and guns in complete silence and withdrew to the east, toward their comrades in Chichagof Harbor. They crossed the ridges without being discovered; by morning they had linked up with the main force.

At sunrise Jarmin Pass lay undefended, wide open to an American advance. But the advance did not take place. In the fog, the Americans could not see that the enemy was gone.

FOR THE FIFTH DAY IN A ROW, a Japanese torpedo-bomber group waited at Paramushiro for a weather break that would give them a chance to bomb the Americans at Attu. There was no such break in sight.

In Paramushiro's harbor, a Japanese task force had assembled around a heavy cruiser and two light cruisers—Admiral Koga, Yamamoto's successor, had finally persuaded high command to act. He had obtained the Imperial Fifth Fleet and had turned it over to the North Pacific's Admiral Kawase, who was already at sea off the Kuriles in heavy cruiser *Maya,* with seaplane carrier *Kimikawa Maru* and a small convoy of reinforcements which he intended to take to Attu.

The Fifth Fleet steamed out of Paramushiro toward a rendezvous with Admiral Kawase south of the Komandorskis. But radio reports from Attu had informed Kawase that the Americans had forty ships there, including three colossal battleships and a carrier. Kawase, with four cruisers, a seaplane carrier and a few destroyers, would be hopelessly outgunned if he went up against that. And so, unaware that the American fleet was out of ammunition, he continued to circle 300 miles west of Attu, hoping for some break.

ABOUT NOON MAY 17, COLONEL WAYNE Zimmerman walked up to an advance observation post and searched the summits above Jarmin Pass. The fog had lifted almost to the top. Zimmerman saw no sign of life.

He gathered a patrol and went forward to reconnoiter the pass. He recalls:

> I found most of a platoon—all dead—and identified Captain Jarmin's body.[10] The Battalion commander was almost in a state of shock. I relieved him and shortly moved the battalion back to reserve.

There were no Japanese anywhere in the pass, except for the bodies of dead Japanese soldiers huddled in grotesque piles of three and four.

Zimmerman brought up a fresh infantry company to occupy the pass and scout the far side; meanwhile he went back to his headquarters to greet the new commanding general, who had just come ashore to take charge after having spent the night aboard *Pennsylvania.*

General Landrum brought with him a motto—"The Japanese soldier can be whipped"—and the desire to convince the 7th Division Staff that he did not intend to steal the credit for any of his predecessor's accomplishments or plans.

TUESDAY, MAY 18, 1943.

At midnight, Colonel Frank Culin had called Captain Willoughby to his tent and asked if Willoughby felt well enough to lead a patrol. Willoughby said he felt fine. Two days' recuperation had been all he had needed.

Willoughby called for volunteers from the remnants of his Scout Battalion; in a matter of minutes he had 150 men lined up. Some of them had sore feet but they were all ready to go.

Willoughby set out to explore the northern approaches to Jarmin Pass. At 2:30 a.m., his advance platoon met a patrol from Colonel Zimmerman's outfit which had come down from the other side of the pass.

The two American forces thus achieved the rendezvous that had been their goal for eight days. Now the American line formed an unbroken semicircle that enclosed the enemy against the sea on the northeastern

---

10. It was not until midway through the Battle of Attu that the pass between Holtz and Massacre Valleys became known by the name of Captain Jarmin, the ranking American officer killed there. The same was true of Austin Cove, where Willoughby had landed. For the sake of consistency I have used these placenames throughout, since that is the way they appear on modern maps.

corner of Attu. Albert Brown was no longer there to see it, but his plan had worked out.

THOUGH THE JAPANESE HAD LOST Jarmin Pass, they had withdrawn in order. Still intact, they were well prepared to defend the jagged high terrain around Chichagof Valley. It would be no easy job to break down their defenses. The heights, several thousand feet tall, were precipitous. Snow, ice, muskeg and fog covered them all. Attu, as Eareckson observed, was no place for human beings.

General Landrum allowed his commanders a day to regroup and reorganize for the new offensive, which was to jump off early next morning. Landrum decided to maintain the present two-part pincer arrangement of forces. Zimmerman would turn northeast along the eastern side of Chichagof, while Culin would strike from the west. Both forces would keep joined at the center to prevent the enemy from breaking out of the trap.

Zimmerman and Culin shuffled exhausted units into the reserve and brought up fresher troops. As always, the vital difficulty was supply: Landing craft and boats had been carrying cargoes from transports to the beaches, but by now, of the ninety-three LCs and boats they had started with, only three were still in operation—two in Massacre, one in Holtz. Ninety craft had gone down, victims of Attu shoals, reefs, williwaws, and surf.

Admiral Rockwell had sent urgent calls to Adak for tugs and barges, but it would take them a week or more to arrive. In the meantime Commander Denny's PT-boats, assigned to pick up downed pilots, pitched in to carry supplies ashore; even PBYs taxied back and forth with hull loads of food, medicine, and ammunition. Rockwell moved the transports dangerously close to shore. The only good thing to come out of it was that the jam of supplies on Massacre Beach had dwindled; by now it was all but exhausted.

Colonel Benjamin Talley's Engineers had begun to build a road up a stream bed, to move artillery inland from Massacre Beach. Overhead, a fixture by now, Colonel Eareckson buzzed Japanese concentrations in Chichagof Valley. In the little Kingfisher Eareckson made several low-level strafing attacks below the fog. "Tunnel-flying" through the narrow canyons, he picked out targets and radioed their locations to Captain Lucian Wernick, who led the bombers circling above the clouds.[11]

11. The original air-liaison plan had called for Eareckson to radio target locations to Butler's Amchitka Control, which was to forward the information to the bombers in the air.

Wernick led several missions down through the soup that day, dumping bombs on enemy positions. It was the only combat that day. By sunset, Zimmerman and Culin were ready to jump off. Landrum ordered an all-out attack as soon as the morning's lifting fog would permit.

WEDNESDAY, MAY 19, 1943.

Landrum's headquarters was a mud-floored tent in Massacre Valley. His washed socks hung outside on tent ropes. His broken leg had not healed completely and Landrum could only hobble around with a knobbed walking stick; his assistant, Brigadier General Archibald V. Arnold, had to assume some of the commanding general's duties.

Arnold went up front with Colonel Zimmerman. Shortly before 10:00 a.m. they kicked off with an artillery barrage and sent the infantry toward the high ground to the northeast. Simultaneously, three miles to the west, Frank Culin pushed two battalions against the Chichagof foothills. The steep trails took the slogging soldiers into morasses of half-melted snow.

Enemy opposition was fierce enough to halt Culin's forward platoons; strength at the spearhead went up from a single company to two battalions, but the Japanese held fast. From here, for a week to come, it would be a grim inch-by-inch battle for every bloodstained hill.

During the afternoon Zimmerman's Southern Force advanced a half mile toward the enemy stronghold and rapidly overran the first high ground. But directly ahead stood a great mountain, Point Able, defended by a tough Japanese infantry company reinforced with guns and mortars. Its leader was Lieutenant Honna—the same young officer who had held Jarmin Pass for the past week. Honna yelled derisively (in excellent English) while he fended off attack after attack. It was Jarmin Pass all over again; it would take Zimmerman three days of fighting right out of the Stone Age, with bayonets, to clear Honna's single line company off the summit.

THURSDAY, MAY 20, 1943.

By noon of the tenth day, the only Japanese resistance in Zimmerman's area was Lieutenant Honna's tenacious company high on the 2,000-foot

---

But Butler's command post neither acknowledged nor forwarded Eareckson's orders. Wernick recalls, "It was as if they had a hearing aid that was turned off. They just didn't respond at all." Perhaps radio static interfered with the messages. At any rate, Eareckson had recognized the husky roar of Wernick's voice on the bomber radio frequency, and had independently directed Wernick to take over and bypass Amchitka Control.

rock of Point Able. Flanking units pushed north past the fortress; and Culin, northwest of them, gained a few hundred yards, no more.

Under the rolling blackness of the overcast a thin cold drizzle soaked the soldiers. The light was bad for shooting. Shadows were troubled and uncertain; long frigid winds moaned along the snow. The shapes of fighting men flitted from cover to cover, their bodies and faces as gray as the rain. One by one as they pushed forward, the soldiers overcame snipers and machine-gun bunkers. Gunshots cracked and echoed across the summits; the distant growl of artillery was muffled by the rain and fog. Here and there bodies lay motionless, half-covered by drifting snow.

ITS LANDING CRAFT DECIMATED, the American force scrambled for supplies. Soldiers risked being shot by their own comrades by wearing caps, hoods, and waterproof boots they had stripped from Japanese dead. At the beaches, platoons threw grenades into the surf to kill fish.

They had to stop grenading long enough to let lifeboat loads of troops come ashore from an ancient transport: Buckner's 4th Infantry Regiment had at last arrived, to swell the ground force to 16,000 men. The troops had been three weeks on shipboard without exercise; they could hardly walk. At snail's pace the regiment writhed through the mountains to join the fighting lines.

In the air, Eareckson spent the day in search of holes in the fog. His little Kingfisher was nimble enough to dart among the mountains at low level. Eareckson was pioneering a technique that would assume great importance in future wars, when pilots like Eareckson would carry the official designation, "Forward Air Controller." But the job crackled with danger. Eareckson carried a cockpit load of rubber plugs and cement "bullet hole kits" for his airplane; more than once he had to beach the Kingfisher to keep it from sinking, its floats sieved by ground fire.*

---

*1995 ADDENDUM: Navy weatherman Paul Carrigan wrote, in a recent letter to Lawrence Reineke, "I met your Col. Eareckson. Great guy and very knowledgeable about weather. He operated a borrowed Kingfisher scout plane from our tender. Col. Eareckson spent quite a bit of time in our weather shack, reading hourly weather, discussing our analyzed map with us, going over forecasts etc. This several times a day. He would take off early in morning, back in forenoon or lunch time, rest for few hours and take off again in afternoon. He flew three times on several days. He'd pancake his shot-up Kingfisher almost alongside *Casco*, taxi hurriedly to boom and hook; plane would be hoisted out and swung onto back deck. Many times when plane emerged from water it was already sinking. As boom swung it inboard, water would pour from dozens of bullet holes or jagged tears in pontoon. Looked like a giant sprinkling can. How we all admired that guy. Great leader of men."

Late in the day he found a break, and called in Wernick's bombers. The attack had to be visual and pinpoint-accurate, to avoid hitting American troops; Wernick took no chances. Pilots bombed with care.

The Aleutian Campaign had been a year-long bombardment siege, but now, at its climax at Attu, air power played the subordinate role. Angry but cautious, the Eleventh Air Force held back.

IMPERIAL HEADQUARTERS TOOK A HARD LINE. "The Navy...will take action to apprehend and destroy the enemy's surface strength."

Circling off the Komandorskis, Admiral Kawase replied by describing the overwhelming size of the American fleet that was massed around Attu. Imperial Headquarters considered his information and signaled, later the same day, "At the last possible moment, every effort will be made to evacuate the Attu Island Defense Force, or even a part of it, by submarine."

Admiral Kawase relayed the order to his I-boat pack, which closed slowly toward Attu.

FRIDAY, MAY 21, 1943.

Wheeler reported: "There was only one area open and Wernick stalked it like a tiger. A lot of damage resulted as several large fires were observed in the Japanese camp."

Eareckson called down the B-25 and P-38 attacks; by noon every building in Chichagof Village, the old Aleut settlement, had been destroyed, with the exception of the church. But coming out of the last raid, two Lightnings collided over Massacre Bay; one fell straight toward the battleship *Pennsylvania*, where a visiting Simon Buckner stood on the bridge and watched tons of steel careen past the superstructure and plummet into the green-black water, close enough to splash the battleship's decks.

Buckner, who wanted a closer look at the battle, went over to tender *Casco* with Colonel Lawrence Castner and asked Eareckson to give them a lift in his plane.

They squeezed into the one-passenger observer seat. Eareckson flew them up Massacre Valley and past Point Able, where Buckner manned the observer's machine gun and strafed the Japanese trenches.

Aboard *Nevada*, Colonel William Alexander watched the plane corkscrew up into the soup and felt apprehensive. "Who were the replacements to be if those three piled up?"

But the three returned without mishap. The weather had socked down in a solid drizzle by the time the Kingfisher had been hauled aboard *Casco.* With no more flying possible that day, Eareckson accompanied Buckner ashore.

To the airman, the face of ground war was remote. Eareckson wanted to learn for himself what things were like on Attu. He walked up to the front line, borrowed a rifle and started shooting at Point Able.

He had fired three shots when a Japanese sniper's bullet creased him across the back. Eareckson emptied his rifle in a furious barrage; several witnesses claimed he killed the sniper. His wound was dressed at an aid station, after which Eareckson walked back down to the beach. Simon Buckner was there, looking after his 4th Infantrymen. Buckner found a Purple Heart medal, pinned it on Eareckson's chest, and then turned Eareckson around and kicked him with a hard combat boot in the buttocks, "for being where you had no business being."

ZIMMERMAN'S BATTALIONS KEPT PUSHING north into the mountains against strong resistance. At Point Able, nothing had moved for three days. The Americans now controlled every inch of Massacre and Holtz Valleys and some of the ridges near Chichagof Valley. On the left flank, a battalion of the newly arrived 4th Infantry had clawed northwest in a pincer toward Culin; despite their exhaustion from shipboard confinement, Buckner's well-trained infantrymen made good headway against heavy Japanese opposition; by nightfall they were half way to their objective.

In the evening, Company E of the 32nd Infantry made a final bold charge up the slopes of Point Able. A rifleman cut down young Lieutenant Honna in his tracks. Honna's outfit (2nd Company, 303rd Japanese Infantry Battalion) was wiped out to the last man; when the Americans crawled onto the top they found not a single Japanese soldier left alive.[12]

SATURDAY, MAY 22, 1943.

The only beach Colonel Yamasaki still held was in Chichagof Harbor, and even that was under American artillery and air attack. But Yamasaki ordered his men to hold the beach at all costs. Submarines were on the way to evacuate them. Help would come.

Help did come, but not in the expected form. In midafternoon nineteen "Betty" bombers from Paramushiro found a patch of clear sky over Holtz Bay, dived through it, and surprised gunboat *Charleston* and destroyer *Phelps*. The two ships rang up flank speed—the jerk almost threw them out of the water—and wheeled into violent evasive

12. Company E, 32nd Infantry, earned a Presidential Unit Citation for its successful charge up Point Able on May 21.

maneuvers while their flak guns cranked toward the diving Japanese bombers.

The two ships fired a concentrated hail of flak. It shot down a Betty and exploded a torpedo in midair. Twelve other torpedoes hit the water and churned forward, but none hit its mark. Flak crippled a second plane, which wheeled away burning, and crashed; the seventeen other Bettys turned away. They dropped packages into Chichagof Valley and zoomed up into the clouds.

AT 6:40 THAT TWELFTH MORNING Colonel Zimmerman found his advance blocked by a powerful enemy concentration on a peak called Sarana Nose. Zimmerman called down a barrage from every available piece—howitzers, mortars, even light machine guns. From field artillery that had been rope-dragged up Colonel Talley's makeshift road, from guns stalled on the distant beaches, and from positions in the front lines, a hail of projectiles arched onto Sarana Nose. It seemed to explode every foot of enemy ground.

The bombardment roared for thirty minutes, after which Zimmerman's infantry began to move out under the ceiling of overhead artillery fire. By 7:30 the soldiers had crossed a flat valley floor and begun to climb Sarana Nose.

On the left flank, a battalion of the 4th Infantry went into action along a parallel ridge. Its scouts spotted troops coming forward over a ridge from the north, and for a while it wasn't clear if they were friend or foe. Mist drifted across the ridge; the Americans held their fire while a platoon leader radioed Culin and learned that Culin's right flank had pulled back during the night. Thus the advancing soldiers must be Japanese. The Americans opened fire.

The advancing troops, Japanese in fact, took cover behind rocks and put up a blast of fire that stalled the Americans. After a half hour's motionless shooting, the Americans called down an artillery bombardment. Blasting 105s drove the Japanese back from the rocks; the 4th Infantrymen drove them down the far side of the ridge with rifles and machine guns.

The main assault against Sarana Nose continued all morning. The Japanese were dug in; the morning's artillery barrage had merely forced them to keep their heads down. Their strength was only a rifle company—fewer than two hundred men—while the American Northern Force was pushing forward with more than two battalions. Against those lopsided odds, the Japanese began to fall back in order; but that was when Zimmerman called in another bombardment.

As Northern Force climbed Sarana Nose, artillery shells walked uphill ahead of them. By the time Zimmerman reached the Japanese second line of defense, where the enemy had paused to wait out the barrage, the fog had broken into pockets of mist. The artillery had shaken the Japanese. Dazed, they had lost the capacity to put up effective resistance.

Afraid to surrender, the Japanese fought or ran, one by one. Those who stayed, died. By nightfall, Zimmerman had decimated the Japanese company and taken Sarana Nose with only a handful of casualties.

The day's northward advances opened the way for a direct attack against the southern gate into Chichagof Valley, where Colonel Yamasaki's entire force had its back to the sea and its front against Culin, to the west, and Zimmerman, to the south.

Culin faced the heaviest resistance, and General Landrum saw no point in pressing the attack hardest on that front. If Culin could hold his ground, it would be enough. With two regiments abreast, Landrum would make the main attack from the south, with Zimmerman's force.

The day's aerial photos showed that a direct attack up the valley floor would bring Zimmerman under devastating fire from the ridges that overlooked the valley. Landrum would have to take that high ground first. With that in mind, he ordered an attack on the steep razorback that ran north along the western side of the Japanese stronghold—Fish Hook Ridge. Covered with ice, these heights were among the most rugged the soldiers had seen in almost two weeks of fighting on Attu. But with the 4th Infantry on the west face and Southern Force on the east face, it ought to be the place where the strongest American attack could meet the weakest Japanese defenses.

The assault would jump off at daybreak.

SUNDAY, MAY 23, 1943.

Trapped behind his innermost defensive perimeter, Colonel Yamasaki had seen his area shrink drastically. But that made him harder to dislodge than ever, since he had more soldiers to defend each yard of ground. Yamasaki's brilliant delaying action had cost him hundreds of casualties, but it left him in possession of a defensive firepower more concentrated than ever before.

A good part of it was dug in on the jagged summits of Fish Hook Ridge.

The fog was worse than usual. Light snow fell all morning. Zimmerman waited most of the day for enough visibility to attack; meanwhile he sent small units to make exploratory probes toward the ridge.

Two companies of Buckner's 4th Infantry got pinned down at the base of the ridge by nine Japanese machine-gun nests. Private Fred M. Barnett remarked to a companion that he was fed up. He walked up into the snowfall, carrying only his rifle and a string of grenades. He disappeared, climbing, and his companions heard furious volleys from machine guns, rifles, and grenades. The racket faded toward the distance; there was a single ragged aftervolley, and then silence.

Private Barnett reappeared and walked unhurriedly downhill. When he was in full sight he stopped and waved the two companies forward. The troops stepped from cover and climbed cautiously. Barnett turned and joined the front rank. The companies found the Japanese trenches free for the taking—Barnett had charged nine successive Japanese emplacements, wiped them all out and emerged without a scratch.

THE SNOWFALL LASTED WELL INTO the afternoon. General Landrum took advantage of its cover by shuffling his battalions. Zimmerman replaced Buckner's weary infantrymen with a battalion from Massacre Bay; Private Barnett and his companions went to the rear while the new battalion, less exhausted but far from fresh, moved into positions early in the afternoon.

Some of the limping men had not removed their boots in thirteen days. At four o'clock they jumped off toward Fish Hook Ridge. Two hundred yards upslope they were stopped cold.

Zimmerman was stalled there for the rest of the day, beaten back by enemy mortars and machine guns. Meanwhile, to the west, Frank Culin's stubborn battlers pressed toward a junction beneath Fish Hook Ridge. By evening, after five days' hard fighting on the western ridges, Culin was at last in position to join Zimmerman in a coordinated attack on the Fish Hook. During the night the two forces exchanged intelligence and gathered for a morning assault.

THE 36TH SQUADRON'S HEAVY BOMBERS had taken off that morning, led by Colonel Earl DeFord, who had spent more than a month flying regular combat missions, to the embarrassment of the pilots who had maligned him. But the snowstorm and fog at Attu scrubbed the day's bomber strike. DeFord led them back to Kiska, the alternate target, but it too was socked in. Wheeler wrote, "We returned to base in disgust."

An hour later a radio signal reached Amchitka Control from a destroyer prowling the western ocean. Its radar had picked up sixteen aerial bogeys 75 miles off Attu and closing. Amchitka scrambled five P-38 fighters, the only ones ready for immediate take-off, and Lieutenant

Colonel James R. Watt led the undersized interceptor mission at top speed to Attu.

Just off the coast, at 14,000 feet, they found the targets: sixteen twin-engine Mitsubishi bombers.

It was the second Japanese air strike from the Kuriles in two days. When the American fighters appeared, the Bettys jettisoned bombs and took violent evasive action. The Lightnings charged. Lieutenant Frederick Moore dropped his pod tanks, went to combat pitch and chased the dodging Japanese bombers with the P-38's superchargers sounding their characteristic shrill whine. The recoil of the four .50-caliber machine guns and the 20-mm cannon between his legs made the stick chatter in his gloved fist. He shot one Betty, watched it torch out and go into a spin; he broke toward a second bomber, shot it down with a sustained burst, and wheeled toward a third target. Powder's sulphur stink filled the cockpit; he made a straight run for a third Betty and opened fire at maximum range. Just short of cloud-cover the Betty shot back a plume of smoke, broke to the side and fell off on one wing. Moore saw it go into the sea, his third kill in as many minutes.

Off Moore's wing, Lieutenant Harry C. Higgins flamed a Betty into the sea; the Squadron Commander, Colonel Watt, chased another fleeing bomber, raked it with shells and blasted it apart.

Lieutenant John K. Geddes sewed a tight stitch of bullet holes across another Betty before its top gunner got the range on Geddes and rocked his plane badly. Geddes fought the crippled P-38 down 14,000 feet to a belly-landing in Massacre Bay. He was hardly out of the cockpit when a Kingfisher seaplane landed beside him on the water. The Kingfisher picked him up so quickly that Geddes hardly got his feet wet.

The Bettys fled, some smoking; the P-38s turned for home. Somewhere on the journey to Amchitka, Colonel Watt disappeared in the fog. He was never found.

The Americans had lost two planes and one pilot. At Paramushiro that night, of the sixteen Bettys that had set out, only seven came home. In the only air battle of the Attu conflict, Japan had suffered heavier losses than in any previous dogfight of the Aleutian Campaign.

Shaken by the furious American response, Paramushiro's air command canceled further air raids against Attu. The effect was to pound another nail in the coffin of Colonel Yasuyo Yamasaki, who had just been informed that Admiral Kawase's reinforcement convoy would not be coming to his aid. There was only one hope left:

evacuation by submarine. So far, no submarines had appeared. Yamasaki reassured his men and asked them to fight on.

MONDAY, MAY 24, 1943.
The combined American infantry attack on Fish Hook Ridge was launched at ten o'clock in the morning. The soldiers had to fight hard for every inch of ice-crusted muskeg. During the day Landrum added a battalion and a half to his front-line strength by marching part of the 4th Infantry back up from Massacre Valley, where it had hardly settled down to rest after yesterday's withdrawal from the front.

Progress was agonizing. Bayonets fixed, soldiers sent grenades into each hollow of ground before they ventured into it. The instructions from field commanders were stark and blunt: "If they don't stink, stick 'em." Stalled for hours at a time (sometimes days), infantrymen huddled trembling in captured Japanese blankets and tent cloth. Colonel William Alexander wrote in his notebook, "High sick rate, high missing rate." There was no shelter for troops at the front. The temperature hung in the twenties; the fog had thinned but there was no sign of the sun.

WHEELER WROTE: "CAPTAIN WERNICK and Major Speer flew alongside Fish Hook Ridge on a level with the Japanese trenches and within 200 yards of them, while the turret gunners raked them with .50-caliber machine-gun fire." The heavies bombed a troublesome enemy gun on Buffalo Nose, below the Fish Hook; they silenced the Japanese gun. Eareckson buzzed the position to make sure.

While Eareckson was occupied there, a separate flight of B-25s and P-38s went over the Fish Hook to bomb the enemy. The American artillery smoke designed to mark the enemy positions was blown back over an American battalion by a sudden wind shift; the bombs dropped on American positions. One disgusted soldier had to be dug out from under half a ton of muskeg; but by luck no one was hurt.

Pilot fatigue had reached the airmen. Several P-38s did not return from the mission. The Navy lost a Ventura bomber, taking off from Amchitka, and a PBY which crashed landing at Adak. West of Attu a PBY pilot dropped two depth charges on a crash-diving enemy submarine, but they failed to explode because the jaded crewmen had forgotten to arm them.

Weariness and cold tortured the ground troops far more. Before nightfall the numbed soldiers were compelled to withdraw to their starting positions below the Fish Hook. Landrum ordered that every available artillery piece be dragged up from the beach by hand, along Talley's new road, but the men were too tired; the best they could do was to manhandle one small 37-mm gun into firing position on a ridge facing the Fish Hook. A few 105-mm howitzers came a little way up Talley's creekbed road in Massacre Valley and stopped at spots where General Arnold hoped their trajectories would reach the Fish Hook. The 105-mm shells that had to be hand-carried to these guns weighed 54 pounds each.

The night was bitter cold, with a dusting of snowflakes. At the front, soldiers waited for the fifteenth day and yet another assault on the Fish Hook.

TUESDAY, MAY 25, 1943.

The Japanese had not stirred all night. By morning they were concealed by so much fresh snow they were invisible.

An American battalion jumped off early in the morning, into a mass barrage. The soldiers advanced into the teeth of it, cleaned out part of one enemy trench, and advanced past it onto a narrow ledge half way up the Fish Hook.

They had left part of the lower enemy trench intact. When the men of Buckner's 4th Infantry moved up to secure the rear, they walked into a crossfire. It took the rest of the day to dig the enemy out of the trench; by then the weary 4th Infantry had taken scores of casualties.

At noon an outpost at Scarlet Beach captured two Japanese soldiers, the first prisoners taken on Attu. They were interrogated that afternoon by American Nisei soldiers. Colonel William Verbeck wrote:

> The Japanese prisoner…has never been told not to talk in event of capture, because the possibility of capture is never considered by the enemy. As a result, this well-disciplined Japanese soldier obeys orders and answers any questions that we direct at him.

Verbeck learned from the prisoners that the enemy was far weaker than it appeared from the strong resistance he was putting up. When Verbeck so informed General Landrum, Landrum sent the information forward to his front-line commanders in the hope it would encourage them and their men.

But it was hard to build up the morale of hungry, exhausted, frozen men. The attack on the Fish Hook inched upward all day, supported by minor air strikes and a few shells lobbed over by field guns. By nightfall

Zimmerman had control of the base of the ridge, and isolated slopes were in the hands of scattered companies. But regardless of what the prisoners said, there was no sign at all that enemy resistance was breaking down.

WHEELER WROTE:

> The 36th Squadron flew two missions today, with Col. DeFord in command.[13] He was concerned lest the advancing American troops be bombed by us, but nothing of the kind happened.
>
> When our planes reached the I.P. [Initial Point of bomb-aiming run over target area] our troops were within 200 feet of the top of the last big ridge, some 2,100 feet high; they were held up there. Along the ridge were various targets assigned by the Command plane. Bombing was from 2,200 feet, below the overcast.
>
> After bombing, we strafed targets where the Japanese were dug in on the mountainsides. The guns of Chichagof have all been silenced except one.
>
> The outcome of the battle is sure, but the time of the end cannot be predicted. The aspect of things is of the greatest desolation with great areas of beach and back-areas blackened and smoking.

WEDNESDAY, MAY 26, 1943.

For once, the weather was good. Sixty-two Air Force planes attacked targets pinpointed by "Viceroy"—Eareckson in his hedgehopping Kingfisher. The bombers drummed along the Chain in relays all day long; they flattened the Japanese camp in Chichagof Harbor, where Lieutenant Nebu Tatsuguchi wrote in his diary:

> Am suffering from diarrhea and feel dizzy.... It felt like the barracks blew up, things shook up and rocks and mud flew all around and fell down; strafing planes hit the next room; my room looks like an awful mess from the sand and pebbles that come down from the roof. Consciousness becomes insane. There is no hope of reinforcement. Will die for the cause of Imperial Edict.

---

13. Earl H. DeFord, fifty-two, was awarded the Air Medal at the end of May 1943, for having led several bomber missions against Attu, and dozens against Kiska. The citation stated in part that DeFord had "displayed heroism and superior leadership while engaged in bombardment missions against heavily defended positions...[and] set a fine example and inspiration for his command." Soon after, he received a promotion to brigadier general.

On the Fish Hook, Japanese soldiers lay concealed by snowdrifts and rocks. They held the Americans back by rolling grenades down on them. On the American center, a battalion of the 4th Infantry broke into squads, elements, and individuals who inched up through the cold rocks in deadly hide-and-seek. On the right, two of Zimmerman's platoons flanked a snow trench which had held up their advance the day before; they got above the trench and attacked from the high side. They had wiped out its defenders by noon. On the left, Culin attacked the Holtz Bay side of the Fish Hook and gradually pushed the enemy back, foxhole by foxhole.

Private Joe P. Martinez, from Taos, New Mexico, was an automatic rifleman in Company K of the 32nd Infantry. With the company stalled by enemy trenches, Martinez walked into the enemy fire, slaughtered five Japanese soldiers with grenades and his BAR, and reached the crest of the ridge before he collapsed with a mortal wound he had taken fifty yards down the hill. Northern Force followed him up, and took the northwestern razorback of the Fish Hook, which Martinez had cleared; but it was too late for Martinez, whose posthumous reward was Attu's only Medal of Honor.[14]

THURSDAY, MAY 27, 1943.

The seventeenth day. Most of the Fish Hook had fallen to the Americans, but the Japanese still held isolated peaks along the ridge. Weather socked down once more; it hid the peaks from view and allowed Colonel Yamasaki to dispatch reinforcements to the ridge. They held the Americans to their previous gains, except for a dogged advance by two of Zimmerman's battalions which crawled toward the top of a hog-back called Buffalo Ridge, east of the Fish Hook. The Buffalo lay in range of Zimmerman's artillery in Massacre Valley, where guns had come almost three miles up from the beach along Colonel Talley's road. With support by the hard-hitting 105s, Zimmerman's men inched up within 200 yards of the crest; but here Zimmerman had to call a halt. The top of the Buffalo was dominated by the higher elevations of neighboring Fish Hook, and until that could be secured from the far side, Zimmerman could not take the lower ridge.

Still, he was only 200 yards from what might well be the end of the Battle of Attu: for the crest of the Buffalo was the Japanese final line of defense above Chichagof Valley.

---

14. Private Joe P. Martinez posthumously received America's highest military decoration (popularly but erroneously called the "Congressional" Medal of Honor), "For conspicuous gallantry and intrepidity in action above and beyond the call of duty on 26 May 1943."

FRIDAY, MAY 28, 1943.

Showered by all the cruel confetti of war—shrapnel, bullets, mortar fragments, grenades—the 4th Infantry finally pushed the last Japanese soldiers off the Fish Hook early in the afternoon. After six days' bitter fighting, the whole of the ridge was in American hands.

Zimmerman promptly called down an artillery barrage on Buffalo Ridge. Howitzers systematically pounded the heights for more than an hour before he ordered his men forward. There was no air support; clouds sat right down on the passes. By grueling one-yard advances, the infantrymen pushed the enemy back. By nightfall, Zimmerman held most of the Buffalo. The only part still in Japanese hands was a circle of peaks that commanded their main camp in Chichagof Valley.

In his command tent that evening, General Landrum studied his maps. Americans had occupied almost all the high ground south and west of the Japanese base. No Japanese positions threatened the southern gate to Chichagof Valley any longer. During the evening, without opposition, a battalion of American troops moved into the valley. It marched north between the Fish Hook and the Buffalo, set up camp just behind the Japanese-held tip of the Buffalo, and dispersed its companies across the valley floor, sealing it off.

The tactical situation had become a mirror-image of the first days of battle, two and a half weeks ago. Then the Japanese had surrounded the Americans from the high ground above Massacre Valley. Now it was the Japanese who were surrounded by enemy positions on the high ridges. Their backs to the sea, the Japanese had been pushed into a crowded little area of low, flat ground.

The bloody struggle was close to its end. Landrum would close for the kill at daybreak—a mass assault by the entire division and all its reinforcements. He ordered all reserves brought forward to the front; every piece of artillery was to be dragged as near as possible. Colonel Talley had almost completed a sled road up Engineer Hill, near the Fish Hook; Landrum's heavy artillery was to be rope-hauled up there during the night.

It would be annihilation. In the hope he could forestall unneeded slaughter by giving the enemy a choice, Landrum dispatched a PBY with a full bomb load of surrender leaflets, which it dropped over the Japanese camp. Surely the enemy commander would admit the uselessness of further resistance, and consider the lives of the men. Surely the men themselves, even if their leadership was fanatical, would surrender in the face of the inevitable.

SURELY THEY WOULD; BUT THEY DID NOT. Colonel Yamasaki knew his situation was dismal; he was as aware of that as Lieutenant Nebu Tatsuguchi, who wrote in his diary:

> The remaining ration is only for two days. Our artillery has been completely destroyed. I wonder if some of the men are still living. Continuous cases of suicide. Half the Sector Unit Headquarters was blown away.

Of the 2,600 men Yamasaki had started with, he had fewer than 800 fighting men left; he had another 600 wounded on his hands. He estimated American strength at 14,000.

There was no hope of reinforcement; and he had just received word that Admiral Kawase's fleet of evacuation I-boats had been turned back by the American destroyer screen. There would be no evacuation.

Yet surrender was not the only option. Yamasaki could make a last stand in Chichagof Valley, though it would serve no real purpose; he could withdraw farther into the northeastern peninsula and fight on for a few more days until he ran out of food and ammunition; or he could do one other thing.

He could attack.

YAMASAKI'S PLAN WAS AS INGENIOUS as it was simple. He had only one possibility of success, no matter how remote; that was in counterattack. He would hit the weakest point in the enemy's encircling line, break through it, and raid the enemy's supplies.

The obvious weak point was the valley floor between the Fish Hook and the Buffalo. It was enfiladed by both ridges, but Yamasaki would attack during the night. What the Americans could not see, they could not shoot.

Yamasaki would charge through the thin American line; he would sweep up Engineer Hill, capture the American howitzers there and turn them on the Americans. With those guns he would pin the enemy down long enough to get his men through to Massacre Valley, where he would overrun the feebly defended American supply camp, replenish his stores, destroy what he did not take, and retire into the southern mountains. Without their supplies the Americans would be slow to follow; they might even be forced to re-embark. Yamasaki would have time for Admiral Kawase—time to reinforce or evacuate.

The slim chance of victory depended on speed. The charging troops could not secure areas, mop up, or fight American positions they had passed. They would charge and keep charging until they had taken the American guns.

The reward could be victory; the certain penalty for failure would be mass death. Yamasaki's gamble was forthright, brilliant, and desperate. It just might work.

AT DUSK YAMASAKI SENT HIS last radio message to Japan, burned his records, gathered his soldiers, and told them, "We are planning a successful annihilation of the enemy."

Lieutenant Nebu Tatsuguchi returned to his post at the hospital and made the last entry in his diary:

> At 2000 we assembled in front of headquarters. The last assault is to be carried out. All patients in the hospital are to commit suicide...
>
> Gave 400 shots of morphine to severely wounded, and killed them.... Finished all the patients with grenades....
>
> Only 33 years of living and I am to die here. I have no regrets. Banzai to the Emperor.... Goodbye Tasuko, my beloved wife.

SATURDAY, MAY 29, 1943.

Company B of the U.S. 32nd Infantry had set up camp dead-center in Chichagof Valley. At 3:00 a.m. Battalion sent down the order that Company B was to march back to the battalion kitchen in the rear and get a hot breakfast before going into the attack at daybreak. Squad leaders awakened their men and began to march them toward the rear. A few sentries remained behind; except for them, the center of the valley was left wide open.

Half a mile northeast of Company B's deserted bivouac area, under the foggy shadows of Buffalo Ridge, Colonel Yamasaki had assembled the last of his Imperial Army troops. He had withdrawn his flankers and advance guards from the top of the Buffalo and all other outposts; he had every one of his soldiers in the silent assembly—every one of the eight hundred who had survived American bullets, Aleutian weather, and the commanded mass suicides of the wounded.

The key to the plan was to get past the two enfilading ridges before sunrise. Yamasaki gave the order. The phalanx moved up the center of the dark valley, silent and swift. Ammunition had fallen so low that many of them were armed only with bayonets and empty rifles.

By 3:15 they had reached the American front line, expecting a fight. Fog drifted across the flat; there was no sign of the enemy. Yamasaki kept walking upvalley. A prowling patrol at the point surprised a few American sentries in the fog and bayoneted them without sound. Yamasaki passed through the American line without being discovered.

It was better than he had dared hope.

At 3:25 a runner came back from the point: the forward patrol had picked up the sound of marching from the slope ahead. An American company appeared to be climbing toward Engineer Hill.

Yamasaki gave the order to charge.

COMPANY B WAS MARCHING THROUGH wisps of fog toward breakfast when hundreds of voices, disembodied in the night, began to shriek. The dread *"Banzai"* cry rolled at them from all directions at once. A roaring horde swarmed out of the fog with fixed bayonets. Rifles chattered; grenades exploded in the rear guard; the yelling Japanese throng rushed and loomed.

In the calamitous confusion, the astonished Americans ran.

Company B fled into the fog. Its men dispersed. They poured away in disorder, up the sides of the Fish Hook and the Buffalo. They scrambled in terror; there was no thought of resistance.

Yamasaki let them go. He pressed on toward Engineer Hill.

Sixteen Americans in a forward observation post at the base of the hill heard the howling below. One of them was Captain William H.

Willoughby of the Scout Battalion: "I had dug my hole deep that night and only loosened my boots. With the first yips, I cut a hole in my tent."

Willoughby and his fifteen companions, most of them officers, reacted instantly with the habit of long training: they took cover and fought. They tried to stem the juggernaut; but they were just sixteen men. Willoughby was hit:

"I got a machine-gun bullet across my face and then a hand grenade came into the hole with me. It put some hunks of heavy metal in me, tore up my chest and arm."

Within five minutes, eleven of the sixteen men in the OP were dead, including Battalion Commander Major J. E. Siddons and his executive officer. The Japanese rushed on without pausing to finish the last men off: Willoughby and four others, all of them wounded, survived.[15]

Yamasaki's timing was brilliant. There was no organized resistance. The surprise assault swept up the base of Engineer Hill and was easily

---

15. Willoughby was not found until the next day. He had lost a great deal of blood. Medics administered plasma and evacuated him. He spent six months in hospital, finally regaining his health, and returned to duty as a major. For his outstanding heroism at Attu he was awarded the Silver Star, Bronze Star, Purple Heart, and several other decorations.

beyond the enfilading fire from the ridges by daybreak. Yamasaki hurtled through the weakest American points, hardly slacking speed. He overran an American command post, killing Lieutenant Colonel James Fish, and brought his men forward in a tight Roman square to charge the hilltop. On the right flank, a Japanese platoon crested a hump of ground at first light and charged into a medical clearing station; stabbed the wounded, bayoneted a chaplain, and slaughtered every patient who moved. Captain George S. Buehler, Captain James W. Bryce, and ten wounded men lay in a tent beside the station; they played dead, hoping the Japanese would not butcher them. Japanese soldiers charged through the tent several times, but the twelve men lay asprawl, held their breath, and survived.

High on Engineer Hill several noncombatant units were camped—parts of the 50th Engineers, the 7th Medical Battalion, the 13th Engineers, the 20th Field Headquarters, and a scattering of frostbitten 4th Infantrymen awaiting evacuation. At the brow of the hill, Brigadier General Archibald V. Arnold had set up the command post from which he was to control his artillery in the planned morning attack.

Medics and disorganized infantrymen streamed uphill out of the dawn fog. As they ran by, General Arnold heard them shouting that the enemy was coming.

The general walked out to the rim, planted his feet and bawled orders.

Within minutes the Engineers and service troops had sprung to arms. Cooks, litter bearers, roadbuilders, and staff officers took shoulder-to-shoulder positions at the crest. General Arnold borrowed an M-1 rifle and crawled to a high point from which he could see the Japanese charging up the hill toward him. With calm, precise hand signals he directed the hand-grenade throws of his hidden troops as if he were calling artillery targets. The grenades blew gaps in the Japanese line but the charge did not falter.

General Arnold dispatched a runner to bring up the nearby 37-mm gun and get it into action. Yelling encouragement to his men, he called grenade targets with deliberate care.

Yamasaki was within rock-throwing distance of the top of Engineer Hill when the banzai charge finally slowed and stopped, brought to heel by a withering point-blank concentration of bullets and grenades from the hasty, improvised American line.

The Japanese faltered, fell back a few yards, then gathered themselves and charged with a frenzy that propelled them to the top.

The 50th Engineers, rushing forward to man the lines, met the charge head-on with bayonets and clubbed rifles. In desperate hand-to-hand fighting they broke the onslaught. The Japanese phalanx fell apart. A few small detachments got through to a point just short of the American 105-mm howitzers—Yamasaki's vital objective—but Arnold's 37-mm gun, and a company of Engineers, stopped them in their tracks. They never reached the all-important big guns.

The Japanese fell back into the fog, down the face of Engineer Hill. They regrouped at the American medical station. Captains Buehler and Bryce and the ten wounded men waited in breathless silence inside their tent while the Japanese survivors milled all around them, tried to reorganize and make another stab at the artillery.

General Arnold's 37-mm gun, and the howitzers from above, began to pummel the hill. The light grew stronger; fog squatted implacably on the lower slopes. Isolated Japanese platoons charged uphill again, and several more times that day, but Yamasaki was never able to concert them for another all-out attack. He knew his attempt had failed.

Early in the day five hundred men, the bulk of his force, committed mass suicide by pulling the pins of their grenades and holding them against their chests.

LATER IN THE DAY YAMASAKI HIMSELF led a last foredoomed attack on Engineer Hill. His handful of exhausted troops struggled upslope with him, against an American line that was now strongly manned. At the point where General Arnold's hand-grenade artillery had killed sixty attackers in the morning charge, the final blow was struck.

The charge broke. Colonel Yasuyo Yamasaki, sword in hand, was killed by a .30-caliber bullet.

CAPTAINS BUEHLER AND BRYCE AND their ten patients crawled out of their tents. Numbed and shivering, not knowing how or why they had survived, they stumbled to the top of Engineer Hill over the massed bodies of Japanese dead.

On the point of victory, the Americans had come frighteningly close to losing everything they had gained in three weeks of ferocious, bloody fighting. Only the precarious line of the 50th Engineers, desperate but steadied by discipline, had kept Yamasaki's charge from reaching the all-important artillery.

But the Engineers had held. It was over.

SUNDAY, MAY 30, 1943.

General Landrum's men still had to mop up. Individual Japanese soldiers held out in the hills; some were not flushed out until three months later. When cornered they all chose to kill themselves.

In all, twenty-eight Japanese prisoners were taken alive on Attu. Not one was an officer.

American burial parties counted 2,351 Japanese bodies, many of them maimed and disemboweled by their own grenades. Several hundred more enemy dead were presumed to have been buried in the hills by the Japanese during the three weeks of battle.

Burial crews scraped open cemeteries for the American dead—549 men.[16] Chaplains sang "Rock of Ages" against the clank and grind of excavating tractors. Two buglers played taps, and the damp earth was rolled over the bodies. Simon Buckner and Governor Ernest Gruening placed wreaths on the Attu graves.

THE PRICE OF WEATHERBEATEN ATTU had been high. In proportion to the numbers of troops engaged, it would rank as the second most costly American battle in the Pacific Theater—second only to Iwo Jima. Total American casualties amounted to half again the number of Japanese troops on the island; the Japanese force suffered annihilation, almost to the last man.

Landing Force Attu had suffered 3,829 casualties: killed, 549; wounded, 1,148; severe cold injuries, 1,200; disease (including exposure), 614; other casualties (including self-inflicted wounds, psychiatric breakdowns, drownings and accidents), 318 men.

The largest single classification of agony—severe frostbite and trenchfoot—represented the first combat cold injuries suffered by American troops in the Second World War. To avoid making the same grisly mistakes in the forthcoming Italian campaign, Army doctors studied Attu veterans with close clinical attention, and submitted voluminous findings to the Surgeon General. As a result, important changes were soon made in Army footgear, clothes, tents, bedrolls, and food. In the next two years' global fighting, the experience of Attu would save thosands of limbs and lives. It did not, however, save hundreds of Attu veterans from amputation.

Command councils subjected Attu's costly mistakes to microscopic study. Most of them would be rectified before the next American joint

16. Both the American and Japanese dead, originally buried in common graves at Attu's Little Falls Cemetery, have since been reinterred at the military cemetery at Fort Richardson near Anchorage.

amphibious operation, which was the invasion of Rendova in June. The "A-frame" cargo hoist, developed in Massacre Bay; Eareckson's Forward Air Control; and dozens of other makeshift Attu experiments soon became standard in the increasingly sophisticated weaponry of the continuing war.

The invasion of Rendova proceeded well, largely because of the Battle of Attu. Attu not only provided the mistakes from which U.S. planners learned; it also caused a shift in Japanese forces which played into American hands. Admiral Koga had moved the Imperial Fifth Fleet north from Truk to support his intended reinforcement or evacuation of Attu. That operation had been aborted because of the unseemly size of the American task force at Attu; by the time the bulk of the Imperial Fifth Fleet was ready to set out for the North Pacific, it was too late to affect the outcome at Attu. But the shift depleted Japanese naval strength in the Solomons and left Rendova virtually undefended by naval ships. Thanks to the Battle of Attu, the American invasion at Rendova was all but unopposed by the Japanese Navy.

Attu had been the only important military operation in the Central or North Pacific since the Battle of Midway a year earlier. It had been the United States Infantry's first amphibious island assault. In ratio to the sizes of forces, it had been the costliest ground battle yet fought in the Pacific. It had been the biggest Pacific invasion since Guadalcanal. The lessons it taught were numerous and important. It had required the commitment of 100,000 men, of all the services, at the front and in support echelons back down the Aleutian line.

Clearly then, it had been anything but a minor skirmish. Yet it attracted little attention at the time, and even less later. Why?

Attu veteran George F. Noland recalls wryly: "No Marines—otherwise it would have been world history." Attu did receive some press coverage, provided by the nine American war correspondents on the scene, the belated and superficial announcements of the Navy in Washington, and the daily accounts broadcast by Radio Tokyo on short-wave. But the battle was soon eclipsed by developments in other theaters. Meanwhile Washington's official information offices, embarrassed by the mistakes and failures of Attu, were not eager to encourage the public to ask questions. And so, if the story of Attu was not swept under the rug, at least it was played down by the ministries of war propaganda.

In the meantime, Allied high command assessed the strategic significance of the victory at Attu. In the context of the times' over-all war plans, that significance was substantial. The capture of Attu (together with nearby Shemya and Agattu, which were occupied simultaneously) gave control of the westernmost Aleutians back to the Allies. This would provide air bases within easy striking distance of Japan's northern perimeter. And it would very likely give the Allies a jumping-off point for the ultimate invasion of Japan.

Only one obstacle remained: the single Japanese fortress left in the Aleutians—Kiska.

ON MAY 31, 1943, IMPERIAL HEADQUARTERS conceded the loss of Attu. "It is assumed the entire Japanese force has preferred death to dishonor." A few days later Radio Tokyo admitted it, with appropriate attention to the heroic example that had been set by Yasuyo Yamasaki and his beleaguered soldiers.

The Japanese had always been enamored of the American legend of the Alamo. Tokyo's propagandists tried to make of Attu a home version of the Texas siege. But the Alamo defeat had been prelude to victory by comrades of its Anglo defenders; Attu, it was all too clear, presaged nothing of the kind for Japan. The Imperial General Staff had neither the power nor the desire to retake Attu. Japan's main concern in the North Pacific was what to do about Kiska; and now most of the discussions revolved around ways to abandon Japan's last Aleutian possession without loss of face.

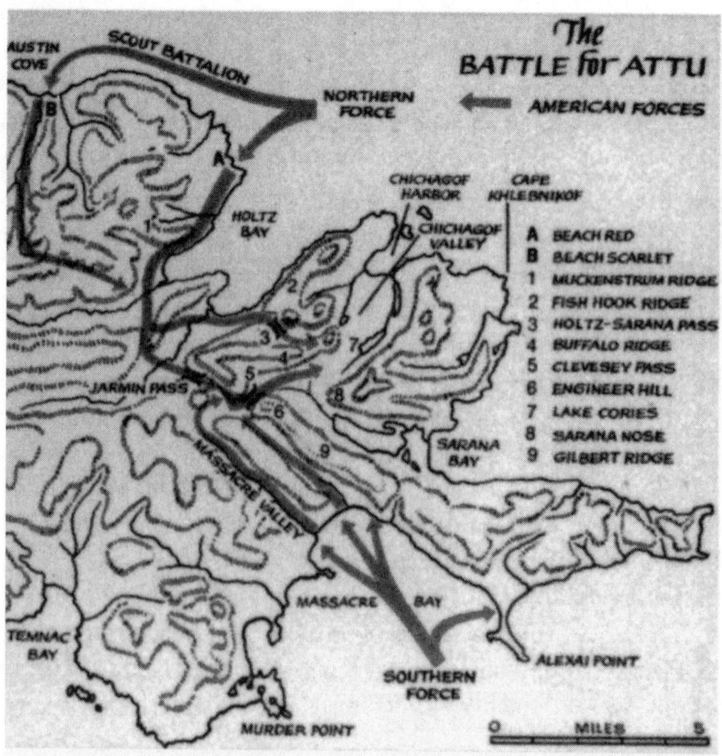

CHAPTER
EIGHTEEN

The Raids on Paramushiro

DURING THE BATTLE OF ATTU, Colonel Benjamin Talley's wizard Engineers had been busy. Under Brigadier General John E. Copeland, a landing force including detachments of Buckner's 4th Infantry and Talley's 18th Engineers had landed on Shemya, a tiny (2 1/4 x 4 1/2 miles) atoll just 25 miles east of Attu. They had gone ashore in a tough, storm-whipped landing to survey the little island, the only flat one in the Aleutian Chain, and to start building the first attack air field expressly designed for the experimental new long-range B-29 Superfortress bomber.

At the same time, with the battle still in full fury, Talley's Engineers had marked out an airstrip on the east side of Massacre Bay (disdaining the northern bogs where the Japanese had tried, and failed, to build a runway).

They built with their usual blinding speed: By June 8, Air Station Attu was open for business; the air field at Shemya was activated less than two weeks later. The Navy established air facilities for both PBYs and land-based Ventura bombers on the two islands, it also built a submarine base at Attu. And Simon Buckner's infantrymen made unopposed landings on Semisopochnoi and Rat Islands (the latter near Kiska), covered by PT-boats.

Bombers and fighters, ships and submarines, construction men and shore-defense batteries moved into the far western Aleutians as fast as Buckner and Kinkaid could get them there. For the two of them were preparing to invade Japan.

LONG BEFORE THE GUNS OF ATTU had gone silent, the Allied Combined Chiefs had met at the Trident Conference in Washington. The outcome at Attu was not seriously in doubt, though it was possible the

Japanese might counterattack. Still, the Combined Chiefs went ahead with the final strategic decision to recover Kiska, make the Aleutians secure by late summer, and build staging bases from Adak and Amchitka to Shemya. Buckner wanted to invade Japan by late 1943. He was overruled by circumstances, and by the Joint Chiefs of Staff, who reset the planned date to early 1945 for an invasion of Japan from the Aleutians.

The far-reaching decision had an electric impact on Alaska. The Territory's early problems of making do with a niggardly War Department budget disappeared immediately. The incoming stream of men and equipment became an avalanche. Up the Inside Passage, the Alaska Highway, and the Northwest Air Staging Route came a flood of supplies, machinery, planes, ships, weapons, and men.

Admiral Kinkaid reinforced the Kiska blockade with an all but impenetrable screen of destroyers, cruisers, and great battleships—and ordered the Eleventh Air Force to bomb Kiska around the clock.

It was a tough order to carry out. The weather gave no quarter. The months from June through August were normally characterized by extra-dense fog, and 1943 was no exception. Williwaws wrecked PBYs and Venturas and all but capsized a 5,500-ton LST at anchor; bombers crashed regularly into unseen mountains. On June 5, during a severe storm at Attu, Colonel Albert Hartl signaled HELLAVA WIND AND RAIN X TENTAGE DOWN X COMMUNICATIONS LINES OUT X BRIDGES OUT. But the bombers flew that day—five missions against Kiska—and almost every other day.

At the flying crews' mess huts, meals were served around the clock. Each morning, charts and recon photos went up at 4:30; crews were briefed at 5:00. First flare (start engines) was fired at 5:30.[1] The fog was as bad as ever, but now they had a new weapon in the arsenal: Commodore Gehres' new squadrons of twin-engine PV-1 Ventura bombers were equipped with the latest and most sophisticated airborne radar yet devised. It gave not only target distance and bearing, but a clear picture of topographical contours—a visual map. By matching that against aerial photos it was possible to pinpoint enemy guns, structures, and other targets in spite of thickest fog.

---

1. At Amchitka, Air Force Captain Richard Lavin would receive a weather signal from Bomber Command every morning at four. He would then up-end an Army cot in front of his tent to indicate that there would be a mission—but usually the fog was so thick the pilots had to get dressed and walk within a few feet of Lavin's tent to find out whether the signal cot was up or down. If it was down, they played wind-driven volleyball near the operations shack until the weather improved and the mission was called.

Starting June 1, the Venturas went into operation as seeing-eyes to guide Air Force bombers through weather previously classified as unfit for flying, and locate targets for them. At the same time, on a suggestion from Eareckson, the combined missions adopted a technique that soon became standard procedure for the Eighth Air Force in Europe: all bombardiers on a mission would "bomb on" the lead bombardier, instead of making their own independent calculations. Now a single bombardier controlled the placement of all bombs in the flight. If the risk of a total miss increased, so did the concentration of lethal bombardment that did hit the target. The key, Eareckson emphasized, was to put the best bombardier in the lead ship.

Increased technological sophistication was not one-sided. Target Kiska quickly found its own answer to the invisible bombers. One of the last supply ships through the blockade had brought a vital weapon to Kiska: radar.

More primitive than the American-English version, the Japanese radar nonetheless had no trouble picking up American bombers as they took off from nearby Amchitka, and following them to target and back. Guided by ground radar, Kiska's seventy antiaircraft batteries put up a curtain of flak with withering accuracy. Brigadier General Earl H. DeFord recalls: "Kiska had the heaviest antiaircraft defense I have ever seen," and Billy Wheeler reported, "Kiska and its often terrible AA fire are a constant mental hazard to us all." He added:

> Major Speer had a close call. One engine was shot out and a shell went up through the bomb-bay and imbedded itself in the top of the ship. Speer has had over 1,000 hours of combat time—he has been in Alaska 26 months. He bears a charmed life, but this is too long a time for anyone to be in this theatre.

AS ALLIED FORCES CROWDED FORWARD for the final push, the tempo of life in the Aleutians gained speed. During these few months of anticipation, boredom was not the problem it had been. Still, groundlings deeply envied the airmen, who were the only men who got to see much of the sun.

But the airmen's lives were anything but glamorous. Some squadrons, on detached service from the States, were not regular parts of the Alaskan command structure; hence promotions were frozen and pay often did not come through. Lieutenant Colonel Lawrence Reineke (then a 2nd lieutenant with the 21st Bomb Squadron) recalls, "The only way to get home solvent was to get orders the day after you'd had a winning night in a poker game." Since very few were rotated home, the problem was usually academic.

The quality of life was best (or at least less-bad) at Adak, where soldiers and airmen lived four to a Quonset hut. Each hut had wooden signs on the door, bearing the occupants' names. A few soldiers had planted flower gardens. Sled dogs stood guard outside many huts; the canine population had mushroomed, and there was a definite pecking order among Adak's dogs, based on the ranks of their owners: General Buckner's hunting dogs[2] were supreme, followed by General Butler's springer spaniel pup, Colonel Eareckson's husky Skootch, and Lieutenant Colonel Verbeck's Irish setter. Retrievers and other pets had the run of the base. Toward the bottom of the ladder of command, enlisted Seaman Lee Early had adopted an Aleutian mutt, named it SeaBee, and taught it to stand up and salute officers.

(In July, dogs proved their worth in the Aleutians. Rats had become a menace at Dutch Harbor—an estimated half million teemed in the port. The services declared unconditional war. Poison and traps were set out; published regulations protected foxes, eagles, hawks and owls; and the Post Medical Inspector, Major W. J. Perry, requisitioned a large pack of terriers trained to kill rats. The concerted effort finally won the Rat Campaign.)

In spite of the heavy injection of invasion-geared new shipping, incoming supplies never quite caught up with the continuing shortages that had plagued the Aleutian theater from the start. Everything, particularly food, was scarce; several times the mess halls were reduced to serving roast halibut for supper. As a result, the general quality of life had not improved much at the front. Wheeler wrote:

> Our base at Amchitka is only 70 miles from Kiska, the sinister volcano of which becomes visible on rare occasions (none recent). Our big Y-shaped fighter strip was finished in March, and now the bomber strip 5,000 feet in length and surfaced with steel matting is another tribute to the Engineer Corps. Some day these Aleutian strips will be 10,000 feet long to accommodate the great B-29's being prepared to convert the Japs to our way of thinking.

---

2. Buckner was fanatical on the subject of hunting—in recommending one officer's promotion he described the man as "one of the best bear hunters I have ever seen"—yet during the hectic three and one half years in Alaska he seldom had a chance to go hunting himself.

Meanwhile our area lies in a swamp dotted with about twenty ponds. Between them lies mud, lightly coated with tundra. Tents are the only shelter from the foul weather and we wallow in mud inside them as well as out.

The electric light generator goes off every few hours and those who have candles are lucky indeed. The S-2 double-tent does service for briefing, interrogation and pilots' alert tent, as well as the routine work of the S-2 [Intelligence] section. A few benches for the flying officer personnel are ranged against the soggy walls; the floor is soft mud and the approaches to the tent are churned by countless boots. Sometimes the entire floor area is covered with tired flying officers lying on the muddy floor around the inadequate stove.

The mess tent stands on a dreary hillock vainly trying to repel the incessant rain, flapping and groaning in the Aleutian gales. The failure of the cursed generator was the last straw, and a few flickering candles dimly light the faces of the boys who from these quarters daily are attacking the stubborn enemy.

Today officers must stand in line outside the mess tent in mud while our too-few plates and utensils are washed so others can eat. Two or three days ago, Capt. Lewis visited Anchorage to requisition more crockery and knives and forks and the like from the Quartermaster there. He was finally ushered into a well-appointed office and the presence of a well-dressed colonel solemnly rocking back and forth behind a glass-top mahogany desk. He seemed not to have heard of us in the Aleutians. The request, he said, was impossible to entertain, as our crockery must certainly have been carelessly tended.

Capt. Lewis was moved to say, "Sir, for the past year we have been engaged in a dispute with some people called the Japanese of whom possibly you have not heard."

The colonel retorted, "Captain, your sarcasm will get you nowhere."

Lewis fired the last shot: "Neither will my good manners. Sir." He made a dignified exit.

TO IMPROVE MORALE, LIEUTENANT Colonel Sam Dows sponsored a contest in which servicemen were asked to compete for a $100 War Bond by writing answers to the question, "Why Are We Here?"

The prize was never awarded.

One of those who sought his own private answer to that question was Air Force Lieutenant Lawrence Reineke, recently arrived Assistant Intelligence Officer of the 21st Bomber Squadron. The answer, to Reineke, was that his main reason for being in the Aleutians was the contribution he could make in carrying the Aleutian air war into Japanese home territory.

Reineke made it a private project to find out all he could about the nearest Japanese target—the huge Gibraltar-like base at Paramushiro Island, which guarded the northern approach to Japan. He learned from staff officers that the Air Force had virtually no intelligence information about Paramushiro (General Butler wasn't even sure where it was), and that no one had ever seriously proposed to bomb it, even though it was now within practical air-striking distance from Shemya and Attu.

Without specific authority, Reineke* went over to the Navy and found that, as he suspected, the Navy had a variety of maps and charts of the northern Kuriles. He collected an armload of them and went on to Army headquarters, where as an authorized intelligence officer he was given access to the bundles of Japanese diaries that had been captured on Attu. For weeks he pored over the diaries, jotted notes and compared diary notations with place-names on the Navy maps. When he was done, Reineke's astute detective work had produced an amazingly complete chart of the Japanese bases at Paramushiro.

A few high-ranking officers roasted Reineke for having ignored regular channels in obtaining his information, but Reineke was an amiable man with an infectious grin and a quick way of talking; it did not take him long to talk a few staff officers into slipping his summaries onto the desks of Generals Butler and Buckner and Admiral Kinkaid.

Kinkaid liked the idea of bombing Paramushiro. Even if it didn't have an important physical effect it would surely have great propaganda and morale values. But the proposal would have to be cleared through CINCPAC and Washington.

In time that too was done. The Joint Chiefs authorized a raid on Paramushiro; the Eleventh Air Force called for volunteer pilots and crews; and Lieutenant Reineke was given the job of briefing them.

Pappy Speer would lead. Lucian Wernick and four other volunteer pilots from three squadrons would fly the mission. Early on July 10, 1943—the day Eisenhower's Allied troops invaded Sicily—the six B-24 Liberators drummed out to Attu to refuel before making the 650-mile

---

*1995 ADDENDUM: For further discussion of the Paramushiro raids see Appendix One.

run across the North Pacific to the Kuriles. Spirits were high: if the attack came off, it would be the first bomber attack on Japanese home soil since the Doolittle raid, and the first ever flown from an American land base.

The mission took off. At the same time, a PBY on western patrol spotted four wooden Japanese transport ships midway between Paramushiro and Attu. It looked as if they intended to run the Kiska blockade. At Adak, General Butler immediately ordered a flight of B-25s to sortie from Attu and hunt down the four transports; to make sure, he radioed Major Speer to divert from his intended mission and go after the ships instead.

Enraged, Speer and Wernick turned the Paramushiro mission off course and headed southwest. Ahead of them, six Mitchell bombers reached the scene and sank two of the Japanese ships. By the time Speer brought his heavies onto the scene, the two remaining ships were taking evasive action and heaving a mass of flak into the sky.

Dutifully the six B-24s went in to attack at deck level. But it was no good. A light ocean vessel could turn faster than a ponderous four-engine Liberator. This was a job for smaller, more maneuverable planes. Never presenting good targets, the Japanese ships turned back to squall cover; and Speer, too low on fuel to continue, angrily ordered the Paramushiro mission to abort and return to base.

They were banking when one of the retiring Japanese transports got in a parting shot. One of its flak bursts blew up in Lucian Wernick's face.

It injured no one, but the plane filled with smoke. Quick examination showed that the explosion had destroyed the nose-wheel and entire hydraulic system. Wernick was in trouble: if he tried to land—and he could hardly stay up forever—he would have no brakes, and only two wheels. Coming down on only two wheels was as bad as coming down on none: a belly-landing on a sparking steel-mat runway would guarantee a holocaust of fire.

For months Wernick had refused to carry life preservers; he considered them useless, knowing the limits of life expectancy in North Pacific water. Now, even though regulations and common sense both suggested an ocean ditching, Wernick gave his crew a solemn promise: he would set them down on solid ground.

Wernick had behind him a year's combat flying in the world's toughest air theater; he was not given to empty boasting. But to set the crippled Liberator down without cracking up in flaming wreckage would require magical, if not miraculous, luck; and after a thousand combat hours, how much luck could a man still count on?

Wernick had developed a firm conviction that no harm would ever come to him or anyone with him in an airplane,[3] but it was a conviction not based on luck or caprice. Experience had developed in him a keen resourcefulness based on talent and self-confidence. It was this skill, not luck, that Wernick's crew depended on while the droning bomber clawed toward home base trailing a vapor of leaking hydraulic fluid.

He radioed Adak Tower to ready crash crews, and gave his nine-man crew careful instructions. They cranked down the two wheels of the main underwing gear by hand. Then, copilot and all, they assembled in the fuselage between the training edges of the wings, to add weight behind the wheels.

It was a daring gamble. Few pilots would risk it; fewer still would succeed.

Approaching Adak, Wernick went down to sea level to get an upward shot at the runway. Ocean froth spattered the metal belly. The big plane splashed awkwardly across the bay. At stalling speed, Wernick manhandled it a few feet into the air—barely enough to clear the lip of the runway. Alone at the controls, Wernick struggled to stall the plane down while keeping the nose high. The two wheels touched and screeched. And, at Wernick's signal, the crowded crew walked—*walked*—slowly through the fuselage toward the tail.

Their steady movement put more and more weight on the tail, shifting the plane's center of gravity as it rolled wildly down the runway, balanced on two wheels.

Maintaining that precarious balance with elevator controls and rudder, Wernick let the plane roll; he had no brakes, and if he had had them, using them would have plunged the nose onto the macadamized steel mat and flipped the plane over.

The tail gunner crawled into his turret; the crew crowded tight aft. Balanced on its main gear, the huge plane careened down the runway, a big sweating man at the controls; slowed, began to tilt, and bumped to a halt within a few feet of the mountain end of the runway.

Slowly, gently, the shattered nose settled to the ground.

The ten men climbed out and looked at their airplane. No one had much to say.

---

3. Eareckson and Wernick shared the belief that no injury would ever befall them in airplanes. Their confidence, if arrogant, was not misplaced. Eareckson retired unscathed from the Air Force after the Korean War, his only combat injury the bullet crease he had suffered while playing infantryman on Attu. Wernick, now a ground-bound math teacher, has not flown a plane in years.

General Butler had watched. Wernick walked away; later, in private, he bawled the general out furiously for having ordered the useless mission. Awed by the spectacle of heroism he had witnessed, Butler took the diatribe without retorting. (Three days later, by sheer coincidence, Wernick's promotion to major came through.)

WHILE WERNICK AND SPEER HAD diverted their Paramushiro-bound mission to attack the Japanese transport ships, a flight of eight Mitchell bombers from Attu had taken off independently with the idea of getting in the first lick at the enemy on his home ground in the Kuriles. By authorizing missions against Japan, Washington had given the Aleutian pilots an every-man-for-himself spirit; everybody wanted to get there first, to have the honor of flying America's first land-based bombing attacks against the enemy homeland.

Without benefit of Lieutenant Larry Reineke's detailed maps or briefings, the eight B-25 free-lancers found a vague land mass obscured by overcast, dropped eight tons of bombs and headed home, not quite sure whether they had hit Japan, the Kuriles, the Kamchatka Peninsula, or some uninhabited North Pacific Island.

Neither the Japanese nor the Russians ever made any mention of having been bombed. Wherever the bombs landed, they did no harm. The off-the-cuff mission made no practical change in the fact that no American pilot had attacked any Japanese home base since the Doolittle raid.

It was left to Speer, Wernick, and the other original volunteers to change that state of affairs. After waiting a week in rain-soaked Attu tents for the weather to clear, they made their second attempt on July 18, 1943. Wheeler wrote:

> The mission was to have left at 0400 but Speer's plane had engine trouble and the major had to take a spare ship that was in doubtful shape. The delay was vexatious, and serious because it lessened the chance of surprise. At 0632…our six B-24's took off in the cold gray Attu dawn and winged westward to unknown adventure.
>
> Our plotted course was to cover a round-trip distance of about 1,700 miles—not excessive so far as Aleutian missions go. Whatever qualms we had over the lack of emergency landing spots en route were compensated for by the knowledge that we were carrying the offensive home to the enemy. It was our first crack at the Jap in his native haunt.

> ...We climbed to 12,000 feet as we approached the Kamchatka peninsula of Siberia, which is mountainous, somewhat like the Aleutians, but quite thickly wooded. We rubbed our eyes at seeing trees, some of us for the first time in a year.

It was a warm 68° even at 18,000 feet, where the mission leveled off. Over Shimushu (a small island just north of Paramushiro) the weather was broken; a low-lying haze was moving in from the southwest. The Liberators followed the Shimushu coast around to the south side of the island and crossed the narrow strait to Paramushiro.

Three Liberators peeled off to bomb the air base; three others—Major Frederick R. Ramputi, twenty-seven; Major Lucian K. Wernick, twenty-six; Major Richard Lavin, twenty-seven—made a straight run over the harbor strait, sighting on a big concentration of several dozen warships, transports, and fishing vessels. Paramushiro was the headquarters of all Japan's northern commands; it was a big base.

Startled Japanese stared up, not sure what was happening. At first they thought the planes were off-course Russian patrol ships. But then the bomb-bay doors yawned open and sticks of 500-pounders tumbled toward the air field. The Japanese ran for cover. In his headquarters office, Vice Admiral Shiro Kawase heard the first string of bombs explode on a nearby taxiway and wheeled to the window, incredulous.

Paramushiro's defenses were not on the alert (even though the American submarine *Narwhal* had shelled the nearby air field at Matsuwa only three days before). A few antiaircraft guns went into frantic operation, but only managed to fire four or five bursts. Pilots ran to their planes and fired up cold engines, but they would be too late to get up to the high bombers.

Bomb explosions rocked several buildings. Craters pocked the main runway. Over the harbor, Ramputi, Wernick, and Lavin circled to make a second bomb run on the anchored ships—their bomb racks had frozen the first time, and Lavin was having engine trouble.

Wernick and Ramputi triggered their bombs by hand while their cameras clicked at high speed. The bombs blew up one ship and damaged two or three others. Lavin could not release his bombs. With one engine feathered, he followed the flight away and shoved his throttles forward, trying to keep up.

The other flight—Major Robert E. Speer, twenty-eight; Major Edward C. Lass, twenty-seven; Captain Jacques Francine, thirty-four[4]—

---

4. The six American pilots of the first Paramushiro mission, all long-time Aleutian combat

was just completing its bomb run over the air base. Thick smoke unrolled across the field. Five Zeroes dodged craters, taxied down a secondary (unhit) runway and reached takeoff speed. On a nearby lake, twenty seaplane-fighters rested at their moorings, but only two were manned; these chugged into life and swung out onto flat water to take off.

Speer gathered his planes, circled east and headed home. Lavin, on three engines, fell behind. The Zeroes appeared to be catching up to him, but none of them was fully fueled or armed; they gave up the chase after a few minutes. Speer cut speed to accommodate Lavin, and at dusk the six planes reached Adak in neat formation and landed at regular two-minute intervals. They had not suffered a single bullet hole or flak scratch.

Film negatives were rushed inside for processing, and the crews trooped into Operations for debriefing. A subdued friend took Speer aside and informed him that one of his Adak pilots, on a routine flight, had cracked up on a hill in the fog, within a few hundred yards of the runway. Such occasions were not uncommon in the Aleutians but that did not change men's emotional reactions to the sudden useless deaths of friends. Morose and silent, Speer went right from debriefing to the funeral, trailed by the other pilots and a handful of reporters.

The funeral dampened what otherwise would have been a satisfying day. After nearly fourteen months' Aleutian warfare, the U.S. Air Force had finally taken the fight into the enemy's home ground. Rush prints of the strike photos showed that the raid on Paramushiro had inflicted more damage than the Japanese had inflicted on Dutch Harbor in June 1942.

Paramushiro had not suffered grievous harm, but in one stroke the raid proved to Japan that Imperial home soil was no longer immune to attack.

For the first time in World War II, the Allies were within hard-hitting bombardment distance of the Empire. It was a sobering revelation. Henceforth Japan would have to defend its whole coast from Paramushiro to Hokkaido. No longer could she depend on distance, Russian neutrality, or her Aleutian bases to act as buffers.

Imperial Headquarters would have to reinforce the Kuriles and Hokkaido by radical measures. The only way to obtain forces was to

---

veterans, were a varied lot. Speer was blond and windburned. Wernick was huge and husky. Ramputi was hawk-nosed and dark, a former wrestler said to be the only Aleutian pilot strong enough to fly a B-24 with one hand. Francine, the oldest at thirty-four, was a former Northwest fur trader who had flown with the RCAF and in Iceland. Lavin was a quiet flier from Spokane. Lass was a limber Coloradan. Together, they represented the pick of three top Eleventh Air Force heavy-bomber squadrons.

withdraw them from other fronts. Speer, Wernick and their companions in one stroke had forced a profound decision upon Japan's leaders—a decision which altered the entire strategic alignment of Imperial forces in the Pacific, as Japanese men, guns, ships and planes moved out of the Solomons and Philippines, bound for the Kuriles.

GENERAL BUTLER ASKED LUCIAN WERNICK to lead a second Paramushiro raid, identical with the first. Wernick refused to volunteer for the job: he pointed out that the first raid had only succeeded because it had taken the enemy by surprise. Next time the enemy would be waiting.

When the second Paramushiro mission took off on August 11, 1943, Wernick was not part of it. The only veteran of the first raid was Major Louis C. Blau, who had been a co-pilot in Speer's flight. Blau led the mission; there were nine planes.

Paramushiro, and the alternate target at the Kataoka naval base on Shimushu, were overcast at 2,000 feet. The nine bombers circled down to make low-level bomb runs—and found that Wernick had been right. The enemy was waiting.

Puffs of barrage flak smoke covered the sky above the targets, flung up by dozens of ground batteries and every ship in the harbor. Zeroes and Rufes were already in the air and climbing.

Once again, flame and smoke spread rapidly across Paramushiro. Bombs—incendiaries and high explosives—struck a dozen buildings, a waterfront pier, a cargo ship, warehouses and supply depots. But just outside the savage flak barrage, thirty-seven Japanese fighters waited to pounce on the emerging B-24s.

Captain Harrel F. Hoffman's Liberator, cornered by Zeroes, torched into a death spin. For the next forty-five minutes the eight remaining bombers fought a running battle with swarms of Japanese fighters—Zeroes, Rufes, Oscars, Haps. They attacked the B-24s from five- and seven-o'clock angles where the bombers' vertical stabilizers shielded their own turret and tail guns.

Japanese cannon and tracers slammed through every bomber; the fighters made thirty and forty passes at some of the fleeing B-24s. The sky was a chugging battlefield. Lieutenant Robert Lockwood's plane, limping on three engines, was punctured from every angle. His gunners hurled back fusillades, but the B-24 lost altitude. The crew threw everything overboard but couldn't lighten the ship enough—and then, at 200 feet, fuel starvation muzzled Lockwood's carburetors and all three engines stopped dead.

With instant presence of mind, Lockwood jabbed booster pumps to get the engines going. The belly turret took a frosting of ocean spray; and the three engines roared into life. Lockwood nursed it forward at zero altitude.

Lieutenant Leon A. Smith, last plane in "C" flight, was an easy target for the enemy; for more than ten minutes he had three fighters on each wing and four on his tail. His gunners raked the air and Zeroes went down flaming on all sides—by the end of the incredible fight, the American bombers had shot thirteen Japanese fighters into the sea.

Somehow, all eight B-24s, including Lockwood's, made it back to Attu. Through great good luck and uncanny flying, the mission had lost only one plane. But that sort of luck could not be expected to hold. The Japanese were beefing up their defenses drastically. In future, any raids against the Kuriles would have to be maximum efforts with strong fighter escorts.

The second Paramushiro raid proved nothing the first hadn't already proved, except that Wernick had been right in expecting the enemy to be alert and tough. Still, General Butler wanted to continue the raids.

But they would have to wait. First, Admiral Kinkaid wanted all his air strength concentrated for the big push—the invasion of Kiska.

CHAPTER
NINETEEN

Battle of the Pips

JAPAN'S IMPERIAL HEADQUARTERS WANTED the 6,000 soldiers on Kiska withdrawn to Paramushiro, where they could be used to reinforce the Kuriles. But the American blockade, which made it almost impossible to supply Kiska, made evacuation equally difficult. How could Admiral Kawase get his men off Kiska if he could not get ships to the island?

The only chance was to use submarines. Since the beginning of March, Kawase's big 5,000-ton I-boats had been Kiska's only source of supply; by June 9 they had made a score of round-trip voyages from Paramushiro. Now, the Chief of the Imperial Naval Staff ordered, "The defense unit on Kiska will be evacuated as quickly as possible by submarine."

Kawase had his misgivings. In view of the limited passenger capacity of the I-boats, it would take forty or fifty round trips to evacuate the entire Kiska garrison. Kawase had only eight I-boats. He had started in March with thirteen but one had been sunk at Attu and four others were missing in action.

At their present rate of operations, the Allies could be expected to invade Kiska by the end of July. Kawase had to get his men off before that. It didn't look as if he would be able to do it in time. And it began to look even less likely when his I-boats kept disappearing at an alarming rate.

Off Shemya on June 10, en route away from Kiska with 150 evacuees, Commander Hanabusa's *I-24* was discovered by an American picket boat's sonar. The little craft, PC-487, under Lieutenant Wallace G. Cornell, dumped five depth charges which exploded under the submarine and blew it to the surface. Cornell put about and aimed his boat on a collision course, intending to ram the 5,000-ton submarine with his 675-ton boat. At 19 knots he crashed into the submarine—but his bow rode up over *I-24's* hull, the keel clattered across her deck, and

PC-487 slid back into the water on the far side. She had hardly dented the tough submarine.

Gunners pumped 20-mm and 3-inch shells into the sub, and Cornell circled to ram again. This time he smashed into the submarine's conning tower, half-expecting the impact to sink his own boat. But the patrol craft stayed afloat, and the Japanese submarine rolled over and sank.

Three days later U.S. destroyer *Frazier* sank *I-31,* carrying evacuees, in the same waters. Then, on June 22, Commander Nagai's *I-7* was just approaching Kiska when destroyer *Monaghan* shelled her at long range and holed her conning tower. She could not submerge without filling. She escaped into Kiska Harbor, where she unloaded a cargo of emergency supplies, but there was no point in taking any evacuees aboard when she probably would not get home.

She tried. She came out at night, running on the surface. But *Monaghan* had waited for her. Shelled, *I-7* went aground on Little Kiska. About forty men from her crew reached shore; they assembled a platoon of workers and tried to get her refloated, but American bombers drove them back and destroyed the submarine.

So far, the I-boats had evacuated 820 men, of whom 300 were at the bottom of the sea. Kawase still had 5,183 men on Kiska—and only five submarines left.

THE U.S. AIR FORCE PLASTERED KISKA—407 bombing sorties in foggy June, even more in July. Navy Venturas made regular night-bombing attacks by radar, leaving Japanese soldiers sleepless and jittery. PBYs patrolled a 500-mile circle in pie-shaped sectors, to detect Japanese ships and fix them for bombers, destroyers, or American submarines. Ancient American S-class submarines, due for retirement within weeks, sank Japanese vessels with frightening regularity. And on July 6, Rear Admiral Robert C. "Ike" Giffen steamed toward Kiska with his "Alley Cats"—four blooded cruisers and four destroyers.

Giffen and his battered flagship *Wichita* ("The Witch") had become Arctic veterans on the deadly Murmansk convoy runs in the wolf-packed North Atlantic. They had fought with Halsey and the *Enterprise* at the recent Battle of Rennell Island. Now, summoned to the Aleutians by Admiral Kinkaid, Giffen took his miniature fleet along the Chain and subjected Kiska to its first naval bombardment in nearly a year.

The twenty-two-minute shelling caused only a handful of casualties ashore, but it convinced Admiral Kawase—if he still needed convincing—that the Americans would invade Kiska very soon. Kawase wrote,

"We cannot be...dependent on the submarines any longer, [since] the evacuation has to be completed as soon as possible before mid-July."

Under unenviable pressure, Kawase grasped at a reckless plan put forward by Naval Captain Rokuji Arichika: to steam boldly into the Aleutians with a surface fleet. He would "make an assault on the enemy in the vicinity of Kiska, and, taking advantage of the dense fog...evacuate all men simultaneously."

It was the same kind of gamble Colonel Yamasaki had made at Attu. When a good commander had only a long shot, he had no choice but to shoot it.

ADMIRAL KAWASE WOULD ACCOMPANY the force, but only as an observer; the commander would be Rear Admiral Masatomi Kimura, Commander of Imperial Destroyer Squadron One. The convoy assembled at Paramushiro, while at Kiska soldiers frantically laid out a road from their underground base to the harbor piers, to facilitate the evacuation.

The underground city had grown to astounding size. It had miles of tunnels, pervaded by the odor of incense which even penetrated the buried ammunition dumps. Barracks, three hospitals, dental clinics, offices, mess halls, machine shops, warehouses, photo labs, telephone switchboard centers, and recreation rooms—all had been excavated laboriously with picks and hand shovels, and shored with wood. Overhead ventilation pipes connected the maze of caves and tunnels.

Soldiers wore heavy fur-lined greatcoats to dash outside on errands, some of which were quietly humane: when an American P-40 fighter crashed on the mountain, the Japanese buried the pilot and put up a wooden cross and a round Japanese grave marker with the inscription, *Sleeping here, a brave air hero who lost youth and happiness for his motherland.*

As they prepared to withdraw, the men of Kiska suffered painful deprivation. Supplies dwindled to nothing. They were so short of food that when American bombs blew dead fish to the harbor surface, soldiers rushed out to net them. The base menu described them as "Roosevelt's Rations."

The furious increase in American bombing attacks convinced Rear Admiral Shozo Akiyama, the ranking officer on Kiska, that the enemy was about to land troops at any moment. And coming on top of that, a rumor that U.S. invasion transports had been sighted by an I-boat was enough to make Akiyama prepare his ceremonial dagger and throw the whole garrison into fatalistic despair. There was little hope the Japanese evacuation fleet could arrive before the enemy landed.

The fleet itself left Paramushiro at dawn Wednesday, July 21, 1943—cruisers *Tama, Abukuma* and *Kiso*, oiler *Nippon Maru*, and a pack of eleven destroyers. It steered due east, to pass far south of the Aleutians and avoid detection by American planes. At a point 500 miles south of Kiska the fifteen ships would refuel and wait for fog; when the fog got thick enough to conceal them, they would dash into Kiska.

THE ALLIED INVASION OF KISKA was set for the second week in August. In the meantime Admiral Kinkaid threw every plane and ship he had into the bombardment and blockade. On July 19, just two days before the Japanese evacuation fleet left Paramushiro, Kinkaid dispatched a two pronged naval attack force—the biggest the Aleutians had yet seen—to pummel Kiska with shells. Under Rear Admirals "Ike" Giffen and Robert M. Griffin, the force included battleships *Idaho, Mississippi,* and *New Mexico,* cruisers *San Francisco, Portland, Louisville, Santa Fe,* and redoubtable *Wichita,* and a screen of nine destroyers.

It was far different from the early days when NORPACFOR had gone to war with a handful of antique cruisers and tin cans. The seventeen men-of-war reached Kiska on July 22, and found the big island bathed in crystal sunlight from harbor to volcano cone. It was the first clear day in two months. The battleships and cruisers opened up with 6- and 14-inch guns.

Colonel William Alexander, who had hitched a ride aboard *New Mexico* to find out what size shore batteries the enemy had, recalls, "The usual snafus were in order. Somebody in Main Plot put the wrong range strip in the system. One of the 5-inch guns opened up on an unsuspecting whale; looked like a hit." But the battlewagons and cruisers lobbed 424,000 pounds of high explosive onto Kiska, and even though nobody was injured it was more than enough to convince the Japanese that their fate was sealed. They fully expected to suffer the same fate as Attu's defenders had; the terrific naval shelling, and the bombardment a half hour later by forty American and Canadian planes, looked like the immediate prelude to infantry landings.

LESS THAN AN HOUR AFTER they had shelled Kiska, Admirals Giffen and Griffin received radio orders to speed west and intercept a force of seven enemy ships reported by a PBY in a sector southwest of Attu.

Waiting for the fleet to come up, the circling Catalina maintained radar contact through the overcast for six straight hours, from 12:24 to 6:25 p.m., before it had to break off and return to Attu for fuel.

There could be no mistake that it had found seven unidentified objects on the surface of the ocean, headed east. The number of radar blips—seven—would loom in significance during the next few days. This first contact, on July 22, foreshadowed an eerie phantom battle that has yet to be explained.

Kinkaid thought he knew what the seven ships were. The daily Intelligence bulletin from CINCPAC said DATE OF ATTEMPTED ENEMY OPERATION IN ALEUTIANS IS...ESTIMATED AS JULY 25...ENEMY OBJECTIVE AND STRENGTH IS UNKNOWN. Tokyo Rose was predicting a Japanese reinforcement, and victory, at Kiska. American aerial photos showed a big increase in activity around Kiska Harbor, and there were disturbing reports throughout the North Pacific—a periscope sighted near Attu, heavy naval movement in the Kuriles, an unprecedented volume of radio traffic to and from Kiska.[1] It all suggested the Japanese might try to beef up Kiska before Kinkaid could land his invasion force.

To forestall that kind of reinforcement, he sent the Griffin-Giffen fleet after the seven ships reported by PBY radar; and to strengthen the fleet still more, he ordered the two destroyers blockading Kiska Harbor—*Aylwin* and the ubiquitous *Monaghan*—to pull off their station and join Griffin. It indicated how vital Kinkaid considered the need to stop the approaching enemy ships.

But at the same time, it was risky to leave Kiska Harbor unguarded. On July 23, Kinkaid tried to fill the gap by ordering four PT-boats to go to Kiska and "remain on patrol stations until necessary to return to base for fuel." But heavy storms blew in from the west. The PT-boats pitched wildly; they would not have seen an enemy task force unless it had collided with them. Regretfully, next day Kinkaid had to order "that MTB's patrolling off Kiska return to and remain at Bird Cape, Amchitka." It left the gates to Kiska Harbor wide open.

BY THE AFTERNOON OF JULY 24 it was clear that Griffin and Giffen had missed the seven radar-spotted enemy ships in the Attu area. If the seven ships had slipped past, they might be already on their way to Kiska. Exasperated, Kinkaid ordered Giffen and Griffin to return to Kiska at top speed and "cover the southerly and westerly approaches to Kiska until contact [is] made." At the same time, Kinkaid sent destroyer *Hull* out from Adak "to proceed to the vicinity of Kiska, assuming patrol north of

1. By this time the Japanese had changed their naval codes and CINCPAC's intelligence, while it still gleaned a certain amount of information from Japanese radio transmissions, was no longer able to read them as if they were plain English broadcasts.

[it] … to prevent enemy forces from reaching Kiska undetected from the northward."

Kinkaid hoped the battleship force would not run out of fuel until after it intercepted the enemy fleet; but just in case, he dispatched oiler *Pecos* with destroyer escort to the waters southeast of Kiska, and signaled ORDERS FOR RENDEZVOUS AND FUELING OF TASK GROUPS WILL BE ISSUED LATER.

That was Sunday, July 25. By nightfall, the Giffen-Griffin task force had steamed to a point within 90 miles of Kiska, south-southwest of the island.

At that moment, the Japanese evacuation fleet under Admirals Kawase and Kimura lay 400 miles due south of the American warships—still waiting foggy weather. The night was clear at both places. The wind was west at 8 knots, the sky cloudless, barometer 30.00 inches and steady, sea calm, air temperature 52° Fahrenheit, water temperature 49°.

Under these conditions—freakish good weather for the Aleutians—the oddest battle of the Aleutian Campaign took place: the mysterious Battle of the Pips.*

MONDAY, JULY 26, 1943.

Shortly before 1:00 a.m., with moonrise yet an hour away, *New Mexico* steamed at fleet center with *Mississippi* half a mile astern. Cruisers and destroyers fanned out across a wide area, some of them as far as twelve miles from the battleships.

At seventeen minutes before one, *Mississippi's* SC radar picked up seven radar echoes to the northeast, fifteen miles distant.

Within seconds, *New Mexico, Portland, San Francisco* and *Wichita* recorded the same radar images. From the high superstructures, radar antennae piped images into the Combat Information Centers, where information was analyzed and flashed to the bridges. *New Mexico's* radar log marked "seven distinct indications on the screen.… Plotting room tracked target first on course 140° T speed 17 knots.…"

Topside, bullhorns squawked the order to General Quarters—and added with studied calm, *"This ain't no drill!"* Men rushed to their battle stations.…

The fleet commenced fire at ranges from eight to twelve miles, the distance determined by each ship's position in the widely scattered group. All the radar bearings converged on a point about 22,000 yards

---

*1995 ADDENDUM: For further discussion regarding the "Battle of the Pips," see Appendix Two.

off *Mississippi's* bow, at a true bearing of 58 degrees from her. At the moment the dispersed ships had no time to compare notes on bearings and ranges, but soon afterward the question would assume great importance.

Admiral Giffen called for a fleet turn to the left, to intercept the radar targets on their southerly heading (and to foil possible enemy torpedoes). While the ships made their ponderous turn, guns salvoed across the night. Great flame lances stabbed the dark. Destroyers spun away to launch torpedo attacks; radar plotters grunted salvo corrections; below decks, men felt concussions like near-misses by enemy shells. *Portland* sighted what looked like a torpedo wake; soon afterward she spotted "illumination by star shells, source unknown." *New Mexico's* radar was still tracking seven radar pips until she fired her twentieth full salvo, when concussion jarred loose a tube in her SC radar. It took seven minutes to find the trouble, shove the tube back in place, and get the radar working again. But *Mississippi* was still tracking the seven pips on all three of her radar systems.

The terrific concussion of *Mississippi's* broadsides put both her catapult observation planes out of commission. *New Mexico's* planes suffered the same disablement, while the premature explosion of a hastily loaded shell ruined one of her 14-inch guns.

Twenty minutes after the shooting started, the targets made a turn. *Mississippi* logged, "Target changed course to 340° True, zigzagging about 20 degrees." *Wichita,* with the targets still on screen, also picked up a radar contact on the peak of Kiska volcano, 76 miles away. The image was easily distinct from the seven moving pips at which her main batteries were shooting.

No human eyes had yet seen the targets. By now the images were weak, winking in and out on the radar screens. By twos and threes they disappeared. Half an hour after the fleet had opened fire, the last pip winked out, and Admiral Giffen ordered the guns to cease firing.

AT 2:13 A.M. THE MOON ROSE. Neither moonlight nor illuminating star shells, fired by several ships, showed any sign that enemy ships ever had been there. At dawn *Wichita* launched a catapult plane, which searched a wide area but found nothing—not even debris.

It was baffling. What had they been shooting at?

Whatever it was, it hadn't shot back. The only damage to the American ships had been caused by the concussion from their own salvos.

Some officers suggested it could have been radar-beam reflections off ionized clouds.

But there hadn't been a cloud in the sky.

Others insisted it had to be a strange bending of radar beams that had caused the antennae to pick up atmospheric reflections (like mirages) of distant peaks on Amchitka and Semisopochnoi.

But radar, which sometimes picked up distant echoes and magnified them, never lied about bearings—only distances. And the radar beams from all but one or two of the American ships had not been pointed toward any mountains, no matter how distant. Nor would a distant mountain give seven pips, or change course and speed.

Other officers maintained that it must have been a radar malfunction, since some of the ships had not picked up any pips at all. *Idaho*, a few miles west of the fleet, had detected nothing, and had not fired. None of the destroyers had made radar contact. Didn't that suggest there probably had been no real targets?

But if there had been something—seven somethings—on the ocean surface at twelve to fifteen miles' range, the tall antennae of the cruisers and battleships in the main fleet would have just reached them on the edge of the horizon. For more distant *Idaho*, and the less-tall destroyers, the targets would have been beyond the horizon—hence, no radar contact. Radar was a line-of-sight device.

There was also the key fact of triangulation. If the ships that recorded radar pips had compared their logged bearings and ranges (there is no evidence they ever did so), they would have found—as any examination of the logs will show—that all the bearings and ranges converged on one point 22,000 yards off *Mississippi's* bow. That could not be explained by malfunction, ionized cloud layers, or bent-beam reflections from distant mountain peaks. It could only be explained by the actual presence of seven concrete objects on the surface of the ocean 22,000 yards off *Mississippi's* bow (a fact the Navy has *yet* to concede).

JAPAN HAD NO KNOWN SURFACE ships in those waters. Her evacuation fleet was hundreds of miles away to the south.[2] But she did have a naval presence in the waters where the Battle of the Pips took place: her patrolling fleet of I-class submarines.

---

2. Because a great many Japanese records were destroyed in 1945, hours before the Empire surrendered, it cannot be said with absolute certainty that no Japanese surface ships were in the area during the Battle of the Pips. Nor are Russian records available at the present time. Yet the weight of circumstantial evidence seems convincing enough. No

For Operation KE-GO, the evacuation of Kiska, Admiral Kawase had added several submarines to his undersea fleet, bringing it to a strength of eleven pigboats. Commander Northern Force Submarine Group had ordered,

> The primary duty of the submarine group will be to harass enemy warships attempting to obstruct our evacuation group in the advance to, and withdrawal from, Kiska Island.

Squadron Five—submarines *I-21, I-169, I-171*, and *I-175*—presumably obeyed orders to "take disposition…by 12:00 [noon] of the 26th," in their assigned positions along a patrol line south of Amchitka—approximately the area of the Battle of the Pips. Of those four submarines, none survived the war; but a fifth submarine, *I-2,* was nearby. Her captain, Mitsuba Ikatura, recalls:

> On July 22nd I received information that the evacuation would take place, so I should start weather reports again. I received a message (date unknown)…that I was to return to Unori Island by the same route. On the way back we heard firing [off] the southeast end of Amchitka Island. We saw the flashes of the guns. We submerged immediately to avoid being hit.

The only existing record, provided after the war by memory by the sub-fleet commander, Vice Admiral Shigeyoshi Miwa, states, "During the operations, Northern Force submarine group patrolled without fighting the enemy, though a few of the submarines were subjected to enemy …attack." Miwa later told Captain James S. Russell, "On the operation in the Aleutians, the Japanese Navy found out your radar was very good because our submarines…received much gunfire from your ships."

The log of U.S.S. *San Francisco* stated: "It is considered that if enemy units were present, they most probably were submarines bound for Kiska on the surface, submerging upon commencement of fire, and possibly resurfacing at intervals [because of uncharged batteries and low air supply]."

Japanese veterans have yet come forward to testify to the contrary. I have been unable to substantiate, or rule out, nebulous hearsay evidence reported by Colonel William Alexander and others that later South Pacific interrogations of Japanese naval prisoners revealed a mysterious Japanese surface-decoy fleet, or a towed-balloon "window" device attached to submarines to attract U.S. radar.

MORE THAN 2,500 FEET UP THE side of a Kiska mountain, the Japanese had installed a naval radar scanning antenna. It was used to track U.S. planes as they took off from nearby Amchitka; but its maximum range from that altitude was about 90 miles across the earth's curvature. The Battle of the Pips took place within the range and scope of that antenna.

It was not unlikely that Kiska radar had spotted the American fleet. Knowing the Japanese evacuation force would have to approach as soon as possible through those very waters, Kiska command could well have requested a distraction by submarines under authority of *Imperial Headquarters Directive No. 246*, which said, "Decoy convoys or the like, depending on the situation prevailing, will make feints...." while the Chief of the Imperial Naval Staff had directed that "dummy convoys will simulate a decoy maneuver...." Had it been Submarine Squadron Five, running on the surface and towing targets?

In the end, though the U.S. Navy admitted that "the possibility [that it was] submarines cannot be ignored," it concluded that "due to peculiar atmospheric conditions, considerable bending of the radar beam was present."[3]

The mystery was never solved. But its immediate aftermath was stark and indisputable.

Every shot fired by a battleship's 14-inch gun burned 1,500 pounds of gunpowder. Battleships consumed almost 200,000 pounds of fuel oil every day at cruising speed, and at combat speed the rate went up rapidly. All summer, a dozen Navy oilers had made regular 5,500-mile round trips from San Pedro, California, to the Aleutians, to provide Kinkaid's ships with oil. One of those oilers, *Pecos,* now waited to rendezvous with the Griffin-Giffen fleet. Because they had used up a great deal of fuel and ammunition in pursuit of seven radar pips (first west to Attu on a PBY radar report, then back for the Battle of the Pips), the ships were forced to turn east and meet *Pecos*.

The rendezvous took place the day after the Battle of the Pips. It was twenty-four hours before all the ships were refueled, on July 28. During

3. The Navy's conclusions regarding the Battle of the Pips are quoted from *Secret Information Bulletin No. 12* of February 12, 1944. Admiral Robert Griffin still agrees with the atmospheric-disturbance theory, though several authorities on the properties of radar have pointed out that the kind of beam-bending described by supporters of the theory is scientifically so unlikely as to be virtually impossible. Admiral Kinkaid says, "I've come to the conclusion that it takes a scientist, not just a line officer like me, to provide an intelligent answer to it." Now, twenty-five years after the Battle of the Pips, the most accurate summation is that offered by Lucian Wernick: "Nobody really knows what they had on that radar."

those twenty-four hours, Admiral Kawase's evacuation task force made its move toward Kiska. It steamed straight across the waters where the American battleships would have been if they had remained on station.*

A FEW HOURS AFTER THE BATTLE of the Pips, Admirals Kawase and Kimura started their northward dash. The fifteen-ship convoy had been reduced by a typical Aleutian mishap: five of the ships had rammed one another in a foggy chain collision. Two of them were damaged so badly that Kimura had to send them back to Paramushiro. The loss would make the embarkation of Kiska's 5,183 men a tight squeeze.

The task force followed a billowing fog front, much as Rear Admiral Kakuji Kakuta had done almost fifteen months earlier when he made his run-in toward Dutch Harbor to launch the opening attack of the Aleutian Campaign. Now, to bring an end to the Campaign, the Japanese fleet steamed north with the weather (while an American battleship force, big enough to destroy it, retired from the path ahead of Kawase). During the night of July 27, while the American ships made rendezvous with their oiler a hundred miles to the east, Kawase crossed the area of the Battle of the Pips and reached a point about 50 miles southwest of Kiska. He paused here, to wait for the weather to thicken.

Reports from Radio Kiska described an unbroken round-the-clock fury of aerial bombardment; every American plane in the theater had been in use during the past thirty-six hours. On July 26 alone, Kiska had received 208,000 pounds of bombs.[4] It looked as if the Americans would invade momentarily.

---

*1995 ADDENDUM: Retired intelligence officer Lt. Col. Lawrence Reineke has unearthed an interesting item in this regard. From a copy of Reineke's notes, sent to me in early 1995: "Kawase's evacuation fleet included SHIMAKASE, a recently commissioned experimental high speed destroyer, the only ship in the Japanese Navy at the time equipped with the latest model radar. It was SHIMAKASE that led the dash into Kiska using this radar to skirt around the north end of Kiska and come in from the Bering Sea side… Upon leaving by the same route after troops were embarked, SHIMAKASE's radar picked up a surface contact and the ships changed course. This contact was [the American submarine] S-33, at a distance of 1500 yards. Unlike [some S-boats], S-33 had no radar. S-33's bridge watch did not see the evacuation fleet pass by less than a mile away. This is a good example of the blindman's bluff game played by our search patrols. Weather again…and little chance of success without radar. Even radar was not the total answer because of malfunction, so-so operators unable to tune properly, moisture, atmospherics etc.

4. That night (July 26, 1943) Commodore Leslie Gehres' Fleet Air Wing had flown an overnight "Black Cat mission" with black-painted PBYs. The Catalinas remained over Kiska all night long. They made bomb runs at ninety-minute intervals to keep the Japanese on edge. They dropped a variety of fragmentation bombs, incendiaries and flares, and on the final run they dropped three cases of empty beer bottles.

If Kawase didn't move instantly, he would probably be too late. He gave up the idea of waiting for a storm, and ordered the fleet to proceed. Shortly before noon on July 28 the evacuation group set out to cover the last 50 miles to Kiska.

About 20 miles in, Kawase (in cruiser *Tama*) peeled off and took station to cover the rear. Rear Admiral Kimura and the rest of the fleet plowed ahead through a thin mist while Kimura radioed Kiska to get ready.

Kiska was ready—had been, for a week. The garrison set demolition charges and booby traps, chalked insults in English on the walls of their abandoned underground quarters, and assembled by the harbor beaches to meet the approaching ships.

On her final run-in to the harbor, cruiser *Abukuma* spotted what looked like an enemy ship in the mist, and launched a spread of four torpedoes. Another ship started to shell the same target. The noise was intense until they drew closer and discovered the "enemy ship" was an outcrop on Little Kiska Island. Meanwhile, the explosions made the assembled troops think they were being bombed through the overcast.

The low overcast covered the area; if there were American planes above it, they made no indication of having spotted the convoy, which steamed into harbor while demolition charges went off throughout the base camp. Installations blew up, fires licked through supply and ammunition dumps; shops and hangars collapsed in flames. The Japanese intended to leave nothing of use for the enemy.

Carrying only their rifles and personal belongings, the soldiers waited at the beach. Admiral Kimura ordered them to leave their small arms behind, because he was two ships short. By the hundreds, rifles and automatic weapons were dumped into the shallow water; then, embarking on scores of smallboats that sped from beaches to ships, the 5,183 defenders of Kiska climbed aboard eight ships in less than an hour's time.[5] Last to leave the beach was Lieutenant Commander Mukai, who had led the occupation forces onto Kiska in June 1942.

The convoy steamed out of Kiska Harbor at 7:30 p.m. while the thin fog broke into tendrils and cleared away behind them. Admiral Kimura sped south, picked up Kawase on the way, and made full flank speed through the clear night. By dawn he was more than 200 miles from Kiska. *Tama's* radar-interception gear picked up what seemed to be an enemy ship's search radar; *Abukuma* sighted a periscope; but the

5. Two Japanese cruisers took on 2,400 of the Kiska evacuees; the rest went aboard six destroyers carrying from 400 to 500 each. The overcrowding was painful, but the entire Kiska garrison got home without a single injury.

convoy took evasive action, steamed into a squall, and avoided contact with the enemy.

Four days later, without having fired a shot, Kawase steamed triumphantly into Paramushiro.

Kawase had brought off one of the war's most imaginative and daring maneuvers, without a single casualty. But the full effect of his brilliant operation would not be felt until three weeks later, when the Allies would play into Kawase's hands beyond his wildest imaginings.

CHAPTER TWENTY

The Invasion of Kiska

THE DAY AFTER THE JAPANESE had evacuated Kiska, a PBY on sector patrol in the fog made radar contact with seven target pips on the North Pacific, southwest of Kiska. Contact was maintained for two hours. Were these the seven phantom ships that had decoyed the American battleships? No one ever found out. But after this last sighting, the ring around Kiska was drawn up tighter than ever before.

Operation Cottage, the invasion of Kiska, was set for August 15, 1943. During July, both before and after the Battle of the Pips, naval ships had bombarded the island eight times. Now task groups under Rear Admiral H. F. Kingman (*Idaho, Tennessee* and four destroyers) and Rear Admiral Wilder D. Baker (*Salt Lake City* and nine other ships) shelled Kiska—ten times in two weeks. When they were not shelling they circled the island.

The Eleventh Air Force, up to 359 combat planes—the most it ever possessed—used them all to keep up a continuous three-week air raid. On August 4 alone, 135 sorties dumped more than 304,000 pounds of explosives on Kiska. Accompanying planes on "garbage detail" dropped surrender leaflets by the tens of thousands.

There was nobody on Kiska to read the leaflets—but the Americans did not know that. No Allied planes had seen the evacuation take place. Since then, the island had been covered by fog; during the few clear moments, bomber pilots spotted no activity on the ground, but that was not particularly surprising—the Japanese had always gone underground during air attacks.

Gradually, nagging clues began to appear. Strike photos showed that new bomb craters hadn't been filled in. No repairs had been made above ground. Vehicles and barges stayed put in identical positions several days in a row.

Air crews were still submitting reports of flak and small-arms ground fire; but the reports came from crews of the green 407th Bomber Squadron, an A-24 dive-bomber outfit freshly imported from the States for the Kiska invasion. The only veteran fliers who thought they saw anti-aircraft fire were conceded to be "flak happy" anyway. Most of the veterans, like those of the 36th Squadron, reported a complete lack of enemy opposition. Wheeler wrote:

> No AA fire reported at Kiska since July 27.... We flew six B-24's with 100-lb bombs today [August 11th] and made numerous individual bomb-runs at low altitude, 2,000 feet. No AA whatever, though our B-24's offer big and tempting targets. A 3-ship mission this afternoon also drew no AA. There has been none for fifteen days encountered by our squadron. The island appears desolate and unoccupied. We wonder if they have somehow withdrawn.
>
> The whole thing looks suspicious and baffling.... The Navy expects heavy casualties, I remember Col. Eareckson's opinion expressed in June that Kiska has no strategic value and isn't worth a single life. We are told that five thousand or more may die in taking the sinister island, but we wonder. G-2 claims there are five to eight thousand Japanese on Kiska. The Navy has been in a cordon about the island. Yet there was a lot of radar activity on July 22—did the Japs evacuate by submarine?

A SUSPICIOUS SIMON BUCKNER TOLD his intelligence staff to compile a thorough report. The result was a massive document containing itemized air-crews' reports of flak and ground fire—perhaps, as Eareckson argued, they saw what they expected to see. At best, the evidence was inconclusive. The enemy might be there; he might not.

General DeWitt thought the Japanese had holed up in mountain tunnels, waiting for an invasion. The others were not so sure. Major General Holland M. "Howlin' Mad" Smith pointed out that the last 11,000 Japanese defenders of Guadalcanal had evacuated secretly on twenty destroyers under cover of darkness on the night of February 4; the American ground forces hadn't realized it until five days later.

General Butler retorted that his Air Force pilots had been fired at over Kiska, and that the dogs—the only living beings sighted on the island—couldn't have been throwing up flak. General Smith replied that the Japanese might have left small detachments behind, to be evacuated by submarine before the American landings.

Smith and Simon Buckner suggested that Kinkaid send the Alaska Scouts ashore from rubber boats at night, before the invasion. That kind of operation had worked successfully on other Aleutian Islands. Colonel Verbeck, now Acting Commander of the Scouts, agreed and put in a formal request to make a preliminary nighttime reconnaissance of Kiska.

But again, the decision was Kinkaid's to make, and his alone.

Often in the last seven months, Kinkaid had made fast, final decisions; his hipshooting later drew sharp criticism from those armed with hindsight. His decision to send Admiral McMorris west with an undersized blockade force had been reckless and could have caused the loss of the fleet; it had not—it had, on the contrary, brought Allied naval supremacy to the North Pacific. His decision to relieve General Brown at Attu had been equally quick; he had been accused of making assumptions on insufficient grounds. But in Kinkaid's philosophy the risk of making a mistake had to be weighed against the risk of not acting at all.

The principles from which Kinkaid acted were always consistent; they were what made him, in the textbook military sense, an excellent commander. The results he obtained were not so consistent. But then, in war nothing was certain.

Kinkaid's decision was to go ahead with the planned full-scale invasion of Kiska.

If the enemy had evacuated, he said, the troop landings "would be a good training exercise, a super dress rehearsal, excellent for training purposes." If the enemy had not evacuated, but had dug into the mountains, then a small Scout party would probably be ambushed and cut to pieces. Either way, putting Scouts ashore did not look like the kind of calculated risk that Kinkaid espoused: the risk, to the Scouts, would be greater than the potential reward.

Kinkaid recalls, "I couldn't see that it would hurt anything to go ahead with the landings whether or not there were Japanese on Kiska. It was all right with me if they wanted to get off the island."

WHEN SIMON BUCKNER HAD FLOWN over Adak a year ago, there had been nobody on the island. Now its population was 90,000. A city had risen by Kuluk Bay; the harbor was crowded with more than a hundred ships. Back down the line—Atka, Umnak, Dutch Harbor, Cold Bay, Kodiak, Anchorage—a quarter of a million Allied servicemen provided support for the impending assault.

The hard lessons of Attu had impressed Kinkaid and his commanders. This time there would be a big enough force, enough equipment, and the right clothing and food to get the job done properly.

The force would include 15,000 Californians, about half of them the 7th Division's surviving Attu veterans; it would include more than 5,000 men from Buckner's Alaskan 4th Regiment; 5,000 men of the 87th Mountain Combat Team (trained to fight the anticipated winter campaign in Italy); 5,300 troops of the 13th Royal Canadian Infantry Brigade; and 2,500 paratroops of a guerrilla unit of commando rangers, the First Special Service Force.

Altogether, Invasion Force Kiska numbered 34,426 combat troops.

The Canadian brigade was led by Major General George Randolph Pearkes, Commanding General of the Canadian Army Pacific Command. Many of the soldiers were conscripts, drafted "for home defense only," and Ottawa had had to issue a highly unpopular order for their use in the Aleutians.*

Some of the units were English-speaking—the Rocky Mountain Rangers, the Winnipeg Grenadiers and Canadian Fusiliers—and others, like Le Régiment de Hull, spoke French. Thrown into training at Adak with American staffs and soldiers, the Canadians found the differences vast—not only in language, but in equipment, terminology, organization, and even insignia of rank.[1]

In their black berets, the Canadians decided to adopt American

*1995 ADDENDUM: The Kiska invasion was the first overseas operation conducted by Col. Robert T. Frederick's 1st Special Service Force, a joint Canadian-American unit (later dramatized in the 1968 movie "The Devil's Brigade," an action entertainment which—understandably?— neglected to mention the Force's Aleutian baptism of non-fire.) In its debut assault, the brigade's 1st and 3rd Regiments landed on Kiska; the 2nd remained in reserve at Amchitka. The quasi-commando FSS Force, in which each American soldier was paired off with (and exchanged uniforms and weapons with) a Canadian counterpart, later saw heroic action in Italy and France; by the time it came through the ferocities of Naples, Anzio and Mentone, half its complement had been killed or lost (MIA), but it had been in the thick of some of the most vicious fighting of World War II and came to be regarded as a triumph of international cooperation. In some ways, however, the less-publicized teamwork of Canadian and American air, sea and ground units throughout the Aleutians Campaign, and in extensive air rescue operations throughout Alaska, western Canada and the states of the U.S. Pacific Northwest, provided even stronger evidence of the two countries' long-standing inter-reliance and kinship. Jokes and bureaucratic snafus and individual rivalries aside, the forces of the two nations blended into a healthy interdependence that was one of the few elements of the North Pacific War that did NOT go wrong at every other opportunity.

1. Canadian Air and Navy forces had participated in the Aleutian Campaign from the beginning; the RCAF had four air squadrons on regular duty in the Aleutians. By August 1943, the RCAF had lost seventeen pilots in the campaign.

insignia to end the confusion; RCA lance corporals and leftenants blossomed forth in stripes and bars in addition to their own crowns and pips. By the time they boarded ship for the assault, the Canadians were equipped with their own battle dress and shoes, American cold-weather gear and artillery, and a mixture of rifles and equipment.

The Army issued a 52-page *Soldier's Manual* to all troops. Based on the experience of Attu, it was a guide to survival in the Aleutians. It talked about feet, blood, foxholes, food, ways to keep warm and dry, and ways to fight. Some of the veteran 7th Division soldiers did not need to be told. Among them were Colonels Wayne Zimmerman and Albert Hartl, with their commands from Attu. At higher level, Eugene Landrum had been replaced by Major General Charles H. Corlett, who had served under Buckner at Kodiak. Corlett would command the ground forces; Rear Admiral Rockwell would command the naval force, as he had at Attu; Kinkaid would command the entire operation, advised by Generals DeWitt, Smith, and Buckner. Since the operation would mark an important milestone on the road to Tokyo, a high-command representative was on the scene in the person of Assistant Secretary of War John J. McCloy.

Equipped with new Arctic gear, the force trained at Adak, practiced amphibious landings from LCIs and LCTs, and accustomed itself to muskeg travel. Planners studied the map of Kiska—based on aerial photos and a chart made in 1935 by the U.S.S. *Oglala*—and made plaster models of the island for unit commanders and troops to study.

The force left Adak on August 13, 1943. It was Friday the thirteenth. More than a hundred warships supported the transports (one of which was the redoubtable *St. Mihiel*). The day before, the Navy had shelled Kiska with sixty tons and the Air Force had dropped a hundred tons on the island. Support forces stood ready—Eareckson would be Forward Air Control, Wernick and Ramputi his bomber commanders in the air. Squeaky Anderson would run supply distribution at the main beachhead. PBYs and PT-boats would stand by for rescue and ferry duty.

D-day was August 15. On the eve of the assault, the transports gathered off Kiska in a light fog. Soldiers sharpened bayonets, cleaned rifles, repacked field packs and studied maps—General Corlett sent a staff lieutenant on the run to find a set of colored pencils to mark his maps. Loudspeakers announced briefing hours. Before dawn, battleships and cruisers drummed vast broadsides onto the island. Minesweepers prowled into the harbor. On their transports, combat troops were awakened and served a steak dinner. On the unstable LSTs many were too nervous, or too seasick, to eat. It was assumed that by the end of the fight, one out of every five men in the first assault waves would be dead.

AT DAWN LIEUTENANT COMMANDER DENNY'S five hapless PT-boats joined a group of transports in an elaborate feint at Gertrude Cove. The transports landed a detachment of Alaska Scouts while the torpedo boats strafed the beach from 100 yards offshore. The object was to fool the Japanese into thinking the invasion beachhead was here at Gertrude Cove: the PT-boats were masked with plywood silhouettes to resemble loaded landing craft, even down to cutouts of helmeted soldiers' heads.

The actual main landing was at a beach on the far western side of the island. LCs separated from their ships and growled through the surf toward shore. Their passengers squinted through the mist. They saw nothing, heard nothing but their own diesels and the roll of offshore naval guns. Overhead a 2,000-foot total overcast prohibited much air activity.

First to hit the Kiska shore were the recon patrols of the Alaska Scouts (led by Colonel Verbeck) and the Mountain Infantry (led by Colonel Robert T. Frederick) at Gertrude Cove. Frederick earned the dubious distinction of being the first American to set foot on Kiska since the departure of William C. House a year ago. Verbeck's and Frederick's missions were similar to Willoughby's at Attu: they were to explore the island, cross its length, and join up with the main force.

When Verbeck came ashore, a fox barked and a few birds flapped up into the foggy dawn. Verbeck found a deserted machine-gun nest above the beach and told his men, "There's nobody here anyway. Let's get across the island." They walked into the mountains, investigated caves and ravines, and found nothing but destroyed equipment and a cache of bamboo gin, which they appropriated. "We had a high old time on the way," recalls Sergeant Joe Kelly.

At the main beach, 7,300 combat troops landed without trouble. Their only encounters with living creatures were with a half dozen dogs, one of which wagged its tail and ran up to Ensign William C. Jones. The uncanny meeting stunned Jones with amazement: the dog was the same pup he had given to the ten-man Kiska weather-station crew fifteen months ago. Jones never learned how "Explosion" had survived the endless bombardments of Kiska.

Through the rest of that day, August 15, soldiers moved into the foggy mountains. The "fanatical" enemy would never risk loss of face by withdrawing without a fight—would he? He was up there in the hills, they felt, saving his ammunition, waiting to ambush them.

They were not dissuaded by Eareckson, who buzzed the hills in spite of fog and muttered into his radio that he would give a case of good Scotch to anybody who could find one single Japanese on the island.

It was a big island. The troops climbed slowly and settled down at sunset. Here and there, a boot touched off a mine or booby-trap. The explosions startled soldiers, who began to shoot into the fog. Brian Murphy recalls, "That night we heard a lot of shooting in the hills. The troops were shooting at anything that moved." Sporadic volleying kept up all night.

In the morning a second big landing force landed on a beach a few miles from the volcano. Brigadier General Joseph L. Ready, the force commander, had never been in combat. The men fanned into the fog in battalion columns of approach (like the parallel fingers of a probing hand). The probes found each other and started shooting in the fog.

One infantryman attacked an "enemy" patrol, whose members shouted at him to stop. When he began to throw grenades he was shot down.

In Sergeant Arthur Brindel's patrol, an automatic rifle broke a pin and fired off a full magazine of ammunition by itself.

Seventeen Americans and four Canadians died (shot by accident or booby-trapped). Fifty were wounded—booby-trapped or shot by mistake. One hundred and thirty men got trenchfoot.[2]

Patrolling destroyer *Abner Read* struck a Japanese mine moored in a Kiska cove. It crushed her stern plates and filled her hold with asphyxiating smoke—several men died there, and then the ship's stern broke off and sank, carrying men down. The final toll from *Abner Read* was seventy-one dead, thirty-four injured.

By August 18, 1943, General Corlett was confident the enemy was nowhere on Kiska, though a radiogram from the War Department insisted that a doctor who had visited Kiska in 1902 had seen mountain caves big enough to hide whole combat divisions. Corlett kept his disgusted soldiers searching for those caves until August 22, the eighth day of the invasion, but all they found were a few foxes and one or two more dogs.

Not until after the war would the Americans learn how, and when, the Japanese had evacuated Kiska.

"You are dancing by foolische *order of Rousebelt,*" said the scrawled message on an underground barracks wall. "*We shall come again and kill Yanki-joker.*"

2. The Canadians at Kiska suffered four dead, four wounded. Equipped with good footgear, they had only one case of trenchfoot.

Japanese food stood congealed on mess-hall plates. The Americans explored the miles and miles of tunnels with head-shaking amazement. Bomb-disposal teams took booby-traps apart; Navy divers salvaged an I-class submarine from the harbor bottom for study; crews gathered the remains of midget submarines, wrecked airplanes, guns, vehicles, and a host of other equipment.

Corlett quickly converted his landing force from an armed combat outfit to an occupation-construction team. Bulldozers went to work long before the topmost peaks had been reconnoitered. As usual, the Talley-trained Engineers (Colonel Talley had moved on by now, to the European Theater of Operations) had an air field operating in less than two weeks (where the Japanese had labored more than a year and never finished their runway).

Corlett said, "I'm tickled pink we didn't have to fight," and Kinkaid agreed—"of course we had no way of anticipating our men would shoot each other in the fog."

The outcome was satisfactory, but nothing could disguise the fact that for more than two weeks the Allies had bombarded an abandoned island, and that for a week thereafter they had deployed 35,000 combat soldiers and sailors—306 of whom became casualties—across the deserted island.

Simon Buckner observed, "To attract maximum attention, it's hard to find anything more effective than a great big, juicy, expensive mistake." The Kiska operation reddened faces from Anchorage to Ottawa to Washington. It did indeed attract maximum attention in the press—for the first time, the Aleutian Campaign got headlines. For years thereafter, when the average American thought of the Aleutians (if he did at all) he automatically thought of the blunder at Kiska.

The Japanese high command enjoyed a hearty laugh, spiced by the knowledge that while the Allies had tied up 300,000 men and hundreds of ships in the Aleutians, a struggling Allied amphibious force had invaded Vella Lavella in the Solomons on the same day as the Kiska landing. With the Kiska force, the Vella Lavella troops wouldn't have had to struggle.[3]

MacArthur struggled too, in the Bismarck Barrier, and Halsey pressed toward New Georgia. Both operations went more slowly than they would have with the addition of the Kiska forces. Tokyo felt there was ample cause for satisfied laughter—but it soon dwindled. Evacuations, no

3. Patterned after the Attu-Kiska order of operations, Vella Lavella was the first of the Central Pacific leapfrogging operations. By taking Vella Lavella first, the Allies deliberately bypassed the Japanese strongpoint at Kolombangara, and left it to wither and starve.

matter how brilliantly executed, could bring no victories. If there was a question of dignity—who had lost face?—there was also a question of strategy: Who had lost ground?

THE INVASION OF KISKA MARKED the official end of the Aleutian Campaign. After 439 days of warfare, the Chain was scratched off global maps as a combat theater.

The bitter laughter over the fiasco at Kiska obscured the long hard fight that had gone before, the brutal struggle for Attu, and the fact that the Aleutian Campaign had given the United States her first theater-wide victory of the Second World War. Japan's adventure in the Western Hemisphere was ended.

A year ago, Japan had threatened America's northern flank. Now the Allies threatened Japan's. To carry that threat forward, General DeWitt submitted to the Joint Chiefs of Staff a plan to use the combined Attu-Kiska forces, reinforced to about 54,000 men, to invade Paramushiro. The JCS discussed the proposal for ten days in September 1943.

It was tempting, but there were three causes for caution. First, Russia had not gone to war against Japan. Siberian Kamchatka was so close to Paramushiro and Shimushu (about 30 miles) that operations would be very tricky without Soviet support. Second, a northern attack on Japan would leave intact the Empire's lifeline to the rubber, rice and oil of the East Indies, over which Japan had gone to war in the first place. Third, and most compelling, the windy fog and miserable wet cold of the Aleutians would make it difficult and hazardous to maintain supply lines or launch operations.

The Joint Chiefs settled on a tentative compromise. They rejected the plan for an immediate Paramushiro invasion, but they did order Kinkaid and Buckner to submit detailed plans for it, and to keep beefing up their staging bases so that the plans could go into quick operations if and when Russia came into the war against Japan. The tentative target date was June 1, 1944, by which time Buckner was to complete facilities for a wing of B-29 Superforts at Shemya, as well as camp areas, warehouses, hospitals, depots and dumps for at least two divisions of amphibious infantry. Meanwhile the Navy was to beef up its Aleutian bases too.

ADMIRAL NIMITZ PLACED THE ALEUTIANS in a "Non-invasion Status" and reduced the North Pacific Force to a purely naval role. Lieutenant General Buckner assumed total military control of the Alaska-Aleutian region, including all Air Force operations. His force reduced, Admiral

Kinkaid said his farewells and went south to take command of the U.S. Seventh Fleet under General Douglas MacArthur. For the rest of the war he would boss "MacArthur's Navy."

There was a quick exodus of familiar faces. Major General William O. Butler left to become Deputy Commander of the Allied Expeditionary Air Forces in Europe (while in Alaska, Buckner himself took command of the Eleventh Air Force). Brigadier General Earl DeFord of Bomber Command went to England with Butler, and soon became Air Chief of Staff in the Mediterranean Theater. Colonel William O. Eareckson stopped off at Pearl Harbor, where Admiral Nimitz pinned a Navy Cross on his tunic; it kept company with Eareckson's Silver Star, Distinguished Service Cross, Distinguished Flying Cross, Air Medal, and the Purple Heart Buckner had given him at Attu. From there Eareckson went into the South Pacific to become Support Air Controller in the New Guinea campaign. Colonel William Alexander took the same route, and spent the next two years serving on Halsey's and MacArthur's staffs.

Major General Holland M. "Howlin' Mad" Smith took command of the Marines who would invade Tarawa in November. Lieutenant General John L. DeWitt went back to San Francisco to continue running the Western Defense Command. Major General Charles H. Corlett, commander of the Kiska invasion force, took the 7th Division south to prepare it for further combat. Having been the first U.S. combat division to recapture American soil, the Hourglass 7th would also be the first to capture Japanese soil (Kwajalein). Later, at Okinawa, it would serve under Simon Buckner's command when Buckner took over the Tenth Army.

Four veteran Air Force squadrons were rotated back to the States. Among them was the weary 36th Squadron. It had served 28 months in Alaska without leave. Four out of every ten of its original flying personnel had been killed. Its handful of fliers had dropped 1,500,000 pounds of bombs and earned 300 combat decorations.[4]

---

4. In all, the Eleventh Air Force had flown 3,609 combat sorties during the Aleutian Campaign—an average of eight a day in the world's foulest weather. Seldom had more than a hundred of its airplanes been in flyable condition at any one time. It had lost forty planes in combat and 174 planes to weather and mechanical failure; 192 of its planes were badly damaged. It had dropped 7,000,000 pounds of bombs on the enemy in a grim campaign of aerial attrition which, detractors to the contrary, had prevented the enemy from building air fields or bringing in reinforcements, and which had contributed crucially to the Japanese decision to evacuate Kiska without a fight.

The Navy's Fleet Air Wing of PBYs and PV-1 Venturas had flown 704 combat sorties and uncounted thousands of patrols, dropped 590,000 pounds of bombs, lost sixteen planes in combat (most of them in the Kiska Blitz) and thirty-five others in fog. Altogether,

Billy Wheeler wrote of the trip home:

> We spent twenty days on that packed Liberty Ship with terrible food and no escort from Dutch Harbor to Seattle. The four small lifeboats could only accommodate 100 men out of the 1,000 aboard. This certainly is a fine way to treat two of our best squadrons, and the men were sore....
>
> Home again. How strange it seems to see trees—and women!

No brass bands welcomed them. On November 20, 1943, the 36th Bombardment Squadron (Heavy) was disbanded. Its men received a few weeks' leave and were shipped to new squadrons and training commands; these veterans of the bitter thousand-mile war were among the best combat fliers in the world, and the Air Force had need of them.

THE WAR'S TIDE HAD LAPPED at Alaska in June 1942. By September 1943 it had receded, but the war in the North Pacific was far from over. It still had two years to run.

Most of the combat troops who had been brought in for the Attu-Kiska operations were quickly withdrawn—7th Division went south, the Canada Brigade returned home (after four months' occupation at Kiska)—but their places were filled by Engineers, SeaBees, occupation forces and service troops. Benjamin Talley's successors floated permanent concrete runways on Adak, Amchitka, Shemya, and Attu (they are still there and in use); and from the westernmost islands, the Eleventh Air Force carried the war into the Kuriles.

Exploratory missions had probed Paramushiro before the end of the Campaign. Now, as one of his last acts as Alaskan air commander, General Butler ordered a full-scale bombardment mission, to hit Paramushiro on September 11,1943. As a parting shot, it was to prove the Eleventh Air Force's greatest disaster of all.

The withdrawal of squadrons had left Butler severely understrength. He could assemble only seven B-24s and twelve B-25s for the strike.

The Japanese were waiting for them. During a 50-minute dogfight against sixty enemy fighters, the Americans dropped about twelve tons of bombs on Paramushiro and Shimushu-To and shot down thirteen enemy planes, but lost three of their own planes on the spot—and seven shot-up

---

including transport planes and warplanes on noncombat flights, the Allied air services lost 471 airplanes in the Aleutians during the campaign. Japanese losses had been sixty-nine planes in combat and approximately two hundred in fog and storms.

American bombers had to crash-land at nearby Petropavlovsk in Soviet Kamchatka. The Russians impounded the bombers, and only after horrifying and heroic misadventures were the seven air crews able to make their way home to the United States.

Of the nineteen planes that flew the mission, only nine came home. In one stroke the Eleventh Air Force had lost more than half its striking power.

Butler left the Aleutians, dumping the remnants in Simon Buckner's hands, and Buckner spent the fall and early winter training his green replacement crews in the handful of remaining airplanes. The Kuriles suffered no further action in 1943, except for a few photorecon flights by Navy planes.

PBY SQUADRON VP-43 HAD SERVED an early hitch in the Aleutian Campaign. Now, with Lieutenant Marshall C. Freerks as exec and soon-to-be commander, the experienced Aleutian pilots headed north from the States for a second North Pacific tour of duty. They started with twelve planes. Two cracked up in storms; they reached Kodiak with ten. Commodore Gehres sent the squadron to Attu to commence search patrols. When they arrived on October 10, 1943, they heard Tokyo Rose announce that the Japanese were on their way back to retake the Aleutians.

Three days later it looked as if she meant it. At 6:00 p.m. Wednesday, October 13, nine four-engine Japanese bombers made a bomb run on Attu from 10,000 feet.

Flak went up and a few P-40s roared off the airstrip. Bombs fell in Massacre Bay and around the air field. Terrific noise and smoke drove ground crews toward the mountains on the run. The only American fighter that got up fast enough to make contact with the enemy ran into an American flak burst and had to make a quick forced landing; the other fighters lost the bombers in the soup.

The bombs had damaged nothing of importance, but they demonstrated that the easy striking distance between Attu and Paramushiro worked both ways. From then on, Attu kept alert, but it proved fruitless; there were no more air raids.

Freerks' squadron moved immediately to Shemya. On October 20 one of his PBYs brushed with a Japanese bomber off Attu. The Catalina evaded the Betty's enormous 20-mm tail cannon and both planes retired with dignity, shot up but crews unhurt. It had been the last aerial skirmish in the Aleutians.

SIMON BUCKNER HAD TURNED a big job into a small one. It was time to move on. He still wanted to march into Tokyo. In June 1944 he stepped toward that goal by going to Hawaii to organize the new Tenth Army for the final Pacific offensive against Japan.

Buckner's postwar plans were set. He had fallen in love with Alaska; he planned to retire from the Army and settle at the farm he had bought at Homer, on the Kenai Peninsula, where bears and wildfowl teemed. Perhaps he would seek appointment to the Territorial governorship when Ernest Gruening decided to step down.[5]

As head of the Alaska Defense Command for four grueling years, Buckner had built up Alaska's military strength—and Alaska itself. He left his mark on the Territory; it is still there.

When he left, his successor had to overcome the handicap of the Buckner legend. Major General Davenport Johnson took on the Alaska Command, the Eleventh Air Force, and the challenge. It was not easy. The war had gone by; morale on the western bases was terribly low—there was nothing to do and nothing to look forward to. Inspection teams from the States observed that Alaska's troops would need complete retraining before they could be useful anywhere. With the enemy threat gone, the forward bases had degenerated into wretched bickering camps—Army against Navy, Negro against white, officers against enlisted men, noncoms against privates, military personnel against civilian workers.

General Johnson found that four hundred officers had spent more than two years in the Aleutians. He sent them home along with thousands of enlisted men, but that didn't explain to their replacements, and to those who remained, whether their presence served any worthwhile purpose. The Aleutians were no more comfortable than they had ever been. By now the U.S. government had spent more than a billion dollars in Alaska and the Aleutians; thirty-two Army and air bases, and scores of outposts, had been built; nearly a half million U.S. military personnel had served, or were serving, there. To what end?

The sense of uselessness only deepened when the Joint Chiefs ordered General Johnson to keep his Northern Invasion plans dusted off and up-to-date, but take no action. The Soviets had not come into the war, but Roosevelt would negotiate soon with Stalin at Yalta. The

5. Buckner's gubernatorial ambition was never firm, but if he had achieved it, it would have been another parallel with his father's record as a distinguished lieutenant general who later became a governor (of Kentucky). It has been suggested that Buckner's insistence on superhuman achievement, and his ambitious drive, were part of an attempt to live up to the image of his patriarchal father.

Paramushiro invasion project might be revived at any time. At the moment it looked as if it might be launched in the spring of 1945.

Snafu operations were no help to morale. General DeWitt had ordered the construction of a staging base for the Attu invasion at Excursion Inlet, 70 miles from Juneau, but it had not been completed in time to be any use. DeWitt had insisted on finishing the job. Governor Gruening pointed out that the base ought to be at Juneau, which already had docks, power, and the harbor facilities which had to be built from scratch at Excursion Inlet. DeWitt stuck to his guns, and the base was built. It was completed late in 1944, and after the last touches were put on, it was demolished.

While an uncompleted base was a sore monument to error, the completion and subsequent destruction of the base was a means to justify the expense and at the same time destroy the evidence of folly.

By the law of averages, most construction in Alaska had to be more useful than that. The Alcan telephone line—2,000 miles of wire strung by Signal Corps men—went into operation between Fairbanks and the States. The Alaska Scouts made a pipeline survey from Fairbanks to Point Barrow, and mapped the entire 34,000-mile coastline of Alaska by foot and dogsled. LORAN (Long Range Radio Navigation) systems were installed throughout Alaska and out the Aleutians as far as Attu, to provide homing navigation beams for airplanes. The beams saved countless planes, particularly those returning from the Kuriles. Air Force Lieutenant David Irwin developed a squad of parapups—sled dogs trained to be parachuted from planes on rescue flights. Quarters and food on the western islands improved considerably, and General Johnson provided a good many recreational facilities never before seen in the Aleutians. Even genuine female nurses were to be found at Adak. But none of this was compensation enough. Service in the Aleutians, the grey place of williwaws and terrible seas, could never be anything but penal servitude.

THE NORTH PACIFIC FORCE BECAME a roving naval task group of obsolete cruisers and destroyers. Its job was to harass the defenses of the Kuriles. During the last two years of the war NORPACFOR bombarded Paramushiro and other Kurile bases fifteen times with big-shell salvos, and made constant offensive sweeps of the North Pacific and the Okhotsk Sea to sink enemy shipping. In one sweep near the end of the war, the force (under Rear Admiral J. H. Brown Jr.) destroyed eleven small enemy ships off the Kuriles. All told, the enemy lost about thirty ships to U.S.

submarines, ships, and planes in northern waters (while the United States lost fifteen ships, patrol craft and submarines, most of them in bad-weather accidents). But the United States had won complete mastery of the northern seas.

Air Force operations against the Kuriles had been suspended after the disastrous raid of September 11, 1943. Commodore Gehres' PBY-Ventura wing resumed the attacks on a small scale at the end of the year with night-bombing missions over Paramushiro. The Catalinas bombed and took pictures by the light of magnesium photoflash bombs. Gehres' "Empire Night Express" continued irregularly for months.

Soon the Air Force's medium and heavy bombers resumed daytime missions. They were, at the time, the longest over-water missions of the war. (The theater's longest mission flew on June 19, 1945, when the B-24s of the 404th Squadron made the 2,700-mile round trip from Shemya to Kruppu. The planes were aloft 15 ½ hours.)

The promised B-29 Superforts never arrived. Only one, an experimental model up for cold-weather tests, touched down at Shemya's new 10,000-foot runway. It did not fly in combat. General Johnson described the flight as a "morale run" but any effect it had in that capacity was negligible. The Kurile campaign was flown by a scattering of replacement B-24s, B-25s, PBYs and Venturas. Johnson's air strength never increased to more than a few dozen planes. They flew about 1,500 sorties against the Kuriles before war's end.

But the effect of the small harassing campaign was out of all proportion to its size. It tied up 500 Japanese planes (toward the end, that was one-sixth of the combined Imperial air forces) and 41,000 ground troops, who deployed against the threat of an invasion in the Kuriles. These were men and planes that MacArthur, Halsey, and Simon Buckner himself did not have to fight in the south. The invasion never did take place, but its threat was enough. The Kurile campaign was of far greater value than the bored Aleutian servicemen imagined.

LATE IN 1944 JAPAN LAUNCHED the first of almost 10,000 bomb-carrying balloons into the upper atmosphere, where prevailing winds carried them across the Pacific toward America. Several hundred reached the United States (one killed five children and a woman in Oregon). About two hundred reached the Aleutians and Alaska. At Adak a radar-tracking station kept an eye on them, and fighters went up regularly to shoot them down, more in disgust than in anger. The few balloon-bombs that did get through to the Alaskan mainland caused negligible damage and no injuries.

IN APRIL 1945, ALASKA'S ATTENTION turned toward the Central Pacific—Okinawa, where Simon Buckner led his Tenth Army into battle. It was the last important land offensive of the war.

Buckner hit the beach Easter morning and bulled into the Pacific's bloodiest battle. It lasted two and a half months. Buckner fought the Japanese into a corner and then, on the eve of victory (June 18) he went up to a forward observation post and was hit by shrapnel from a Japanese artillery shell.

He was dead within seconds.

Four days later, the battle was over. Lieutenant General Simon Bolivar Buckner Jr. was one of its 12,000 American dead.[6] (Japanese dead numbered more than 100,000.)

OF THE 7,000 AIRPLANES THAT FLEW into Alaska between 1943 and 1945 along the $60,000,000 Northwest Staging Route through Canada, 6,430 were Lend-Lease planes turned over to the Russians, who picked them up at Fairbanks and flew them to Siberia by way of Nome or Shemya.

Stalin finally reciprocated by declaring war on Japan. It was August 8, 1945—two days after the United States had dropped a nuclear bomb on Hiroshima.

Stalin wanted to be in for the kill. He intended to annex the Kuriles to the Soviet Union (he did); he also hoped to divide Japan and Tokyo into occupation zones (he did not).

Soviet armies invaded Japanese-held Manchuria with brutal speed. In the next month the Russians suffered 8,000 dead and 22,000 wounded, the Japanese 80,000 dead. Half the fighting took place after Japan had surrendered—Stalin wanted to grab as much territory as he could.

The war had reached its end at last. On August 13, 1945, the Eleventh Air Force flew its last bombing mission from Shemya to Paramushiro. Two days later, Japan surrendered.

The long war in the North Pacific was over.

---

6. During the first weeks of the Battle of Okinawa, Time magazine put Buckner's portrait on its cover. Among the superstitious the anxiety rose that the Time "jinx" would hang over Buckner and the Americans on Okinawa. Weeks later Buckner was dead.

Three funeral services were held in his honor—at West Point, at Arlington National Cemetery, and at his home in Kentucky. Vice Admiral Thomas C. Kinkaid attended all three requiems, flying from one to the other, all on the same day.

Kinkaid told me that the only fault he could ever find with Simon Buckner was that Buckner shouldn't have been up at the front line where he was killed. When Kinkaid made that remark, Mrs. Kinkaid pointed out that he was forgetting how he had stood bolt upright with binoculars on the exposed bridge of Enterprise during bombing attacks at Midway, while all the other deck officers were belly flat behind cover.

"That was different," Kinkaid growled. "I had business there."

Epilogue

THE ALEUTIANS HAVE NOT CHANGED in the twenty-five years since their forgotten war was fought. Rusting relics of battle still litter Attu's mountainsides. Giant B-29 hangars and a huge hospital are crumbling into ruin on Shemya. Half-collapsed World War II Quonset huts can be seen on the hills of Adak. The Navy has authorized the sale of 5,253 acres of surplus property at the former naval base at Dutch Harbor.

There are today a number of semi-secret radar and interceptor bases in the Aleutians.* At Anchorage, Elmendorf Air Force Base is now

---

*1995 ADDENDUM: The above section, like the body of this book, was written in the late 1960s. The only deliberate untruth perpetrated in it was the description of Shemya as an island whose military facilities were "crumbling into ruin"; this was written, in a time of Cold War and conflict in Viet Nam, as a courtesy to a government with which I sometimes disagreed but which I did not wish to betray.

In fact I had traveled the length of the Aleutians in 1967 and had seen most of the military installations along the Chain, including not only crumbling ruins on several islands (some are still there in 1995) but also then-busy Navy and Coast Guard stations at Adak, an AEC nuclear weapons test center at Amchitka, and the active U.S. Air Force base at Shemya, where I bunked in one of the enormous underground compounds. A complement of more than a thousand officers and enlisted personnel was stationed there at the time. The mainly subterranean base had all sorts of amenities, from shops to a library to its own closed-circuit television broadcasts. Its long runways and huge aboveground hangars—the same ones that had been built for B-29 Superfortresses—were in use throughout the 1960s as homes for RC-135 planes that flew regular spy missions near the Soviet coast.

I haven't been back to the western Aleutians since those days, but quite a few veterans have rendezvoused there for reunions in the past few years; as they describe it today, any military efforts along the Chain have been reduced to a skeletal minimum. Native Aleuts have resettled several of their former home islands. The much-reduced Shemya base is now called Eareckson Air Force Station; Attu, uninhabited, is a National Battlefield Park. Adak stands by, mainly as a base for Coast Guard sea and air patrols that perform search-and-rescue operations and enforce laws and treaties governing the harvest or protection of seals, dolphins, whales and fish. As always, however, there is warfare in the Aleutians. It is fought by all living creatures against the common enemy: the demon weather.

headquarters of the Alaskan Command; in 1969, C-141 Starlifter jet transports roared through Elmendorf around the clock, shuttling from the States to Vietnam along the Great Circle Route. Aleuts have resettled one or two islands, but for the most part the Aleutians are more deserted today than they were in 1941. Three small trees struggle for livelihood in the wind and fog of Adak.

The Alaskan air is as unforgiving as ever. On June 14, 1967, Lieutenant General Glen R. Birchard, head of the Alaskan Command, was killed when his float plane crashed on an Alaskan lake. The author witnessed the aftermath of a minor eruption at Great Sitkin volcano in the Aleutians in November 1967, and rode an old plane into Shemya in a 60-knot crosswind. The Aleutians, and their williwaws, have not been tamed.

A FEW UP TO-DATE OCCURRENCES CONTINUE to echo the long-ago Campaign. On July 16, 1967, a Japanese trawler was seized in Alaskan waters; several Russian "fishing vessels" have been arrested in the Aleutians, raising the ghosts of prewar Japanese reconnaissances. Veterans held a 25th anniversary celebration at Adak in August 1967, and the members of the Navy's PBY air wing plan a reunion at Seattle, to be chaired by Admiral James S. Russell.

Several principal figures of the Aleutian Campaign, like Russell, went on to significant achievements. Russell became a four star admiral, was appointed Vice Chief of Naval Operations (the second-highest office in the operational Navy), and subsequently became Supreme Commander Allied Forces Southern Europe (NATO). Now retired, the Navy's highest-ranking flying officer, he is a Boeing Company consultant (he studied aeronautics under Theodore von Karmann) and an executive of Alaska Airlines.

Vice Admiral Thomas C. Kinkaid planned and executed the naval phase of the liberation of the Philippines and the Battle of Leyte Gulf. He accepted the Japanese surrender at Seoul in 1945 and later served as commander of several major districts and Sea Frontiers. He retired a full four-star admiral in 1950 and now lives in Washington, D.C.

Colonel William O. Eareckson flew throughout the island campaigns of the Pacific as Forward Air Controller, bomber unit commander, and air staff officer for Admiral Nimitz. But his postwar assignments showed that the Air Force considered him a hot potato. He had earned every decoration short of the Medal of Honor; he was loved by the men who served with him, and respected as a brilliant tactician. Yet he was no politician. His caustic wit and outspokenness held him back in the military bureaucracy of the postwar years. After brief assignments to Labrador and other outposts, Eareckson was still low on the advancement list in 1951 and was regularly passed over for promotion to brigadier general. He retired in 1954, still a colonel after thirteen years in that rank. On October 26, 1966, he died.

THE CAMPAIGN IN THE GRAY AND WINDY Aleutians was the United States' first offensive campaign of World War II—the first to begin, the first to be won. Its major events had included the first extensive aerial bombing campaign in American history; the first mass military airlift ever executed; the longest and last classic daylight surface battle in naval history; the first land-based American bomber attacks on the Japanese homeland; and, in the Battle of Attu, the U.S. Infantry's first amphibious island assault landings and the second most costly infantry battle of the Pacific war (in ratio to the size of the forces engaged).

Attu did for the U.S. Army what the raid on Dieppe in August 1942 did for British-Canadian amphibious forces: by its very mistakes and failures it taught lessons which led to later successes in the Pacific leapfrogging campaign. If the Normandy Invasion was won on the blood-washed beaches of Dieppe, then at least some part of the war in the Central Pacific was won on the steep beaches and craggy mountains of Attu.

ERNEST GRUENING WAS ONE OF THE TWO lonely U.S. Senators who in 1964 opposed the Tonkin Gulf Resolution (which gave the President of the United States authority to extend American armed intervention in Southeast Asia); on March 10, 1964, Gruening made the first major speech ever delivered on the Senate floor opposing the United States' increased military involvement in Vietnam. To a certain extent, Gruening's stand (highly unpopular at the time) was based on personal experience.

The Aleutian Campaign had been a little war, fought without precedent in a Pacific theater with which Americans were unfamiliar. It was not amenable to ordinary methods of warfare. It required the utmost in human resourcefulness merely to achieve survival; it required extraordinary ingenuity to do battle with unproved methods that had to be designed on the spot. It produced unique developments—in navigation and communication; in air-rescue operations in hostile, remote areas; in aerial support methods like Forward Air Control; in assault techniques like radar-controlled air missions and DR calculation bombing; in infantry tactics (Attu was almost a guerrilla campaign and lasted far longer than anyone had anticipated).

Thus the Aleutian Campaign set a pattern that has held true ever since—a strange Pacific theater into which the United States poured the better part of a half million troops to fight a shifting, nebulous enemy over a battleground of dubious worth. It would be dangerous to draw too close an analogy between the Aleutians and Vietnam—the differences are as obvious as the parallels—but the historical comparison does lead to an important question: If there was a lesson in the Aleutian war, have we learned it?

DURING THE ALEUTIAN SUMMER OF 1943, Warrant Officer Boswell Boomhower wrote:

A soldier stood at the Pearly Gate;
His face was wan and old.
He gently asked the man of fate
Admission to the fold.
"What have you done," St. Peter asked,
"To gain admission here?"
"I've been in the Aleutians
For nigh unto a year."
Then the gates swung open sharply
As St. Peter tolled the bell.
"Come in," said he, "and take a harp. You've had your share of hell."

Afterword 1995

THE IRREPRESSIBLE LARRY REINECKE has sent volumes of photocopied records and memoirs, along with a number of audiotaped interviews, some dating back many years. The good Tom Spitler, of Anchorage, has kept my mailbox filled with frequent updates on events in contemporary Alaska that bestir echoes of the war. Numerous other correspondents have sent along everything from bemused anecdotes to lengthy treatises.

On Veterans' Day 1993, roughly the 50th anniversary of the end of the Aleutians campaign, I was privileged to participate with scores of historians and veterans who came to Anchorage to attend several days of symposia, exhibits, films, tours and meetings, collectively dubbed the "Alaska At War" Conference. The undertaking was organized by Joan M. Antonson, John H. Cloe, Carol Burkhart, Georgeanne Reynolds, and Russ Sackett. A wealth of material, much of it new, was brought forward. That fascinating symposium produced its own book and tape recordings; I feel neither a need nor a right to plunder that material. I hope the extended bibliography in this new edition of *The Thousand-Mile War* will be a helpful guidepost to lead searchers in useful directions.

I am delighted to have had some of the errors in the earlier version of this book pointed out and to have this opportunity to correct such matters as the Zero-Hellcat myth. I assure all correspondents that I haven't ignored anyone's input; but in some cases, those who endeavor sincerely to correct my mistakes seem to have documentation that is no more persuasive than that which supported the original supposed mistakes. In those cases, unless an arbiter can be found who can settle the dispute, all one can do is leave open the unresolved difference of opinion, or of recollection, and let posterity try to provide a decision.

John Huston's wartime Technicolor documentary movie *Report From The Aleutians* is now available on videocassette. Also available are the

1986 Alaska Historical Commission documentary *Alaska at War* and a video memento of a veterans' reunion, *The Forgotten Front—Veterans Remember.*

These and other memorabilia are available from the Alaska Aviation Heritage Museum, 4721 Aircraft Dr. Anchorage, AK 99502; to inquire, telephone 800-770-5325 or 907-248-5325; telefax 907-248-6391.

In 1989 the Anchorage Museum of History and Art featured an exhibition of nearly 100 paintings from the Aleutian war from the pens and brushes of artists like Canadian Captain Edward J. Hughes and American Private Don Miller. Many of the evocative works were reproduced in the museum's catalog, *Drawing the Lines of Battle.*

There is a small year-round museum of natural and WW II artifacts on the U.S. Navy's base at Adak (zipcode 99695). Tour companies in the 1980s and 1990s have been taking summer travelers to the islands (mostly to Unalaska/Dutch Harbor), where the intrepid tourist can indulge in photography, kayaking, whale-watching, natural history and archaeology junketing, trophy fishing, birdwatching, flightseeing, and World War II site-visiting.

In both Japan and the United States, numerous veterans' groups have been organized; in some cases they have held joint meetings with their counterparts ("yesterday's enemies"). There have been reunions and memorial meetings—in Seattle (August 1986), Nagoya (January 1986), Anchorage (August 1990), El Paso, Texas (September 1991), Dutch Harbor (June 1992), Fort Richardson (September 1992), NAS Whidbey Island, Washington (September 1992), Colorado Springs, Colo. (October 1990 and October 1992), Attu (June 1993), Kiska (August 1993), and others.

The Eleventh Air Force Association is active and vigorous, its far-flung membership held together by the publication in Ketchikan of Ralph Bartholomew's newsletter. Among active groups are those that include veterans of the navy's Patrol Wing 4—its still-vigorous champion the legendary Admiral Jim Russell—; the 42nd and 54th Troop Carrier Squadrons; the 21st, 36th, 73rd, 77th, 404th and 406th Bomber Squadrons; the 11th, 18th, 54th and 344th Fighter Squadrons; the 54th Fighter Group (42nd, 56th and 57th Squadrons); and the 10th Rescue Boat Squadron.

Veterans of these and other units have shared valuable information, ranging from tidbits to volumes.

Veteran Merle L. Emmons, for example, served in the Aleutians as first mate on tugs, freighters and miscellaneous vessels; for such duties he held an odd rank—he was an army technical sergeant. In 1995 he wrote to me from Manchester, Maine, with a request that this new edition mention "the Army 'fleet', which…was one of General Buckner's doings…. The Army unit, Harbor Craft Detachment (TC) Alaskan Dept At Large, was established with headquarters in Anchorage and covered an area from Seattle north to Alaska and the Aleutians." To some extent this unit is covered (although not by name) in the original book, in mentions of Buckner's unorthodox enterprises and of the transport *St. Mihiel* and her sister craft, but one must sympathize with so many veterans like Emmons whose units (and experiences) seem to have been given short shrift.

Some veterans have gone to extraordinary lengths to compile detailed histories of units or vessels in which they served. Leon T. Davis, for example, has spent fifteen years assembling a working biography of gunboat USS *Charleston,* which some references in the 1969 *The Thousand-Mile War* erroneously described as a cruiser. The venerable *Charleston* served as Captain Ralph C. Parker's flagship from 1940–1942, then as Rear Admiral John W. Reeves' flagship from 1942–1945. Davis writes, "We did anything the COMALSEC could think of—we were his plaything." At one time or another in the Aleutians the sturdy *Charleston* saw impromptu service as seaplane tender, attack raider, ammunition barge, ordnance transport, sub chaser, convoy escort, floating antiaircraft battery, artillery and naval gun fire-control spotter, and advance-scout patrol ship. A sample Davis entry: "May 30, 1942: Gunboat *Charleston* underway for station on surface patrol line via Akutan Pass (not 400 miles south of Kodiak) to 80–85 miles southwest of Otter Point. Wind reached gale force with heavy long swells, heavy fog, couldn't see stars or land (no radar) so didn't know if we were out 60 or 100 miles; we were just looking for the [enemy] fleet…"

According to Davis, *Charleston* has the dubious honor of having fired both the first and the last shots of the war in Alaska: the first "on December 15, 1941, across the bow of a USSR freighter that was trying to run away" and the last on October 13, 1943, when Japanese high-altitude planes bombed the by then Allied port at Attu; *Charleston* was "moored starboard side to Navy Dock #1 Massacre Bay. We expended 755 rounds (no hits by Marine AA guns); bombs just fell into bay with no hits. Last air action in Alaska."

Davis added, "I have logs and action reports from 1727 (Bering) to 1945 end of war. Man have I got it!" And, happily, he has shared it.

A directory of people who served in the military is maintained by the National Personnel Records Center, NPRC/NCPMF-C, 9700 Page Boulevard, St. Louis, Missouri 63132-5000. Where possible, the inquirer should provide the subject's full name, retired or separated grade or rank, military serial number and/or Social Security number, and any specific informational request. The center doesn't have current records on everybody, of course, but usually it's the most promising place to start. The National Archives and Records Administration maintains its Alaska Region office at 654 West 3rd Ave., Anchorage, AK 99501; telephone 907-271-2441.

In May 1993, after lengthy and heroic efforts by Ralph Bartholomew and other veterans, the official name of Shemya Air Force Base was changed to Eareckson Air Force Station.

The 11th Air Force was reformed in 1990, with its headquarters (as always) at Elmendorf Air Force Base; this proud organization has a treasure of a historical unit, headed by the prominent scholar John Haile Cloe, author of the two-volume study *The Aleutian Warriors* (see bibliography). Historian Cloe can be reached by mail at the Office of History, 11th Air Force, 6900 Ninth St. #204, Elmendorf AFB, Alaska 99506-2255.

For years after 1945 there was a general lack of interest in Alaska's war. Many Americans (if they didn't have a relative or a friend in the theater) are utterly unaware that a war was fought in Alaska in 1942–1943, and even among those who served there, few were aware of the larger picture.

Was it the presumed strategic insignificance of the Alaska-Aleutian theater that made it a topic of commensurate insignificance to most writers and publishers?

I think there is more to it than that. When I was digging in the National Archives and the Pentagon's records, I saw that it was mainly after the fact that the importance of the North Pacific theater was downgraded. During the war itself there were times when the theater actually was regarded by high-ranking planners on both sides as having more strategic significance than is justified in hindsight by the realities of the day.

At times during the war no one could be certain whether the Alaska theater was vitally important. When one mixed in such factors as Lend-Lease and the American effort to seduce the Russians into declaring war on Japan, the unimportance of the theater became quite a lot less absolute. At the strategic level, uncertainty and embarrassment and paranoia all may have contributed strongly to the Alaska war's being kept under wraps.

Also, by coincidence, most of the dramatic moments of the Alaska war happened to be eclipsed in public perception by momentous events elsewhere—Midway, North Africa, Crete, Sicily, Guadalcanal, so forth.

Still, if the home fronts in America and Japan remained largely unaware of what was going on in the North Pacific, it was because both governments imposed intense blackouts on news from the Alaska theater. During most of the campaign, neither side allowed journalists anywhere near the battlefronts. Those few who did write from vantage points near ground zero (Corey Ford, Dashiell Hammett, et al.) found their dispatches gutted by censorship so heavy-handed and pervasive that I still had to battle it strenuously many years later when I was trying to learn about the campaign. It is instructive to observe that the Aleutians campaign received more coverage in *National Geographic Magazine* (whose mostly free-lance photographers and reporters were disregarded by the government as insignificant naturalists) than it did in any newspaper.

My own process of research included ridiculous obstacles. Most of the official records I examined in the 1960s had to be declassified—one at a time—before they could be used as sources for this book; they were of no discernible sensitivity at that late date, but getting them declassified was a comic-opera battle that I probably would have lost if it had not been for the heroic assistance of Alaska Senator (and former territorial governor) Ernest Gruening.

Fortunately, some things have changed. Most records have been declassified, and in the years since *The Thousand-Mile War* was first published, a gratifying inventory of new material has come to light. I have received some of it—reams of published and unpublished documents from veterans and history buffs; with their permission, it has been forwarded to the Knight Library of the University of Oregon in Eugene.

There isn't room to thank everybody who has tendered material either to me or to Oregon or to the various archives in Alaska. I'm grateful to each contributor, and am especially grateful for information and wisdom provided by John Andrews, Frank A. Baker, Ralph Bartholomew, Steve Birdsall, William S. Boone, Paul Carrigan, Harold D. "Doug" Courtney, Leon T. Davis, Merle L. Emmons, Frank Fuller, Bill Grant, Otis Hays, Edgar Kaufman, Karl Kaoru Kasukabe, Allen "Red" Miller, Russell J. Petitt, Frederick Ramputi, Benjamin Talley, Gore Vidal, and again those two dedicated keepers of the flame, Lawrence Reinecke and Tom Spitler.

I'm indebted beyond price to John Cloe for his expert assistance, which has extended far beyond any reasonable call of duty; with wonderful generosity he has shared the harvest of his many years' labors as the air war's historian-in-chief at Anchorage. John's keen-eyed diligence and splendidly prolific notes have enabled us to identify and correct a good many errors that appeared in the earlier edition. And he has graciously contributed his entire up-to-date list of published and unpublished sources, so that we have been able to make this editions' new bibliography as comprehensive as possible.

Deep thanks too for their sine-qua-non assistance to the fine faculty and faculties of the University of Alaska Press—including Terrence Cole, Pamela Odom, and steadfast Debbie Van Stone.

I also am very deeply indebted to Admiral James S. Russell, to veteran Alaska pilot John Seamands, and to my good friend Lucian Wernick, who reminded me that not only was his surname misspelled in the caption of a photograph in the 1969 edition, but also the book's index erroneously listed him as a recipient of the Purple Heart. The Air Medal, yes; the Purple Heart, no—Lucian went to war armed with the conviction that neither he nor his crew members would ever be injured in an airplane, and happily he never had to revise that conviction. A few years ago, however, while riding a motorcycle through the mountains of Greece, he went over the edge and tumbled a mighty distance before he and the bike came (separately) to rest. The Wernick luck still holds; he walked away from that one, too.

APPENDIX
ONE

Further Discussion of the Paramushiro Raids

THIS ACCOUNT OF THE EARLY raids on Paramushiro was based on informal conversations with several veterans. As Reineke, John Cloe, and others have advised me, it is inaccurate in several respects. The missions were coordinated and planned, not nearly so independent or off-the-cuff as my 1969 account asserts. Larry Reineke is particularly upset with me: "I will appreciate a more truthful account of my briefing the first Paramushiro raids and [please] list me as a 2nd Lt which was my rank at the time." Larry is eager that I emphasize his unimportance ("I had nothing to do with planning [or] organizing...the mission") but I must demur; Reineke was no "brown nose" but his protestations are far too modest. In spite of his denials I still feel the early Paramushiro missions could not have been initiated and executed as they were without his invaluable input. In fairness let me quote excerpts combined here from Larry's own version, in a letter to me dated July 11, 1994, and in a previous letter (Sept. 28, 1990) he had written to the Adak Museum:

> Actually the 'Brass' on Adak were sleeping. They had no more notion of bombing Paramushiro than of going home early.
>
> The orders as I recall came from Washington and there was the usual hurry up.
>
> This is the sequence: I arrived at Adak on May 7th 1943. I was assigned to the 21st Bombardment Squadron as the assistant Combat Intelligence Officer under a Capt. Herald, a reserve officer who used to run a laundry in Texas. He gave me no duties other than to stay in the Intelligence hut, and he didn't allow me to do any briefing or interrogations (as it was called in those days—now [known as] de-briefing). I had nothing to do. I read and

re-read all the intelligence material in the hut. I was desperate for a project to keep my sanity.

On May 11, 1943, American troops landed on Attu. Via the short wave radio in the hut I was able to follow the air commanders' broadcasts and I sketched in the progress on the Attu map (now at the Library of University of Oregon). This same map gave an indication of the Kurile Islands and I became intrigued by the distance from Attu to Paramushiro.

Irwin Smith, navigator on Capt. Wadlington's crew, worked out the mileage, winds and gas consumption, and told me that the B24s and the B25s could make the mission from Attu and return with enough gas to fly all the way to Adak if necessary.

So I had my project. Study the Kuriles.

However I soon drew blanks. Bomber Command had no information at all. Neither did Air Force command.

Next I went to Navy Intelligence…I struck up a conversation with an Ensign who…found some Navy charts and books, dated in the 1880s but they had the outlines of the two islands, and more important to the Air Force the elevations on the islands. He made a chart for me. I made several trips to the Navy, reading the books and studying the charts. One day the Ensign said, 'We're translating the diaries we got on Attu. Like to read them?'

As the Japanese wrote detailed diaries, and a lot were from soldiers who had been stationed [previously] on Paramushiro, the information enabled me to produce a pretty good situation map on the chart, and also get an overall view of the haste with which the Japanese were fortifying the islands.

There was nothing secret about my project. The chart hung on the bulletin boards in the S-2 hut—it was in full view for anyone to study… but no one did except me. Certainly not Capt. Herald—he was gone all day playing cards and only appeared at the hut when a mission was briefed.

Then one day Washington sent the order: Bomb Paramushiro.

The job of briefing the mission was given to a Major [Herman or Herbert] in the 404 Bomb Squadron. Normally a first time mission like this would have been done at least at Bomber Command, if not [11th] Air Force. But as I later realized they had no intelligence, so passed the buck to a squadron S-2. … A mission of that importance…should have been briefed by the Air Force Headquarters S-2, a Colonel. I think Major [Herbert] was the 'fall guy'.

> I came on indirectly when Major Herbert—[who was] to do the briefing for S-2—said [to me], 'What the hell is the use of me learning all this when you know it all already? So you be ready with your chart and when I speak I'll introduce you and then you take over the briefing.'
>
> Which is what happened. He introduced me and I gave the briefing. [It] was held sometime between 4 and 5 [a.m.]...I hung up my chart and started talking.... The hut was dark; the lights were on the briefing boards; and it was not until the [lights came up that I saw] the briefing was being attended by General Butler of 11th AF, General Buckner of Alaska Command and Admiral Kinkaid, Navy, along with lesser brass.
>
> I felt I had repaid the Air Force something on the debt of training me.
>
> ...[But it] seems the top brass chided the Intel sections about a lowly baldheaded old S-2 2nd lieutenant coming up with information—the next obvious head to roll was Reineke's. Two or three days after that, Capt Herald cornered me in the 21st S-2 hut. He wanted to know where I got my information. I told him [it had come] from the Navy. I was then chewed out because I had skipped channels. I was confined to the hut from 8 to 5. My chart was taken away. ... About 2 weeks later I was exiled to Shemya to pull tundra and prepare foundations for Jamesway huts.
>
> So researcher, look at versions you see of this briefing and see how the truth gets mangled. Or as someone said, History is a collection of lies mutually agreed upon.

I'm afraid Col. Reineke is hoist by his own confession. Like it or not, the credit seems in large part to be his own.

Still, as usual there is disagreement amongst veterans about nearly everything, including the date and nature of the first Paramushiro raid. Lieutenant Colonel William Molett (USAF RET) of the 36th Bombardment Squadron says the first Paramushiro raid was launched not in July but on May 25, 1943, from the new 2500-foot fighter airstrip that was still under construction on Attu, with six B-24s making the journey successfully but mistakenly dropping their bombs on a rice field half a mile short of the intended military and naval targets. "General Buckner was not very happy with our bombing," Molett recalled in a 1994 letter to editor Ralph Bartholemew of the 11th Air Force Association Newsletter. "No one on the mission got so much as a good conduct medal for the trip. I am somewhat bitter as our trip seems to have missed the history books. I keep reading…that the first raid on Paramushiro was made in July 1943 when we did it on May 25, 1943. My Form 5 shows an 11-hour combat mission on that date."

Wheeler's diary of the 36th Squadron's activity for that date shows only two missions, both of them flown from Adak to Attu for the purpose of providing air reconnaissance and bombardment in support of the troops who were still fighting on the ground there. The infantry battle was still raging; it didn't end until four days later. It seems unlikely that six four-engine bombers would have been sent to Attu on that day for any purpose other than support of embattled ground troops.

Veteran pilot William Boone, who has been preparing an account of the Paramushiro missions, wrote to me (letter dated March 18, 1995) with regard to the chronology of the first Air Force attacks on the Kuriles, "I was on the two aborted Paramushiro missions of 10 and 11 July 43 and on the successful one on 18 July."

Is it possible that the solution to the mystery could be the inadvertent entry of an incorrect date on Col. Molett's "Form 5" document?

As with certain other incidents, I can't come up with a definitive tie-breaker at the time of this writing (summer 1995); I can only report the discrepancy in accounts.

(Incidental note: Boone offers this correction—"By the way, Wheeler was a pilot, not a navigator.") …Regarding Paramushiro, several veterans felt the previous printings of *The Thousand-Mile War* appeared to give short shrift to the two years (1943–1945) of long-range warfare that the U.S. Navy and Air Force waged against northern Japan. The apparent neglect toward their expeditions wasn't intentional. This book was designed primarily as a history of the Aleutians Campaign, which (technically) ended with the occupation of Kiska in 1943; but the book's title does not suggest that limitation, and veterans are correct in lambasting me for having left them out in the Aleutian cold.

Perhaps the gruelling nature of those two last years of the war is best indicated by a short note I received from Frank A. Baker, dated March 26, 1994:

> I was a radio operator-gunner on a B-25 bomber with the 77th Bomb Sqdn. on the island of Attu in 1944–45. As you know, these missions at that time were the longest over-water missions of World War II… We arrived on Attu in 1944 with three other replacement crews and made our first bomb run on Friday Oct. 13th. Thirty-three days later we were the only crew left out of four.

From the autumn of 1943 on, American airmen faced not only the perils of Aleutian weather and Japanese defenses but also the horrors of Siberian internment. Otis Hays, Jr., in his 1990 book *Home From Siberia,* describes vividly the ordeals of aircrews who were forced to make emergency landings on the Soviet mainland. Although the whereabouts of most of them were known by the U.S. Government, they were listed officially as MIAs ("missing in action"). Eventually some were repatriated; others escaped. Upon their return to the United States they became hapless (and frequently furious) victims of a pre-Cold War policy designed to avoid jeopardizing the fragile American-Soviet alliance: they were instructed by their own government to endure the indignity of signing oaths of silence in which they pledged "that at no time will you give any information whatsoever to anyone—family, friends or military personnel of whatever rank—concerning repatriation from or presence in the country of repatriation. Details concerning your presence in that country, journey to that country and subsequent repatriation therefrom are matters of vital military security." (Quoted from Eleventh Air Force Association Newsletter #17, Nov. 22, 1994.) It is only recently, through publications by Hays and such other writers as John Cloe, William Boone and Stan Cohen (see Bibliography) that the gaps in our knowledge of that period are being filled in.

APPENDIX
TWO

Further Discussion of the Battle of the Pips

REGARDING THE "BATTLE OF THE PIPS"—this addition of new material:

It has been confirmed that the Japanese radar operator on top of Mount Kiska saw, and was bewildered by, the abrupt retirement of the Allied fleet.

Bewildered, but not paralyzed: Kiska signaled the all-clear to the Japanese task force which then came in, unopposed, evacuated all personnel from Kiska and took them home to Japan without a single casualty.

To this day, the U.S. Navy's 1944 published conclusion (peculiar atmospheric conditions—a temporary bending of radar beams) is still the official version.

But on Oct. 4, 1991, George Fulton wrote me a letter that appears to solve, at long last, the mystery of the Pips.

George Fulton is a long-time captain in the Pacific fishing fleet, and author of the book *Good Morning, Captain.* He has been a commercial fisherman for forty years, spent a significant part of his career fishing for crab in the Western Aleutians, and is still alive and navigating, which means among other things that he's a very good skipper.

He is also an expert on shipboard navigation devices, ranging from the sophisticated new GPS design all the way back to the early radar that was used by the United States Navy in 1943.

George Fulton wrote to me as follows:

> The Battle of the Pips.... When I first read your book I checked with three other captains who had read it, and they all had arrived at the same conclusion.
>
> During July [1991], I crossed North Head, on Akutan Island, and with your book in hand, duplicated the Battle of the Pips using color radar.

> There were hundreds of blips on the tube, and the density of the flights changed—as they searched and found the plankton they sought—from red to orange to yellow and finally to [black, providing an exact duplicate of the blips that appeared during the Battle of the Pips].
>
> ...That they would be gone at daylight is no surprise at all since they tend to spread out all over the ocean in their dawn search... They could have been forty to sixty miles away and regrouping by the time the navy could have seen them visually...
>
> ...What you describe...fit[s] exactly the night flight pattern of dense flocks of 'mutton birds,' or Dusky Shearwaters which is their correct name. The Shearwaters migrate annually between New Zealand and Alaska, arriving in the Aleutians in late May, [spending the summer,] and departing in September-October...

ALSO KNOWN AS FULMARS, these petrels are one to two feet long, with wingspans up to four feet. The subarctic seabirds are members of the albatross family; they travel in enormous flocks, they lay one egg a year, they feed on plankton, and when they fly low they appear to "shear the water" with their wings.

Captain Fulton's letter continues:

> Practically every [summer] morning, in the vicinity of Unimak Pass, the birds sleep in massive rafts—sometimes in long streaks and sometimes in individual patches, relative to the density of the plankton layers they were feeding on at dusk... The Dusky [Shearwater] is very hard to see visually at night, and [even a huge flock] would be impossible to see from the distances of 8-to-12 miles the fleet was scanning [in 1943]... With our new radars we 'see' them all the time, and avoid them, since, when startled, or on a moonless night, they will fly directly into our bright lights and land on deck by the thousands.
>
> [Because of its design] a World War II radar would only see these rafts [of birds as massed blobs] if they were airborne [in sizable flocks] and navigating to a new feeding ground at night. The first bearing [in your book] gives a course [that would be consistent with] the logical course [these birds would use] to search for plankton density...
>
> [It] is exactly how modern factory trawlers find massive pollack schools...[We use] the mutton birds...as a clue during the summer months when pollack feed on the same plankton.

> In your next reference the [Pips] change course 'to 340 True zigzagging about 20 degrees.' As mutton birds fly they veer left and right, and once they've decided they've found an interesting feeding area, the hundreds of thousands you are looking at…thin out into [groups of] thousands—settle to the water, start diving, and totally disappear off your radar scope.

And so, 48 years after the fact, Captain George Fulton provided the one explanation that appears to account plausibly for every detail of this little historical mystery.

Bibliographical Remarks

CERTAIN INDIVIDUALS AND ORGANIZATIONS HAVE received disproportionate emphasis in this book—for example, the 36th Bombardment Squadron, which was only one of many Air Squadrons in the Aleutian campaign. I did this, not to detract from the record of any other person or unit, but to provide representative detail without being repetitious or making the book longer than necessary. I hope veterans whose units are not emphasized will understand that I have not meant to minimize their importance. In some cases the choice was arbitrary; in others it was dictated by the availability of thorough records. The 36th Squadron, for example, is represented by the unique Wheeler diary, and I chose it for that reason.

The Alaskan commands had little time for paperwork, and the theater itself was empty in a sense: there were no audiences in the orchestra seats, few innocent or impartial civilians to observe (or, it is worth remarking, to become casualties). There were a few bits and pieces of published material:

During the war, newsmen wrote half a dozen books on the Aleutian campaign. Dashiell Hammett, an Army corporal in the Aleutians, co-authored a brief pamphlet-sized account. Gore Vidal's first book, *Williwaw,* may have been the only war novel to come out of the campaign. All these accounts were distorted by wartime bias, cut to the bone by censorship, ignorant of the Japanese side of the story, and restricted to the worm's-eye view of on-the-scene reporting. The multivolume published histories of each of the U.S. armed services devote a few chapters to the Aleutian campaign, in little more than outline form.

But fundamentally this book has no prior published history to draw on. Therefore it relies heavily on unpublished sources.

Because the campaign was all but forgotten by 1945, and because Russo-American relations have been too sensitive since then to allow security regulations to lapse, the bulk of official material remained classified until recently. Even after twenty-five years, a large number of records had to be declassified expressly for this book.

This account relies mainly on American and Japanese records in the government and private archives that are listed in the foregoing Acknowledgments section. These have been reinforced by interviews and correspondence with many veterans, some of them listed in the bibliography. I have compared Japanese and American records, official and unofficial sources, written records and personal recollections. The correspondence fills many more pages than the manuscript of this book. The accompanying photos have been selected from hundreds, collected from government and private files. The result includes quite a bit of material that has not been previously published, and some that cannot be found in any official records (let alone such surveys as the half-page summary in Winston Churchill's six-volume *The Second World War*).

IN THE BIBLIOGRAPHY IS A PARTIAL LIST of veterans I interviewed either in person with tape recorder, or by correspondence. The list by no means exhausts all the people I consulted; it is restricted to those whose information has been used significantly in the book; remarks following each name summarize the person's position or function during the Aleutian campaign, and topics to which he contributed information.

My deepest gratitude to each of them.

I have not included dates of correspondence or interviews, since the date would be useless to any researcher who did not have the transcriptions of the interviews and letters in front of him. All the interviews and correspondence were gathered in 1967–1968. I will place the entire file (including the letters, tape recordings, and other research materials I collected—like copies of the Wheeler diary) in my collection at the Library of the University of Oregon at Eugene, for use by anyone who would like to study the subject further.

The following bibliography contains only those sources which I used in writing the book. Usually each source's title seems to indicate its contents clearly enough, but where it seems useful, I have added parenthetical remarks to explain what the item covers.

I have not documented this book; I discarded the idea of including source notes for each chapter and subsection, because a book like this is put together much as you would decorate a Christmas tree: you take the basic outline (which can be found in the general histories and surveys) and hang on it a multitude of ornaments and strips of foil in the form of tiny facts gathered in many places. Therefore to document each paragraph thoroughly would be to list a vast number of sources, none of which contributed more than one or two small facts.

I hope the bibliography itself will be specific enough for the interested researcher. There is, of course, a degree of half-hidden documentation in the text, as in the quotes from unit histories and diaries, and in the use of the word "recalls." Wherever that word appears, it indicates that I am quoting from my own interviews with, or letters from, the person being quoted.

Unless otherwise noted, official records and documents listed in the bibliography are to be found at the major archives of U.S. Government and Defense Department agencies, most of them in and near Washington, D.C.

Bibliography

Veterans Interviewed

Alexander, Colonel William, USA Retired. Member of Lieutenant General Simon B. Buckner's staff; participant at San Diego planning conferences for Attu invasion; liaison officer between Buckner and the Navy; observer at Battle of Attu and Battle of the Pips; friend of Colonel William O. Eareckson.

Arnold, Major General Archibald V., USA Retired. Commander of Artillery, and Assistant Landing Force Commander, Battle of Attu; friend of Major General Albert E. Brown.

Brown, Major General Albert E., USA Retired. Commanding General, Landing Force, Battle of Attu, until relieved of his command. Participant in all planning stages, and early operational phases of the Battle of Attu.

Cale, Francis. Enlisted SeaBee; construction worker and foreman on building projects at Dutch Harbor, Umnak, Adak.

Caughey, Frank S. Navy officer, PBY pilot in Patrol Wing Four.

Colodny, Robert G. Enlisted Army soldier in Alaska Defense Command; co-author, with Dashiell Hammett, of *The Battle of the Aleutians.*

Cone, Russell. Air Force officer; bomber pilot and squadron commander at and after the Battle of Dutch Harbor; aide to Lieutenant General Simon B. Buckner, Jr., in 1943.

Corlett, Major General Charles H., USA Retired. Commanding General, Landing Force, Invasion of Kiska; Commanding General, 7th Infantry Division.

Culin, Major General Frank L., Jr., USA Retired. Regimental commander; Commander of Northern Force, Battle of Attu.

Davis, Nathan. M.D. Army officer; medical doctor, Alaska Defense Command.

Dawson, Captain William "Bull," USN. Navy officer; staff officer, PBY Patrol Wing Four, 1943.

DeFord, Brigadier General Earl H., USAF Retired. Commander of Eleventh Bomber Command, January–September 1943 (succeeded Colonel William O. Eareckson); bomber pilot.

Donley, Robert L. Navy officer; PBY pilot in Patrol Wing Four.

Eareckson, Mrs. Frances. Widow of Colonel William O. Eareckson.

Freerks, Marshall C. Navy officer; PBY pilot and patrol squadron commander, 1942 and 1943–1944.

Griffin, Vice Admiral Robert M., USN Retired. Naval task group commander, bombardment of Kiska and Battle of the Pips.

Gruening, Senator Ernest. Territorial Governor of Alaska; friend of Lieutenant General Simon B. Buckner, Jr.

Hartl, Major General Albert V., USA Retired. Regimental and battalion commander, Northern Force, Battle of Attu.

Haugen, Jack O. Enlisted Navy man; PBY plane captain in Patrol WingFour.

Ikatura, Mitsuba. Japanese Navy officer; captain of I-class submarine.

Inaba, Michimune. Japanese Navy officer; captain of I-class submarine.

Kelly, Joe. Army sergeant; member of Alaska Scouts ("Castner's Cutthroats").

Kinkaid, Admiral Thomas C., USN Retired. Commander, North Pacific Force, January–September 1943; conceived and executed (was in over-all command of) blockade of Kiska and Attu and the invasions of those islands by the Allies.

Marston, Lieutenant Colonel Marvin R. "Muktuk," USAR Retired. Arctic explorer; special service officer on staff of Lieutenant General Simon B. Buckner, Jr.; founder of Eskimo Scouts.

Meyer, Jack. Army sergeant; served at Attu and Kiska.

Morinaga, Masahiko. Japanese Navy officer; captain of I-class submarine; witness to Battle of the Pips.

Murphy, Brian. Army lieutenant (infantry), Kiska.

Murphy, Desmond (his brother). Army lieutenant (artillery), Attu.

Newman, Edward. Army sergeant, Adak.

Noland, George F. Army enlisted man; Signal Corps photographer, Battle of Attu.

Quintrell, Thomas A. Army officer; staff officer with Major General Archibald V. Arnold, Battle of Attu; witness to General Arnold's leadership during final Japanese assault on Engineer Hill.

Ramputi, Colonel Frederick R., USAF. Air Force officer; squadron leader and heavy bomber pilot throughout Aleutian Campaign.

Reeve, Robert C. Pioneer Alaskan bush pilot; helped train prewar Air Force pilots in Alaska; flew cargo to Buckner's air bases; flew passengers and cargo into the Aleutians during the Campaign.

Reeves, Rear Admiral John W., USN Retired. Commander, Alaska Naval Sector (replaced Captain Ralph C. Parker).

Reineke, Lieutenant Colonel Lawrence, USAFR. Intelligence officer, 21st Bombardment Squadron; conceived and planned first Paramushiro bombing missions.

Reitman, Norman, M.D. Air Force captain; medical officer at Ladd Field, Fairbanks.

Russell, Admiral James S., USN Retired. Commander of PBY Patrol Squadron 42 at Battle of Dutch Harbor; PBY pilot; compiler of Japanese interrogations and records of Aleutian Campaign in Tokyo in 1945.

Sillin, Major General Norman D., USAF Retired. Air Force officer, composite group commander; commanding officer, 11th Fighter Command; Eleventh Air Force staff officer.

Talley, Brigadier General Benjamin B., USA Retired. Commanding officer of U.S. Army Engineers for the Alaska Defense Command; built air fields and bases at Cold Bay, Umnak, Adak, Amchitka, Attu, Shemya, many others.

Webster, Lieutenant Commander William S., USN Retired. Navy officer and pilot; PBY pilot with Patrol Wing Four; builder of LORAN air navigational system in Aleutians in 1944.

Wernick, Lucian K. Air Force officer; B-17 and B-24 pilot, 36th Bombardment Squadron; tactical bomber commander at Battle of Attu and Invasion of Kiska; friend of Colonel William O. Eareckson.

Willoughby, Colonel William H., USA Retired. Infantry officer; Commander of Provisional Scout Battalion at Battle of Attu.

Zimmerman, Major General Wayne C., USA Retired. Infantry officer; Chief of Staff to Major General Albert E. Brown at Battle of Attu; Commander of Southern Landing Force, Battle of Attu.

Unpublished Documents and Offical Records

"Action on Attu." Report by G-2, Alaska Defense Command, July 30, 1943. Prepared by Lieutenant Colonel W. J. Verbeck.

"Action Report, CINCPAC: Operations in Pacific Ocean Areas, March 1943: Parts I & II." Report by Chief of Staff, CINCPAC, June 9, 1943. (On Battle of the Komandorskis.)

"Activities of Shore Fire Control #1, 11 April–15 May 1943." Report to Commander Attu Invasion Force, May 16, 1943. Prepared by Lieutenant Jakie L. Mann. (On naval gunnery control and Willoughby's Scott Battalion; typescript in files of Desmond Murphy.)

"Administrative History of the Ferrying Command, 29 May 1941–30 June 1942." Report by Ass't Chief of Air Staff, A-2, June 1945. *Army Air Force Historical Study* #33.

"Alaskan Air Defense and the Japanese Invasion of the Aleutians." Report by Ass't Chief of Air Staff, A-2, June 1945. Army Air Force Historical Study #4.

"Aleutian Campaign, The." Summary by Office of Naval Intelligence. Combat Narrative, 1945.

"Aleutian Campaign, The." Report by Captain James S. Russell, USN: pp.

78–103 in *The Campaigns of the Pacific War,* edited by Rear Admiral R. A. Ofstie and compiled by members of the U.S. Strategic Bombing Survey; Washington, 1946. (On the Japanese side of the Campaign as developed through interviews and interrogations with Japanese officers, and analysis of surviving Japanese documents, in Tokyo in 1945.)

"Aleutian Islands Campaign—Operation Record." Volume XVI of Reports by First (Japanese) Demobilization Unit; Tokyo, 1946.

"Aleutian Naval Operations (March 1942–February 1943)." Office of the Chief of Military History, Japanese Monograph No. 88. (Records of Japanese operations.)

"Aleutian War, The." Prepared by Leonard Barnes and AndrewThompson for the Chief of Military History, 1944.

"Aleutians, The: Secret Memorandum, 27 October 1943." Prepared by Intelligence Division, Western Defense Command.

"Aleutians Operations Record, May 1942–August 1943." Office of the Chief of Military History, Japanese Monograph No. 46. (Records of Japanese operations.)

Air Campaigns of the Pacific War. Prepared by Military Analysis Division,U.S. Strategic Bombing Survey. Washington, July 1947. (Scattered statistical references.)

"Attu Operation, The." Report to Headquarters, U.S. Army Forces, Pacific Ocean Area, prepared by Captain Nelson L. Drummond, Jr., G-2, Historical Subsection, May 24, 1945. Three volumes.

"Battle Experience (January–July 1943)." Reports to Headquarters, Commander in Chief U.S. Fleet—Secret Information Bulletins 6, 7, 8, 9 and 12. (On Komandorskis, Attu, Pips).

Biographical Information on officers and personnel, supplied by the Armed Services and by the Personnel Records Division of NARS in St. Louis.

"Bombardment—Two Years in Alaska: The Combat Diary of the 36th Bombardment Squadron (Heavy)." By Lieutenant Billy J. Wheeler, Historical Officer, 36th Bombardment Squadron. October 1943. (Wheeler's title; throughout this book it is referred to either as "Wheeler" or the diary of the 36th Squadron.)

"Building Alaska with the U.S. Army, 1867–1962." Report to Headquarters, U.S. Army Alaska, prepared by Alaska Command Information Office, August 10, 1962.

"Chronological Journal of Enemy Operations in Alaskan Area Beginning 24 May 1942." Report to Commander of Patrol Wing Four, prepared by officers of Squadrons 41 and 42. (n.d.) (On U.S. analysis of Japanese moves before Dutch Harbor.)

"Chronology of Eleventh Air Force Operations: 7 December 1941–7 December 1943." Report to Headquarters, Alaska Defense Command, prepared by "Research Section, AFOPN-2." (n.d.)

"Cold Injury, Ground Type." Report to the Surgeon General, prepared by Medical Department U.S. Army, 1958. (On the lessons learned at Attu.)

"Command History, North Pacific Force." Report to CINCUS, prepared by NORPACFOR staff officers from war diaries, 14 August 1945.

Correspondence in the files of Admiral James S. Russell, USN Retired:

From Commander Paul F. Foster to Chief, BuAer, July 26, 1942;
From Foster to Director, Plans Division, Navy Department, May 16, 942;
From Foster to Vice Chief of Naval Operations, July 16, 1942;
From Foster to Vice Admiral Wilson, July 11, 1942;
From Captain I. M. McQuiston (BuAer) to Chief, BuAer, July 21, 1942;
From First Lieutenant John B. Murphy, USAAF, to Air Office, Alaska Defense Command, June 5, 1942.

(Foster was FDR's personal observer on the scene. The exchange of correspondence throws light on the preparations for, and actions of, the Battle of Dutch Harbor, and the reorganizations in Communications etc. that followed.)

Diary of Captain Walter Feinstein, U.S. Army Medical Corps, Alaska Defense Command, 1942–1943. (Typescript from Dr. Feinstein's files.)

Diary of Lieutenant Lawrence Reineke, U.S. Air Force, July 14th to October 3rd 1943. (Holograph from Lieutenant Colonel Reineke's files.)

"Eleventh Air Force, The—Dutch Harbor." Pages 111–117 in *Army Air Forces in the War against Japan* 1941–1942: A.A.F. Historical Narratives, August 1945.

"Eleventh Air Force In The Aleutians, The." Pages 149–156 in Ibid.

"Eleventh Air Force Statistical Summary, June 1942–August 1945." Report to Alaska Defense Command, prepared by "27th SCU." (n.d.)

"Enemy on Kiska, The." Report to the Chief of Military History, prepared by Intelligence Division, Alaska Defense Command, November 24, 1943. (Thick, thorough report on the Japanese base.)

"Enemy Positions, North Pacific." ICPOA Bulletin No. 5-42, prepared by Intelligence Center, Pacific Ocean Area, December 20, 1942.

Extracts of Japanese diaries captured at Attu, May–June 1943, translated by Intelligence Division, Alaska Defense Command, 1943. (Typescripts from government archives and files of Lieutenant Colonel Lawrence Reineke, USAFR.)

"Field Order No. 1, Landing Force 16.8 1 August 1943." Final battle plans and Major General Albert E. Brown's orders, including "Plan E" which was finally chosen and used for the invasion of Attu. (Typescript from files of Major General Albert V. Hartl, USA Retired.)

"Final Report, Attu." Report to Chief of Military History, prepared by Alaska Defense Command. (n.d.—OCMH File No. 91-DC4-2.0.)

"Fleet Problem XVI." Report to Commander In Chief, U.S. Fleet, prepared by Commander Pacific Fleet, 1935. (On naval exercises in the Aleutians in 1935.)

"G-3 Report of Offensive Phases of Aleutian Campaign, 14 September 1943." Report to CG ADC by G-3 Office, Alaska Defense Command.

"Historical Record, 21st Bombardment Squadron (Heavy)." Summary prepared by Historical Officer, 21st Bombardment Squadron, February 22, 1943. (Typescript from files of Lieutenant Colonel Lawrence Reineke, USAFR.)

"History, Alaskan Air Command." Prepared by Historical Division, Office of Information, Alaskan Air Command, October 1, 1963.

"History, Eleventh Air Force." Prepared by Lieutenant Jerry N. Ranschoff, staff of Eleventh Air Force, August 12, 1945.

"History, Fleet Air Wing Four, 11 Aug. 1941–15 Dec. 1944." Prepared by staff of Fleet Air Wing Four, 1945.

"History of 11th Fighter Squadron, 1941–1943." Unit history prepared by First Lieutenant William S. M. Johnson, 1944. (Typescript in files of Alaskan Air Command, Elmendorf AFB.)

"History of Elmendorf Field, Fort Richardson, Alaska, 8 June 1940 to 31 May 1944." Prepared by Captain Henry E. Fleischer, 1945. (In files of Elmendorf AFB.)

"History of Service in Alaska, 406th Bombardment Squadron (Medium)." Prepared by Historical Officer, 406th Bombardment Squadron. (n.d.—typescript from files of Lieutenant Colonel Lawrence Reineke, USAFR.)

"History of the Medical Department in Alaska in World War II." Report to the Surgeon General by Gordon H. McNeil. (n.d.)

"History, 28th Composite Group." Prepared by Historical Officer, 28th Composite Group. USAAF, April 23, 1943. (Typescript in files of Lieutenant Colonel Lawrence Reineke, USAFR.)

"History, 73rd Bombardment Squadron." Prepared by Historical Officer, 73rd Bombardment Squadron. (n.d.)

"History, 77th Bombardment Squadron (Medium)." Prepared by Historical Officer, 77th Bombardment Squadron, 1943. (Typescript from files of Lieutenant Colonel Reineke.)

"History, 404th Bombardment Squadron (Heavy)." Prepared by Historical Officer, 11th Fighter Squadron, 1944. (Typescript from files of Lieutenant Colonel Reineke.)

Interrogations of Japanese Officials. Prepared by the staff of the U.S. Strategic Bombing Survey (Pacific), Naval Analysis Division; 2 volumes, 1946.

"Invasion Upon Aleutians" by Mikizo Fukazawa (Japanese Army War Correspondent), July 1942. Translated by Intelligence Division, Alaska Defense Command, from printed copies captured at Attu in June 1943. (Typescript, files of Elmendorf AFB.)

"Japanese Naval Charts of Aleutian Operations, June 1942–August 1943." Charts in files of Admiral J. S. Russell.

Logs of United States Navy ships *Casco, Gillis, Idaho, Mississippi, New Mexico,*

Portland, Richmond, Salt Lake City, San Francisco, Wichita; others to lesser extent.

"Memorandum." To Army Air Forces historians (Wesley Craven and James Cate, author-editors of The Army Air Force in World War II) regarding errors in the published history of the Aleutian Campaign, written by Captain J. S. Russell, USN. (n.d., probably 1948.) (Typescript carbon copy in files of Admiral J. S. Russell.)

"Memorandum for the Record." Evidence presented to the Chief of Staff, U.S. Army, in his own defense by Major General Albert E. Brown, May 4, 1948.

Navy Department, United States: News releases and dispatches, 1941–1945, regarding the North Pacific and Alaska Sector.

"Navy Directives No. 1 to No. 315 (5 Nov. 1941–23 Dec. 1943)." Issued by Japanese Imperial General Headquarters; translated by Headquarters, U.S. Army Forces Far East, 1945.

"Night Action of 26 July 1943: Action Report of U.S.S. *Mississippi* (BB 41)." (With ship's log; on Battle of the Pips.)

"Night Firing on Radar Contact, 26 July 1943: Action Report, U.S.S. *New Mexico* (BB 40)." July 27, 1943. (With ship's log.)

"No Mean Victory: The Saga of the Army Air Forces in Alaska and the Aleutians." Prepared by Colonel William S. Carlson and Major George D. Brodsky, May 30, 1945. (Typescript, 5 volumes, evidently prepared on the authors' own volition in hopes of getting it published; in files of NARS in Alexandria.)

"Northern Area Naval Operations (February 1943–August 1945)." Office of the Chief of Military History, Japanese Monograph No. 89. (Records of Japanese operations.)

"Officers and EM killed in Action, 21st Bombardment Squadron (Heavy)." Report to HQ, 11th Bomber Command, prepared by staff of 21st Bombardment Squadron, May 18, 1943. (Typescript from files of Colonel Lawrence Reineke.)

"Official History of the Alaskan Department June 1940–June 1944." Prepared by Historical Section, Alaskan Department, Alaska Defense Command. Two volumes, 1945.

"Operations against Attu—May 1943." Report to CINCPAC prepared by Rear Admiral Francis W. Rockwell. (n.d.)

"Operations in Aleutian Islands." Volume XV of Reports by First (Japanese) Demobilization Unit, Tokyo, 1946.

"Operations Reports of 73rd Bombardment Squadron (Medium)." Reports to 11th Bomber Command and Eleventh Air Force by staff of 73rd Squadron. (n.d.)

Order of Battle of the United States Army Ground Forces In World War II: Pacific Theater of Operations. Prepared by the Office of the Chief of Militar History, 1959.

"PatWing Four in the Battle of the Aleutians." Unit history prepared by "Gustafsen," 1944. (From files of Admiral James S. Russell.)

Pieces of Eight: A Memoir of the Eighth U.S. Naval Construction Battalion. Prepared by members of the 8th Construction Battalion, 1945. (SeaBees.)

"Preliminary Report on Attu Landing." Report to Western Defense Command, prepared by Lieutenant Colonel Lynn Davis Smith, Assistant Chief of Staff for Operations, Fourth Army, 1943.

"Report of Action on Attu." Report to Commanding General, Attu Landing Force, prepared by Lieutenant Colonel Albert V. Hartl, CO 17th Infantry Regiment, June 1943. (Typescript from files of Major General Hartl.)

"Report of Commanding General, Attu Landing Force." Report to CINCPAC and Western Defense Command and COMNORPACFOR, prepared by Major General Eugene M. Landrum, June 25, 1943.

"Report of Firing on 26 July 1943: Action Report, U.S.S. Portland." (With ship's log; on Battle of the Pips.)

"Report of Operations—Attu." Report to Commanding General, Alaska Defense Command (Buckner), prepared by Major General Eugene M. Landrum, June 1943.

"Report on Aleutian Campaign." Joint Army-Navy report prepared for the Chief of Military History by Advanced Intelligence Center, North Pacific, December 15, 1944. (AIC NORPAC No. 880.)

"Secret Sailing Directions for U.S. Bases, North Pacific." JICPOA Bulletin No. 31-43, October 14, 1944.

"Shemya History: The Black Pearl." Prepared by 5073rd Air Base Squadron, Alaskan Air Command. (n.d.—probably 1960s. In files of Shemya Air Force Base.)

"Short History, Battle of Attu." Prepared by Colonel B. W. Boyes, November 1944. (Files of Elmendorf AFB.)

"Strength in the North: The Alaskan Command." Prepared by Truman R Strobridge, 1966. (Files of Elmendorf AFB.)

"Submarine Operations in Operations Phase III (March to November 1943)." Office of the Chief of Military History, Japanese Monograph No. 163. (Records of Japanese operations.)

"Tactical History of 21st Bombardment Squadron." Prepared for the *mimeographed Shemya Squeal* (No. 6—1943). (From files of Colonel Reineke.)

"Translations of Extracts from Japanese Documents—15 December 1945." By Captain James S. Russell, USN, Naval Analysis Division, U.S. Strategic Bombing Survey (Pacific,) 1945–46. (Typescripts in files of Admiral James S. Russell.)

"War Diary, Commander North Pacific Force, Pacific Fleet, 22 May 1942–31 December 1943." Prepared by Admirals Theobald and Kinkaid; 9 volumes.

"War Diary, Fleet Air Wing Four." Prepared by Office of Naval Records, Chief of Naval Operations. July 31, 1946.

"War Diary, U.S. Naval Operating Base, Dutch Harbor, Alaska—December 1942–December 1943." Prepared by Base Commander, Dutch Harbor U.S. Naval Base, 1944.

"War Diary, U.S.S. *Gillis.*" Prepared by Commander N. F. Garton, USN. (n.d. In files of Admiral Russell.)

"War Diary, VP-43." Prepared by officers of PBY Patrol Squadron 43. (n.d., probably January 1943; typescript from files of Admiral Russell.)

"World War II in Alaska and the Aleutian Islands." Thesis for the University of Alaska, prepared by Captain Lee S. Cohen, USAF, April 1965. (Files of Elmendorf AFB.)

Published Works

Andrieu d'Albas, Emmanual M. A. *Death of a Navy: Japanese Naval Action in World War II.* New York, 1957.

Arnold, Maj. Gen. Henry H. "Our Air Frontier in Alaska." *National Geographic* LXXVIII (Oct. 1940), 487–504.

Bank, Ted, II. *Birthplace of the Winds.* New York, 1956.

Bishop, John. "My Speed Zero." *Saturday Evening Post* (Feb. 5, 1944), 26–28 & ff. (On Battle of the Komandorskis.)

"Buck's Battle." *Time* VL (April 16, 1945), 32–36. (On Buckner and Okinawa.)

Bulkley, Captain Robert J., Jr. *At Close Quarters: PT Boats in the United States Navy.* Washington, 1962. (See Part V, "The Aleutians—a Battle Against Weather," pages 260–274.)

Capture of Attu As Told By the Men Who Fought There, The. Compiled by the editors of *The Infantry Journal*. Washington, 1944.

Carter, Rear Admiral Worrall Reed. *Beans, Bullets, And Black Oil.*Washington, 1952. (On naval operations and supply.)

Charles, Roland W. *Troopships of World War II.* Washington, 1947.

Cline, Ray S. *The War Department: Washington Command Post: The Operations Division.* Washington, 1951. (Official history.)

Collins, Henry, et al. *The Aleutian Islands: Their People and Natural History.* Washington, 1945.

Conn, Stetson, and Byron Fairchild. *The Western Hemisphere: The Framework of Hemisphere Defense.* Washington, 1960. (Official history.)

Conn, Stetson; Byron Fairchild; and Rose C. Engelman. *Guarding the United States and Its Outposts.* Washington, 1964. (Official history.)

Cooney, Lieutenant Commander David M. *A Chronology of the U.S. Navy: 1775–1965.* New York, 1965.

Craven, Wesley F., and James L. Cate, editors. *The Army Air Forces in World War II.* Volumes I, IV, and VI. Chicago, 1948, 1950, 1958.

Davison, Lonelle. "Bizarre Battleground—The Lonely Aleutians." *National Geographic* LXXXII (Sept. 1942), 316–17.

Day, Beth. *Glacier Pilot: The Story of Bob Reeve.* New York, 1957.

Dimond, Anthony J. "Is Our Neck Out?" *American Magazine* CXXX (Aug 1940), p. 34.

———. "*The Strategic Value of Alaska.*" The Military Engineer XXXIII (Jan.–Feb. 1941), pp. 12–20.

Dornbusch, C. E. *Unit Histories of the United States Air Forces.* Washington, 1958. (A bibliography.)

Dziuban, Stanley W. *Military Relations Between the United States and Canada,* 1939–1945. Washington, 1959.

Easterwood, Thomas J. *The Lights and Shadows of the Rocky Mountains.* Dundee, Ore. n.d.

Engel, Leonard. "PBY Saga." *Air Trails Pictorial* (Feb. 1944), pp. 22–23 & ff. (Mainly on the Kiska Blitz.)

Esposito, Vincent J., editor. *A Concise History of World War II.* New York, 1964.

Ford, Corey. Short Cut to Tokyo: *The Battle for the Aleutians.* New York, 1943. (A journalistic account.)

Fuchida, Mitsuo, and Masatake Okumiya. Midway: *The Battle that Doomed Japan*. Annapolis, 1955. (Okumiya was Air Officer aboard carrier Ryujo at the Battle of Dutch Harbor.)

Fuller, J. F. C. *The Second World War.* New York, 1948.

Gallico, Paul. "The Stubborn Man: Medal of Honor Winner Private Joe P. Martinez." *Esquire* (April 1944), p. 40. (On the Battle of Attu.)

Gilman, William. *Our Hidden Front.* New York, 1944. (Journalistic account.)

Glines, Lieutenant Colonel Carroll V., editor. *Polar Aviation.* New York, 1964.

Griffin, D. F. First Steps to Tokyo: *The Royal Canadian Air Force in the Aleutians.* Toronto, 1944.

Hailey, Foster. "Alaskan Fighting." *New York Times Magazine* (Aug. 22, 1943), pp. 4 5.

Hammet, Dashiell, and Walter Colodny. *The Battle of the Aleutians.* Adak, 1944.

Hammond, Lieutenant Colonel David B. "Aleutian Water Transportation Problems." *The Military Engineer* XXXVI (Nov. 1944), pp. 373–375.

Handelman, Howard. Bridge to Victory: *The Story of the Reconquest of the Aleutians.* New York, 1943. (Journalistic account.)

Hardin, Lieutenant Colonel John R. "Engineers Rush Alaskan Defenses." *The Military Engineer* XXXIV (Jan. 1942), pp. 1–4.

Haugen, Jack O., editor. *The Story of VP-43.* San Bruno, California, 1967. (On the PBY patrol squadron.)

Haugland, Vern. *The A.A.F. Against Japan*. New York, 1948.

Hayes, John D. "War in the Central and Northern Pacific." Pages 268–296 in *A Concise History of World War II* edited by Vincent J. Esposito. New York, 1964.

Hrdlicka, Ales. *The Aleutian and Commander [Komandorski] Islands And Their Inhabitants*. Philadelphia, 1945.

Ito, Masanori. *The Imperial Japanese Navy*. New York, 1962.

Jablonski, Edward. *Flying Fortress*. New York, 1965.

Karig, Walter, and Eric Purdon. *Battle Report*. Five volumes; New York, 1947. (See Vol. III, pp. 259–345.)

King, Fleet Admiral Ernest J. *United States Navy At War: Final Official Report to the Secretary of the Navy*. Three volumes; Washington, 1944–1945.

Kluckhohn, Frank L. "Kinkaid: Master of Sea War." *New York Times Magazine* (Nov. 5, 1944), pp. 16 & ff.

Lane, Colonel Albert L. "The Alcan Highway." *The Military Engineer* XXXIV (Oct. 1942), pp. 492–499.

Long, Lieutenant Hubert D. "The Battle of Attu." *The Aleutian* I (July 8, 1943), pp. 4 & ff.

Lord, Walter. *Incredible Victory*. New York, 1967. (On Battle of Midway.)

Maurer, Maurer, editor. *Air Force Combat Units of World War II*. Washington, 1961.

McMillion, Major Shelby A. "The Strategic Route to Alaska." *The Military Engineer* XXXIV (Nov. 1942), pp. 546–553.

Meyers, George N. "The Alaska Scouts." *Yank, The Army Weekly* (Nov. 8, 1943), pp. 7–9.

Morgan, Murray. *Bridge to Russia*. New York, 1947. (On Lend-Lease.)

Morison, Samuel Eliot. *History of United States Naval Operations in World War II*. Fifteen volumes; New York, 1947–1962. (See volumes IV, V, VII.)

———. *Strategy And Compromise*. New York, 1958.

———. *The Two-Ocean War*. Boston, 1963.

Neuberger, Richard L. "Alaska—Northern Front." *Survey Graphic* XXXI (Feb. 1942), pp. 57–62.

Nolan, William F. *John Huston, King Rebel*. Los Angeles, 1965.

Patty, Stanton H. "Alaska Sprouts Wings." *Aerospace Historian* XIV (Spring 1967), pp. 15–21 .

Pearse, Major Ben H. "Alaskan Offensive." Pages 17–20 in *Air Force Diary*, edited by James H. Straubel. New York, 1947.

Potter, Jean. *Alaska Under Arms*. New York, 1942.

———. *The Flying North*. New York, 1947.

Potter, John D. *Yamamoto.* New York 1965.

Pratt, Fletcher. "Campaign Beyond Glory: The Navy in the Aleutians, 1942–43." *Harper's Magazine* CLXXXIX (Nov. 1944), pp. 558–569.

Reeve, Robert C. "My Friend Squeaky Anderson." *Cook Inlet Historical Society Newsletter* II (Feb. 1966), pp. 1–2.

"Report from the Aleutians." 47-minute motion picture (Technicolor), released by the U.S. War Department August 1943. Produced by Darryl F. Zanuck; narrated by Walter Huston; written and directed by John Huston.

Ringold, Herbert. "Life Line to the USSR." Pages 275–282 in *Air Force Diary,* edited by James H. Straubel. New York, 1947.

———. "Up Where the Soup Begins." Pages 303–305 in *Air Force Diary,* edited by James H. Straubel. New York, 1947.

Roscoe, Theodore. *United States Submarine Operations in World War II.* Annapolis, 1949.

Schull, Joseph. *The Far Distant Ships: An Official Account of Canadian Naval Operations in the Second World War.* Ottawa, 1961.

Smallwood, David W. "Last Match." *Air Force* (Nov. 1943), pp. 37–38.

Stefansson, Evelyn. *Here Is Alaska.* New York, 1943.

Stefansson, Vilhjalmur. "Alaska: American Outpost No. 4." *Harper's Magazine* CLXXXIII (June 1941), pp. 83–92.

Straubel, James H., editor. *Air Force Diary.* New York, 1947.

Sturdevant, Brigadier General Clarence L. "The Military Road to Alaska: Organization and Administrative Problems." *The Military Engineer* XXXV (April 1943), pp. 173–180.

Theobald, Richard J. "The Maiden Voyage of LST 169-V1 1." *The New Yorker* XX (Dec. 9, 1944), pp. 74–76.

Thompson, George R., et al. *The Technical Services: The Signal Corps: The Test (December 1941 to July 1943).* Washington, 1957. (Official history.)

United States Submarine Losses, World War II. Prepared by Commander Submarine Force, U.S. Pacific Fleet, and others; Washington, 1963.

Vidal, Gore. *Williwaw.* New York, 1946. (Novel.)

Watson, Mark Skinner. The War Department: Chief of Staff: *Prewar Plans and Preparations.* Washington, 1950. (Official history.)

Werth, Alexander. *Russia At War,* 1941–45. New York, 1964.

Wheeler, Keith. *The Pacific Is My Beat.* New York, 1943. (Journalistic account.)

Wintermute, Major Ira F. "War in the Fog." *American Magazine* CXXXVI (Aug. 1943), pp. 40 & ff. (Bomber pilot's account.)

Wittels, David G. "These Are the Generals: Buckner." *Saturday Evening Post* CCXV (May 8, 1943), pp. 17 & ff.

Bibliographic Addendum 1995

THIS MATERIAL WAS COMPILED from lists provided by the author, John Cloe, and Terrence Cole. Among the pertinent works published since 1969 or not listed in the original bibliography are the following:

UNPUBLISHED DOCUMENTS AND OFFICIAL RECORDS

Assistant Chief of Staff, G-2, Western Defense Command. Final Report of Reduction and Occupation of Attu From the Combat Intelligence Point of View, Intelligence Memorandum No. 8. 9 August 1943. Summary of combat intelligence on Japanese occupation forces, Attu, 23 October 1942–31 May 1943.

Bush, James D. Jr. *Narrative Report of Alaska Construction, 1941–1944.* N.p: Alaska Defense Command, 1944. Reprinted by Alaska District, U.S. Army Corps of Engineers, 1984. Describes all major construction projects. Includes maps.

Denfield, Colt D. *The Defense of Dutch Harbor, Alaska from Military Construction to Base Cleanup.* N.p.: U.S. Army Corps of Engineers, Defense Environmental Restoration Program, Alaska District, December 1987.

Envirosphere Company. *World War II in Alaska: A Historic and Resources Management Plan,* September 1979. Final Report, prepared in 1987 for the Alaska Region, National Park Service and the Alaska District, U.S. Army Corps of Engineers. Provides a preservation plan and document resources associated with World War II in Alaska.

Faulkner, Sandra. *Dutch Harbor, Alaska.* N.p.: National Park Service, Alaska Region, 1987.

Kirkland, John C. and David Coffin, Jr. *The Relocation and Internment of the Aleuts During World War II.* N.p. 1981.

Northern Pacific Intelligence Center. *Aleutian Campaign.* N.p: U.S. Navy, 15 December 1944.

Office of Information, 172nd Inf Bde (AK). *The U.S. Army In Alaska,* Pamphlet

360-5. 172nd Inf. Bde (AK), May 1976. Sixth edition of history of U.S. Army in Alaska. Pages 85–98 cover World War II.

Office of Naval Intelligence. *The Aleutian Campaign, June 1942–August 1943.* N.p.: Publication Branch, U.S. Navy, 1945. One of a series of combat narratives of U.S. Navy operations during World War II. Valuable reprint of formerly confidential combat narrative written in 1945 by (uncredited) Colin G. Jameson and L. C. Smith. Contains detailed accounts of the Battle of the Komandorskies, and the planning and occupation of Attu and Kiska. Maps, photographs, naval battle tracks, and tasks organizations.

Perrigo, Lyle. "A Study of Deterioration of Abandoned World War II Installations in Resurrection Bay, Alaska," A research proposal for the Arctic Environmental Information Data Center, Anchorage, Alaska, May 1986.

Rust, Frederick E. *Eighteenth Engineers Regimental Diary, 20 January 1943-November1944.* Unpublished typescript from Lawrence Reineke Collection.

Stein, Gary C. "A Transportation Dilemma: Evacuation of the Aleuts in World War II." Paper presented at Alaska Historical Society meeting in Fairbanks 1982 on the forced evacuation of the Aleuts from the Aleutian and Pribilof Islands in the wake of the Japanese occupation of the eastern Aleutians.

Talley, Benjamin B. as interviewed by Charles Hendricks. *Engineer Memoirs of Brigadier General Benjamin B. Talley,* Fort Belvoir, Va.: Office of History, U.S. Army Corps of Engineers, 1994. Limited edition, some copies privately circulated. A copy of this valuable and instructive recollection is in the archives of the University of Alaska at Anchorage, along with General Talley's daily logs from the 1940s, and many others of his papers.

U.S. Army Corps of Engineers. *Debris Removal and Cleanup Study Aleutian Islands and Lower Alaska Peninsula.* Directed study of World War II debris left in the Aleutians. Inventory of facilities, structures, weapons. Maps and photographs.

BOOKS

Amme, Carl H., ed. *Aleutian Airdales.* Plains, Mont.: Plainsman Publishing, 1987.

Binek, Lynn K. and Walter Van Horn et al, eds. *Drawing the Lines of Battle: Military Art of World War II Alaska*. Anchorage, Alaska: Anchorage Museum of History and Art, 1989. Illustrated 48-page catalogue of paintings and drawings.

Carrigan, Paul. *The Flying, Fighting Weathermen*. N.p., n.d. About Navy meteorologists in the Aleutians.

Cloe, John H. *The Air Force in Alaska, Part I: Early Flights and Strategic Importance, 1920–1940*. Anchorage, Alaska: Alaskan Air Command, 1983.

———. *The Air Force in Alaska, Part II: Buildup to Dutch Harbor, June 1940–June 1942*. Anchorage, Alaska: Alaskan Air Command, 1986.

———. *The Aleutian Warriors, A History of the 11th Air Force and Fleet Air*

Wing 4, Part I. Missoula, Mont.: Pictorial Histories Publishing Company, 1991.

———. *Top Cover for America, the Air Force in Alaska 1932–1983*. Missoula, Mont.: Pictorial Histories Publishing Company, 1984.

Coates, Ken. *North to Alaska! Fifty Years on the World's Most Remarkable Highway*. Fairbanks, Alaska: University of Alaska Press, 1992.

Cohen, Stan. *The Forgotten War: A Pictorial History of World War II in Alaska and Northwestern Canada. Missoula, Mont*.: Pictorial Histories Publishing Company, 1981. This 4-volume series of large-format picture books provide an invaluable picture of the Alaskan war in graphic and dramatic detail.

———. The Forgotten War*: A Pictorial History of World War II in Alaska and Northwestern Canada, Volume II*. Missoula, Mont.: Pictorial Histories Publishing Company, 1988.

———. The Forgotten *War: A Pictorial History of World War II in Alaska and Northwestern Canada, Volume III*. Missoula, Mont.: Pictorial Histories Publishing Company, 1992.

———. The Forgotten *War: A Pictorial History of World War II in Alaska and Northwestern Canada, Volume IV*. Missoula, Mont.: Pictorial Histories Publishing Company, 1993.

———. *The Trail of '42: A Pictorial History of the Alaska Highway*. Missoula, Mont: Pictorial Histories Publishing Company, 1988.

Cole, Terrence, ed. *The Capture of Attu: Tales of World War II in Alaska*. Anchorage, Alaska: Alaska Northwest Publishing Company, 1984. This selection of reprints from the 1944 Infantry Journal edition contains the stories as told by the men who fought in the Aleutians, combined with Dashiell Hammett's brief history of the campaign.

Cole, Terrence, et. al. *Alaska or Bust: The Promise of the Road North*. Fairbanks, Alaska: University of Alaska Museum, 1992. A brief history and museum catalog on the 50th anniversary of the building of the Alaska Highway.

Driscoll, Joseph. *War Discovers Alaska*. Philadelphia, Pa.: Lippincott, 1943. Description of Alaskan sociological and economic conditions during World War II. Contemporary example of racial bias against Japanese.

Goldstein, Donald M. and Katherine V. Dillon. *The Williwaw War: The Arkansas National Guard in the Aleutians in World War II*. Fayetteville, Ark.: University of Arkansas Press, 1992.

Grover, David H. *Army Ships and Watercraft of World War II*. Annapolis, Md.: Naval Institute Press, 1992. Lists all vessels that were in the service of the Army during the War, with attention to the craft that made up Buckner's "Army fleet" (Harbor Craft Detachment (TC), Alaskan Dept).

Gruening, Ernest. *The State of Alaska*. New York: Random House, 1954.

Hays, Otis Jr. *Home From Siberia: The Secret Odysseys of Interned American Airmen in World War II*. College Station, Tex.: Texas A&M Press, 1990.

Hutchinson, Kevin Don. *World War II in the North Pacific: Chronology and*

Fact Book. Westport, Ct: Greenwood Press, 1994. Covers day-to-day orders and records; illustrated and indexed; with commentary.

Jacobs, Will A. *A History of the Alaska District, United States Army Corps of Engineers 1946–1974.* N.p.: Government Printing Office, 1976. Prepared from a manuscript researched and compiled by Lyman Woodman.

Long, Everett A. and Evan Negenblya. *Cobras Over the Tundra*. Fairbanks, Alaska: Arktika Publishing, 1992.

Lorelli, John A. *The Battle of the Komandorski Islands*. Annapolis, Md.: Naval Institute, 1984.

Love, Edmund C. *The Hourglass*. Washington, D.C.: Infantry Journal Press, 1950.

MacGarrigle, George L. *Aleutian Islands*. Washington, D.C.: U.S. Army Center for Military History, 1992. A volume in the military's official series "The U.S. Army Campaigns of World War II."

Marston, Marvin R. *Men of the Tundra*. New York: October House, 1969.

Mills, Stephen E. *Arctic War Birds*. Seattle, Wash.: Superior, 1971.

———. Arctic War Planes: Alaska Aviation of WWII. New York: Bonanza Books, 1978.

Morgan, Lael, ed. *The Aleutians*. Anchorage, Alaska: The Alaska Geographical Society, 1980. Excellent 224-page presentation of high-quality color photographs and informative text, plus a fold-out map; includes a good 30-page overview of the war with numerous pictures.

Morrison, William and Kenneth Coates. *Working the North: Labor and the Northwest Defense Projects 1942–1946.* Fairbanks, Alaska: University of Alaska Press, 1994.

Murray, Robert Haynes. *The Only Way Home*. Waycross, Ga.: Brantley Printing Co., 1986.

National Park Service. *World War II in the Aleutians: Alternatives for Preservation and Interpretation of Historic Resources.* Anchorage, Alaska: Alaska Regional Office, National Park Service, May 1992. Nicely illustrated book, in magazine format, reporting on a draft study of "management alternatives for preservation and interpretation of World War II resources."

Nielson, Jonathan M. *Armed Forces on a Northern Frontier: The Military in Alaska's History, 1867–1987*. New York: Greenwood Press, 1988.

Paneth, Philip. *Alaska, BackDoor to Japan*. London: Alliance, 1943.

Rearden, Jim. *Cracking the Zero Mystery*. Fairfield, Pa.: Stackpole Books, 1990.

———. Castner's Cutthroats: *Saga of the Alaska Scouts.* Prescott, Ariz.: Wolfe Publishing, 1990. A historical novel of the scouts in the Aleutians.

Remley, David. *Crooked Road: The Story of the Alaska Highway.* New York: McGraw-Hill, 1976.

Russell, James S. "The Aleutian Campaign," in *The Campaigns of the Pacific United States Strategic Bombing Survey (Pacific).* New York: Greenwood

Press, 1969. A reprint of the original report published in 1947. Details Aleutian campaign Kurile operations. Contains charts, maps, and statistical tables.

Salisbury, C. D. *Soldiers of the Mist: Minutemen of the Alaska Frontier.* Missoula, Mont.: Pictorial Histories Publishing Co., 1992.

Scrivner, Charles. *The Empire Express*. Temple City: Historical Aviation Album, 1976.

Twichell, Heath. *Northwest Epic: The Building Of The Alaska Highway.* New York: St. Martin's Press, 1990. Comprehensive narrative, illustrated, sparked by personal enthusiasm; the author's father was one of the builders of the wartime highway.

Webber, Bert. *Aleutian Headache*. Medford, Ore.: Webb Research Group, 1993.

Ulibarri, George S. *Documenting Alaskan History: A Guide to Federal Archives Relating to Alaska*. Fairbanks, Alaska: University of Alaska Press, 1983. Thorough 304-page guide to National Archives files pertaining to Alaska, including military records; includes photos, reproductions, and guidelines to help researchers find resources.

Unalaska/Dutch Harbor. Anchorage, Alaska: The Alaska Geographical Society, 1991.

Unalaska High School students. *Cuttlefish Five: The Aleutian Invasion, World War Two in the Aleutian Islands.* Unalaska, Alaska: Unalaska High School, 1981. A valuable collection of oral histories and eyewitness accounts of the war.

Unalaska High School students. *Cuttlefish Six: The Unknown Islands, Life and Tales of Henry Swanson.* Unalaska, Alaska: Unalaska High School, 1981. A personal account of the war at Unalaska.

Walkowiak, Tom. *Fleet Submarines of WWII.* Missoula, Mont.: Pictorial Histories Publishing Company, 1989.

Published Periodicals

"Battle of Alaska, Profit and Loss," *Time*, 27 Jul 1942. Account of Japanese attack on Dutch Harbor and occupation of Attu, Kiska and Agattu.

Brandon, Dean. "ALSIB: The Northwest Ferrying Command." Parts 1 and 2. *Journal, American Avaition Historical Society.* Spring and Summer 1975.

Buckner, Simon, Jr. "Cannery That Wasn't There," *Scholastic*, 12 Apr 1943. Personal account of the deceptions used in the construction of airfields at Cold Bay and Umnak to fool the Japanese.

Chihaya, Masataka, "Mysterious Withdrawal from Kiska," *Naval Institute Proceedings*, Feb 1958. An account of the Japanese evacuation of Kiska.

Clemmens, C. "Report on the Aleutians." *Readers Digest*, March 1943. Operations against Japanese in the Aleutians.

Cressman, Robert J. "Desperate Battle at Unalga Pass," *Naval History,* Fall 1990. An account of the Japanese shoot down of the PBY flown by Ensign

Albert Mitchell at Dutch Harbor.

Denfield, Colt D. "Coastal Defenses in Alaska: A Brief History and Status Report," *Coastal Defense Study Group News*, Vol 1, No 4, July 1986.

"Dutch Harbor, U.S. Gets Look at It Destruction," *Life*, 10 Aug 1942.

Fradkin, Philip L. "War on the Refuge," *Audubon*, Nov 1980. Discusses the effect of the war on the Aleutian environment.

Frisbee, John L. "The Forgotten Front," *Air Force Magazine*, Feb 1984. An account of the air war in the Aleutians.

Green, Murray. "The Alaskan Flight of 1934—A Spectacular Official Failure," *Aerospace Historian*, Spring/March 1977.

Gruening, Ernest H. "Strategic Alaska Looks Ahead," *National Geographic*, Sept 1942. Description of Alaska by its territorial governor.

Hatch, Fred John. "Allies in the Aleutians," *Aerospace Historian*, Summer/Jun 1974. Royal Candian Air Force operations in support of the Aleutian Campaign. Map, photographs.

Hays, Otis E. Jr. "The Silent Years in Alaska," *The Alaska Journal, A 1986 Collection*. An account of censorship in Alaska during World War II.

———. "When War Came to Seward," *The Alaska Journal*, Autumn 1983.

Hendricks, Charles. "The Eskimos and the Defense of Alaska," *Pacific Historical Review*, 1985, Vol 1, pp. 271–295.

Jones, Howard. "Etta Jones…POW," *Alaska Life*, Dec 1945.

Kilralfy, Alexander. "Japan's Alaska Strategy," *New Republic*, Jun 29 1942.

Lawler, Pat. "Taking the Territory by Storm," *The Alaska Journal, 1981 Collection*. Biography of Simon B. Buckner.

Lazarus, Allan M. "The Hellcat-Zero Myth," *Naval History*, Summer 1989, Annapolis, Md.: U.S. Naval Institute.

Merritt, Allan. "Crash Boat to the Rescue," *Alaska Life*, Sep 1944.

Morgan, Lael. "Aleutians Legacy From World War II: Clean It Up, But Save The Battlefields!" *Alaska Magazine,* May 1980.

Naske, Claus-M. "The Battle of Alaska Has Ended and the Japanese Have Won It," *Military Affairs*, 1985.

Orr, Robert D. "Operation in the Aleutians," *Military Review*, Jan 1943. Describes the logistical efforts to support operations.

Penny, Charles. "A Military Bush Pilot on the Forgotten Front," *Aerospace Historian*, Spring 1975.

Reeve, Robert C. "I should Have Stayed in Bed," *Aerospace Historian*, Summer/Jun 1975.

Stokesbury, James. "Battle of Attu," *American History Illustrated*, Apr 1979.

Thompson, Erdwin N. "North Star Defense: Alaska World War II Military Bases," *Council On America's Military Post*, Sept 1986.

Index